iMovie™
fast & easy™

Send Us Your Comments

To comment on this book or any other PRIMA TECH title, visit our reader response page on the Web at **www.prima-tech.com/comments**.

How to Order

For information on quantity discounts, contact the publisher: Prima Publishing, P.O. Box 1260BK, Rocklin, CA 95677-1260; (916)787-7000. On your letterhead, include information concerning the intended use of the books and the number of books you wish to purchase.

iMovie™
fast&easy™

Kevin Harreld

A DIVISION OF PRIMA PUBLISHING

©2000 by Prima Publishing. All rights reserved. No part of this book may be reproduced or transmitted in any form or by any means, electronic or mechanical, including photocopying, recording, or by any information storage or retrieval system without written permission from Prima Publishing, except for the inclusion of brief quotations in a review.

A Division of Prima Publishing

Prima Publishing and colophon are registered trademarks of Prima Communications, Inc. PRIMA TECH and Fast & Easy are trademarks of Prima Communications, Inc., Roseville, California 95661.

Publisher: Stacy L. Hiquet
Marketing Manager: Judi Taylor
Associate Marketing Manager: Heather Buzzingham
Managing Editor: Sandy Doell
Acquisitions Editor: Lynette Quinn
Project Editor: Cathleen D. Snyder
Technical Reviewer: Mark E. Loper
Copy Editor: Kelli Brooks
Interior Layout: Marian Hartsough Associates
Cover Design: Prima Design Team
Indexer: Sharon Shock

Balloon Help, FireWire, iMac, iMovie, Mac, Macintosh, Power Macintosh, and QuickTime are trademarks or registered trademarks of Apple Computer, Inc. Photoshop is a trademark of Adobe Systems Incorporated.

Important: Prima Publishing cannot provide software support. Please contact the appropriate software manufacturer's technical support line or Web site for assistance.

Prima Publishing and the author have attempted throughout this book to distinguish proprietary trademarks from descriptive terms by following the capitalization style used by the manufacturer.

Information contained in this book has been obtained by Prima Publishing from sources believed to be reliable. However, because of the possibility of human or mechanical error by our sources, Prima Publishing, or others, the Publisher does not guarantee the accuracy, adequacy, or completeness of any information and is not responsible for any errors or omissions or the results obtained from use of such information. Readers should be particularly aware of the fact that the Internet is an ever-changing entity. Some facts may have changed since this book went to press.

ISBN: 0-7615-2907-1
Library of Congress Catalog Card Number: 00-102903
Printed in the United States of America

00 01 02 03 04 DD 10 9 8 7 6 5 4 3 2 1

To Lisa and Genevieve,

the Best Actresses in my world

Acknowledgments

Special thanks go to Stacy Hiquet and Lynette Quinn for taking me seriously when I said I could do this book. Thanks also to Ben Dominitz and Matt Carleson for having respect and confidence in me. Prima is a wonderful company to work for. Thanks also to rookie editor Cathleen Snyder, who managed the project like a pro, and to Kelli Brooks and Mark Loper for their quality insights. Kudos also to Kelli Crump, my first mentor in book publishing, and Bill Mishler, my Zen master. Final thanks to my parents for always being there for me . . . and buying me a camera.

About the Author

KEVIN HARRELD is a Senior Editor for the Tech Division of Prima Publishing. After years of working behind the scenes editing numerous Tech books, he took a starring role as author of *iMovie Fast & Easy*. He also worked for several years in various roles in the newspaper industry, where he learned the definition of a deadline. Spending a year as a Film Studies minor, living in movie houses and video stores (before he had a child), and listening to Joe Bob Briggs has made Kevin believe that he's an authority on movies. Kevin lives in Indianapolis with his wife, Lisa, daughter, Genevieve, and hound, Dignan. He enjoys fairways and greens, hardwood and hoops, and big screens and artificial butter flavor.

Contents at a Glance

Introduction xvii

PART I
FILM SCHOOL 101 1

Chapter 1   Tools of the Trade 3
Chapter 2   Capturing Footage 11

PART II
THE IMPORTING AND EDITING ROOM 23

Chapter 3   Lights, Camera . . . Starting Your Epic 25
Chapter 4   Beginning the Importing and Editing Process 43
Chapter 5   The Cutting Room Floor—Precise and Polished Editing 63

PART III
IMOVIE SPECIAL EFFECTS AND POST PRODUCTION . 83

Chapter 6   Adding Stylish Transitions 85
Chapter 7   Text in iMovie: Rolling Titles, Credits, and Captions 105
Chapter 8   Audio: Adding Soundtracks, Scores, Sounds, and Narration 123

CONTENTS AT A GLANCE

| Chapter 9 | iMovie and Still Images | 151 |
| Chapter 10 | Compressing and Exporting Your Movies | 167 |

PART IV
OUTSIDE IMOVIEMAKING 183

Chapter 11	Tricks with Text	185
Chapter 12	Using QuickTime with iMovie	229
Chapter 13	Getting Your iMovie on the Web	263

PART V
APPENDIXES 287

| Appendix A | Acquiring and Installing iMovie | 289 |
| Appendix B | iMovie Keyboard Shortcuts | 299 |

| Glossary | 303 |
| Index | 307 |

Contents

Introduction xvii

PART I
FILM SCHOOL 101 1

Chapter 1 **Tools of the Trade** 3
  Digital Video Cameras 4
  The Software 7
  FireWire Cable 8
  Analog Video Converters 9

Chapter 2 **Capturing Footage** 11
  Moviemaking Composition Basics 12
    Including an Establishing Shot 12
    Moving into Medium Shots 13
    My Close-Up, Please 14
  Shooting Better Video 15
    Zooming 15
    Panning 16
    Varying Angles and Shot Lengths 17
    Lighting 18
    Steadying Secrets 18

CONTENTS

Other Non-Static Shots	19
Unique Angle Perspectives and Camera Tricks	19
Part I Review Questions	22

PART II
THE IMPORTING AND EDITING ROOM 23

Chapter 3 Lights, Camera . . . Starting Your Epic 25

Connecting Your Camcorder	26
Starting iMovie	27
Starting iMovie from the Desktop	27
Starting iMovie from the Folder	28
Creating a New Project	30
Previewing Your Video in the Monitor Window	33
Exploring the iMovie Screen	34
Getting Help	37
Getting Help from the Help Menu	37
Getting Help from the Balloons	39
Running the Help Tutorial	40

Chapter 4 Beginning the Importing and Editing Process 43

Switching Modes	44
Importing a Clip from Your Digital Video Camera	44
Storing Clips	47
Selecting the Destination of Your Imported Clips	47
Expanding the Shelf	49
Using iMovie's Scene Detection Feature	51
Adjusting the Quality of Video Playback	52
Exiting iMovie	54
Opening an Existing iMovie Project	56
Importing Analog Video	58

Chapter 5　The Cutting Room Floor—Precise and Polished Editing 63

- Selecting Clips 64
  - Selecting a Single Clip to Edit 64
  - Selecting Multiple Clips 64
- Renaming a Clip 65
- Cropping Clips 67
- Undoing a Crop 69
- Splitting Clips 70
- Copying Clips 72
- Moving Clips from the Shelf to the Viewer 74
  - Dragging Clips to the Viewer 74
  - Moving Clips Using the Edit Menu 77
- Trashing Clips 79
- *Part II Review Questions* *81*

PART III
iMOVIE SPECIAL EFFECTS AND POST-PRODUCTION 83

Chapter 6　Adding Stylish Transitions 85

- Selecting a Transition 86
- Setting Transition Speed 88
- Adding the Transition 90
- Why Use Certain Transitions? 92
- Changing a Transition 93
- Deleting a Transition 95
- Inserting a Clip Where a Transition Exists 96
- Adding New Transitions to the Palette 97

CONTENTS xiii

Chapter 7 **Text in iMovie: Rolling Titles, Credits, and Captions** 105
    Opening the Titles Palette 106
    Selecting a Title Style 106
    Typing Your Title Text 108
    Selecting a Title Background 109
        Selecting Apple's Still Files as Backgrounds 110
    Working with Fonts 112
    Adjusting the Duration of Your Title 115
    Positioning Your Title 116
        Specifying Alignment and Scrolling Direction 117
        Setting the Exact Placement of Titles 117
    Adding the Title to Your Movie 119
    Changing Your Title 120
    Deleting Your Title 121

Chapter 8 **Audio: Adding Soundtracks, Scores, Sounds, and Narration** 123
    Touring the Audio Viewer, Music Palette, and Sound Palette ... 124
    Adding Music from an Audio CD 129
        Adding a Song from a CD 129
        Adding a Portion or a Song 131
    Adding Sound Effects 132
    Adding Voice-Over or Narration 134
    Sound Bytes: Cropping Audio Clips 137
    Moving an Audio Clip 138
    Renaming an Audio Clip 139
    Deleting an Audio Track 140
    Adjusting Audio Levels 141
        Adjusting the Volume of a Clip or Clips 141

Adjusting the Volume within a Single Clip 142
Muting Audio Tracks 143
Fading Your Recording In and Out 144
Expanding Your Sound Effect and Looping Music Library 145

Chapter 9 iMovie and Still Images 151
Extracting Still Images from Your Videos 152
Adding a Still Image to an iMovie 154
Creating a Slideshow 156
Adding Stills to Your Shelf and Timeline 157
Setting or Varying the Duration of the Stills 160
Transition Hints for the Slideshow 161
Title Hints for the Slideshow 162
Sound Advice for Your Slideshow 164

Chapter 10 Compressing and Exporting Your Movies 167
Saving Your iMovie 168
Making a Copy of Your iMovie 168
Exporting Your Movie to Your Camera 172
Making a Copy on VHS Tape 174
Exporting Your Movie to QuickTime 175
Part III Review Questions *181*

PART IV
OUTSIDE IMOVIEMAKING 183

Chapter 11 Tricks with Text 185
Creating an Opening Film Countdown 186
Preparing Your Canvas 186
Creating the First Number 188
Creating the Other Numbers 196

CONTENTS xv

    Adding the Images to iMovie 200
    Adding Transitions 203
    Playing Your Effect 204
Inserting More Exciting Titles 205
    Preparing Your Canvas 205
    Creating the Title 207
Inserting Silent Film Dialog Placards 214
Adding Silent Film Sound Effects 222

Chapter 12   Using QuickTime with iMovie 229
Upgrading to QuickTime Pro 230
Opening a QuickTime Movie 231
Understanding the QuickTime Player 234
Sizing and Playback with Menu Commands 237
Showing Your Movie on Your Computer Screen 241
Editing QuickTime Clips 242
    Cutting, Copying, and Pasting 242
    Extracting, Enabling, and Deleting 247
        Extracting Video and Sound Tracks 247
        Deleting Video and Sound Tracks 250
        Enabling Video and Sound Tracks 251
Importing QuickTime Clips into Your iMovies 252
Adding Special QuickTime Video Effects 256

Chapter 13   Getting Your iMovie on the Web 263
Setting Up an iTools Account 264
Accessing Your iDisk 273
Creating Your Home Page 276
Part IV Review Questions 286

PART V
APPENDIXES 287

Appendix A Acquiring and Installing iMovie................. 289

  Downloading iMovie 290

  Installing iMovie. 292

Appendix B iMovie Keyboard Shortcuts.................... 299

  Glossary 303

  Index 307

Introduction

So, you wanna be in pictures? Home movie Hitchcock wannabes now have a simple and exciting desktop video-editing tool: Apple's iMovie. iMovie is the perfect tool for turning those long, boring home videos into interesting, polished productions that your family and friends will enjoy. Let's face it, without video-editing software to sharpen your home movies, even your own kids and creative filming techniques (of the floor) can be dull.

With iMovie, you can be a modern day Orson Welles and write, direct, and star in your own original short films. Or, you can edit those shelves of dusty, unwatchable videotapes you've had for years. You've probably seen better film on teeth. After you master iMovie, you will start to think like a movie director or editing room technician every time you pick up the camera.

iMovie Fast & Easy will teach you to make better home movies using Apple's exciting video-editing software. You will learn to edit your video clips, add smooth transitions between clips, insert opening titles and closing credits, add soundtracks and sound effects, create special effects, and export your finished production. You'll also learn some camera shooting tricks to help you visualize a better epic. A final section shows you how you can utilize features of photo manipulation programs and QuickTime Pro to enhance your productions, and also create a simple Web page to post your final masterpieces.

Prima Tech's *Fast & Easy* guides are visual solutions to getting started and learning computer-related subjects. The easy-to-follow, highly visual *Fast & Easy* style makes this a perfect learning tool. Computer terms are clearly explained in non-technical language, and numbered steps keep explanations to a minimum to help you learn faster.

Special Features of This Book

Besides the visual and detailed descriptions of useful tasks, this book also contains some additional comments, including

Notes. These give background and additional information about various features.

Tips. These reveal shortcuts or hints that make using iMovie even simpler.

A comprehensive glossary of terms is also included, as well as informative appendixes to help you download and install iMovie from Apple's Web site and learn some useful keyboard shortcuts. Have fun with *iMovie Fast & Easy*, and good luck directing your home movies. Your family and friends will thank you.

PART I
Film School 101

Chapter 1
   Tools of the Trade 3

Chapter 2
   Capturing Footage 11

1
Tools of the Trade

What tools do you need to become a desktop moviemaker? Thanks to iMovie and the plummeting prices of digital video cameras, you can now afford to use state-of-the-art video and computer hardware. It's important to know the peripherals of iMovie, the digital video cameras it supports, and the computer system requirements for using iMovie. In this chapter, you'll learn how to:

- Identify supported digital video cameras
- Understand the software and computer system requirements
- Understand FireWire
- Identify analog video converters

Digital Video Cameras

Apple's iMovie Web site (http://www.apple.com/imovie) has a list of digital video cameras that are supported by iMovie and the iMac DV edition. As of the printing of this book, the list includes the following:

- Sony DCR-PC1
- Sony DCR-PC100
- Sony DCR-TR7000
- Sony DCR-TRV103
- Sony DCR-TRV110
- Sony DCR-TRV310
- Sony DCR-TRV510
- Sony DCR-TRV8

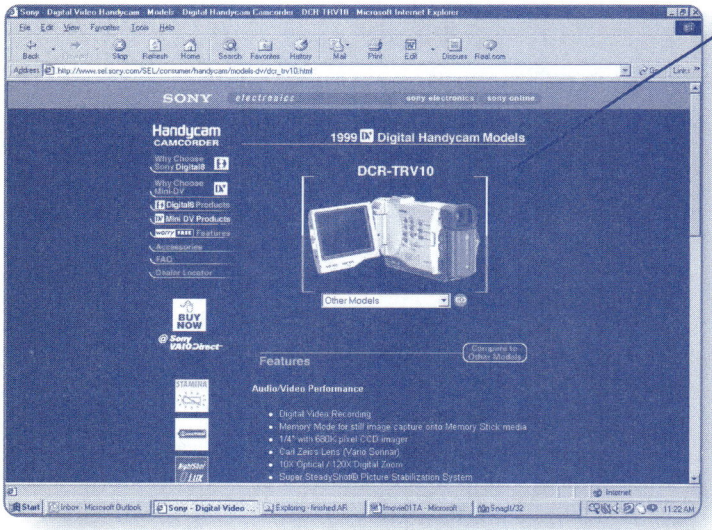

- Sony DCR-TRV10
- Sony DCR-TRV900
- Sony DCR-TRV900e

DIGITAL VIDEO CAMERAS 5

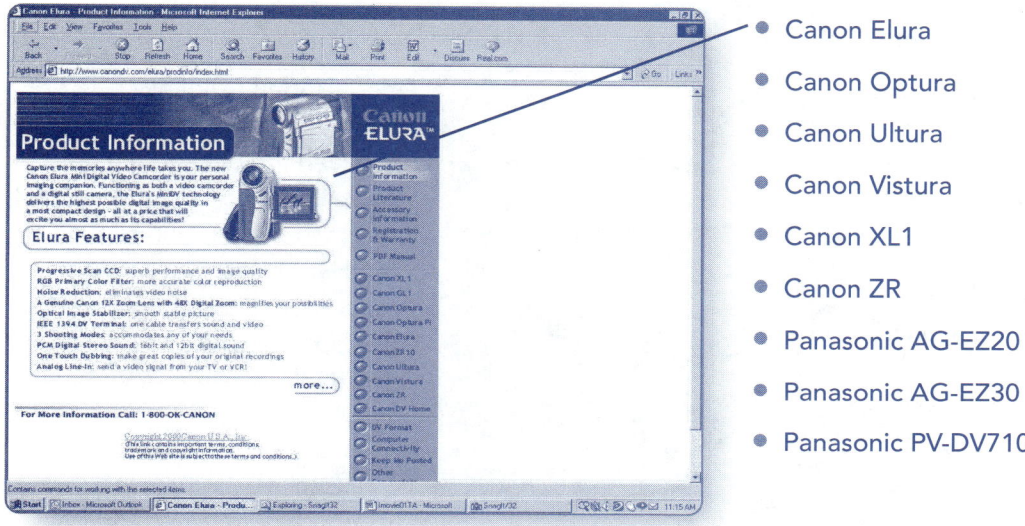

- Canon Elura
- Canon Optura
- Canon Ultura
- Canon Vistura
- Canon XL1
- Canon ZR
- Panasonic AG-EZ20
- Panasonic AG-EZ30
- Panasonic PV-DV710

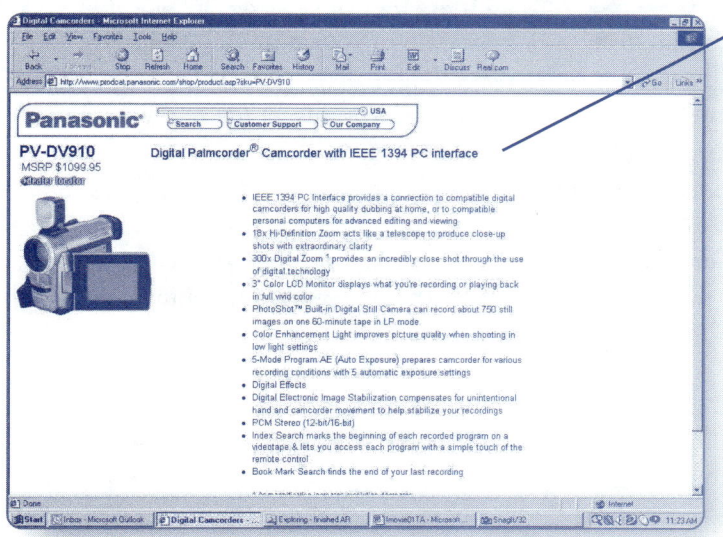

- Panasonic PV-DV910
- Sharp VL-PD3

CHAPTER 1: TOOLS OF THE TRADE

In this book, I use Sony's DCR-TRV510 Digital8 Handycam model. Sony's Digital8 camcorders offer a bridge between the old and the new. Basically, you can capture digital information on standard 8mm and Hi8 videotapes. This is an advantage because 8mm and Hi8 tapes are much more affordable than mini DV tapes for DV camcorder models, and 8mm and Hi8 tapes that contain your old analog video can be played back and imported into iMovie through your Digital8 camcorder. 8mm tapes are still considered the most popular cassette format for camcorders. Sony does recommend that you use Hi8 (Metal Particle) tapes for optimum quality in capturing your digital footage.

If you have a camcorder that is not on this list and you're not sure if it is a digital video camera, you can check with the camera manufacturer to find out. The camcorder also requires a FireWire, iLink, or IEEE 1394 port for importing and exporting video. If you aren't sure whether your camcorder has this capability, check with your camera manufacturer.

THE SOFTWARE 7

The Software

By purchasing an iMac DV or iMac DV Special Edition, you have already acquired the iMovie software—it comes installed on the machines. You can also purchase a CD-ROM for $19.95 (U.S.) or $29.95 (Canada) that includes iMovie and the tutorial files from Apple by calling 1-800-293-6617 in the U.S. or 1-888-295-0653 in Canada.

Finally, you can get a copy of iMovie through a free download from Apple's Web site. It is the same program as the one that is installed on the iMac DVs and available on the CD-ROM, except that it doesn't include the tutorial files. Apple left out these files, which are over 160 MB in size, in order to reduce the download size. See Appendix A, "Acquiring and Installing iMovie," to learn how to download and install iMovie from Apple's Web site.

CHAPTER 1: TOOLS OF THE TRADE

Before you download iMovie, make sure your Macintosh computer has the following minimum system requirements, as recommended by Apple:

- 300 MHz Power Macintosh G4 computer or PowerBook G3

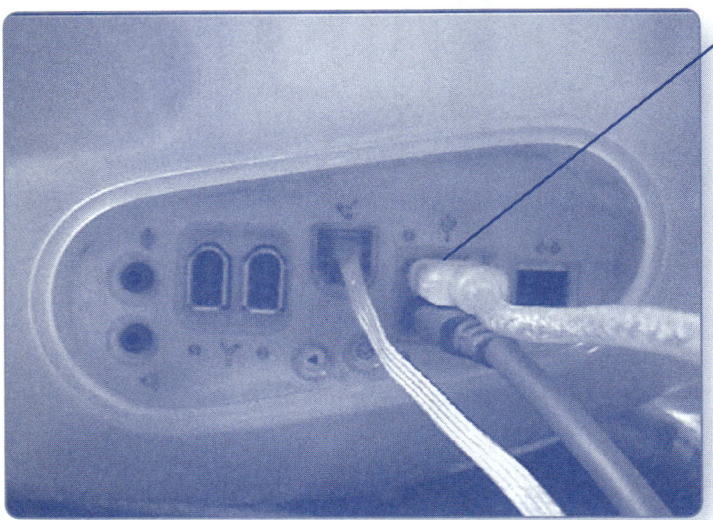

- A built-in FireWire port
- Mac Operating System (OS) 8.6 or later
- QuickTime 4.0 or later
- 64 MB of RAM
- A CD-ROM drive
- 2 GB of hard disk space
- A monitor display that supports 800 x 600 resolution and thousands of colors (1024 x 768 and millions of colors recommended)

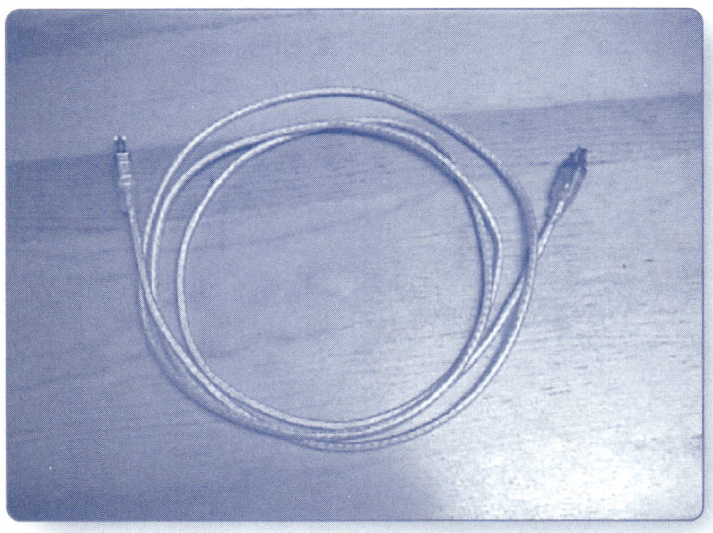

FireWire Cable

FireWire is the multimedia peripheral that allows you to import and export video and audio from your camcorder at tremendous speeds—400 Mbps, to be exact. FireWire has 30 times more bandwidth than USB (*Universal Serial Bus*), which used to be the standard for this type of activity. FireWire is also referred to as iLink or IEEE 1394.

ANALOG VIDEO CONVERTERS 9

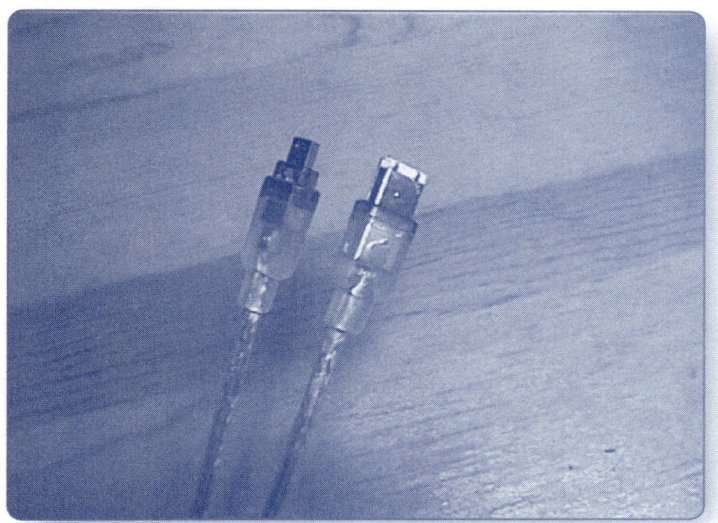

The FireWire cable has 4-pin and 6-pin connectors to connect your digital camcorder to your Macintosh.

Analog Video Converters

iMovie is designed to work with video cameras that support digital video (DV). However, if you have a camcorder that is not DV format, you can convert other formats (8mm, Hi8, VHS, SVHS) to DV format with a special converter box. Sony makes this converter box, and it is available through their Web site (http://www.sel.sony.com/SEL/consumer/handycam/accessories/i-dvmcda1.html).

10   CHAPTER 1: TOOLS OF THE TRADE

This converter box has standard S-Video and RCA input/output ports for video/audio, and a FireWire input/output port. It can therefore convert analog video to a digital video signal, or digital video to analog. You can use all the editing features of iMovie with this box, but you cannot capture video using the box. You must manually capture video, which shouldn't be a problem since you are probably doing it in that manner anyway.

Another way to import analog video into iMovie is to dub the video onto a DV tape, and then import the footage. You'll learn how to do this in Chapter 4, "Beginning the Importing and Editing Process." This solution works for those who have DV camcorders and want to import their old VHS videos into iMovie for editing. If you only have a non-DV camcorder and you want to use iMovie, you'll have to use the Sony converter box. At about $500, it is not cheap, so you may want to consider picking up a DV camcorder for a few dollars more.

2

Capturing Footage

iMovie is a great editing tool, but it alone cannot help you make great movies. A great movie begins with the footage you capture. The nice thing about this powerful editing tool is that you don't have to capture footage in chronological order. Capture whatever you want and piece it together later. Just make sure you capture footage in a variety of angles, zooms, compositions, and so on, so that you put together an interesting video in the end. Hopefully, the hints in this chapter will help you piece together an Academy Award nominated film—or at least keep your friends from falling asleep. In this chapter, you'll learn how to:

- Capture full, medium, and close-up shots
- Improve zooming and panning
- Vary camera angles and shot lengths
- Improve lighting
- Steady your camcorder

Moviemaking Composition Basics

Whether you are capturing video or extracting clips from existing videotapes, it's a good idea to have a picture in your mind of what you want your video to say or accomplish. You don't have to sketch out a storyboard like they do in Hollywood, but some advance thought will help you produce a more captivating finished product.

Including an Establishing Shot

The establishing shot, or full shot, shows the audience the setting of the scene and establishes how the subject of your movie fits in with the background or surroundings. You should have this shot somewhere at the beginning of your movie, so your audience can see the big picture early on.

MOVIEMAKING COMPOSITION BASICS   13

Moving into Medium Shots

Medium shots reveal the action and subject of the movie.

These shots show one to three players within a small area, including their gestures and expressions.

14 CHAPTER 2: CAPTURING FOOTAGE

My Close-Up, Please

Close-up shots introduce the individual players to the audience.

Expressions and emotions are revealed through zoomed-in, tight frames of your actors' faces.

Close-up shots of subtle objects, such as a time clock ticking slowly away at a sporting event, are also very effective.

SHOOTING BETTER VIDEO 15

Shooting Better Video

Techniques such as zooming and panning add to the effectiveness of your movie, but you must use them judiciously and correctly. Here's a quick tour of the camera dos and don'ts that will help you in your moviemaking.

Zooming

It takes a while to get the feel for delicately zooming in and out with your camcorder. It is important, though, to zoom in slowly from a full shot to a close-up, or zoom out from a medium shot to reveal a full shot. Many people make the mistake of constantly zooming in and out, which can confuse viewers.

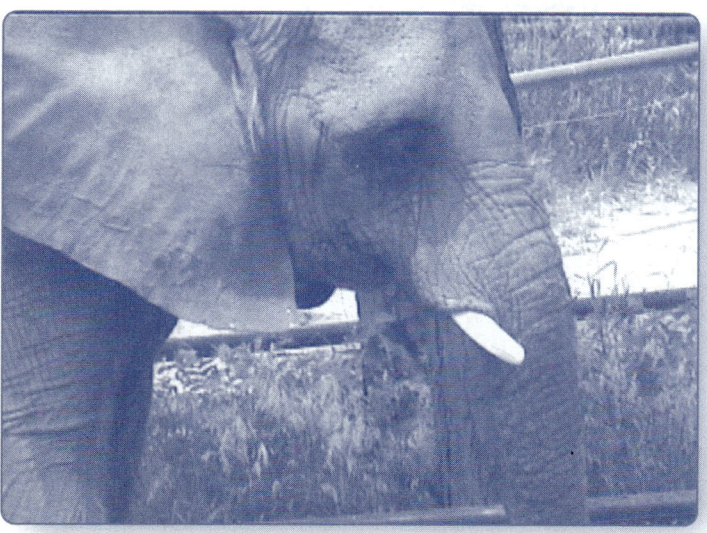

A better way to create this same effect might be to stop recording, move to a new location or change your zoom setting, and then start recording again. This is frequently called a jump cut, or a cut zoom in/out.

16 CHAPTER 2: CAPTURING FOOTAGE

Panning

A panning shot rotates the video camera along a horizontal line, from right to left or vice versa. A common mistake is to quickly sweep back and forth across a scene, dizzying the viewer.

Again, a better practice is probably to stop the camcorder and vary the angles and shot lengths. But panning is effective when done slowly and steadily, and is useful when capturing footage of, say, the Grand Canyon.

SHOOTING BETTER VIDEO 17

Varying Angles and Shot Lengths

As I mentioned before, one of the most effective ways to make your movie more engaging is to vary the angles and shot lengths.

Capture footage from the front, side, above, and straight on. Also, use full shots, medium shots, and close-ups throughout your movies.

Lighting

Bad lighting can easily wash out your videos. This might go without saying, but try to avoid shooting into a bright light, such as sunlight, lamplight, or light blazing through a window. Try to put your main light source behind and to one side of you, so that your subject is well lit and doesn't cast any shadows.

Steadying Secrets

Even though many camcorders have stabilization features that compensate for your shaky hands, it can be difficult to keep the camera still.

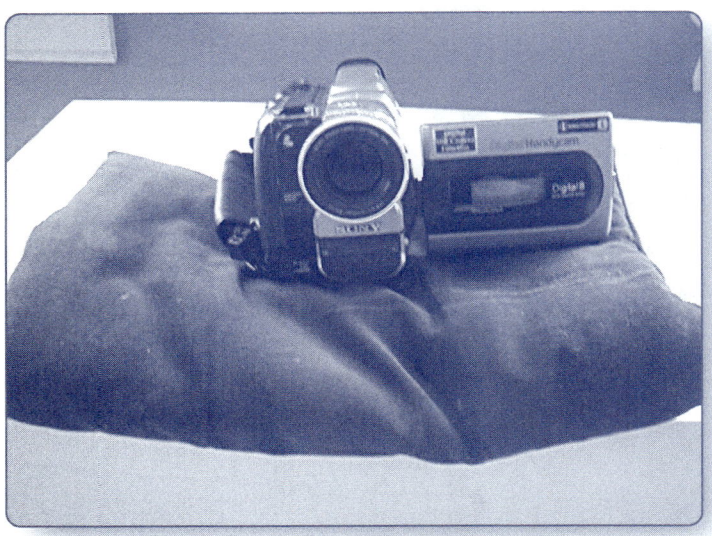

Tripods are the best solution for shots that absolutely need to be steady. You can also use pillows and beanbags for support. Pillows and beanbags mold to fit the contours of your camcorder while you rest it on the ground or other flat surface.

SHOOTING BETTER VIDEO

Leaning on a table to brace yourself also gives you a steadier shot. Or, you can kneel or sit down and rest the camcorder on your free knee or in your lap to reduce those camera shakes.

Other Non-Static Shots

Most of the time, it is your subjects that should be moving, not the camera. In certain situations, though, you might find it effective to use tracking shots, in which you physically move with the camera as it is shooting. Be careful, though. You still have to be very steady and avoid the nauseatingly jerky shots that this type of technique can produce. Think *Blair Witch Project*. Enough said.

Unique Angle Perspectives and Camera Tricks

Don't be afraid to experiment. The way you frame a scene or position, group, arrange, and view your players and objects can add emotional impact to your finished production.

Tilting the camera slightly can add tension to a scene.

Use dramatic angles. Low camera angles can make your characters and objects appear tall and powerful. Diminish your characters and objects with high camera angles.

SHOOTING BETTER VIDEO 21

Use extreme close-ups to frame inanimate objects, as well as your characters.

Using the basic techniques described in this chapter will help you avoid falling victim to some of the classic video-maker blunders (the most famous being never get involved in a land war in Asia). And now that you know some of the camera tricks that the pros use, you're that much closer to becoming the next Spike Lee. Well, at least your videos will be more interesting.

Part I Review Questions

1. What video cameras are compatible with iMovie? *See Digital Video Cameras in Chapter 1*

2. What is digital video? *See Chapter 1*

3. What are the minimum computer system requirements to run iMovie? *See The Software in Chapter 1*

4. Why is FireWire important to iMovie? *See FireWire Cable in Chapter 1*

5. Can you use your analog video in iMovie? *See Analog Video Converters in Chapter 1*

6. What is an establishing shot? *See Including an Establishing Shot in Chapter 2*

7. Why is it important to limit zooming and panning with your camcorder? *See Shooting Better Video in Chapter 2*

8. What is a better way to show the effects of zooming in and out or panning back and forth? *See Varying Angles and Shot Lengths in Chapter 2*

9. What are some tricks to help you keep your camera steady during filming? *See Steadying Secrets in Chapter 2*

10. How can you avoid bad lighting? *See Lighting in Chapter 2*

PART II

The Importing and Editing Room

Chapter 3
    Lights, Camera . . .
    Starting Your Epic 25

Chapter 4
    Beginning the Importing
    and Editing Process. 43

Chapter 5
    The Cutting Room Floor—
    Precise and Polished Editing 63

3

Lights, Camera . . . Starting Your Epic

Now that you know the basics about your equipment and how to capture video, it's time to fire up iMovie and feel your way around the iMovie screen. Quiet on the set, 'cause we're getting ready to roll. In this chapter, you'll learn how to:

- Connect your camcorder to your Mac
- Start iMovie
- Create a new project
- Preview your video
- Get help

Connecting Your Camcorder

The iMac DV comes with the FireWire cable you need to connect your digital video camera to your computer. Two FireWire ports are located on the right side of the machine. If you aren't using an iMac DV, your Macintosh (iMac, Power Mac, or PowerBook) must have a built-in FireWire port or an add-on FireWire card to connect to your DV camera and import digital video footage.

> **NOTE**
> If all you plan to do is edit digital video, QuickTime movies, or still pictures in iMovie, you don't need a FireWire port and cable. Without a FireWire, you can still download, install, and run iMovie on Macintosh computers that meet the minimum system requirements; you just can't import digital video from your camcorder.

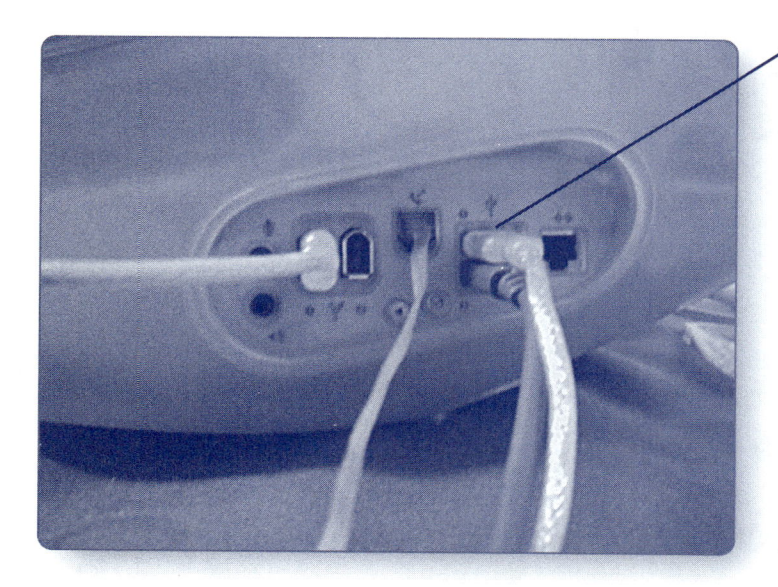

To connect your FireWire, just plug the longer, flatter (6-pin) end into the appropriate port in your Mac . . .

... and the smaller, square (4-pin) end into the appropriate slot in your camcorder. (This will vary depending on the make and model of your camera.) Now you're ready to roll.

Starting iMovie

iMovie is already installed on your computer if you have an iMac DV. All you have to do is fire it up. If you've downloaded and installed the free version from Apple, you can start iMovie from the iMovie folder on your hard drive. Refer to Appendix A, "Acquiring and Installing iMovie," if you still need to download and install iMovie.

Starting iMovie from the Desktop

If you have an iMac DV with the preinstalled iMovie program, then you can simply start iMovie from the desktop.

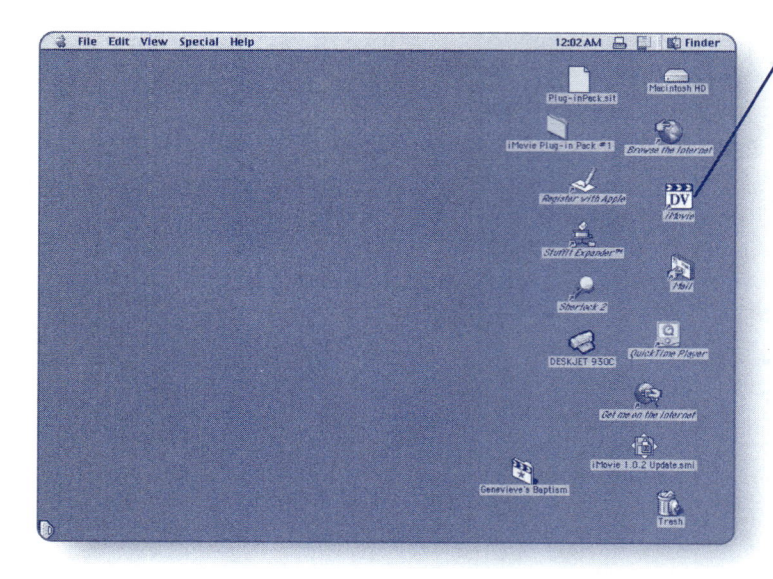

1. Double-click on the **iMovie icon** on your desktop. The program will start. A QuickTime movie will open and offer you three options: New Project, Open Project, or Quit.

You will learn about these options later in this chapter, in the "Creating A New Project" section.

Starting iMovie from the Folder

If you have downloaded and installed iMovie from the Apple Web site (see Appendix A, "Acquiring and Installing iMovie"), you will have to open iMovie from its folder on your Macintosh hard drive (HD).

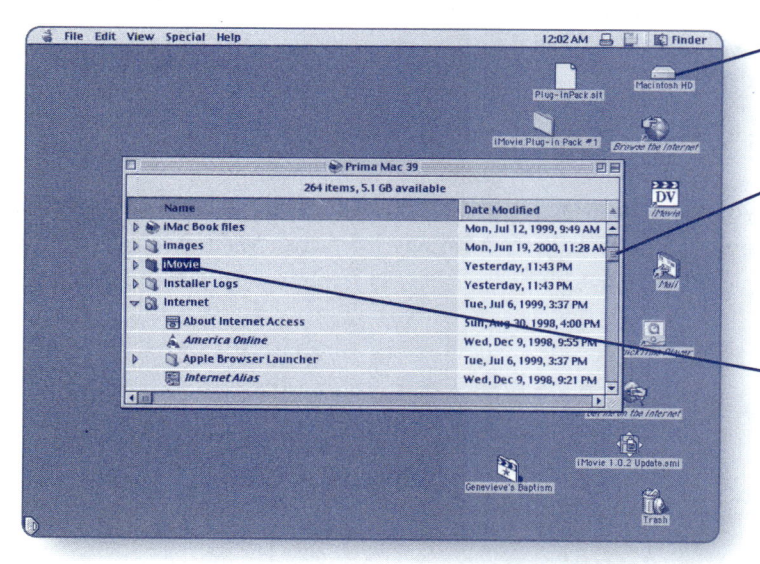

1. Click on the **Macintosh hard drive icon** on your desktop. The hard drive dialog box will open.

2. Press and hold the **mouse button** on the scroll bar and **drag** the **scroll bar** up or down to search for the iMovie folder.

3. Double-click on the **iMovie folder**. The iMovie folder will open.

STARTING iMOVIE

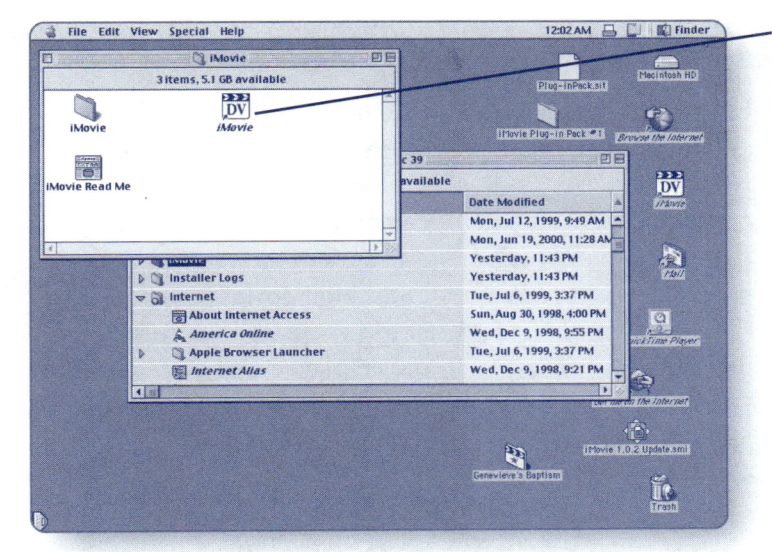

4. Double-click on the **iMovie icon.** The iMovie program will begin.

A QuickTime movie will open and offer you three options: New Project, Open Project, or Quit.

Creating a New Project

Before you begin, make sure you have your camcorder plugged into your iMac and you have some digital video footage loaded in your camcorder. When you started iMovie for the first time in the "Starting iMovie" section earlier in this chapter, a QuickTime movie played and gave you three options: New Project, Open Project, or Quit.

1. **Click** on **New Project**. The Create New Project dialog box will open.

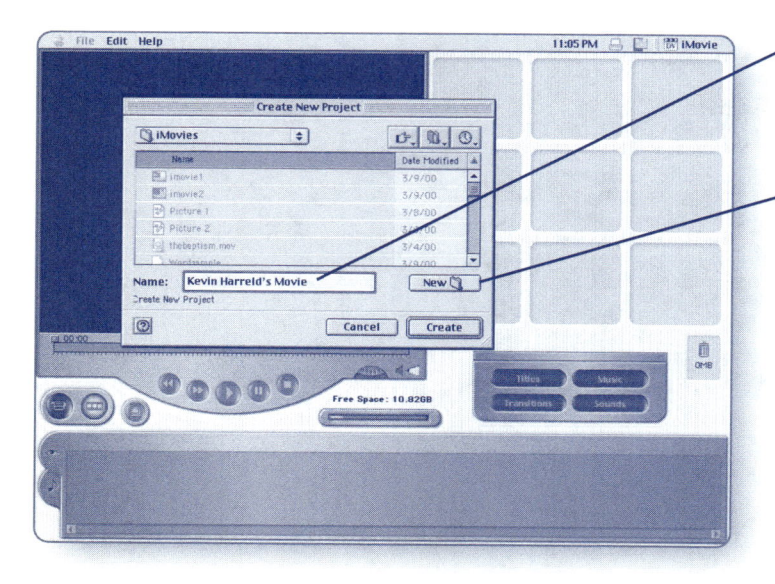

2. **Click** in the **Name text box** and **type** a **file name** for your movie.

3. **Click** on the **New Folder button**. The New Folder dialog box will open.

CREATING A NEW PROJECT 31

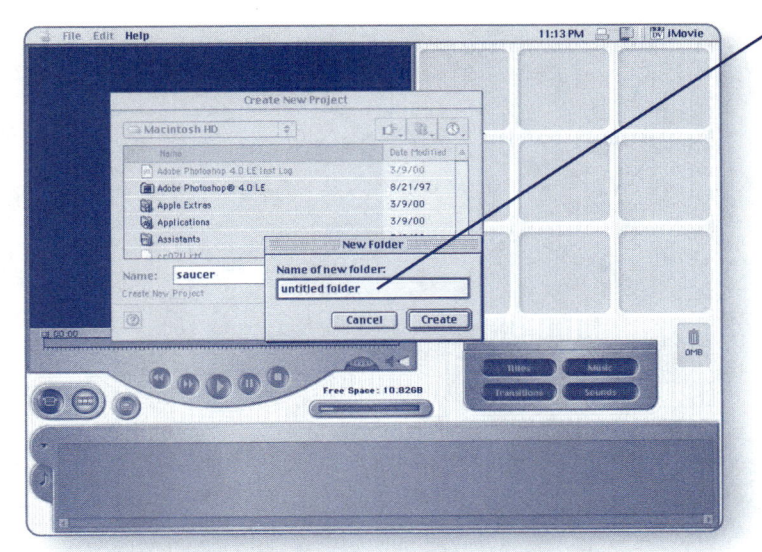

4. Click in the **Name of new folder text box** and **type** a **name** for your folder. This is where you will organize and keep track of all your epics.

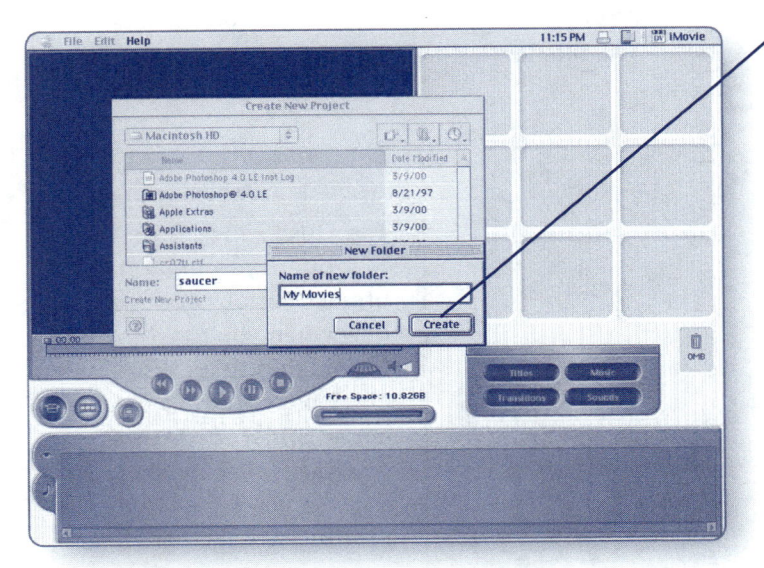

5. Click on **Create**. The Create New Project dialog box will open with your folder title in the destination box at the top and your movie file name in the Name text box.

CHAPTER 3: LIGHTS, CAMERA... STARTING YOUR EPIC

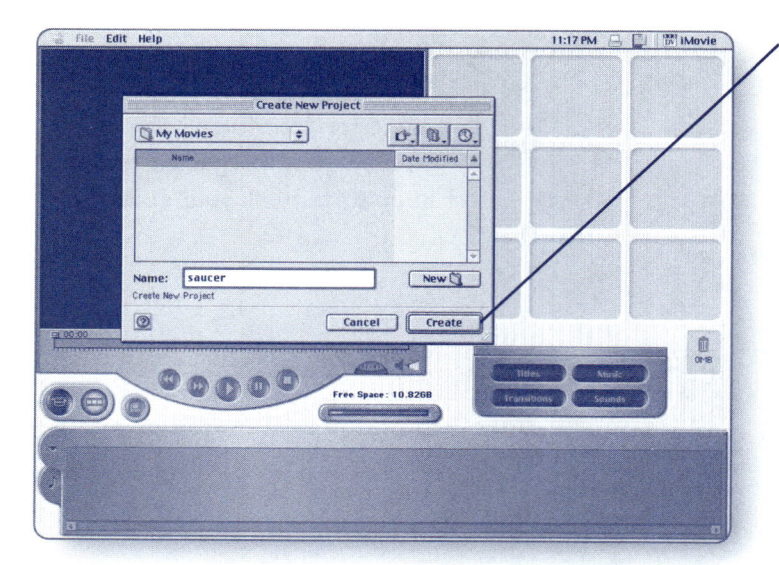

6. Click on **Create**.

The iMovie screen will appear with a blank Monitor window and your movie file name in the Clip Viewer at the bottom of the screen.

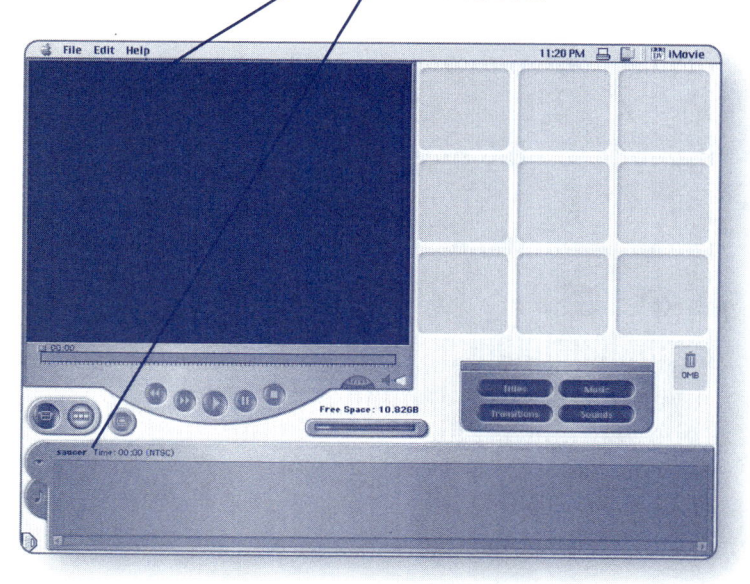

> **NOTE**
> The QuickTime movie that offers you the three project options appears only when you run iMovie for the first time. From now on, in order to create a new project in iMovie, you must click on File, and then click on New Project from the File menu that appears. Then, follow steps 2–6 in this section to create your new project.

Previewing Your Video in the Monitor Window

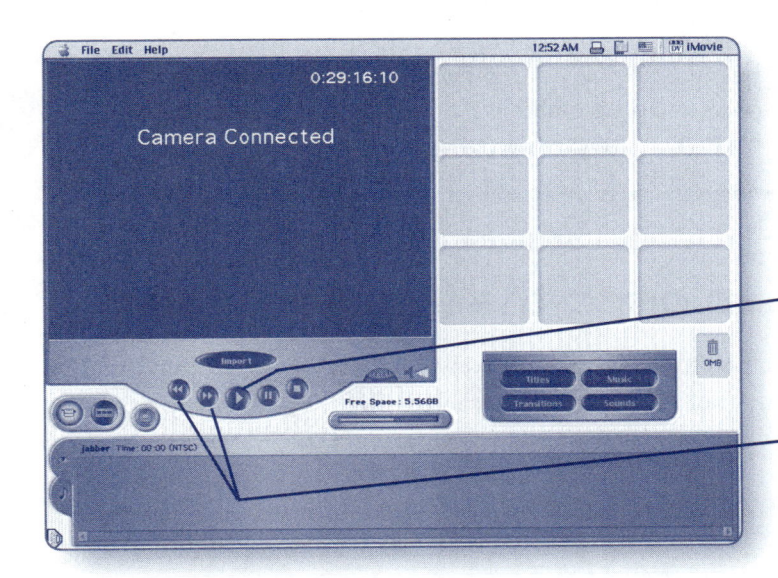

You can start previewing your footage with just a click of your mouse button. Make sure your camera is switched to VTR mode, or you won't be able to import your footage.

1. Click on the **Play button**. Your video will play in the Monitor window.

2. Click on the **Rewind and Fast Forward buttons** to scan through your video. Your video will rewind or fast forward in the direction you chose.

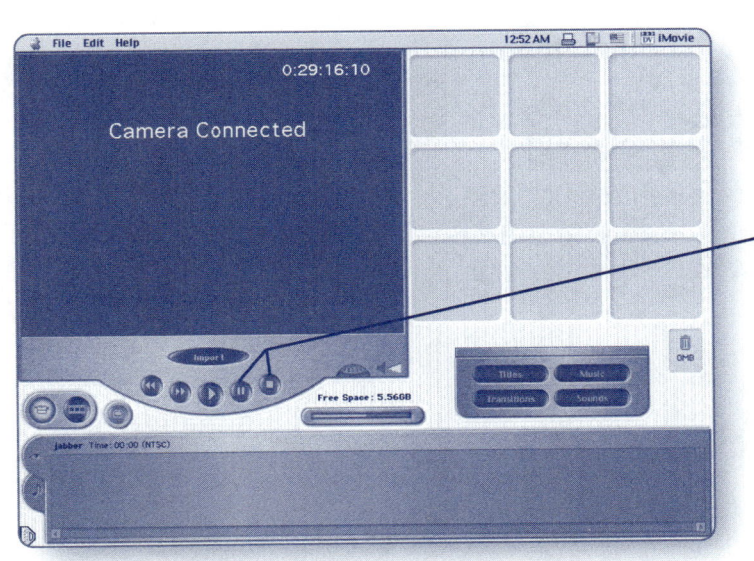

NOTE

You can use the Rewind and Fast Forward buttons on your camcorder to achieve the same results.

3. Click on the **Pause button or the Stop button** to pause or stop playing your video. Your video will pause or stop, depending on which option you selected.

CHAPTER 3: LIGHTS, CAMERA... STARTING YOUR EPIC

> **NOTE**
> The video playback on your monitor will be choppier than the playback you see on the viewfinder or flip-screen on your camcorder. This is because digital video on your computer monitor plays at approximately 20 frames per second, while normal DV plays at about 30 frames per second.

Exploring the iMovie Screen

Now that you've started iMovie, you will want to know all of the fabulous features you can toy with to make the perfect production. Here's a quick tour around the iMovie screen.

- **Monitor window.** This is where you can preview your video directly from your digital camera, using the Rewind, Fast Forward, Play, Stop, and Pause buttons along the bottom of the window. You will also preview your clips and iMovies here.

EXPLORING THE iMOVIE SCREEN   35

- **Shelf**. This is where you'll store clips that you might decide to use in your final epic.

- **Effects palette**. This is where you'll add titles, transitions, music, and sound effects.

- **Trash**. This is where you can discard your unwanted clips and free up that valuable hard disk space.

- **Viewer**. This is where your movie will come together. You will edit and place clips and transitions in the Clip Viewer and edit and place sounds in the Audio Viewer.

CHAPTER 3: LIGHTS, CAMERA... STARTING YOUR EPIC

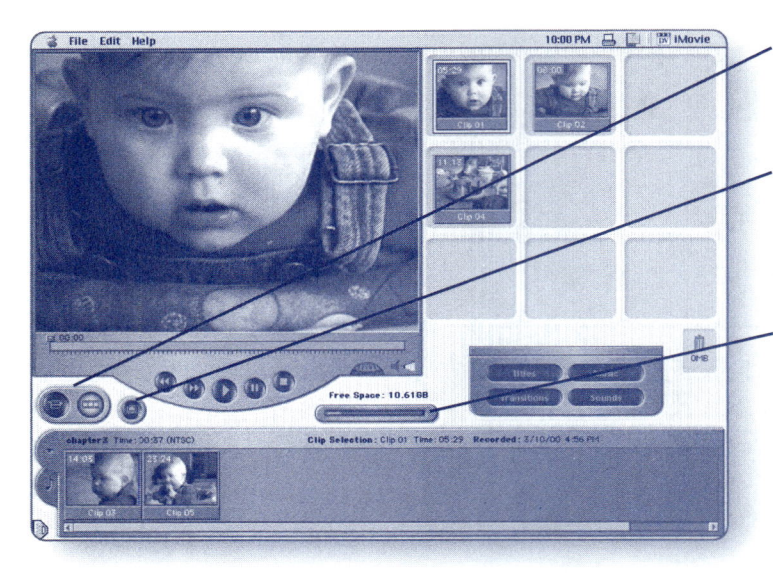

- **Mode buttons.** Click on these to use Camera mode or Edit mode.

- **Full-Screen button.** Click on this button to view your epic on your entire computer screen.

- **Disk Space gauge.** Use this feature to monitor your available hard disk space.

- **Taskbar.** As usual, the File, Edit, and Help menus guide you through tasks.

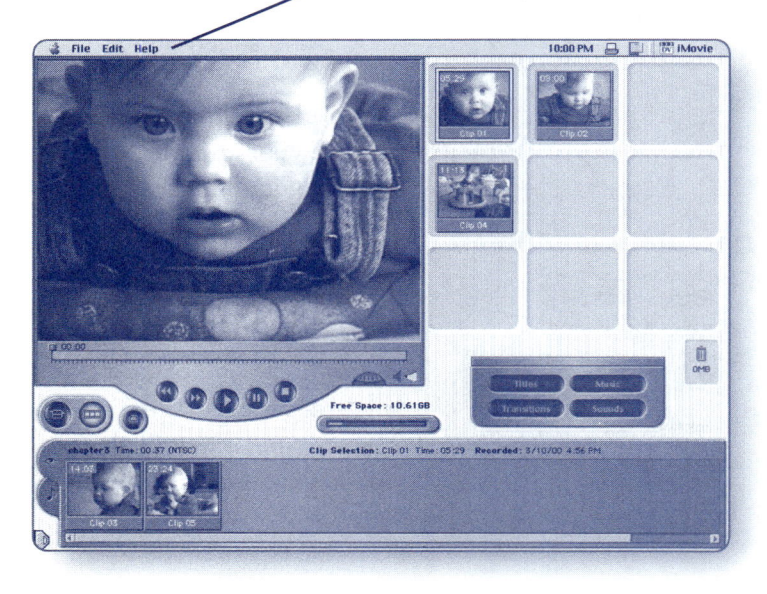

In subsequent chapters of this book, you will learn in much more detail how to use all of these features.

Getting Help

If you run into trouble and need a quick solution to your problem, you can always access the Help files within iMovie. Hopefully, if I've done my job, by the time you finish reading this book you'll never need to use these Help features. But, I've never been one to turn away a helping hand.

Getting Help from the Help Menu

The Help menu offers quick answers to specific questions in iMovie. A simple point, click, and search can yield the information you need.

1. **Click** on **Help**. The Help menu will appear.

2. **Click** on **iMovie Help**. The iMovie Help dialog box will open.

CHAPTER 3: LIGHTS, CAMERA . . . STARTING YOUR EPIC

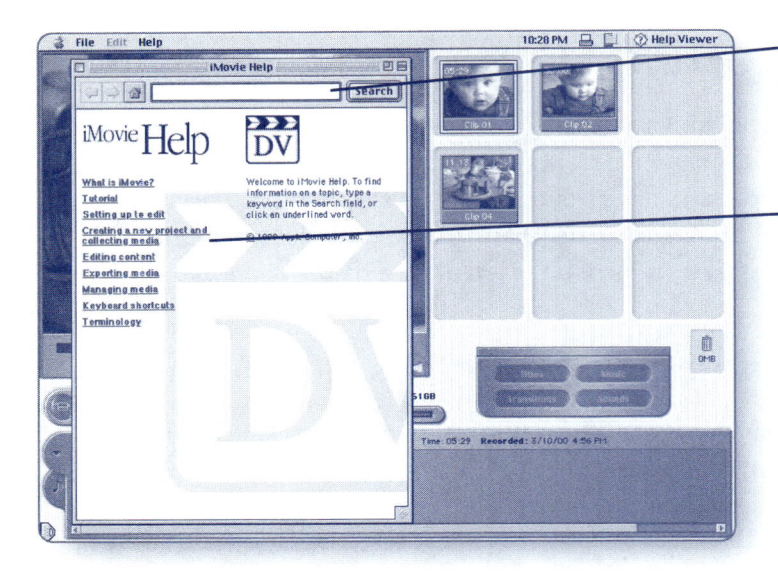

3a. Type a **help topic** in the text box and **click** on **Search**.

OR

3b. **Click** on a **topic** in the list on the left side of the dialog box. The Search Results page will appear and display a list of closely related topics.

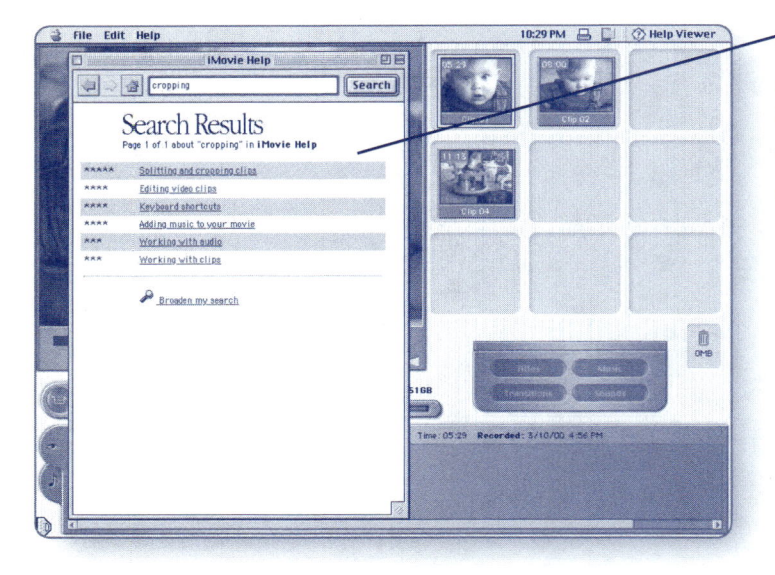

4. **Click** on the **topic** about which you want to learn more. Information about that specific topic will appear in a new dialog box.

GETTING HELP 39

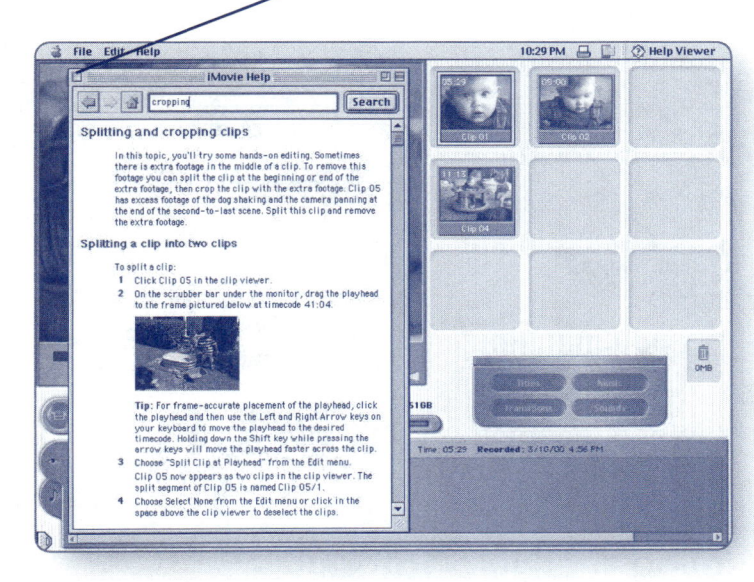

5. Click on the **Close button** to exit Help. The Help dialog box will close.

Getting Help from the Balloons

Macintosh computers also have a help feature called balloons. With this feature, you can hold your mouse pointer over an icon, button, tool, and so on, and a balloon will appear with an explanation of the element.

1. Click on **Help**. The Help menu will appear.

2. Click on **Show Balloons**. The Show Balloons option will be selected.

40   **CHAPTER 3: LIGHTS, CAMERA . . . STARTING YOUR EPIC**

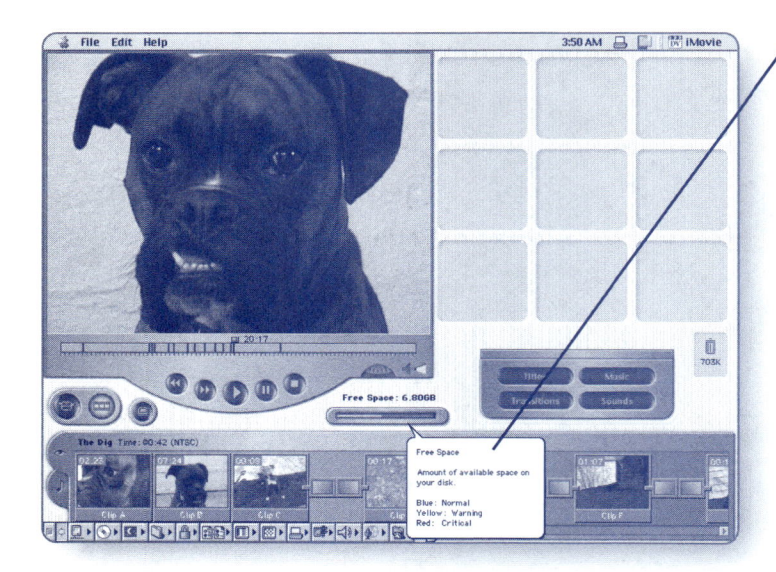

3. **Place** the **mouse pointer** over an area on the screen about which you want more information. A balloon with a brief description of the screen element will appear.

> **NOTE**
>
> To turn off the help balloons, click on File, and then click on Hide Balloons. The balloons will disappear.

Running the Help Tutorial

With the iMovie version that is installed on iMac DVs and the iMovie version that you can order on CD-ROM, there is a built-in tutorial with sample clips with which you can follow along, if you desire.

1. **Click** on **Help**. The Help menu will appear.

2. **Click** on **iMovie Tutorial**. The iMovie Help dialog box will open.

GETTING HELP 41

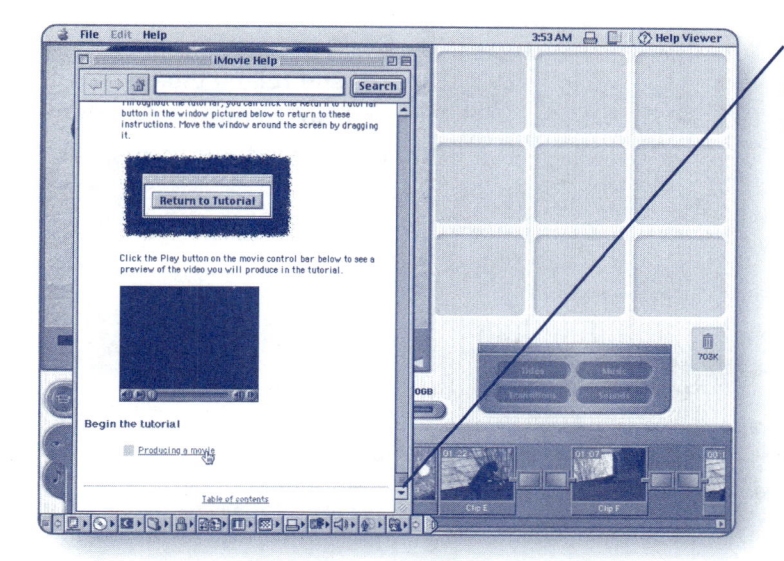

3. Click on the **down arrow** to scroll down to the bottom of the dialog box.

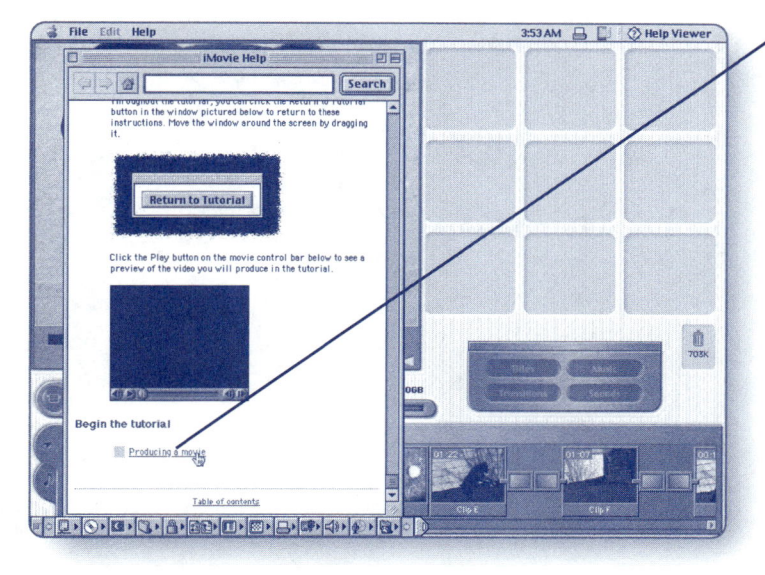

4. Click on **Producing a movie**. The tutorial will begin.

CHAPTER 3: LIGHTS, CAMERA . . . STARTING YOUR EPIC

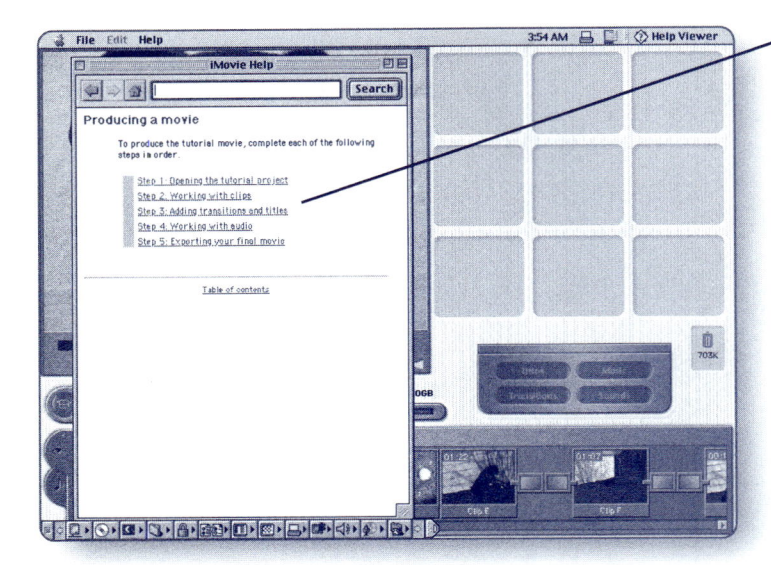

5. Click on a **topic** in the tutorial and **follow** the on-screen **instructions** to view the tutorial for the topic you selected.

4

Beginning the Importing and Editing Process

Before you jump in and start cutting scenes from your movie, you should have a storyboard picture of your epic in your mind so that you know what footage you need to gather and import into iMovie. iMovie will help you make the production, but it cannot provide your vision. After you have planned out all your shots and captured the footage, you're ready to import and begin editing. In this chapter, you'll learn how to:

- Switch modes
- Import a clip from your camcorder
- Store clips
- Use the scene detection feature
- Adjust the quality of video playback
- Import analog video

Switching Modes

iMovie includes two different work modes: Edit and Camera. Before you can begin editing your clips in iMovie, you need to get into Edit mode. If importing digital video clips is on your agenda, you need to jump into Camera mode.

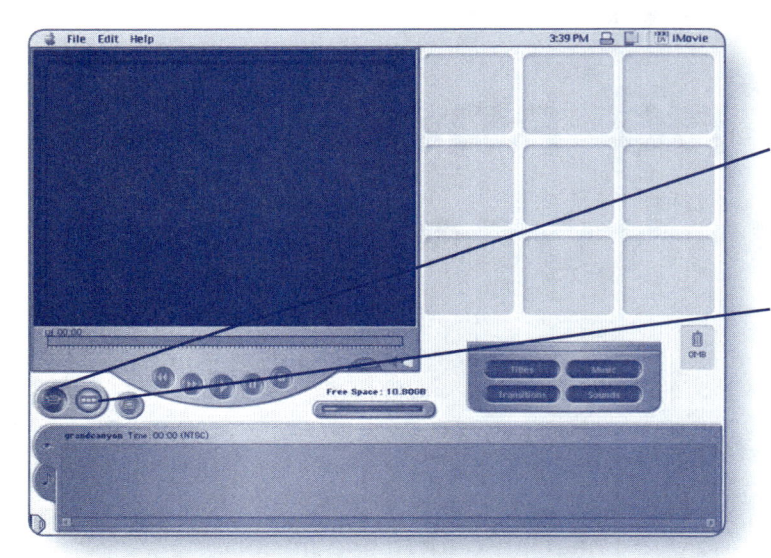

1. Click on one of the following **mode buttons**:

- **Camera.** The blue screen in the Monitor window will indicate whether the camera is connected or not.

- **Edit.** The blue screen in the monitor window will turn to black.

Importing a Clip from Your Digital Video Camera

Now that you've captured your award-winning footage, you need to get it into iMovie so that you can begin playing with this exciting editing tool. Make sure that your digital video camera is connected to your Mac, that your digital videotape of footage is in your camcorder, and that the power is on and the camera is switched to the VTR setting.

IMPORTING A CLIP FROM YOUR DIGITAL VIDEO CAMERA 45

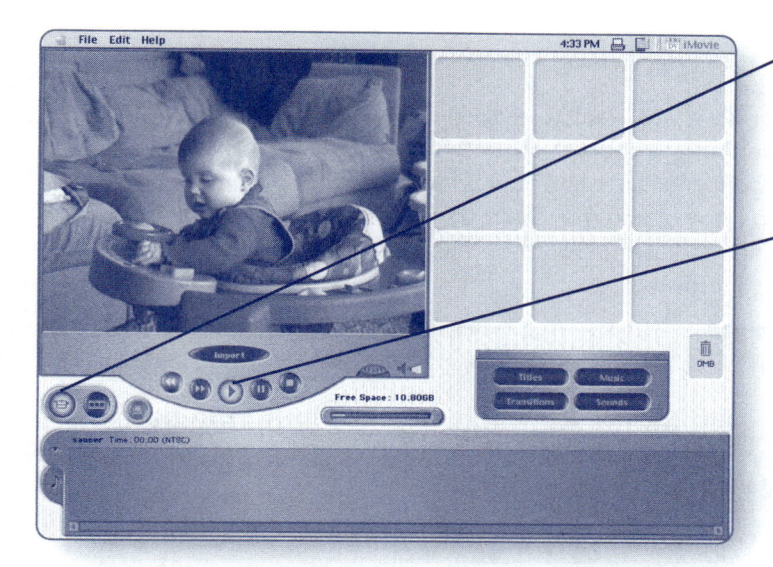

1. **Click** on the **Camera mode button**. You will now be in Camera mode, so that you can import your video.

2a. **Click** on the **Play button** on the Monitor window.

OR

2b. **Press** the **Play button** on your camcorder. You video will play in the Monitor window.

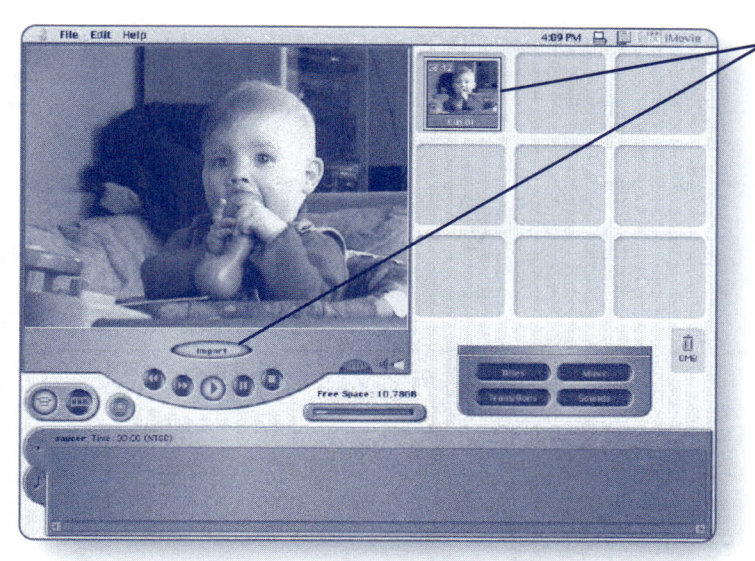

3. **Click** on the **Import button** in the Monitor window. The clip will appear on the Shelf, with a running time count in the upper-left corner and the clip number labeled at the bottom of the clip.

CHAPTER 4: BEGINNING THE IMPORTING AND EDITING PROCESS

NOTE

You can skip steps 2a or 2b if you want to—clicking on the Import button will immediately import the video from your camcorder. But, if you want more control over what footage you want to import into iMovie, you may want to press the Play button first, and then click on Import when you see the footage that you want to import.

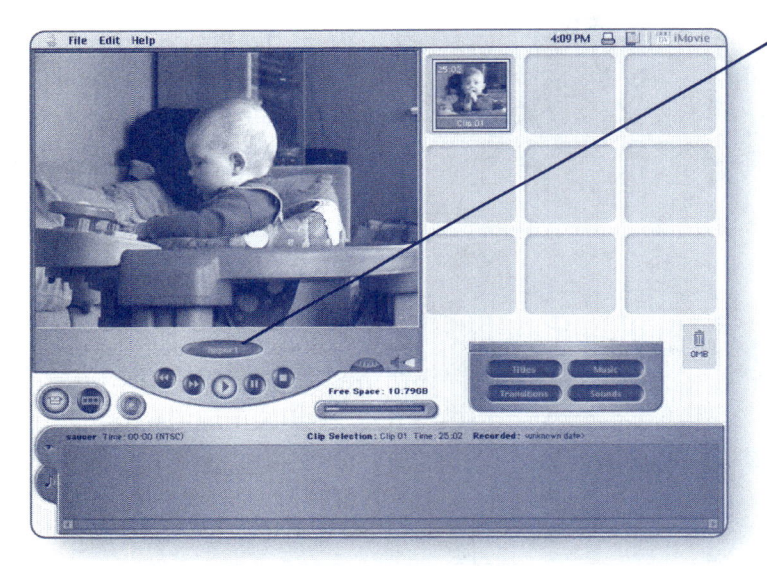

4. **Click** on the **Import button** again when you want to stop importing that particular clip. The final time length of the clip will appear in the upper-left corner of the clip.

TIP

Don't worry about beginning and ending your imported clip exactly where you want it. You'll edit the individual clips with cropping tools later. With that in mind, it's best to give yourself some breathing room. Start importing your video a few frames ahead of where you want the clip to start. Then, stop importing a few frames after where you want the clip to end. This will ensure that you have all the footage you want in that particular clip, and you can always edit it again later.

Storing Clips

As you just learned, when you import digital video to iMovie, the clips that you import are automatically saved to the Shelf. This is the easiest way to manage your clips in the initial stages of your editing. However, you can change this setting to automatically save your clips directly into the Clip Viewer if you desire. You can also increase the number of clips that you can store in the Shelf.

Selecting the Destination of Your Imported Clips

iMovie will automatically save your imported clips to the Shelf unless you tell it to save them to the Clip Viewer. At this stage, it may be easier to see and work on your initial, raw clips in the Shelf. On the other hand, the Shelf only holds up to 12 clips on most monitors, so if you want to continuously add clips without interruption, you might want to tell iMovie to automatically save them to the Clip Viewer.

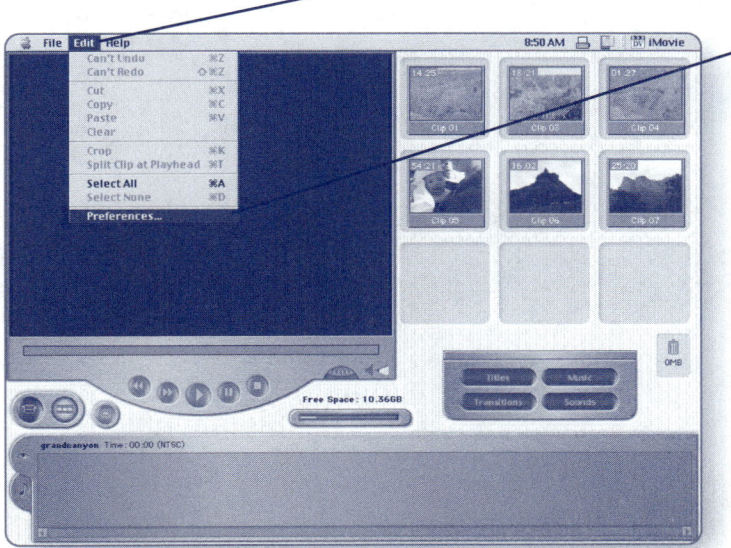

1. **Click** on **Edit**. The Edit menu will appear.

2. **Click** on **Preferences**. The Preferences dialog box will open.

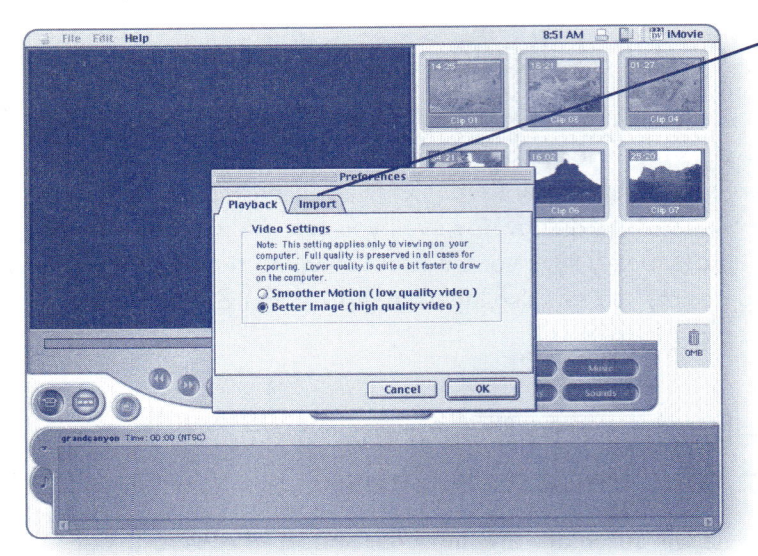

CHAPTER 4: BEGINNING THE IMPORTING AND EDITING PROCESS

3. Click on the **Import tab**. The tab will move to the front. The Shelf option should already be selected, which means that when you import your video, the clip will go directly into the Shelf.

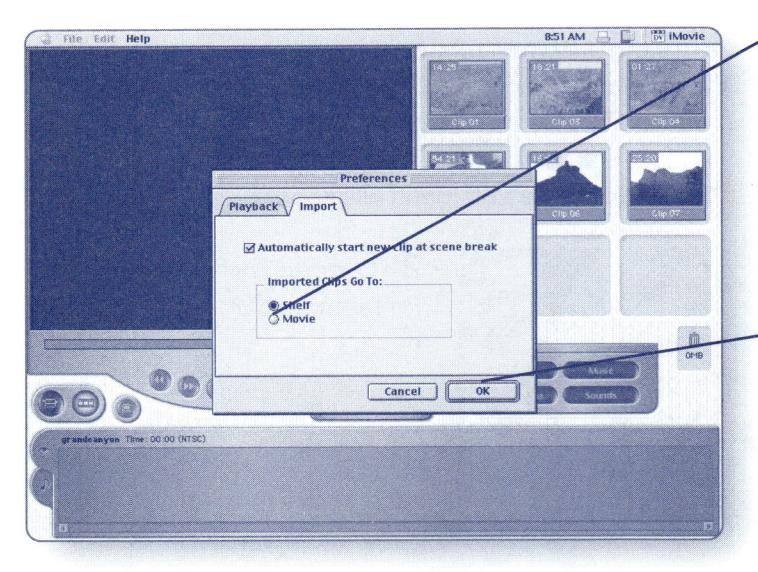

4. Click on the **Movie option** if you want you your imported clips to go to the Viewer. You'll learn more about the Viewer in Chapter 5, "The Cutting Room Floor—Precise and Polished Editing."

5. Click on **OK** to save your changes.

STORING CLIPS 49

Expanding the Shelf

If your monitor resolution is set to 800 x 600, then the number of clips you can store on the Shelf is nine. You can expand this to 12 if you change your screen resolution to 1024 x 768.

1. Click on the **Apple icon** at the top-left corner of your monitor. The Apple menu will appear.

2. Move the **mouse pointer** down to Control Panels. The Control Panels menu will appear.

3. Click on **Monitors**. The Monitor dialog box will open.

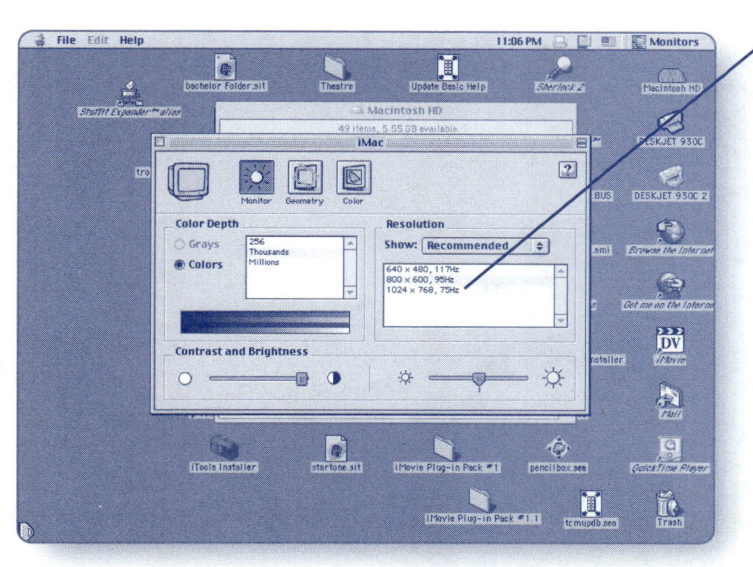

4. Click on **1024 x 768** in the Resolution window. Your monitor resolution will change to 1024 x 768 pixels.

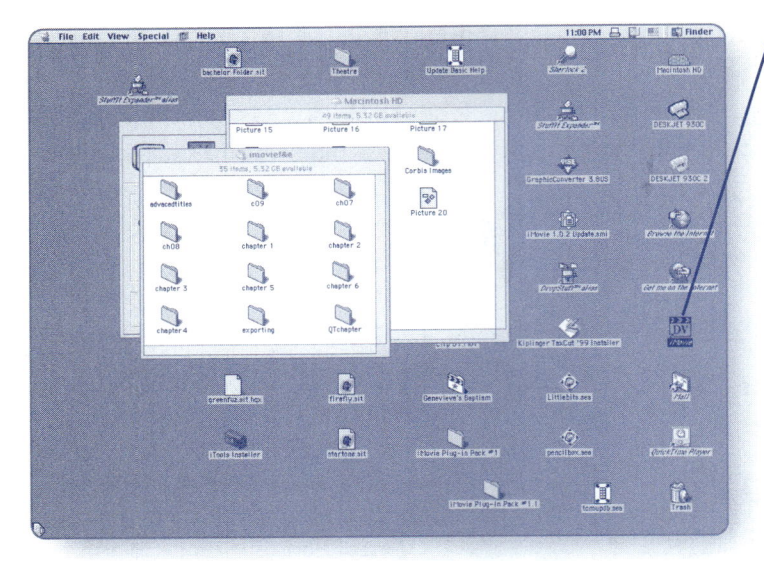

50 CHAPTER 4: BEGINNING THE IMPORTING AND EDITING PROCESS

5. Double-click on the **iMovie icon** on your desktop. iMovie will open.

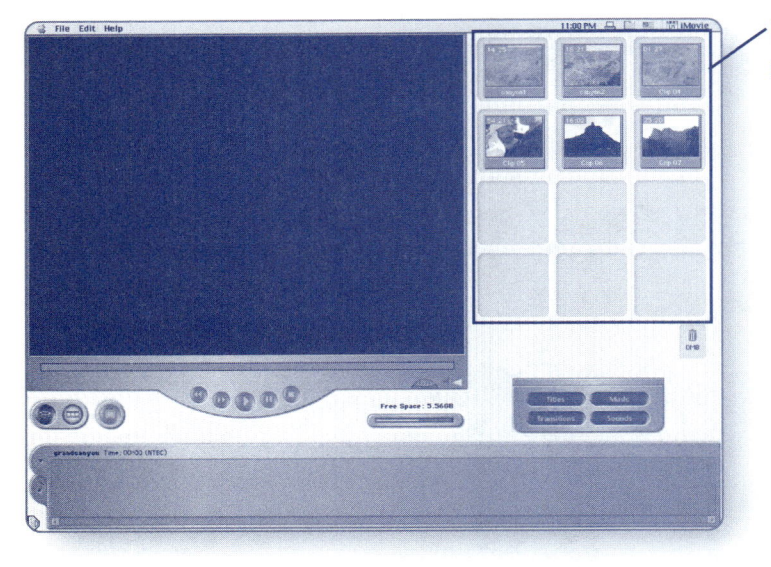

Notice that the Shelf now has space for 12 clips.

Using iMovie's Scene Detection Feature

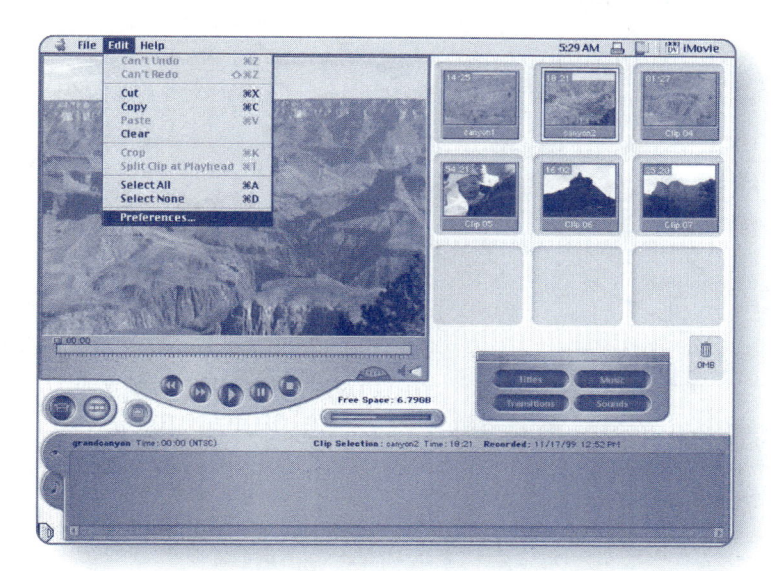

You can capture clips using an automatic scene detection feature. iMovie will automatically find the beginning and end of a scene that you captured and save it as a clip. If you are a moviemaker who likes to stop and start scenes often, this is a great feature.

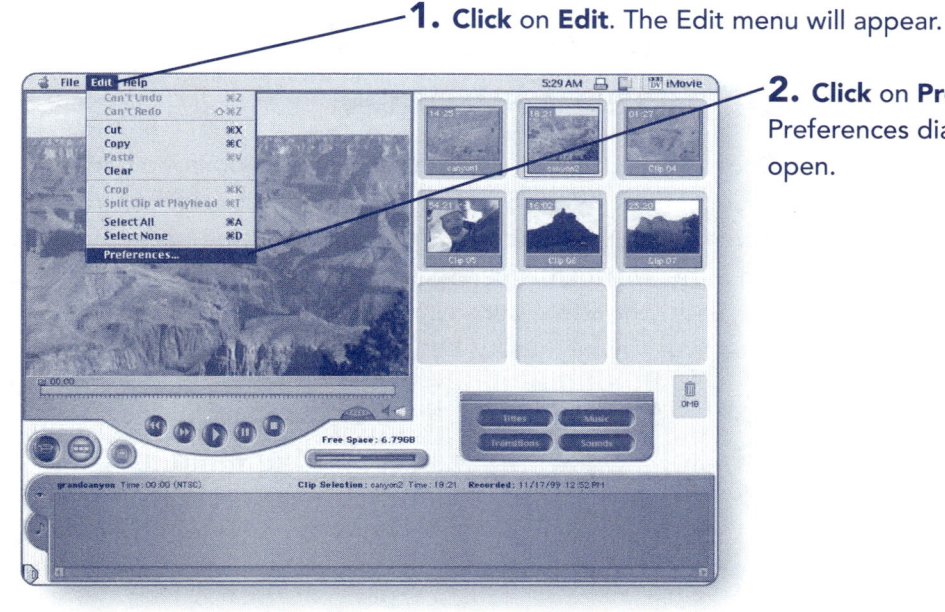

1. Click on **Edit**. The Edit menu will appear.

2. Click on **Preferences**. The Preferences dialog box will open.

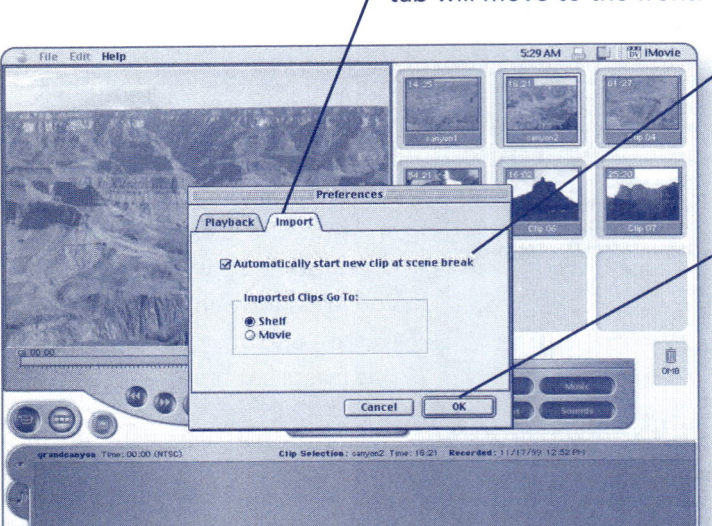

3. Click on the **Import tab**, if it isn't already selected. The tab will move to the front.

4. Click on the **Automatically start new clip at scene break check box**. The option will be selected.

5. Click on **OK**. Your changes will be saved. Now, when iMovie detects where you started a scene, a new clip will appear in the Shelf. When it detects the end of the scene, that clip will stop importing and a new clip will appear with the next scene you captured. You can just sit back and watch iMovie create the clips for you.

Adjusting the Quality of Video Playback

Depending on how you like to see your video played back on your computer, you can make adjustments accordingly. You have two choices: Smoother Motion and Better Image. Smoother Motion basically gives you smoother video playback, but with reduced image quality. Better Image gives you crisper image quality, but choppier video playback.

ADJUSTING THE QUALITY OF VIDEO PLAYBACK 53

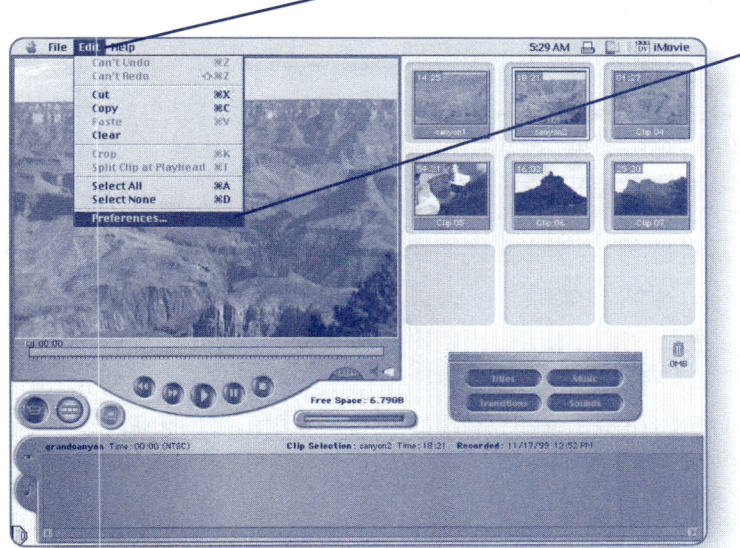

1. Click on **Edit**. The Edit menu will appear.

2. Click on **Preferences**. The Preferences dialog box will open.

3. Click on the **Playback tab**, if it isn't already selected. The Playback tab will move to the front.

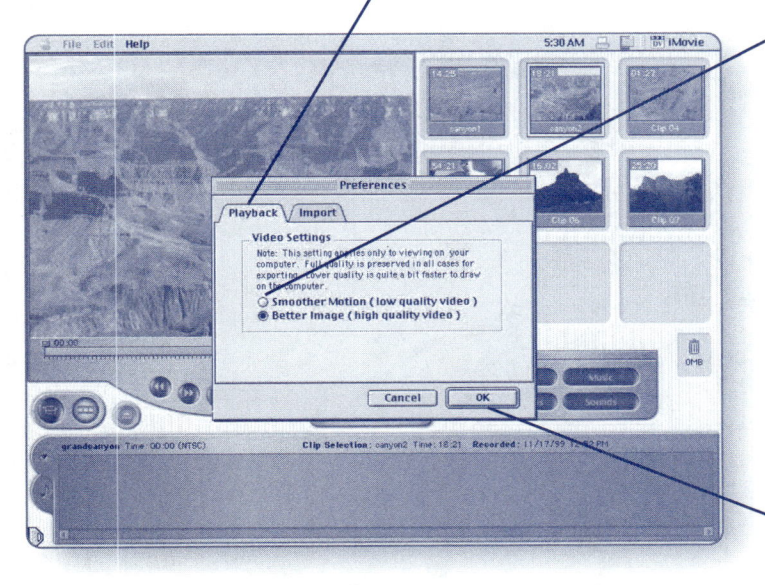

4. Click on **one** of the following:

- **Smoother Motion (low quality video)**. Smoother Motion will decrease visual quality to give you more frames per second during playback.

- **Better Image (high quality video)**. Better Image will give you crisper images, but you will see a choppier playback.

5. Click on **OK**. Your changes will be saved.

CHAPTER 4: BEGINNING THE IMPORTING AND EDITING PROCESS

> **NOTE**
> This feature is only for the video playback on your computer screen. These settings do not affect the quality of the movie you make when you export your finished product to videotape or QuickTime, which you will learn about in Chapter 10, "Compressing and Exporting Your Movies."

Exiting iMovie

Ready to take a break from iMovie? You can easily quit the program and save any changes you have made to your project.

1. **Click** on **File**. The File menu will appear.

2. **Click** on **Quit**. A warning box will appear.

EXITING iMOVIE 55

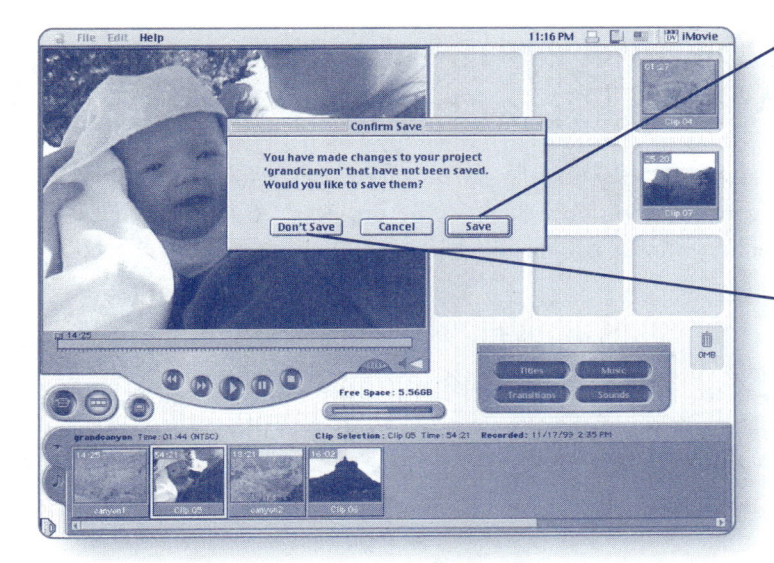

3a. **Click** on **Save** to save any changes you made to your iMovie project. iMovie will save the changes and quit.

OR

3b. **Click** on **Don't Save** to disregard any changes you have made to the project. iMovie will quit without saving any changes.

OR

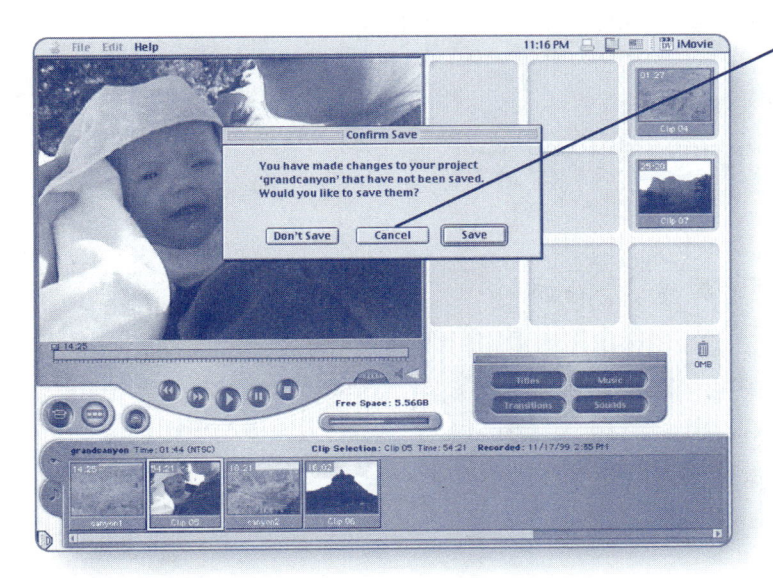

3c. **Click** on **Cancel** if you decide you don't want to exit iMovie. You will return to your iMovie project.

CHAPTER 4: BEGINNING THE IMPORTING AND EDITING PROCESS

Opening an Existing iMovie Project

By now you may have imported hours of footage and saved it as three or four individual iMovie projects. You can open an existing iMovie project by using the Open command.

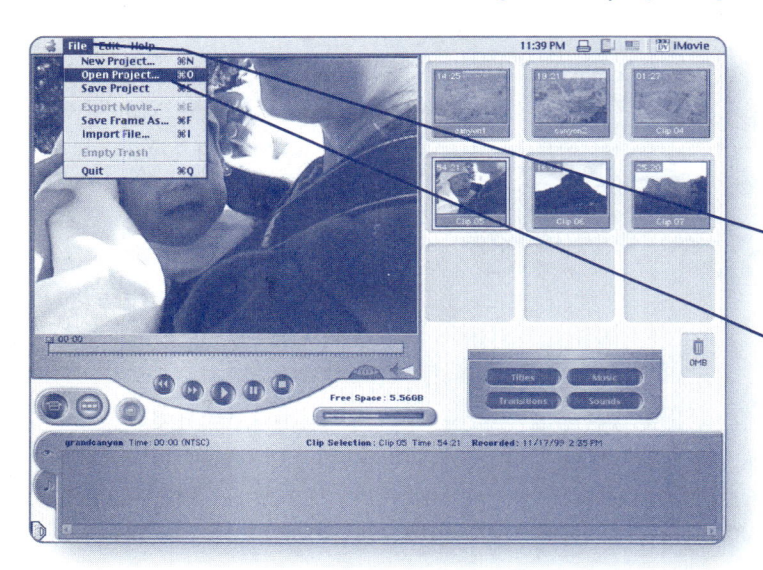

1. Open iMovie, if you don't already have it open. iMovie will open with the last project you worked on in the Shelf.

2. Click on **File**. The File menu will appear.

3. Click on **Open Project**. The Open Existing Project dialog box will open.

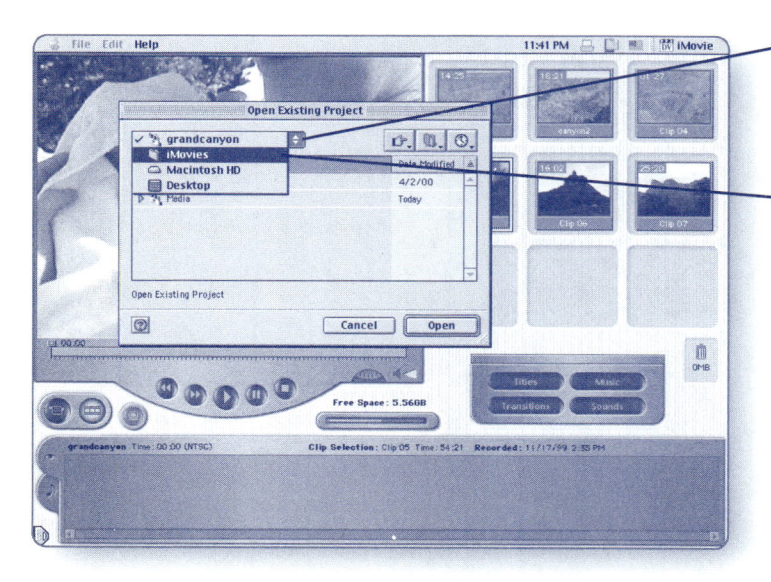

4. Click on the **up and down arrows** to the right of the list box. A pop-up menu will appear.

5. Click on the **folder** in which your movie resides. A list of your movies will appear.

OPENING AN EXISTING iMOVIE PROJECT   57

6. Click on the **movie** that you want to open. The movie will be selected.

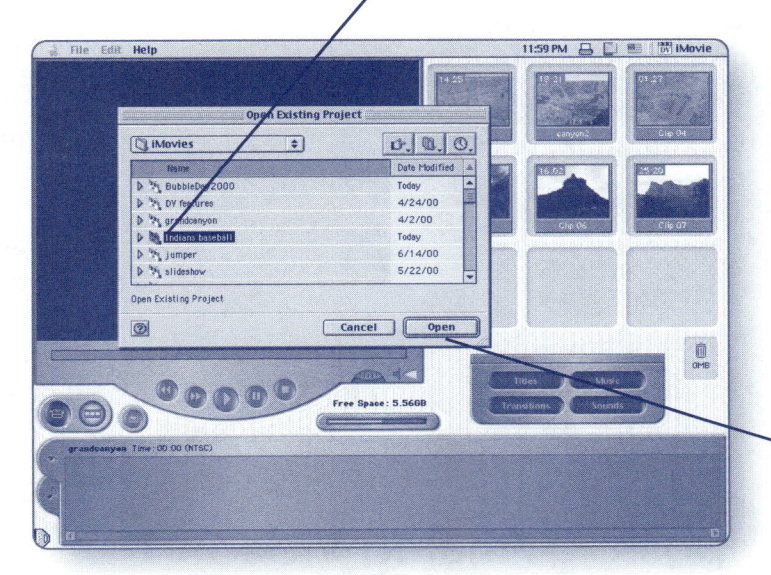

NOTE
The movie icon you see in Step 6 is actually a folder of your movie project. It houses two icons: the actual iMovie and a Media folder that contains all of the individual clips within the iMovie.

7. Click on **Open**. Another dialog box will open, containing the actual iMovie and the Media folder.

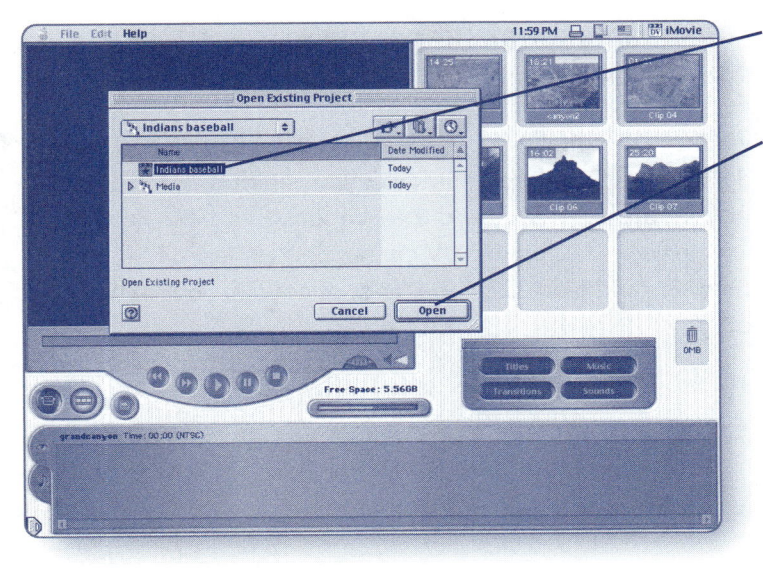

8. Click on the **iMovie icon**. The movie will be selected.

9. Click on **Open**.

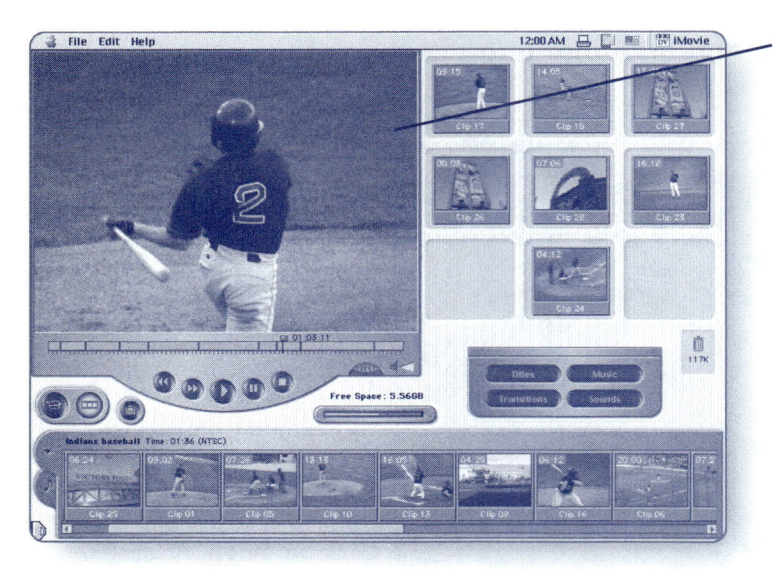

The movie will open.

Importing Analog Video

As I mentioned in Chapter 1, "Tools of the Trade," if you want to import analog video, but you don't have a DV camcorder, you need a special converter box that will convert the analog video to a digital video signal.

If you have a digital video camera and you want to add some old VHS tape footage into iMovie, you can dub the VHS footage onto a DV tape and then import it into iMovie. All you need is a VCR, some A/V connecting cables, a DV camcorder and blank DV tape, and, of course, your VHS footage.

IMPORTING ANALOG VIDEO 59

1. **Insert** your **VHS tape** into your VCR and **insert** a blank **DV tape** into your camcorder.

2. Attach one end of the **A/V connecting cables** to the appropriate ports on your camcorder.

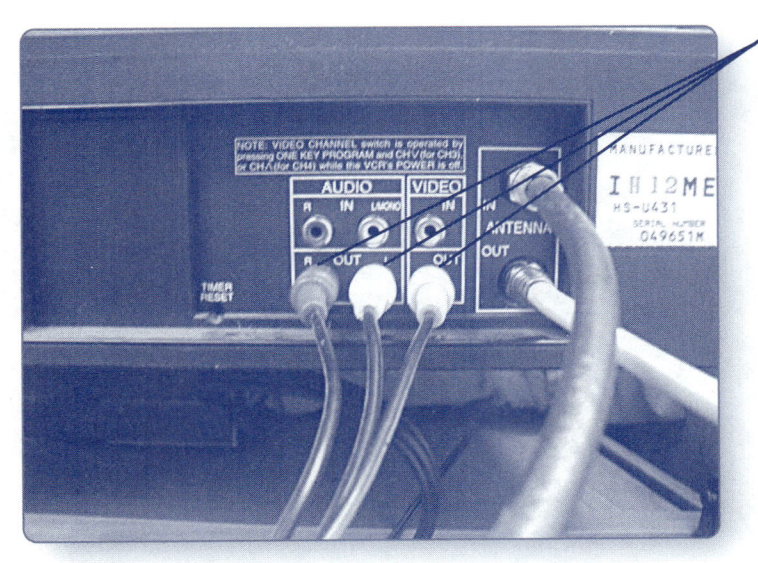

3. Attach the other end of the **A/V connecting cables** to the output ports on your VCR.

60   CHAPTER 4: BEGINNING THE IMPORTING AND EDITING PROCESS

4. Set your **camcorder** to VTR and **press** the **Play button** on your VCR.

The VHS footage will play in your camcorder and . . .

. . . on your television.

IMPORTING ANALOG VIDEO   61

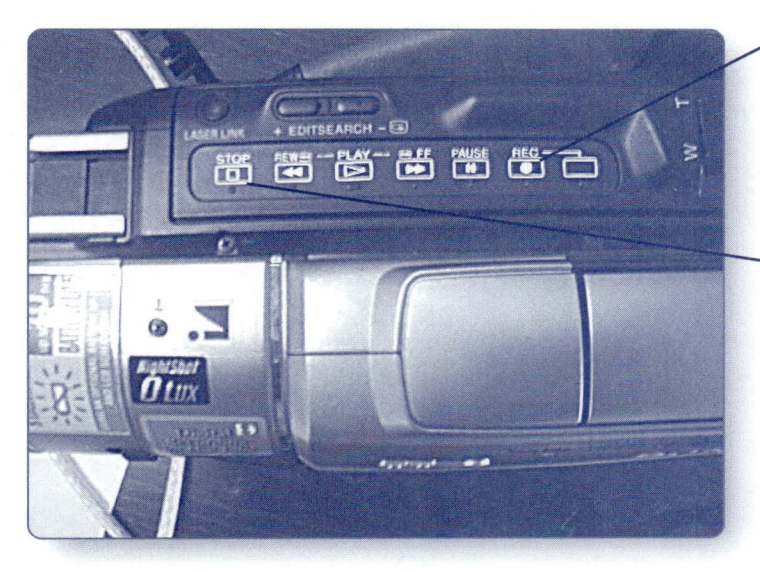

5. Press the **Record button** on your camcorder at the instant you want your footage to start recording onto your DV tape. The footage will start recording.

6. Press the **Stop button** on your camcorder when you want to cease recording the footage. The recording will stop.

You now have your analog video footage on your DV tape, ready to import into iMovie. Just follow the steps in the "Importing a Clip from Your Digital Video Camera" section in this chapter to help you import the clip into iMovie, and you're all done.

> **NOTE**
> You may notice that the analog video you imported is a bit grainy. It's definitely not going to have the sharp quality of your digital videos, but the picture still looks pretty good, and the important thing is that you got the footage into iMovie.

5

The Cutting Room Floor—Precise and Polished Editing

With iMovie, you can edit your clips to filter out hours of the repetitive footage you take while waiting for your seven-month-old daughter to say, "Da-Da." You can make it look as if she said it on cue, even if it did take an entire roll of videotape. You will learn to appreciate what Hollywood film editors do to make a great film. And the next time you watch the Academy Awards, maybe you won't go to the kitchen to make a sandwich when the Oscar for Best Film Editing is announced. In this chapter, you'll learn how to:

- Select and rename clips
- Crop and split clips
- Copy and move clips
- Throw clips in the trash

Selecting Clips

You can edit your clips one at a time or several at once. It's just a matter of selecting one clip or a group of clips, and then starting your work.

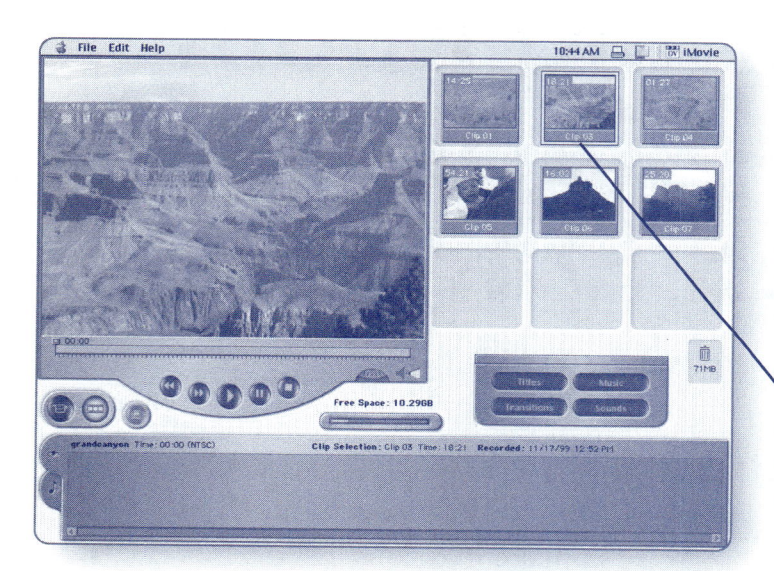

Selecting a Single Clip to Edit

Before you start editing your clips, you have to identify what clip you want to work on. Selecting a single clip is a simple task.

1. On the Shelf, **click** on the **clip** you want to edit. The clip will be highlighted and will appear in the Monitor window.

NOTE

You might notice that a long blue bar appears in the Monitor window after you select your clip. This is called the Scrubber bar. You will learn more about this editing tool later in this chapter, in the "Cropping Clips" section.

Selecting Multiple Clips

There might be times when you need to select more than one clip at a time (for example, when you are moving clips from the Shelf to the Viewer, which you'll learn about later in this chapter, in the "Moving Clips from the Shelf to the Viewer" section).

RENAMING A CLIP 65

1. Click on a **clip**. The clip will be selected.

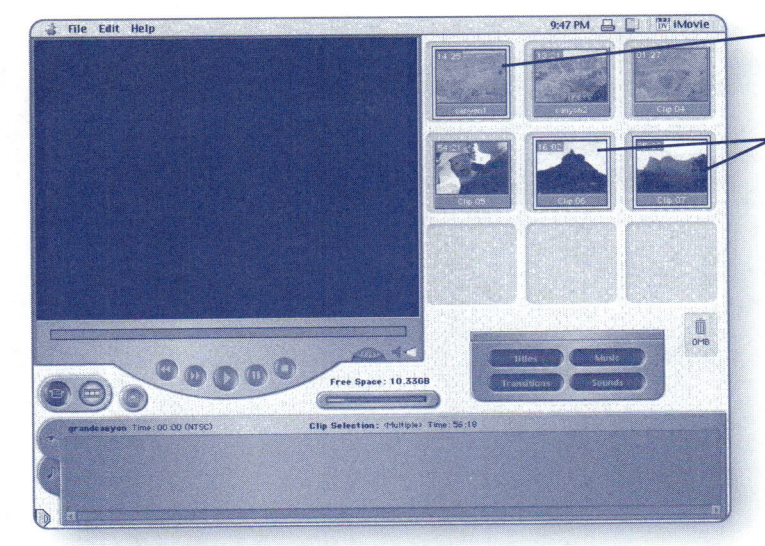

2. Press and hold the **Shift key** and **click** on any other **clips** that you want to select. All the clips that you click on will be selected.

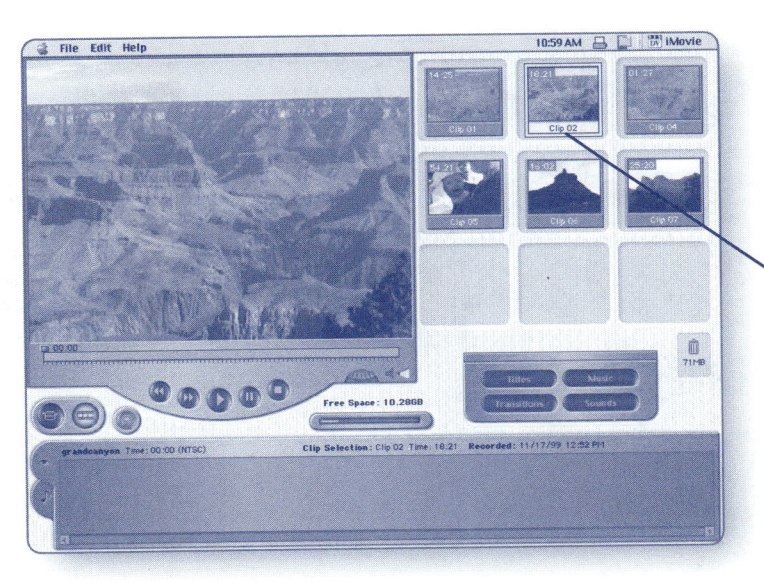

Renaming a Clip

Renaming a clip makes it easier to remember what that clip contains.

1. Click on the **name** of the clip you want to rename (in this case, I've selected Clip 02). The clip will be selected.

66 CHAPTER 5: THE CUTTING ROOM FLOOR

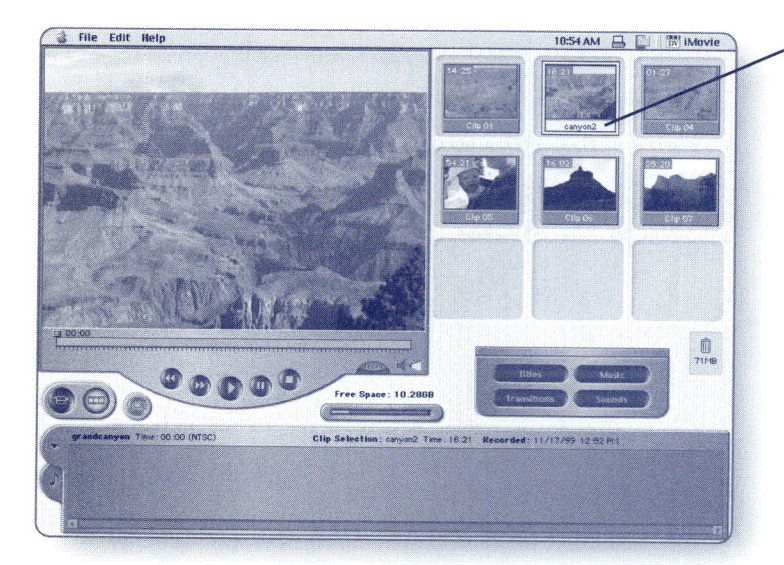

2. Type the **name** of your clip.

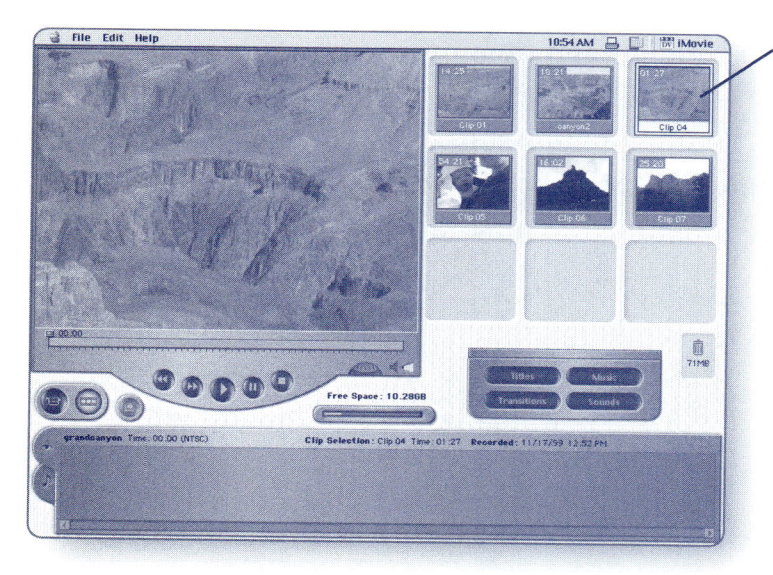

3. Click anywhere on the **screen** outside of the clip, or press Enter. Your new name will take effect.

CROPPING CLIPS

Cropping Clips

Remember when I said you'd get to crop out the unwanted footage from the beginning and end of your clips? Here's your chance.

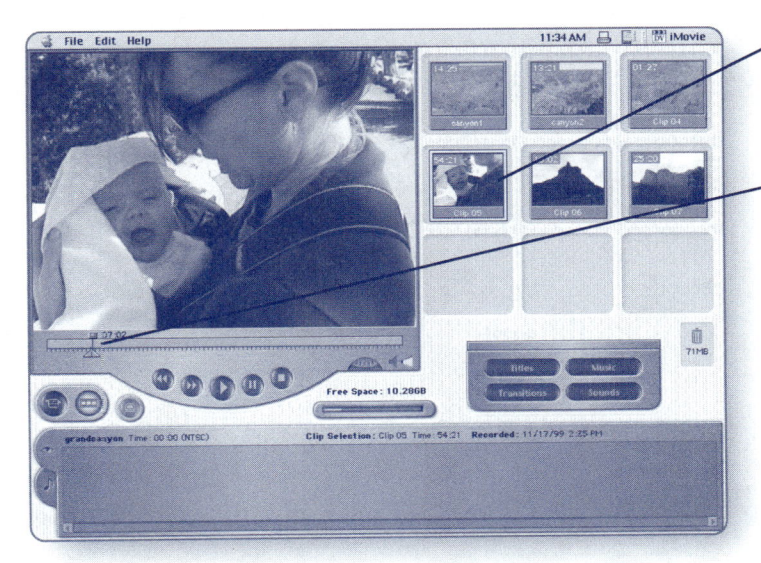

1. Click on the **clip** you want to crop. The clip will appear in the Monitor window.

2. Click just below the blue **Scrubber bar** in the Monitor window. Two triangles called crop markers will appear below the Scrubber bar, and a tiny monitor icon called the playhead will appear just above the Scrubber bar. A time counter will also appear next to the playhead.

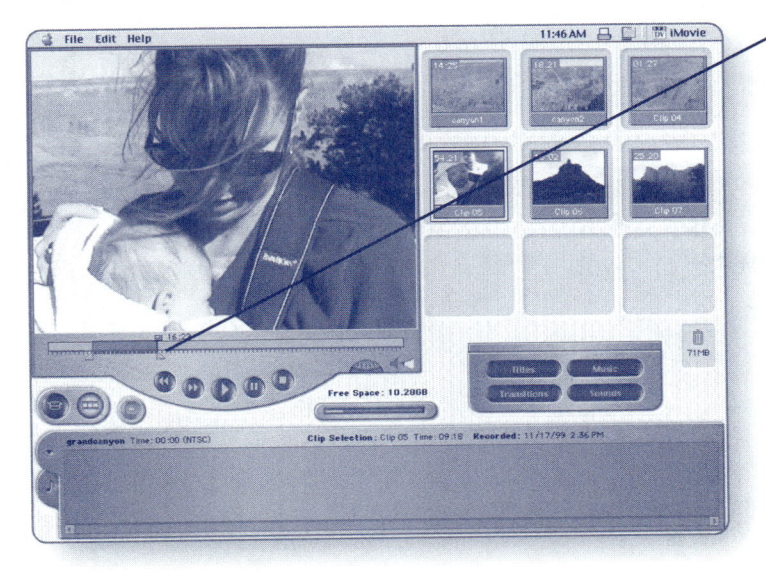

3. Click and hold the **mouse button** on the right crop marker and **drag** the **marker** to where you want to crop the end of the clip. The video in the Monitor window will advance as you drag the crop marker.

4. Release the **mouse button** at the desired end crop location. The video footage in the Monitor window will stop advancing.

CHAPTER 5: THE CUTTING ROOM FLOOR

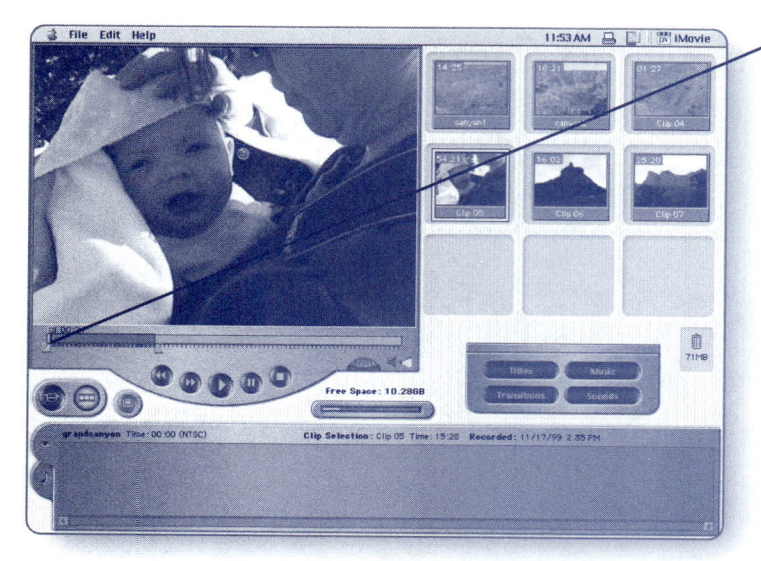

5. Click and hold the **mouse button** on the left crop marker and **drag** the **marker** to where you want to crop the beginning of the clip. The video in the Monitor window will advance or reverse as you drag the crop marker backward and forward.

6. Release the **mouse button** where you want to begin the crop. The beginning of the crop will be marked.

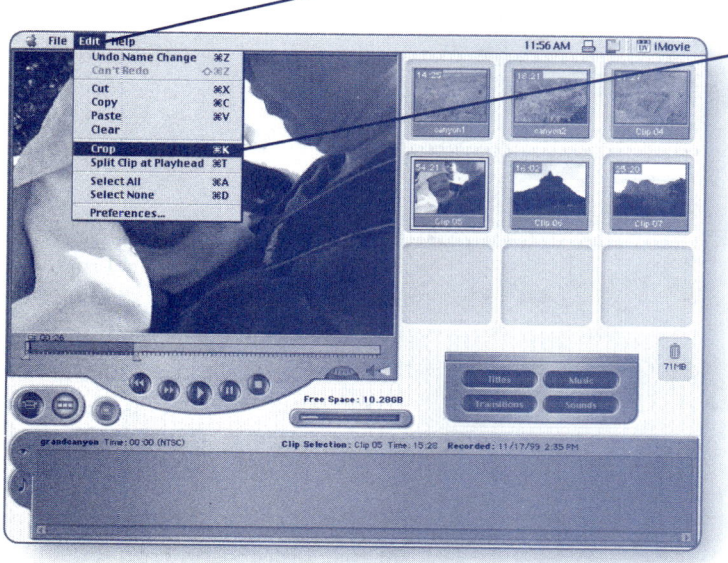

7. Click on **Edit**. The Edit menu will appear.

8. Click on **Crop**. The area outside the two triangles will be cropped.

UNDOING A CROP

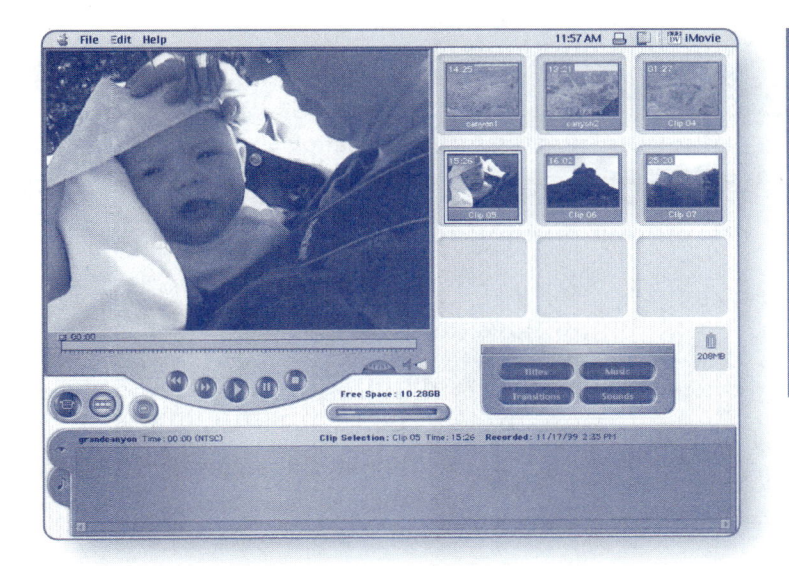

TIP

For more precise cropping, use the arrow keys on the keyboard. Use the right arrow key to advance forward one frame at a time. Use the left arrow key to rewind one frame at a time.

Undoing a Crop

Say you've cropped the clip and you don't like how it looks. You can use the Undo feature to revert the clip back to its previous form.

1. Click on **Edit**. The Edit menu will appear.

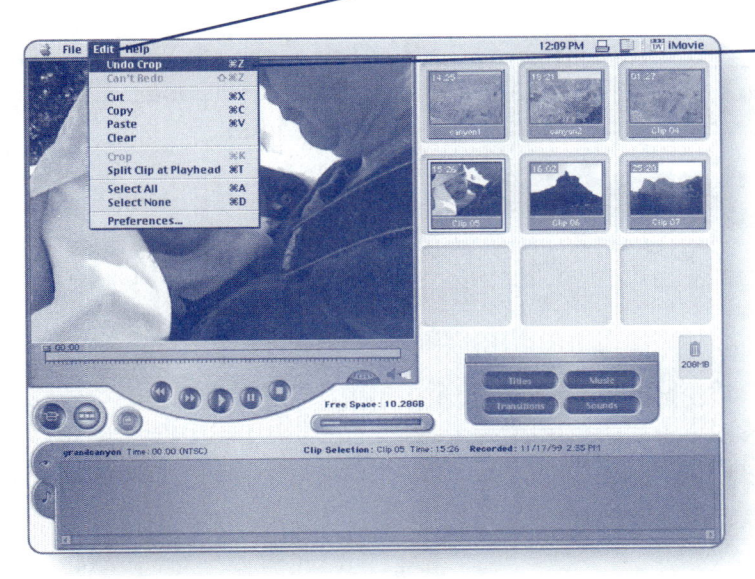

2. Click on **Undo Crop**. The clip will go back to its previously saved state.

CHAPTER 5: THE CUTTING ROOM FLOOR

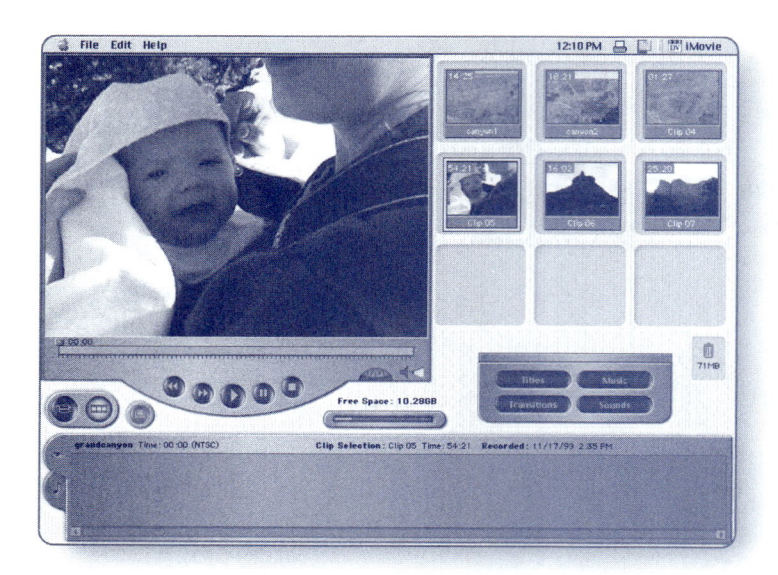

> **NOTE**
> The Undo feature works for any action you've taken that you want to reverse, not just cropping. Follow the previous steps to undo anything.

Splitting Clips

The split-clip feature allows you to take an imported clip and split it into two separate clips. This is important when you have imported a clip of a certain scene, but you want the clip to have a transition (which you'll learn about in Chapter 6, "Adding Smooth Transitions"), or you want parts of the scene to be in different places in your finished movie. Or, you might have footage in the middle of a clip that you want to crop out. By splitting the clip, you create two separate clips, each of which you can crop at the beginning and end.

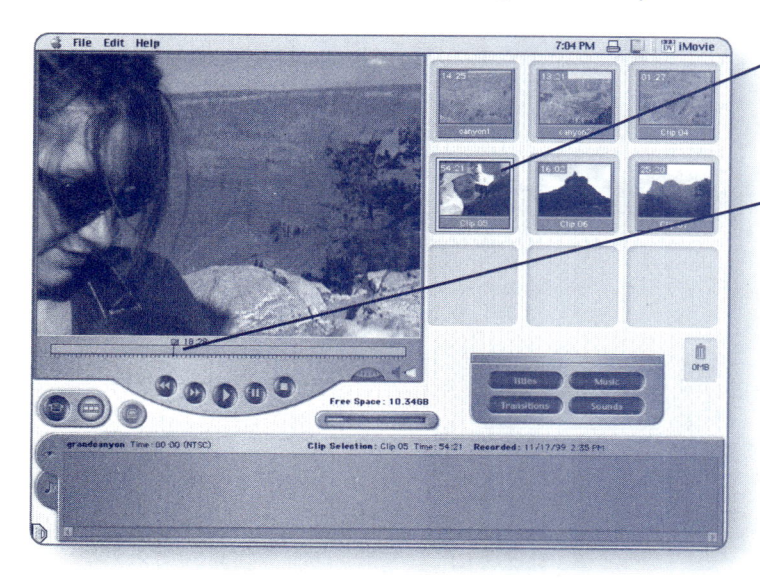

1. Click on the **clip** you want to split. The clip will appear in the Monitor window.

2. Click on the **Scrubber bar** at the approximate area where you want to split the clip. The playhead will appear.

SPLITTING CLIPS   71

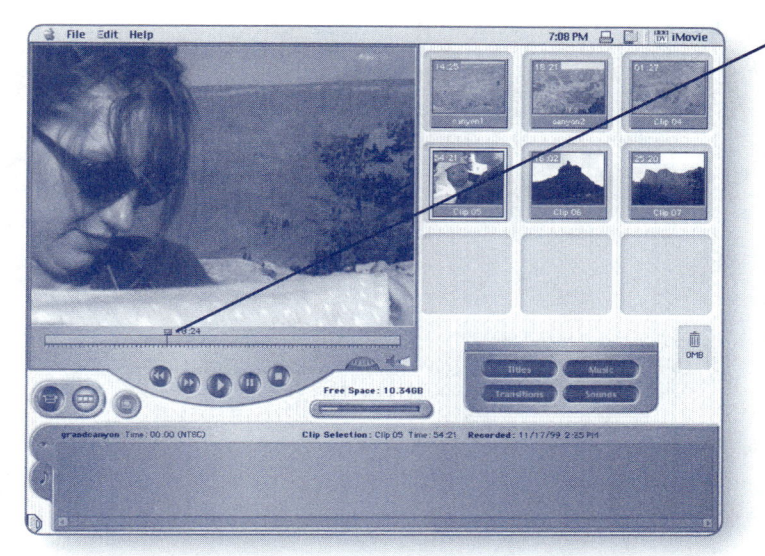

3. Press the **left and right arrow keys** on your keyboard to navigate to the exact spot where you want to split the clip. The clip will move one frame at a time in the direction of the arrow that you are pressing, and the time next to the playhead will adjust as you move.

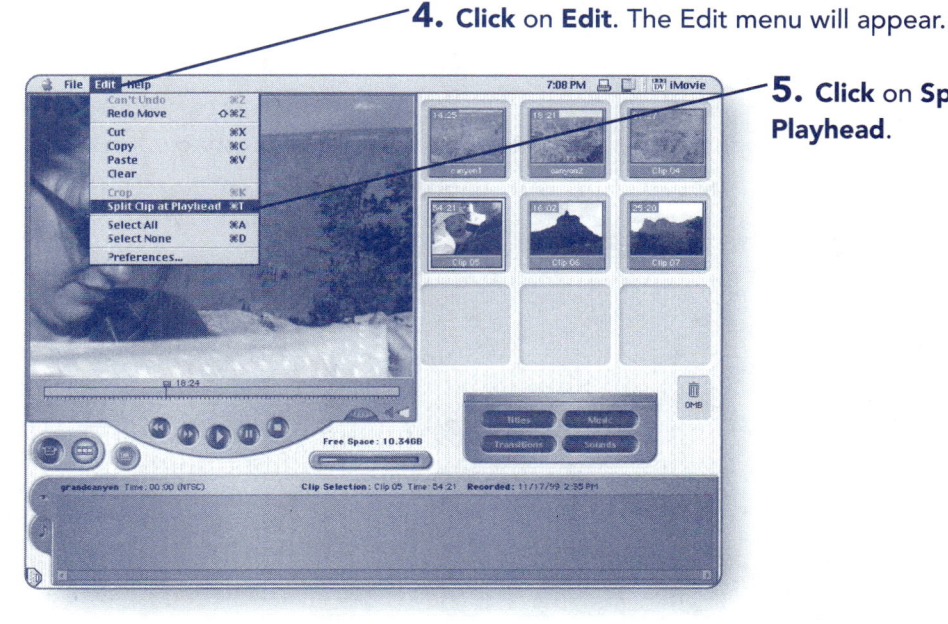

4. Click on **Edit**. The Edit menu will appear.

5. Click on **Split Clip at Playhead**.

CHAPTER 5: THE CUTTING ROOM FLOOR

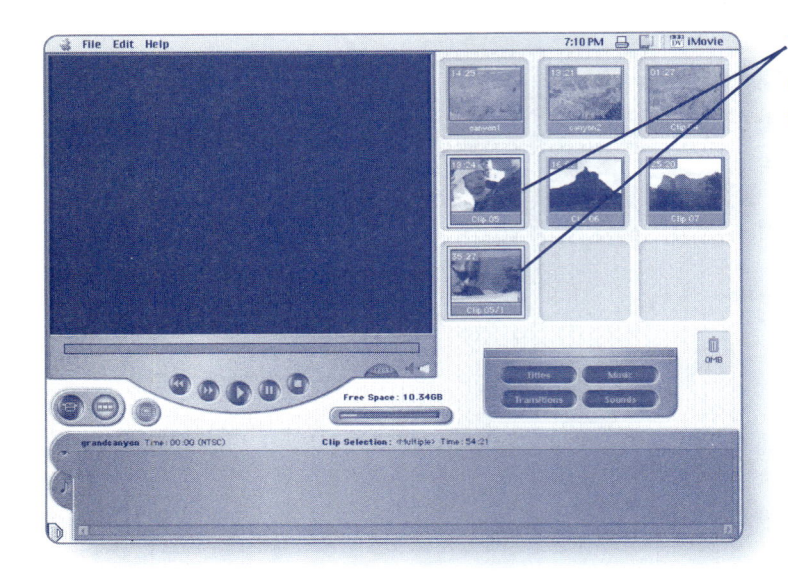

The single clip will become two clips, which both will appear in the Shelf.

Copying Clips

Instead of splitting a clip in two, maybe you want an exact copy of a clip. One reason for copying a clip is to leave one version of the clip in its original form while testing effects and edits on the other version. By making a copy, you will always have the original footage exactly the way you captured it.

1. Click on the **clip** you want to copy. The clip will be selected.

2. Click on **Edit**. The Edit menu will appear.

3. Click on **Copy**. A copy of the clip will be placed on a clipboard.

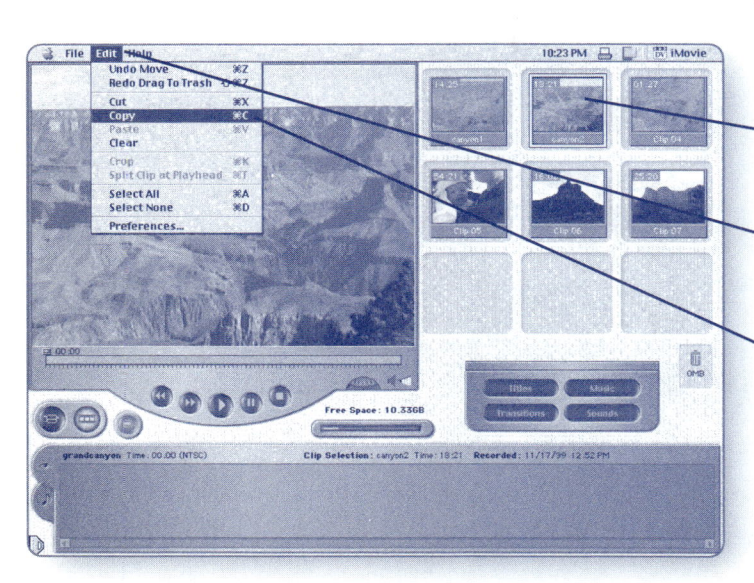

COPYING CLIPS 73

4. Click on **Edit**. The Edit menu will appear.

5. Click on **Paste**.

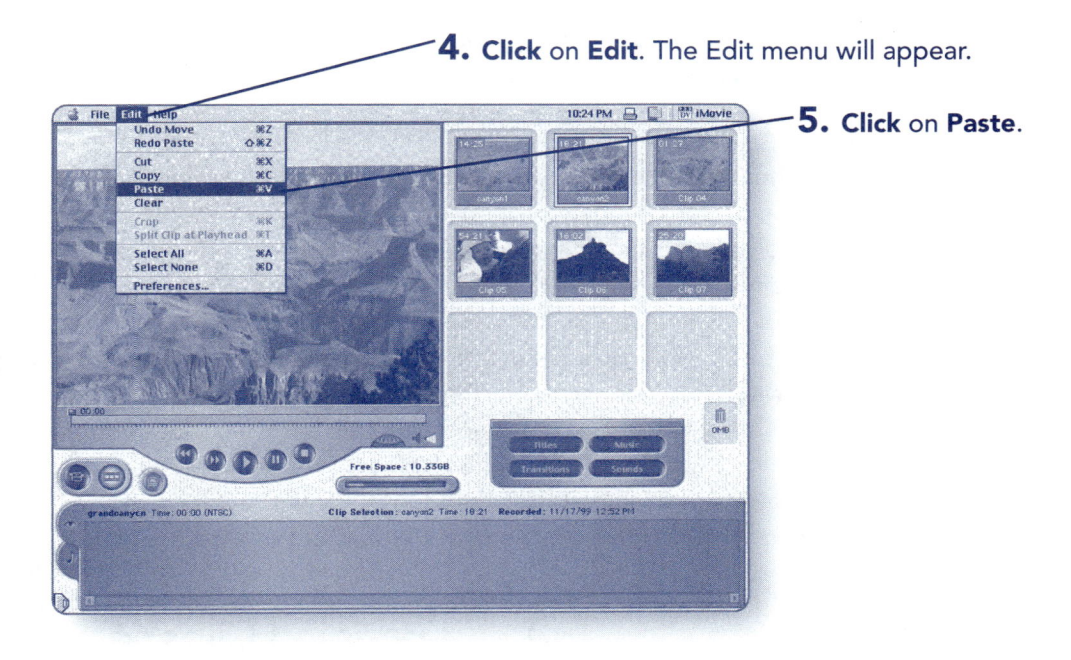

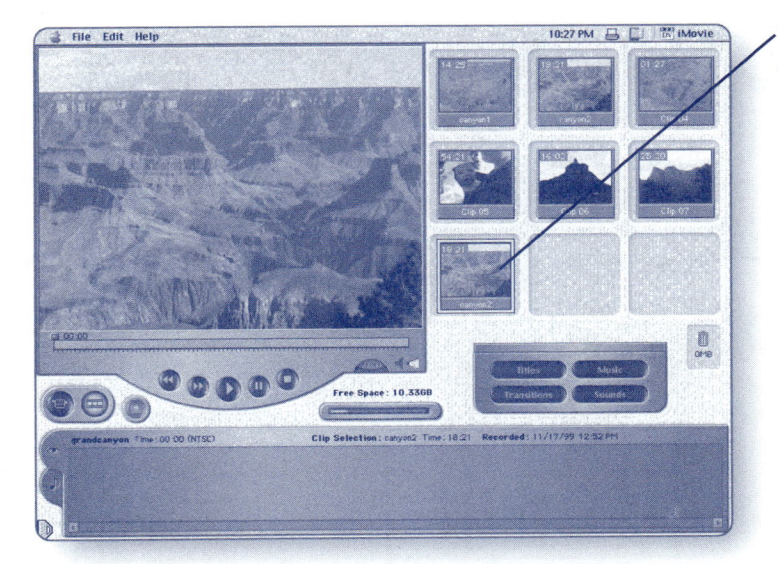

The copied clip will appear on the Shelf.

Moving Clips from the Shelf to the Viewer

After cropping a clip just the way you like it, you might want to put it on the Viewer. The Viewer is a timeline where you can see your movie come together chronologically. You can put as many clips as you want, in any order you want, on the Viewer. This is where you'll shuffle clips around, add transitions between clips, add audio effects, and so on in an endless array. You'll learn all about the special features of this tool as you read the rest of the chapters in this book. For now, you need to get those clips on the Viewer. There are two ways to move your clips from the Shelf to the Viewer: by dragging-and-dropping or by using the Edit menu.

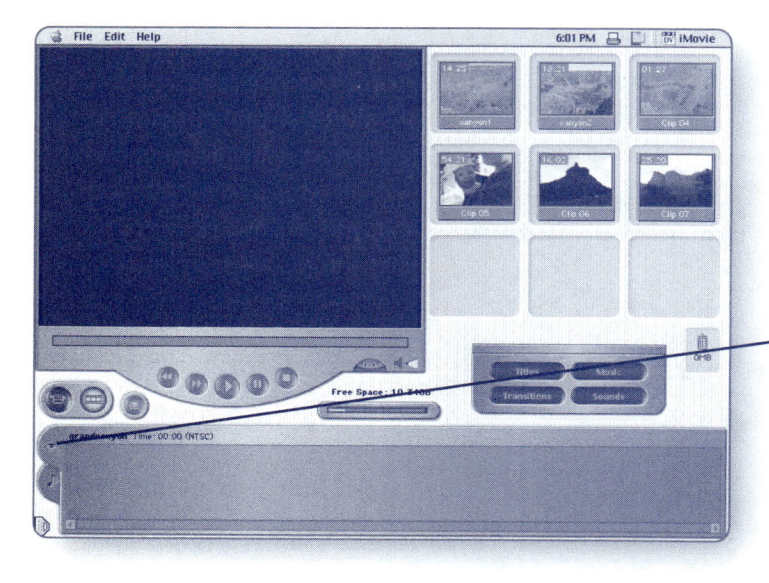

Dragging Clips to the Viewer

If you like to use the mouse, dragging your clips from the Shelf to the Viewer is the way to go.

1. Click on the **Clip Viewer tab** of the Viewer, if it isn't already selected. The Clip Viewer tab has the picture of the eye on it. The Clip Viewer tab will move to the front.

MOVING CLIPS FROM THE SHELF TO THE VIEWER

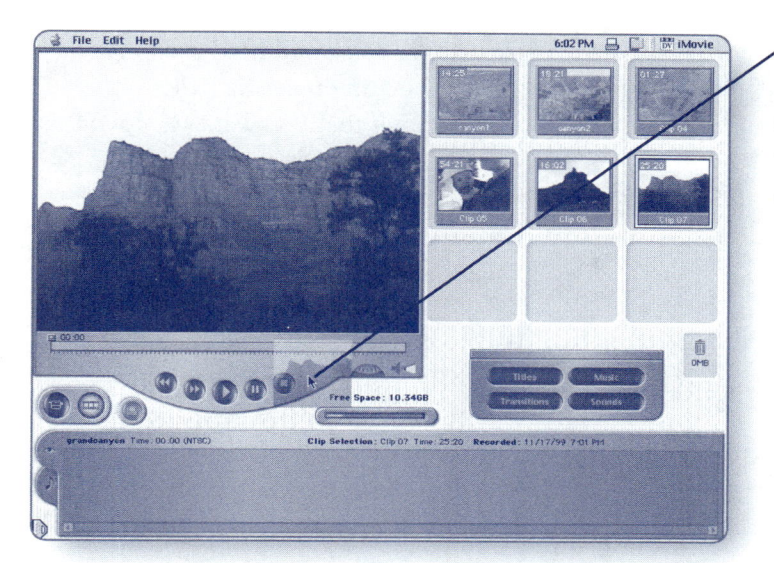

2. **Click and hold** the **mouse button** on the clip in the Shelf that you want to move to the Viewer and **drag** the **clip** down to the Viewer.

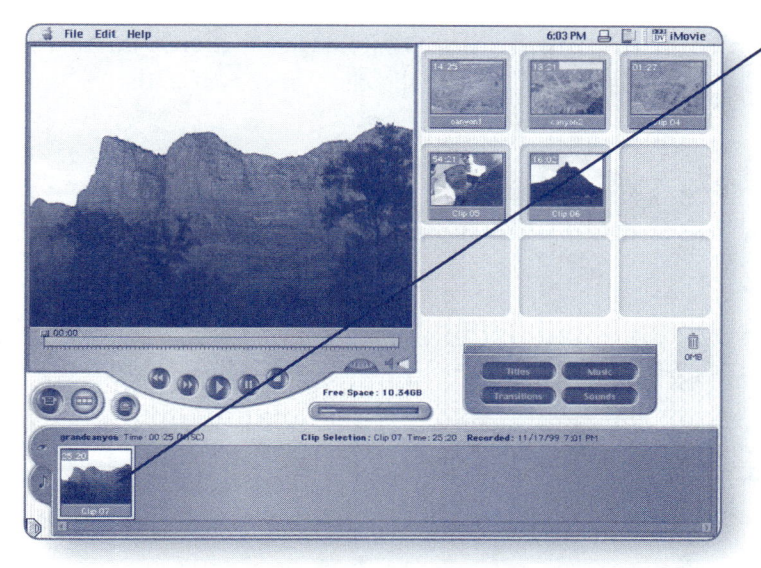

3. **Release** the **mouse button**. The clip will appear in the Viewer.

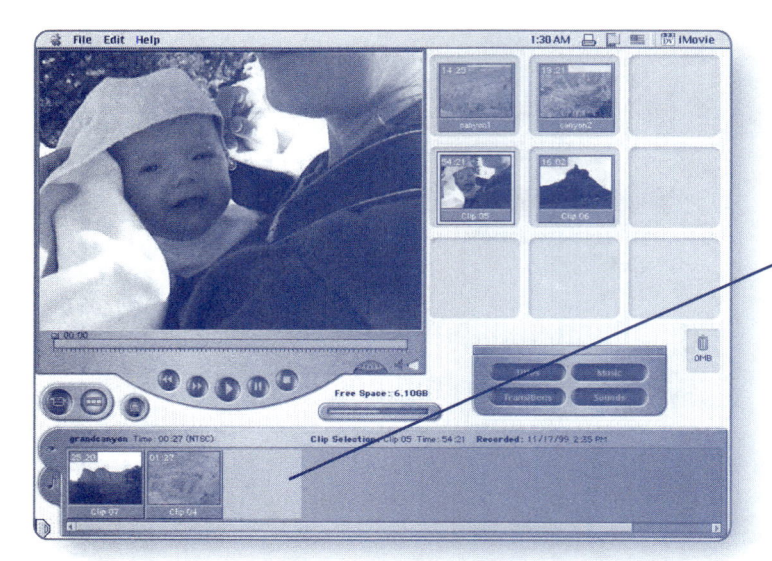

CHAPTER 5: THE CUTTING ROOM FLOOR

4. Click and hold the **mouse button** on another clip in the Shelf that you want to move to the Viewer and **drag** the **clip** down to the Viewer.

5. While still holding down the mouse button, **drag** the **clip** before or after the clip that's already in the Viewer. A box will highlight where the clip will be placed in the Viewer.

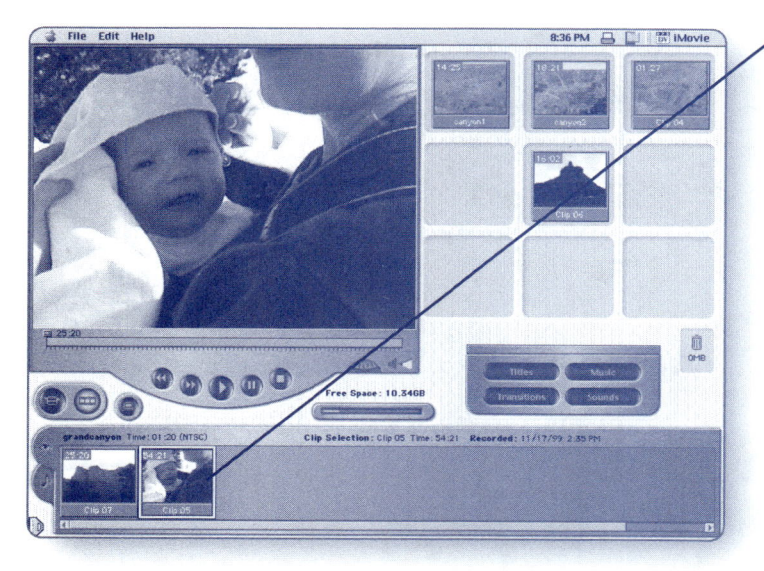

6. Release the **mouse button**. The clip will appear in the Viewer.

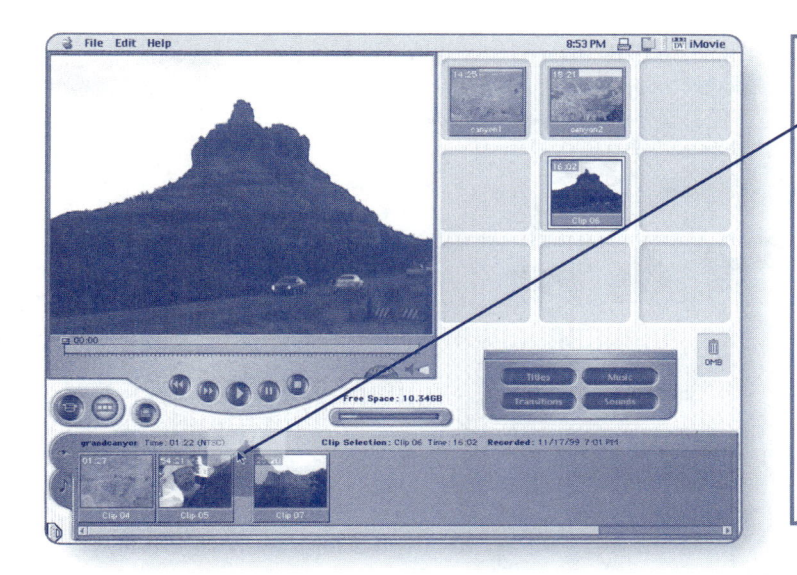

MOVING CLIPS FROM THE SHELF TO THE VIEWER 77

NOTE

Often, you will want to insert a new clip among multiple clips in the Viewer. Just drag the new clip to the desired spot in the Viewer. When the small space appears between the two clips, release the mouse button. Your clip will be inserted between the two clips that are already in the Viewer.

Moving Clips Using the Edit Menu

Moving clips with the Edit menu is basically a matter of cutting and pasting. The only problem with this technique is that you have no control over where your clips are inserted on the Viewer.

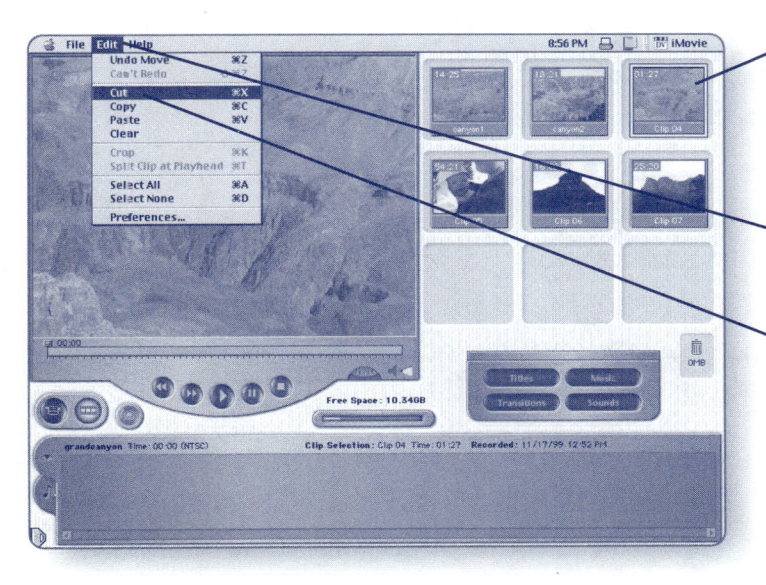

1. Click on the **clip** in the Shelf that you want to move to the Viewer. The clip will appear in the Monitor window.

2. Click on **Edit**. The Edit menu will appear.

3. Click on **Cut**. The clip will be removed from the Shelf.

CHAPTER 5: THE CUTTING ROOM FLOOR

4. Click on **Edit**. The Edit menu will appear.

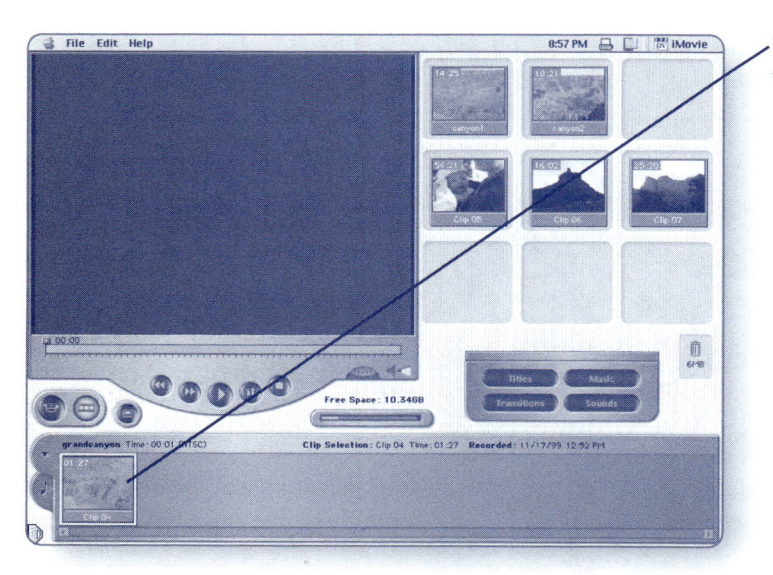

5. Click on **Paste**.

The clip will be added to the Viewer.

TRASHING CLIPS 79

Trashing Clips

Do you have clips that you've decided not to use? Dump them in the trash.

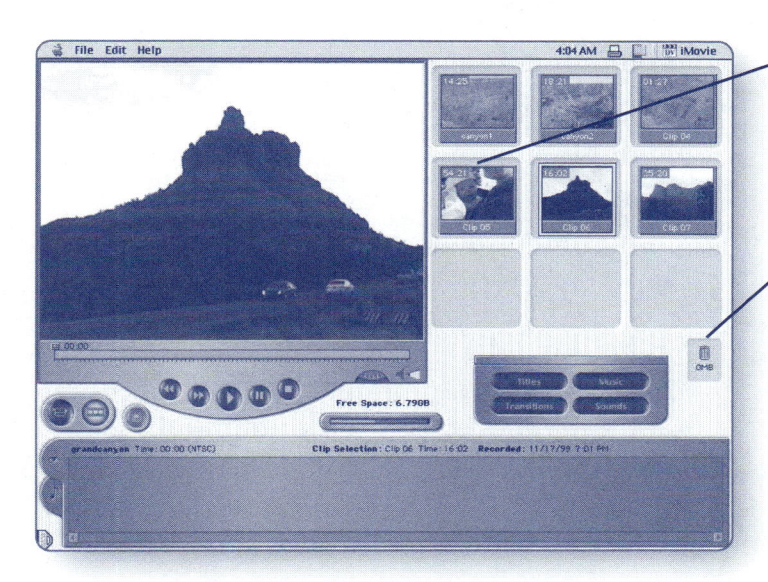

1. Press and hold the **mouse button** down on the clip you want to delete and **drag** the **clip** to the trashcan icon at the bottom of the Shelf.

2. Release the **mouse button** when the trashcan is highlighted. The clip will be thrown away.

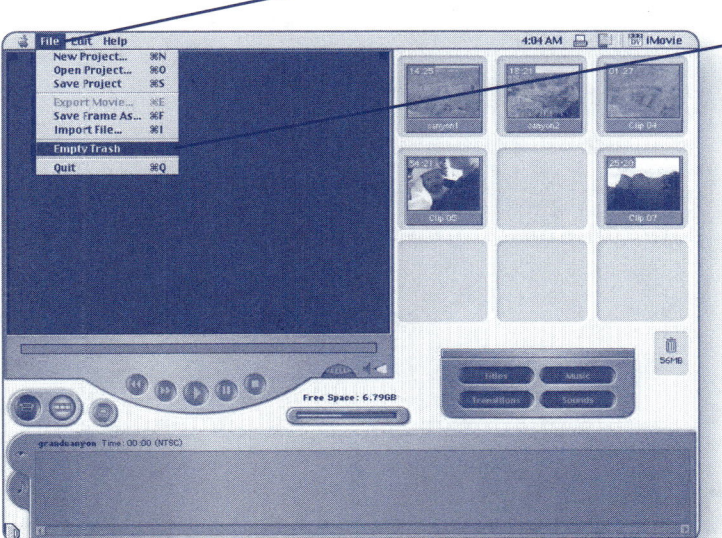

3. Click on **File**. The File menu will appear.

4. Click on **Empty Trash**. The Confirm dialog box will open.

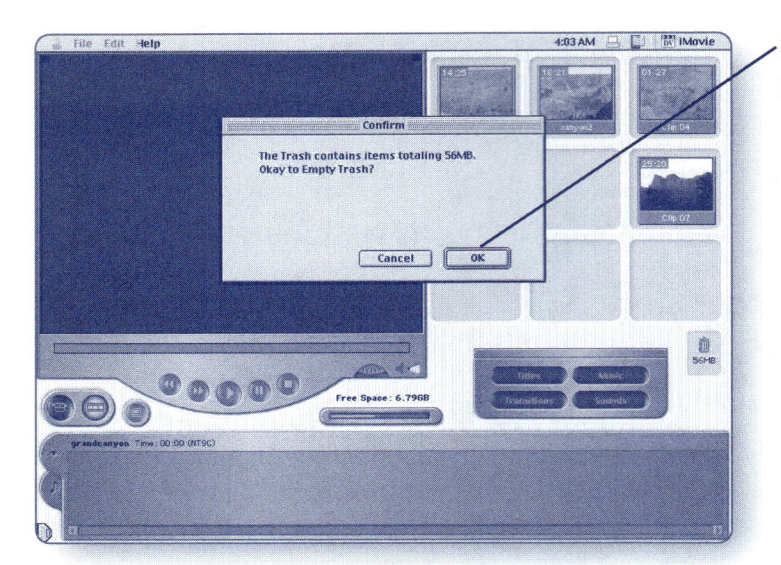

5. Click on **OK**. The trash will be emptied.

Part II Review Questions

1. How do you create your first iMovie project? *See Creating a New Project in Chapter 3*

2. How do you view your video on the computer screen? *See Previewing Your Video in the Monitor Window in Chapter 3*

3. How do you get your video into iMovie? *See Importing a Clip from Your Digital Video Camera in Chapter 4*

4. How do you adjust the quality of your video clips in iMovie? *See Adjusting the Quality of Video Playback in Chapter 4*

5. How do you automatically find the beginning and end of a video scene that you captured and save it as a clip? *See Using iMovie's Scene Detection Feature in Chapter 4*

6. How do you name a clip? *See Renaming a Clip in Chapter 5*

7. How do you cut unwanted footage from individual clips? *See Cropping Clips in Chapter 5*

8. How can you split one clip into two separate clips? *See Splitting Clips in Chapter 5*

9. How do you put a clip in the Clip Viewer? *See Moving Clips from the Shelf to the Viewer in Chapter 5*

10. How do you make an exact copy of a clip? *See Copying Clips in Chapter 5*

PART III

iMovie Special Effects and Post-Production

Chapter 6
Adding Stylish Transitions **85**

Chapter 7
Text in iMovie: Rolling Titles,
Credits, and Captions **105**

Chapter 8
Audio: Adding Soundtracks,
Scores, Sounds, and Narration **123**

Chapter 9
iMovie and Still Images **151**

Chapter 10
Compressing and Exporting
Your Movies **167**

6
Adding Stylish Transitions

Transitions can make your movie look seamless. Instead of straight cuts from one scene to the next, you can apply a number of different transition effects to the breaks in action. The transitions in iMovie add stylistic cross-fades, dissolves, washes, and other effects to your videos. In this chapter, you'll learn how to:

- Select a transition
- Set transition speed
- Add, change, and delete transitions
- Insert a clip where a transition exists
- Add new transitions to the Effects palette

CHAPTER 6: ADDING STYLISH TRANSITIONS

Selecting a Transition

Selecting a transition for your movie takes a bit of forethought. With iMovie, you have the opportunity to play with the different effects to see what works best with your movie. You can mix and match different transitions, but it's usually best to stay simple and consistent and use the same effect throughout. Just try some of the effects to see what works best with your footage.

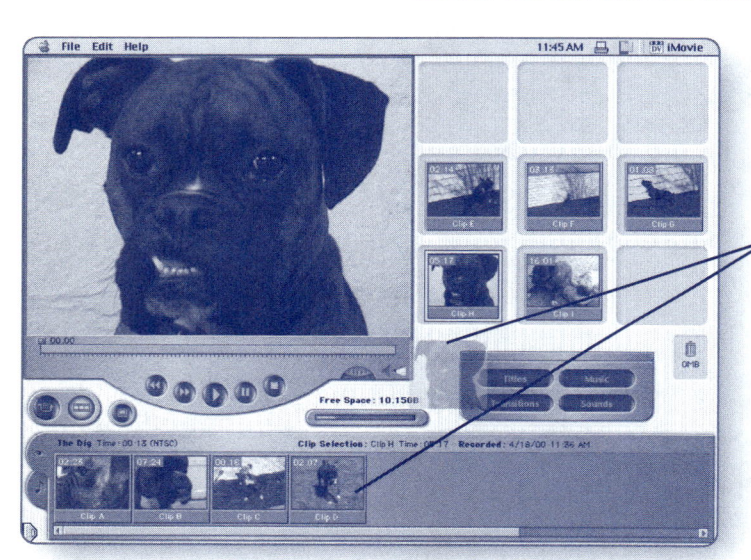

1. Move your **clips** from the Shelf to the Viewer, if they're not already there. Try to arrange the clips, from beginning to end, in the order you want them. You can rearrange the clips later, but it's best to get them close to how you want them at this time.

> **NOTE**
>
> Go back to Chapter 5, "The Cutting Room Floor—Precise and Polished Editing," if you need a refresher on how to move your clips from the Shelf to the Viewer.

2. Click on the **Transitions button** in the Effects palette. The Transitions palette will appear.

SELECTING A TRANSITION 87

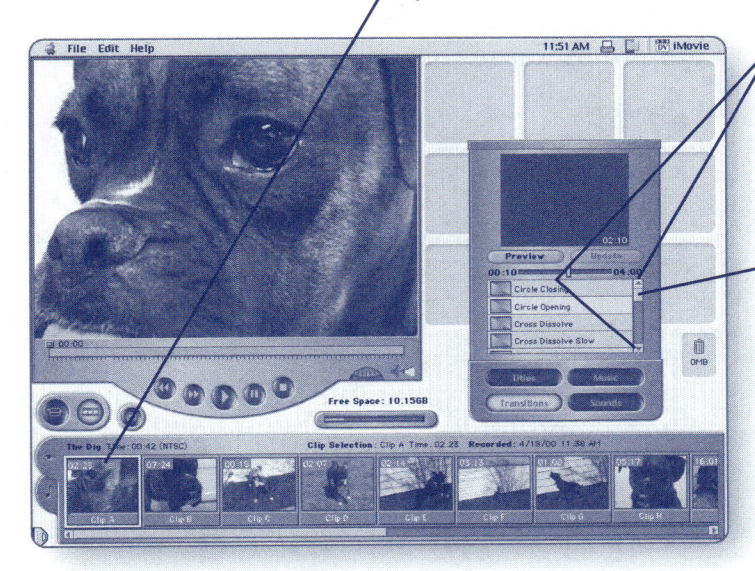

3. Select a **clip or series of clips** on which you want to preview the effects of a transition. The clip(s) will be selected.

4a. Click on the **up and down arrows** in the scroll box to look through the effect selections.

OR

4b. Press and hold the **mouse button** on the scroll bar and **drag** the **mouse pointer** up or down to view the available selections.

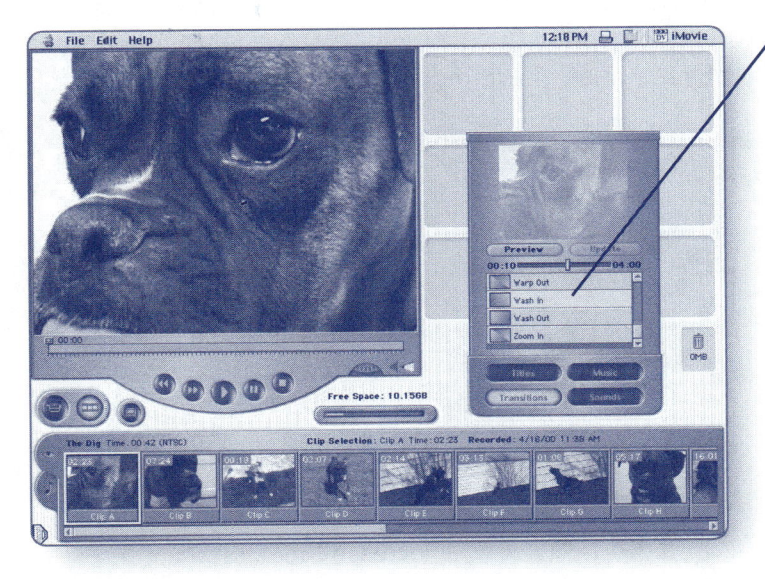

5. Click on a **transition effect**. The effect will appear in the preview window.

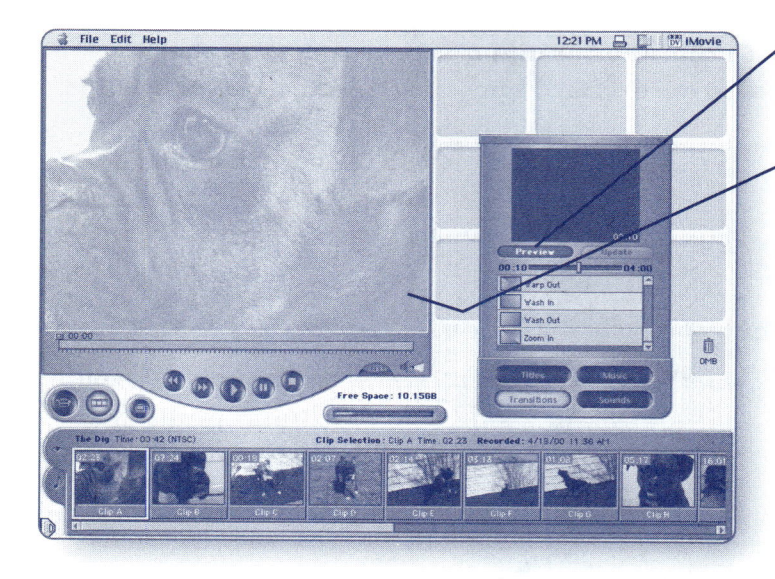

6. **Click** on the **Preview button**.

The transition effect, applied to the clip you selected, will appear in the Monitor window. This will give you a better idea of how a transition looks than you could get by seeing it in the small preview window in the Transitions palette.

Setting Transition Speed

You will need to assign a duration to your transitions. If you want a slow, deliberate transition effect between your clips, you need to increase the duration. If you want just a slight hint of a transition effect, reduce the duration.

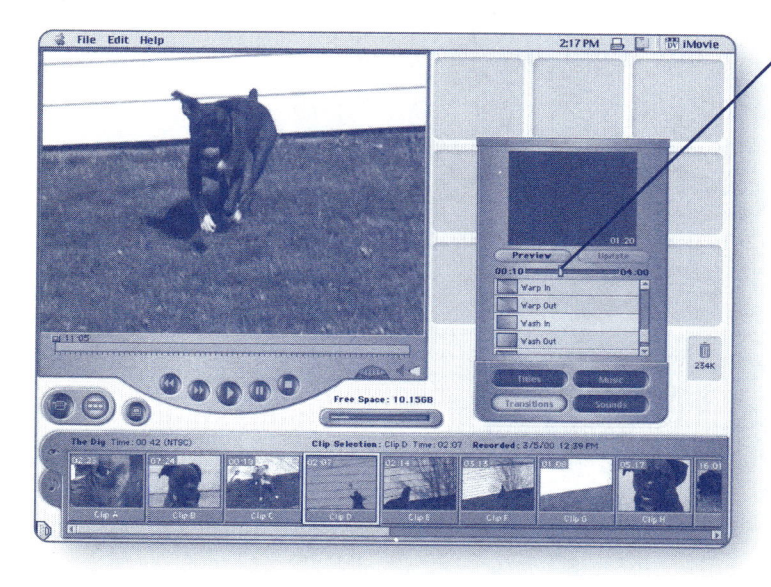

1. **Click and hold** the **mouse button** on the slider in the Transitions palette.

2a. **Drag** the **slider** left to reduce the duration of the transition.

OR

2b. **Drag** the **slider** right to increase the duration of the transition.

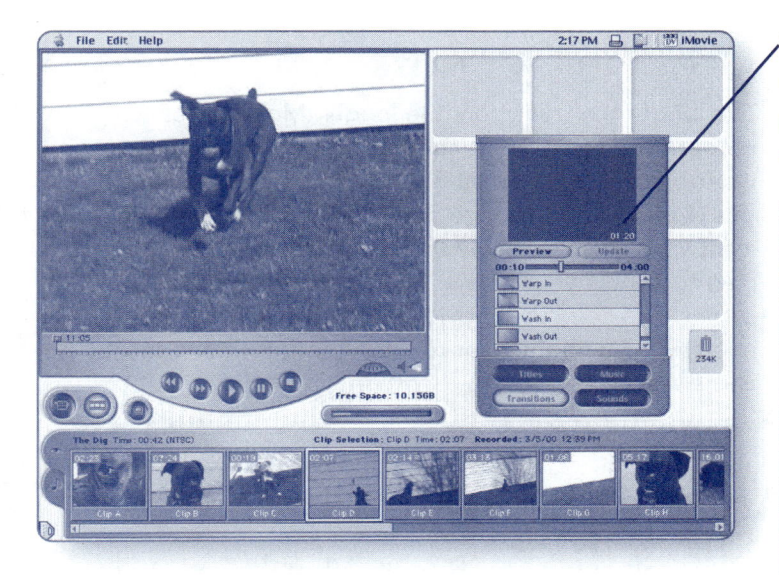

SETTING TRANSITION SPEED

The transition time will appear in the lower-right corner of the preview window as you drag the slider.

> **NOTE**
>
> The number at the left end of the duration slider, 00:10, or 10 frames, represents the minimum length that you can set for a transition. The number at the right end of the duration slider, 04:00, or 4 seconds, represents the maximum length that you can set for a transition. As you drag the slider, the duration will appear in the bottom-right corner of the preview window. For example, 01:20 means that your transition is 1 second and 20 frames in length.

3. Release the **mouse button** when you reach the desired duration. The transition effect you chose, as well as the duration you just established, will be shown in the preview window.

CHAPTER 6: ADDING STYLISH TRANSITIONS

> **NOTE**
> The longer the transition, the longer iMovie takes to render the transition. *Rendering* is when iMovie creates video frames for a transition. You might want to keep this in mind when you are determining how large you want your finished movie to be, and how you eventually plan to export your movie. For example, if you are planning to send this movie in an e-mail to your relatives, you might want to keep the transitions short and sweet.

Adding the Transition

Now that you've thought about the effect that you want for your movie, selected a transition, and set the duration, you need to add the transition.

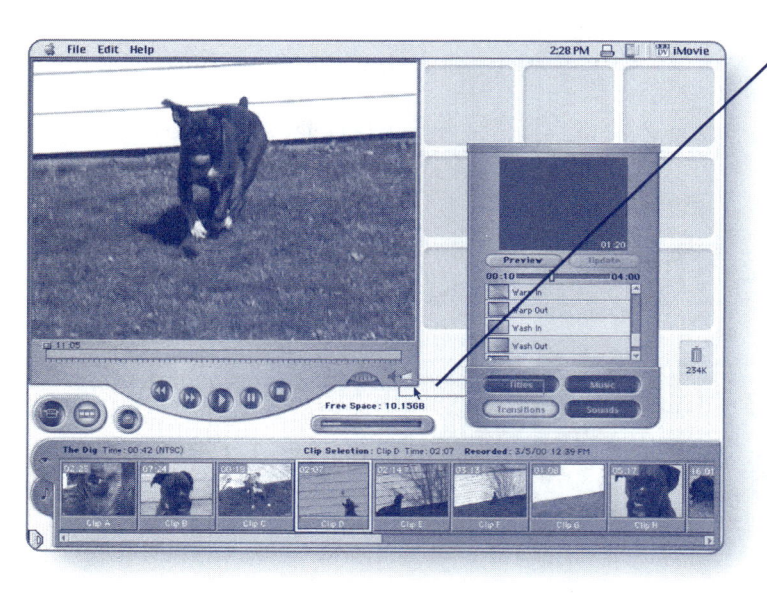

1. **Press and hold** the **mouse button** down on the transition you selected and **drag** the **transition** down between the clips to which you want to apply the effect. The right clip will move over a tad to make room for the transition.

ADDING THE TRANSITION 91

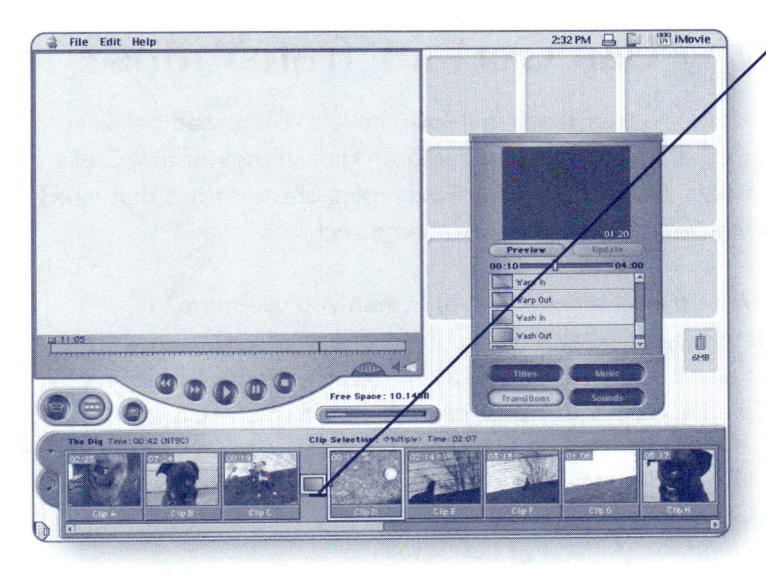

2. Release the **mouse button** and **drop** the **transition**. A monitor icon will appear where you added the transition. A red bar will slowly extend at the bottom of the monitor icon. This is iMovie rendering the transition.

3. Repeat this **process** to add more transitions.

NOTE
You may notice that the clips at both ends of a transition shrink a bit when you add the effect. This is because the transition is using up a few frames at the end of one clip and the beginning of the other to produce its effect.

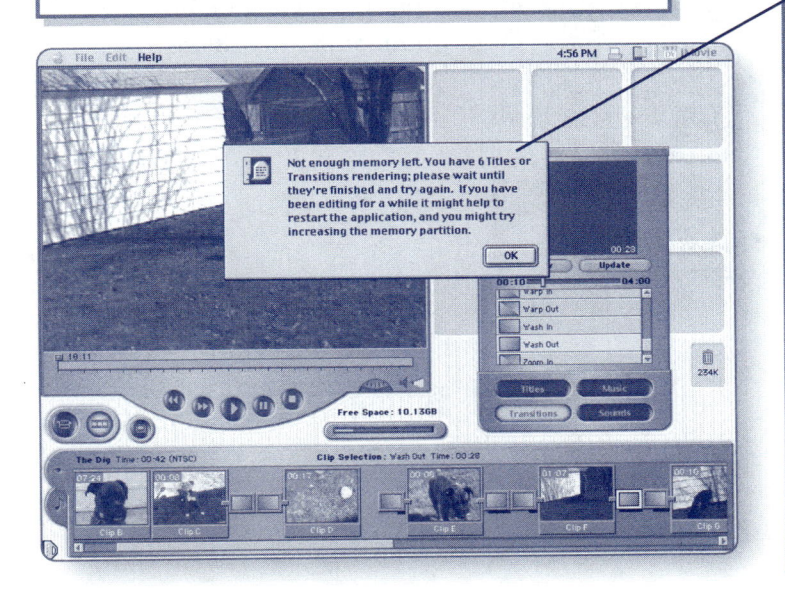

NOTE
Avoid adding several transitions in succession. Transitions take time and memory to render. When you drag multiple transitions down to the Clip Viewer one after another at a rapid pace, iMovie will slow down and might even give you an error message telling you that there isn't enough memory to add anything until rendering is complete. Just wait until iMovie has finished rendering the current transitions to add more.

CHAPTER 6: ADDING STYLISH TRANSITIONS

Why Use Certain Transitions?

Most of the transitions in iMovie have to be placed between two clips because they utilize both clips in their effect. Cross Dissolve and Push Right are examples of transitions that need to use two clips to produce their effect.

Certain transition effects work when you use them in combinations or at the beginning or end of your movie. The Fade and Wash transitions are two such effects. For example, adding a Wash Out transition to the end of one clip and then attaching the Wash In transition to the beginning of the following clip creates a more seamless effect. Or, you can put a Fade In transition before the first clip in your movie, and a Fade Out at the end of the last clip.

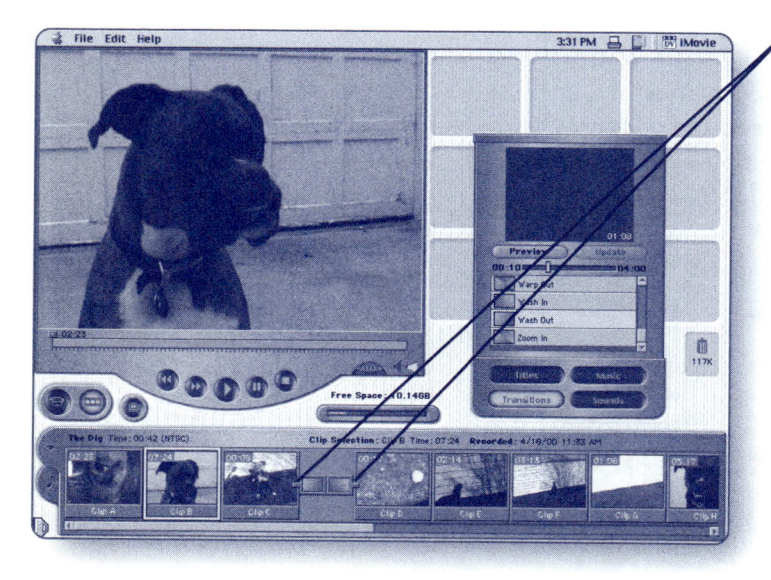

Notice that there is a tab on the transition's monitor icon that attaches to either one or both of the clips associated with the transition. This tab lets you know whether the selected transition effect utilizes one or both of the transitions.

CHANGING A TRANSITION 93

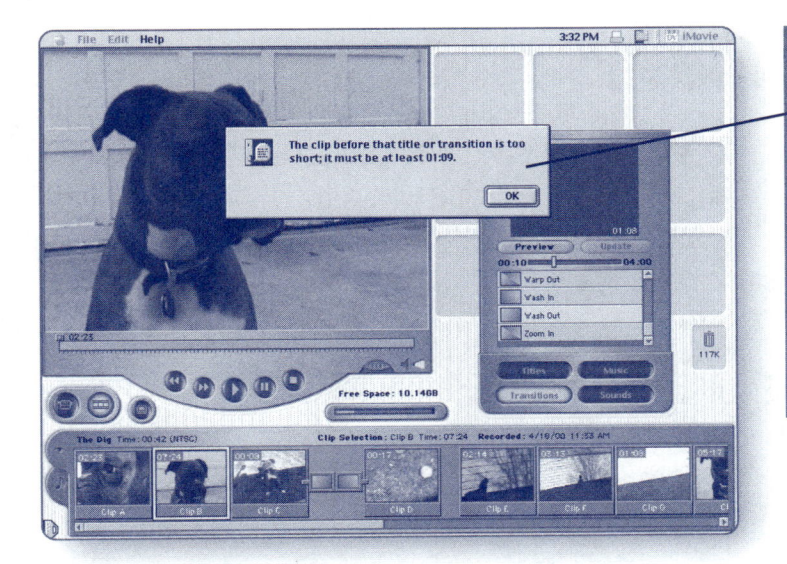

NOTE

The transition duration cannot be longer than the corresponding clip's duration. You will get an error message if you try to attach a transition that is longer than the clip to which you want to attach it.

Another thing to keep in mind is that you don't want to overuse transitions. Often, video editors get overzealous and add transitions everywhere. A straight cut between scenes is effective for many productions. The next time you go to the movies, check out how many times special effects for transitions are used between scenes and how many times just a simple cut is used.

Changing a Transition

Change your mind about using that Wash Out transition? You can change the style and duration of any transition.

CHAPTER 6: ADDING STYLISH TRANSITIONS

1. Click on the **transition** you want to change. The transition will be selected.

2. Click on a **new transition style** in the Effects palette. The new style will be selected.

3. Move the **slider** to a new duration. The new duration will be selected.

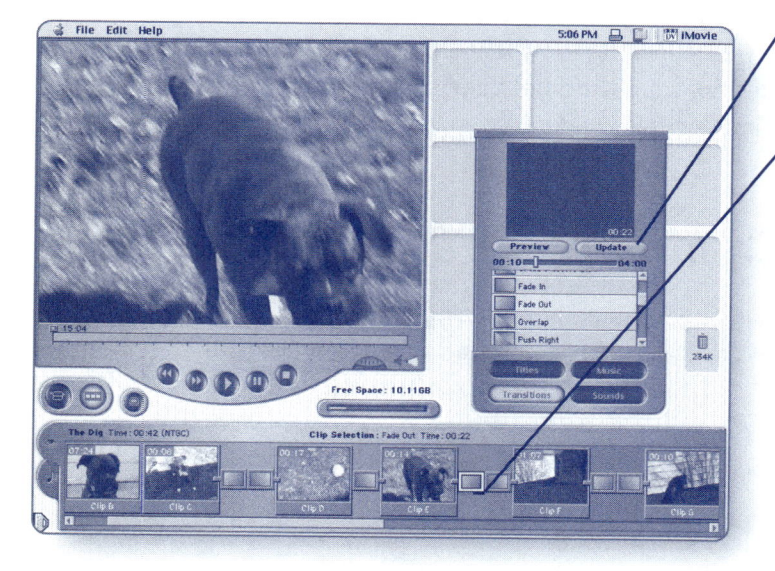

4. Click on the **Update button**. The changes will take effect.

Notice that the new transition is rendering—the red bar is moving from left to right in the monitor icon.

DELETING A TRANSITION 95

Deleting a Transition

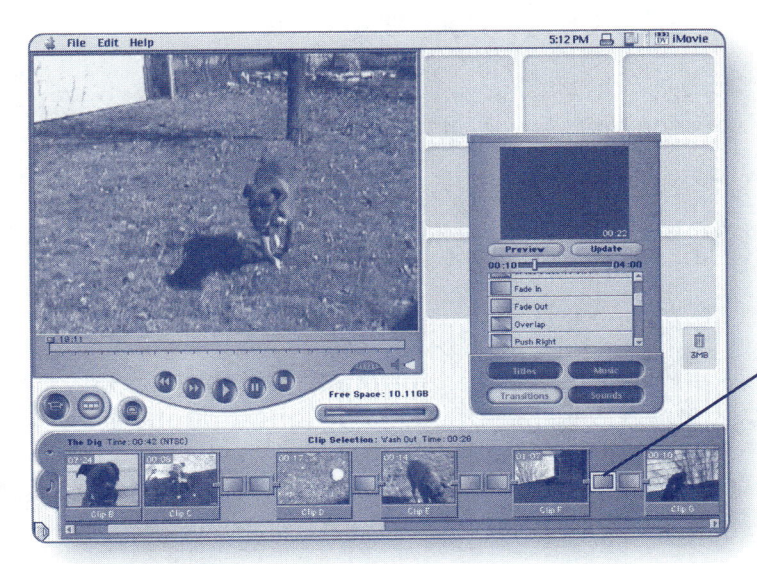

Want to get rid of a transition altogether? You can delete the transition completely. And remember those few frames of the two clips that were used up by the transition? They will be restored after you delete the transition.

1. Click on the **transition** you want to delete. The transition will be selected.

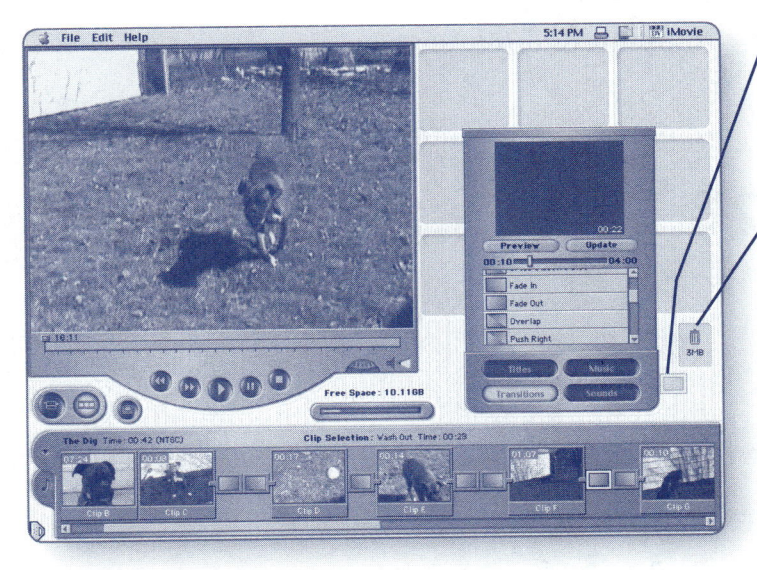

2. Click and hold the **mouse button** on the transition you want to delete and **drag** the **transition** to the trash can.

3. Release the **mouse button**. The transition will be deleted.

NOTE
You can also delete a transition by clicking on the transition you want to delete, and then pressing Delete key.

CHAPTER 6: ADDING STYLISH TRANSITIONS

Inserting a Clip Where a Transition Exists

Let's say you decide that you want to add a new clip between two existing clips connected by a transition. If you drag the new clip to the Clip Viewer, iMovie doesn't open a space for you to drop the clip. Sometimes you just have to improvise.

1. Click on the **transition** where you want to add your new clip. The transition will be selected.

2. Press the **Delete key**. The transition will be deleted.

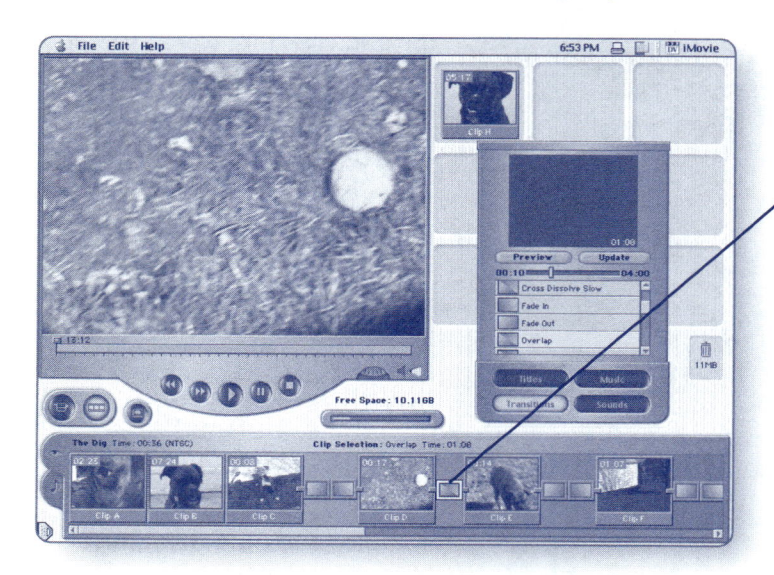

3. Drag your **new clip** from the Shelf to the desired position in the Clip Viewer.

4. Release the **mouse button**. The clip will appear in position between the clips.

ADDING NEW TRANSITIONS TO THE PALETTE 97

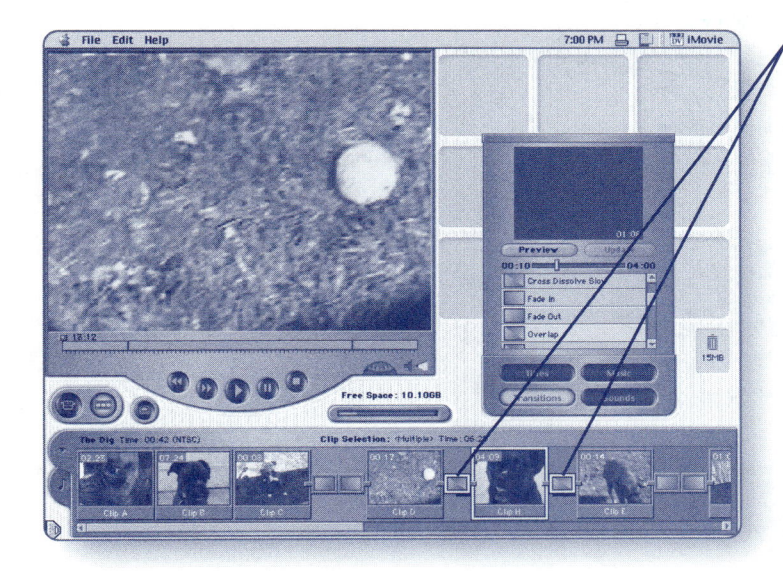

5. Add the **transitions** back in between the first and second clips and between the second and third clips.

Adding New Transitions to the Palette

Apple has a Plug-in pack of additional transitions (and titles) available on its Web site. To download the Plug-in pack, you need to connect to the Internet and go to Apple's Web site.

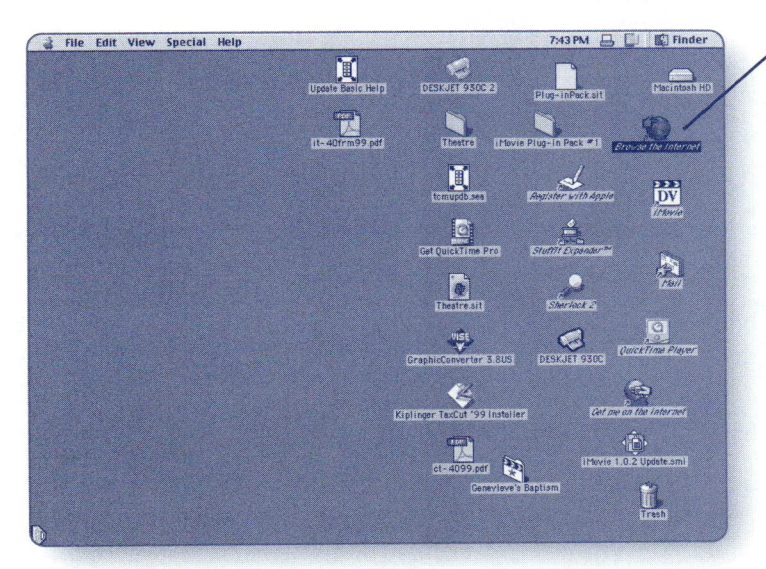

1. Connect to the **Internet**. Your browser window will open.

NOTE

Your steps for connecting to the Internet will vary, depending on your configuration and what ISP (*Internet Service Provider*) you use.

98 CHAPTER 6: ADDING STYLISH TRANSITIONS

2. Type the **URL** for Apple's Web site (http://www.apple.com/imovie) and **click** on **Go**. Apple's iMovie home page will appear.

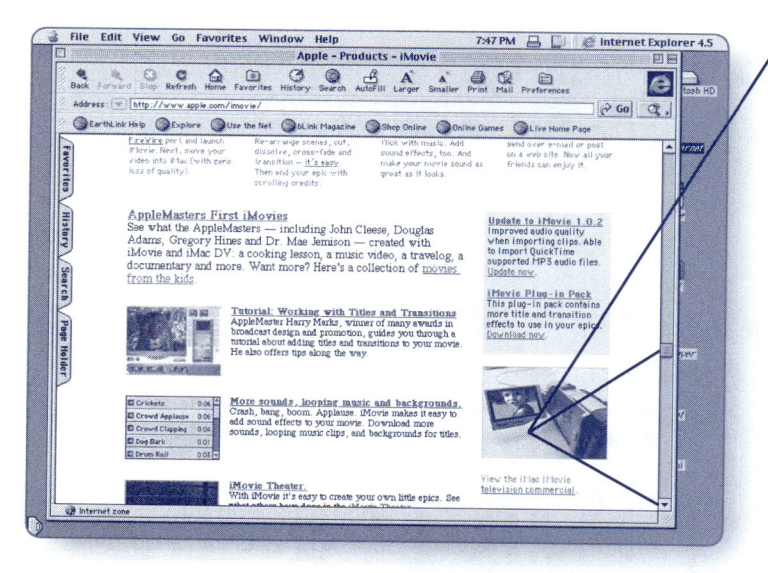

3. Scroll down the **page** until you reach the iMovie Plug-in Pack link.

ADDING NEW TRANSITIONS TO THE PALETTE 99

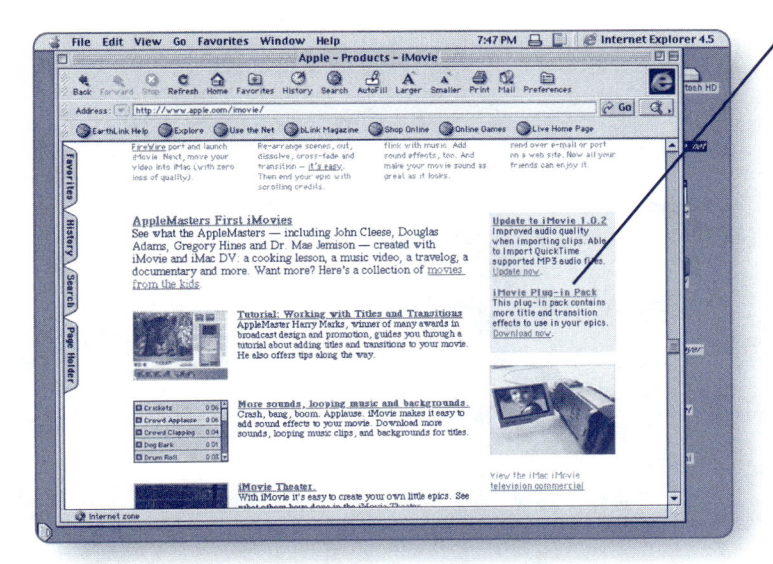

4. Click on the **iMovie Plug-in Pack link**. The Plug-in Pack will download to your desktop.

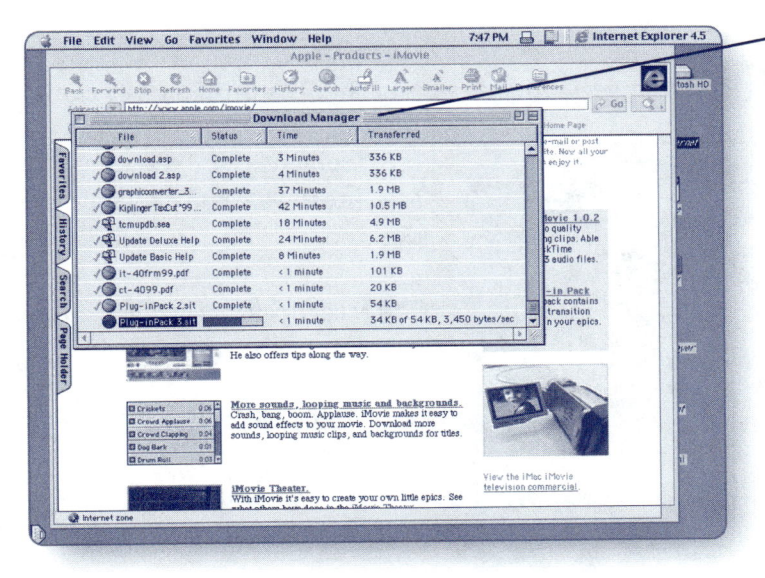

If you are using Internet Explorer, the Download Manager will appear and show you the progress of the download.

CHAPTER 6: ADDING STYLISH TRANSITIONS

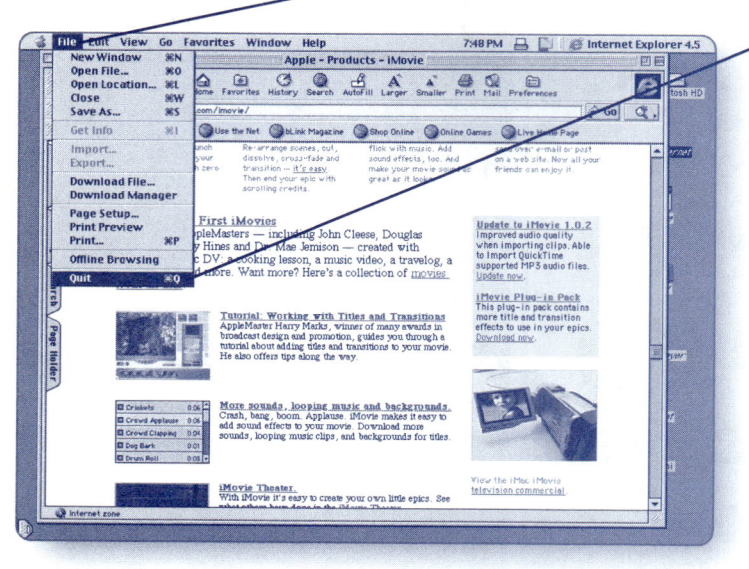

5. Click on **File**. The File menu will appear.

6. Click on **Quit**. Your browser will close.

7. Exit iMovie, if you have it running. The program will close.

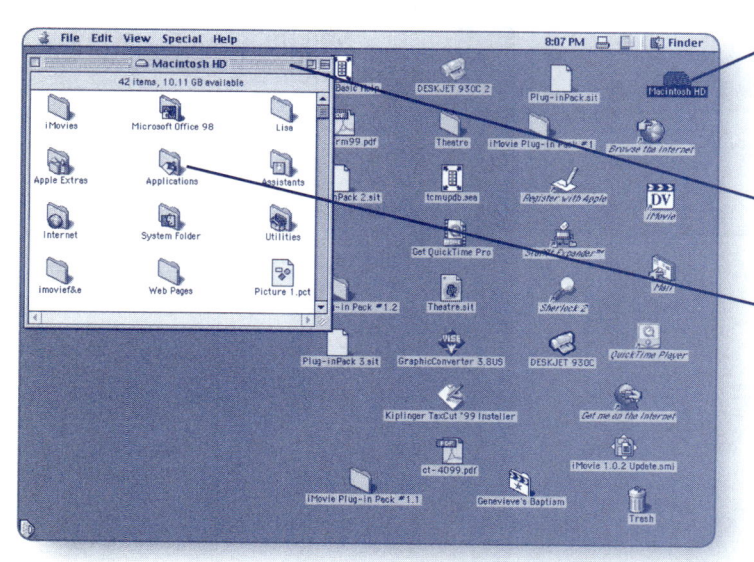

8. Double-click on the **Macintosh HD icon** on your desktop.

The Macintosh HD window and contents will appear.

9. Double-click on the **Applications folder**. The Applications window will appear.

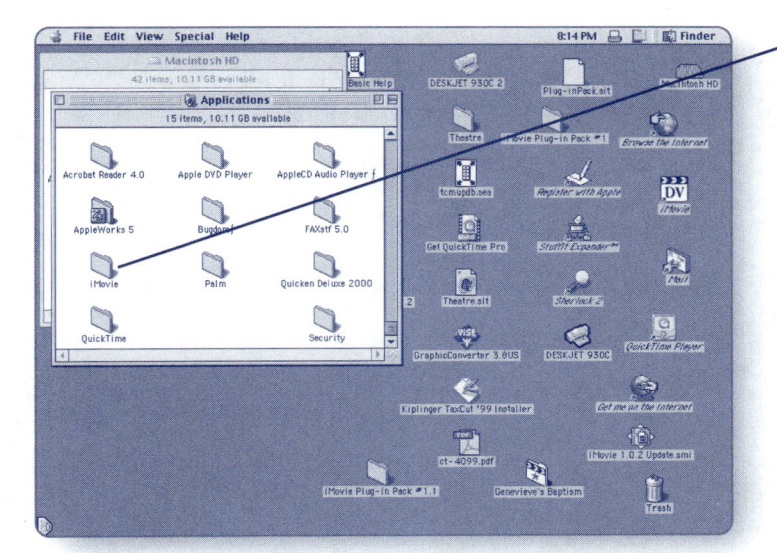

ADDING NEW TRANSITIONS TO THE PALETTE 101

10. Double-click on the **iMovie folder**. The iMovie window will appear.

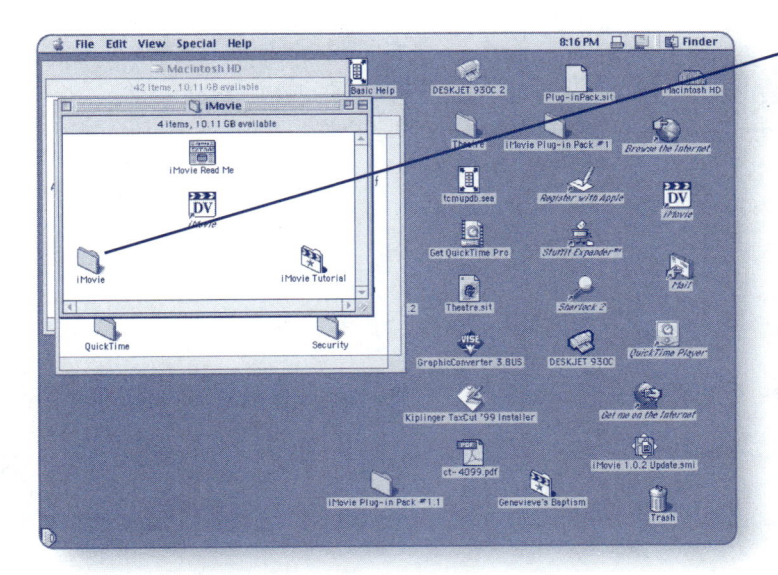

11. Double-click on the next **iMovie folder**. The next iMovie window will appear.

CHAPTER 6: ADDING STYLISH TRANSITIONS

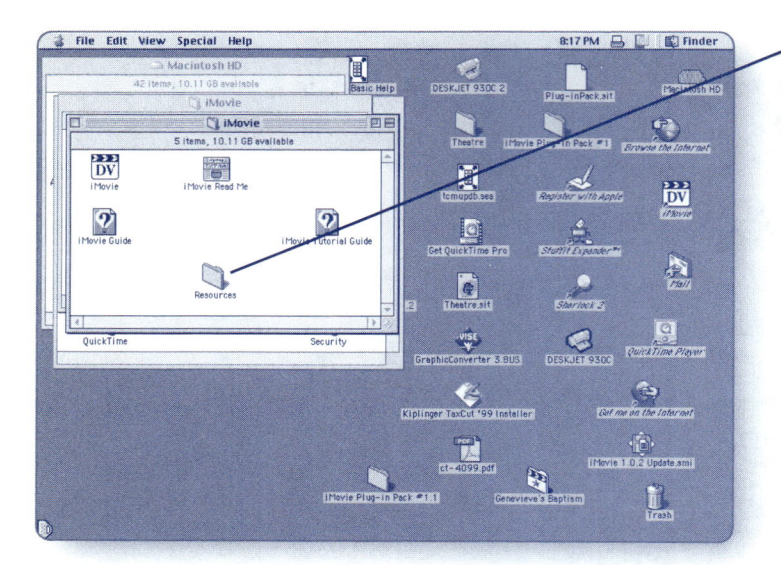

12. Double-click on the **Resources folder**. The Resources window will appear.

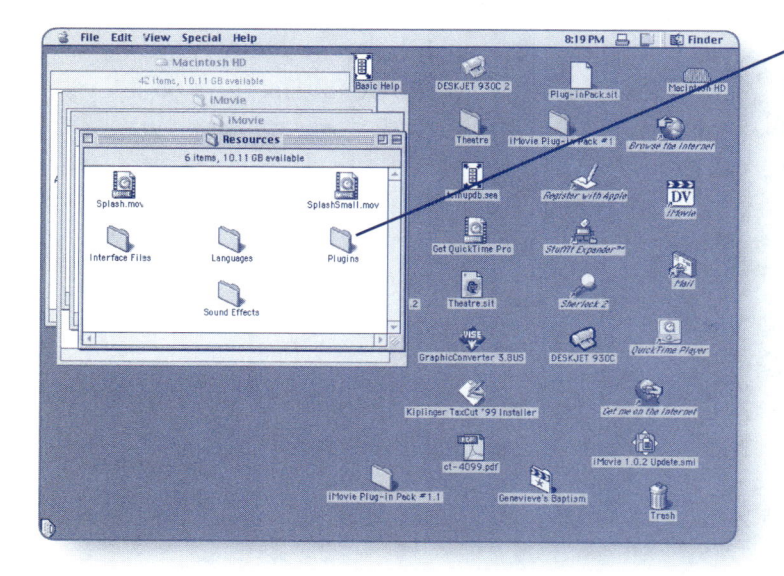

13. Double-click on the **Plugins folder**. The Plugins window will appear.

ADDING NEW TRANSITIONS TO THE PALETTE 103

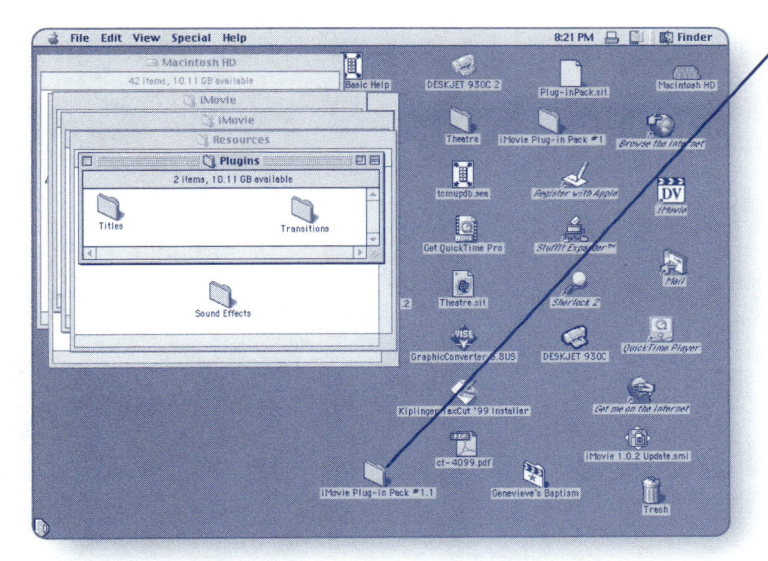

14. **Locate** the **iMovie Plug-in Pack folder icon** on your desktop.

15. **Press and hold** the **mouse button** down on the icon and **drag** the **folder** into the Plugins folder.

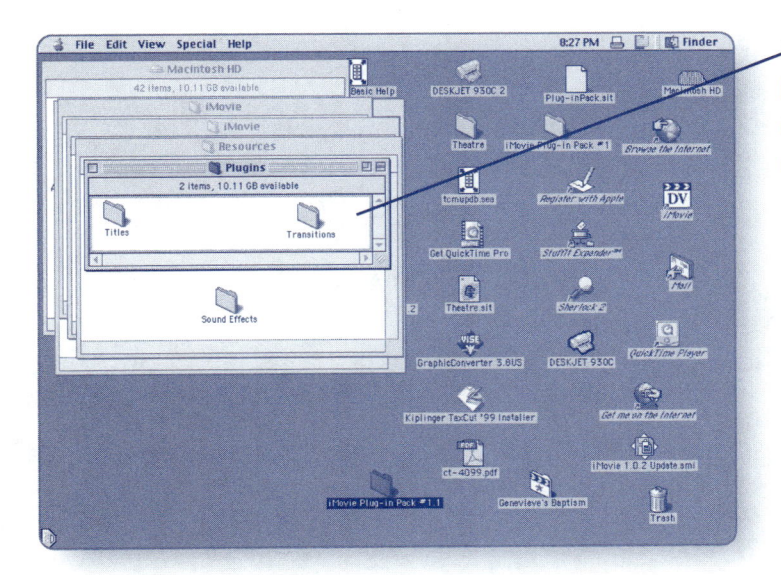

16. **Release** the **mouse button**. The new transitions (and titles) will be available the next time you launch iMovie.

7

Text in iMovie: Rolling Titles, Credits, and Captions

A picture is worth a thousand words, but sometimes you need to spell it out for your audience. Using text in your movies allows you to title your epics, provide explanation, and give credit where credit is due. Titles can add personality, and personality goes a long way. In this chapter, you'll learn how to:

- Select a title style and background
- Work with font styles and colors
- Adjust the duration of your title
- Position your title
- Change and delete your title

Opening the Titles Palette

The Titles palette is located at the bottom of the Effects palette, next to the Transitions palette, Music palette, and Sounds palette. You open the Titles palette the same way you opened the Transitions palette in Chapter 6, "Adding Stylish Transitions."

1. **Click** on the **Titles button** in the Effects palette. The Titles palette will appear.

2. **Click** on the **Titles button** again. The Titles palette will close.

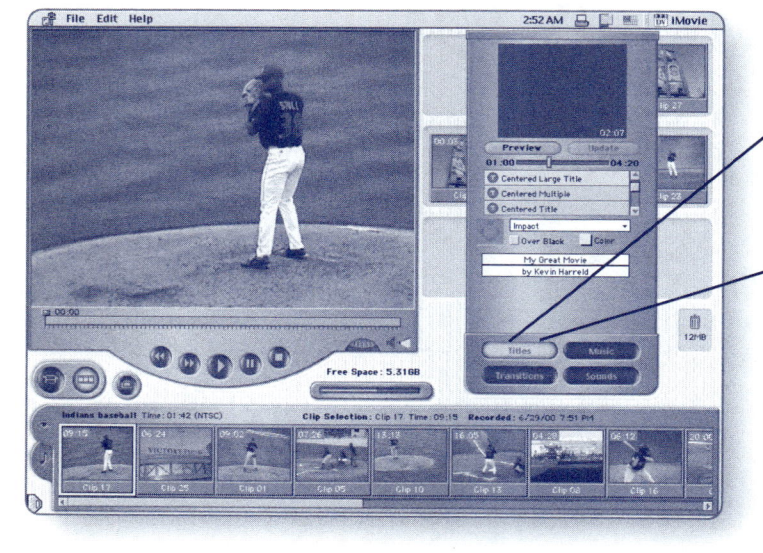

NOTE

After you learn about iMovie's title effects in this chapter, learn what else you can do with text in Chapter 11, "Tricks with Text."

Selecting a Title Style

Just below the preview window and duration slider bar in the Titles palette, there is a list of the title styles available for you to use.

SELECTING A TITLE STYLE

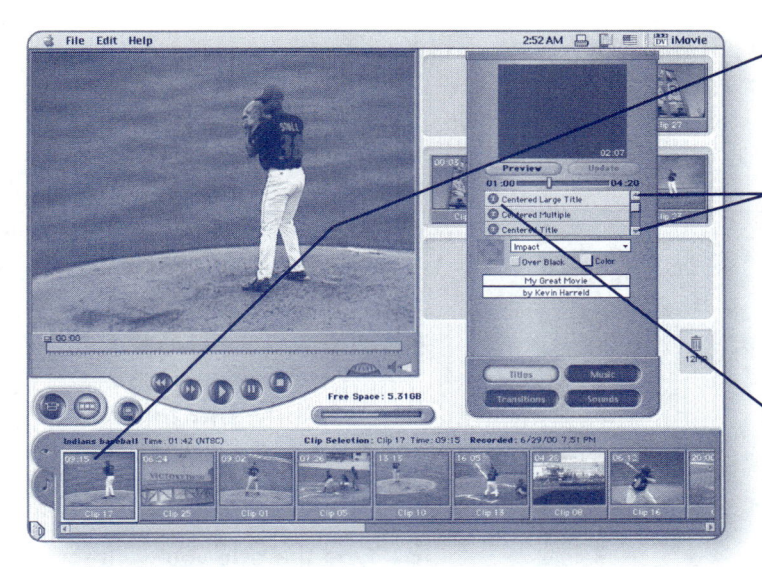

1. Click on the **clip** on which you want your title. The clip will be selected.

2. Click on the **up and down arrows** in the scroll box next to the title styles window to search through the different styles available.

3. Click on a **style**. The title style will quickly preview in the preview window.

4. Click on **Preview** in the Titles palette. The title style will preview in the Monitor window. This will give you a better look at the style.

Typing Your Title Text

Depending on the title style you choose, different title text boxes will be available. Some styles allow you to type in long blocks of text or scrolling credits. Others allow you to simply add a short, one-line billboard. You'll see what's available after you select a style.

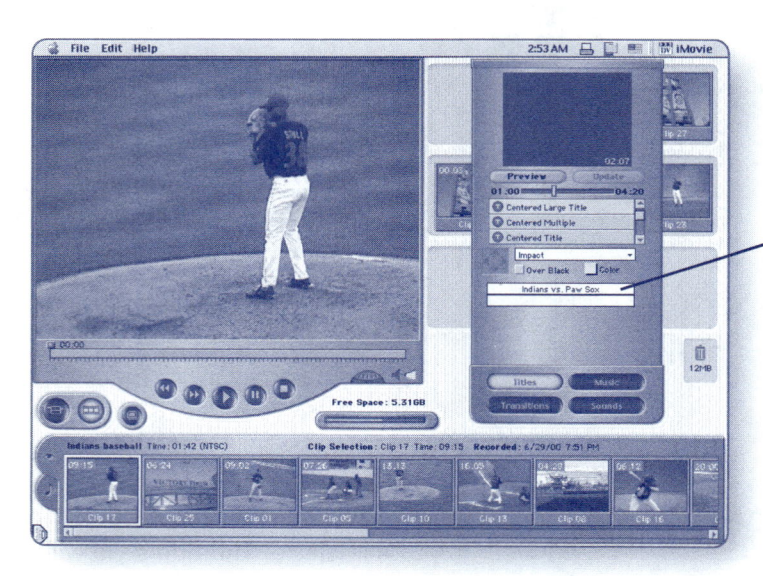

1. **Click** in the **title text box**. The default text will be highlighted.

2. **Type** the **title** you want for your movie.

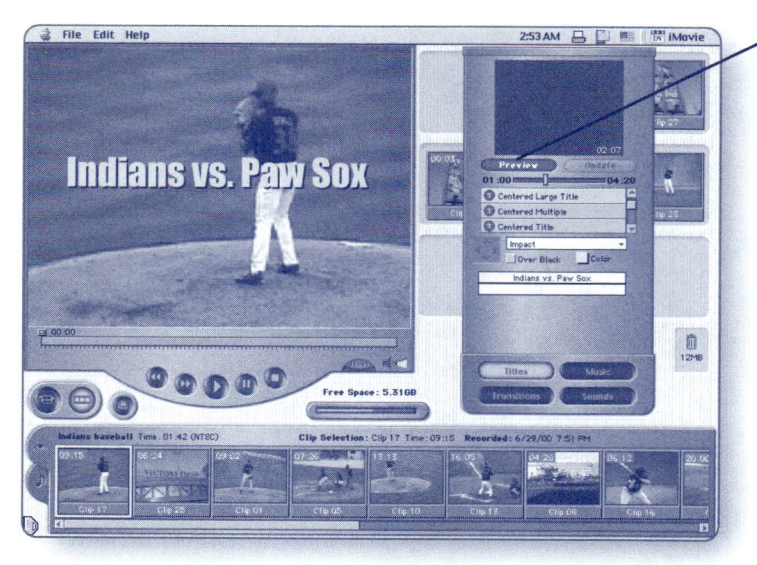

3. **Click** on **Preview**. Your title will preview in the Monitor window.

Selecting a Title Background

There are two ways you can show the opening title for your movie: over a video clip or over a plain black screen.

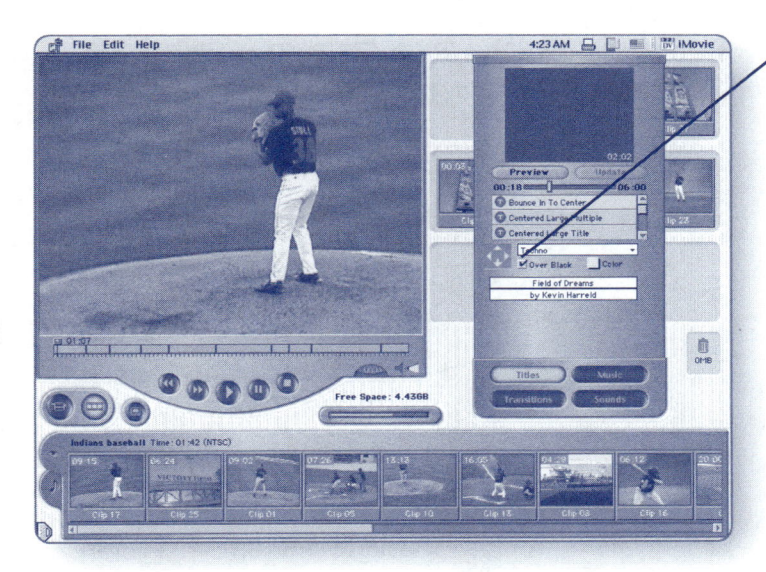

1a. Click on the **check box** to the left of Over Black to insert a check mark. This will allow your title to be shown over a black background, rather than over a video clip.

OR

1b. Leave the **check box** to the left of Over Black unchecked and click on the clip to which you want to add your title. This will allow you to use the video clip as the background for your title.

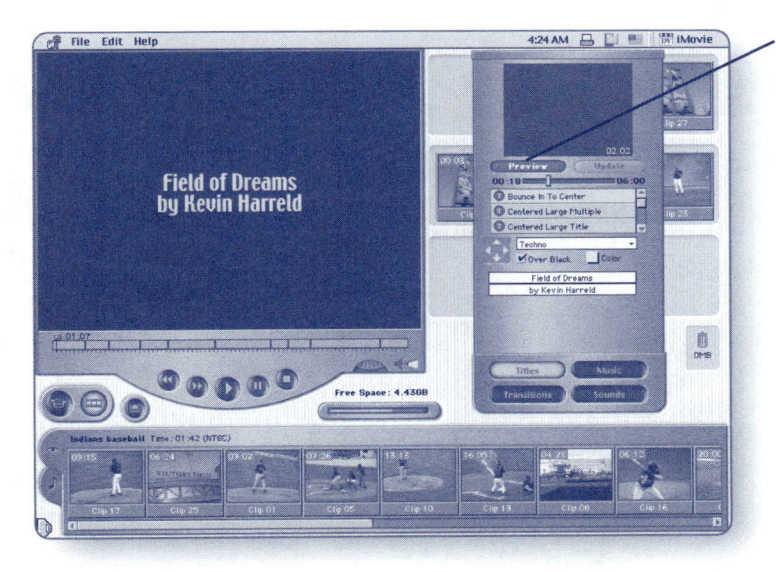

2. Click on **Preview**. The title on the video clip or black background will appear in the Monitor window.

CHAPTER 7: TEXT IN iMOVIE: ROLLING TITLES, CREDITS, CAPTIONS

Selecting Apple's Still Files as Backgrounds

You're not limited to using a black page or a video clip as the background for your title. You can take any still image file (provided that it is in JPEG, PICT, GIF, BMP, or Photoshop format), insert it into your movie, and then add the title to the image. You'll learn how to do this in Chapter 9, "iMovie and Still Images." Apple has a library of appropriate stills that you can use as backgrounds for your titles or credits.

1. Go to **http://www.apple.com/imovie**. The iMovie page will appear in your browser.

2. Click on the **Sounds, Music, Backgrounds link**. The library of backgrounds, sound effects, and looping music page will appear.

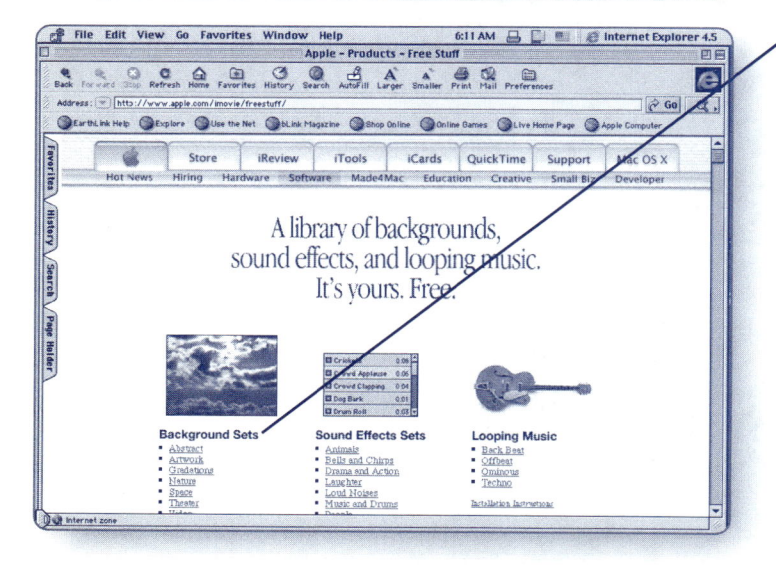

3. Click on a **Background Set**. The Backgrounds download page will appear.

SELECTING A TITLE BACKGROUND   111

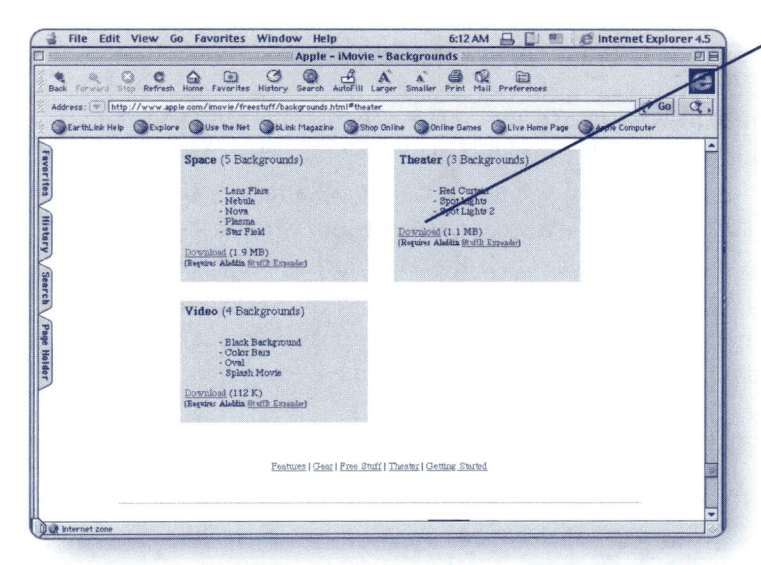

4. Click on **Download** for the Background Set you selected. The Background Set will download to your Desktop.

5. Click on the **desktop icon** for the Background Set you downloaded. The folder will extract to your desktop.

6. Open the **folder** and **click** on a **background image**. The image will appear.

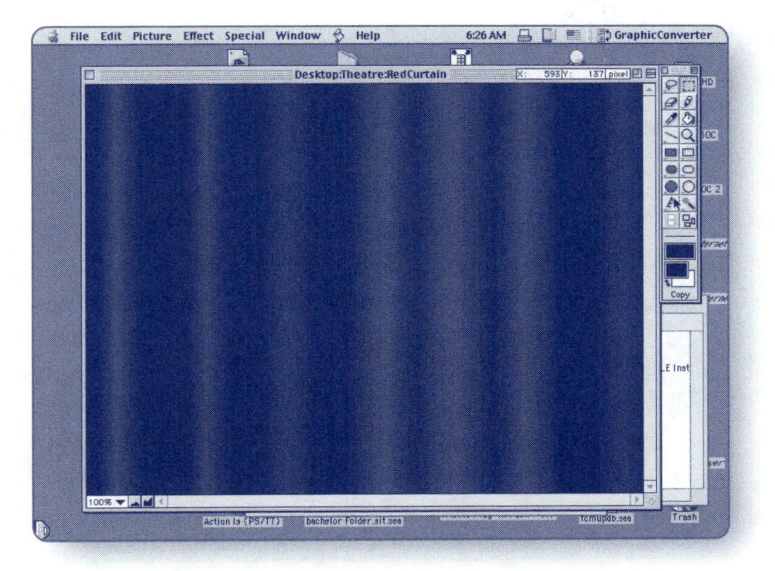

Now you have a cool image to use as a backdrop for a title. Check out Chapter 9, "iMovie and Still Images," to learn how to insert the image into your iMovie.

Working with Fonts

The font you choose for your movie title sets the tone for your whole epic. Certain font styles, sizes, and colors say different things to the audience. For example, a thicker, bolder font makes a strong impression, whereas a smaller, more delicate font sets a lighter mood. Selecting a font color is also something to consider. You need to select a color that will show up well when it is superimposed on your video. You want your fonts to be easily viewed by your audience.

1a. Click on the **clip** to which you want to add your title. The clip will be selected.

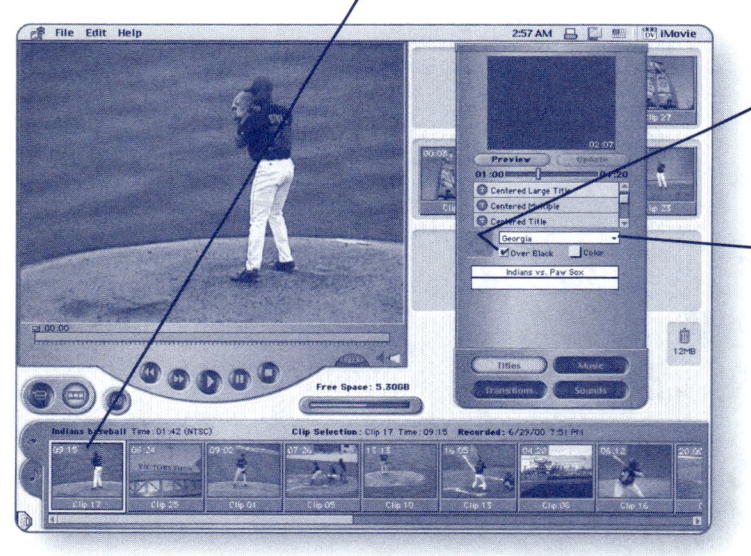

OR

1b. Click on the **Over Black check box** to select a black background for your title.

2. Click on the **down arrow** to the right of the font styles. A list of fonts will appear.

WORKING WITH FONTS 113

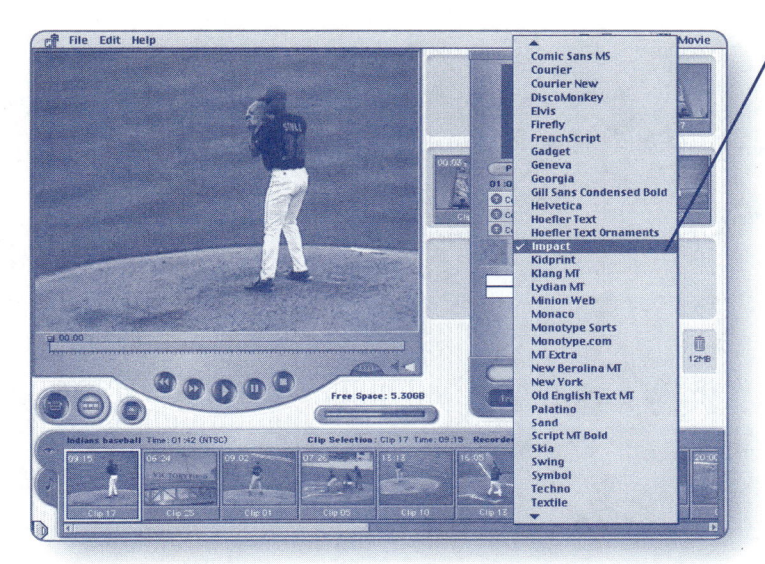

3. Click on a **font** from the list. The font will preview in the preview window.

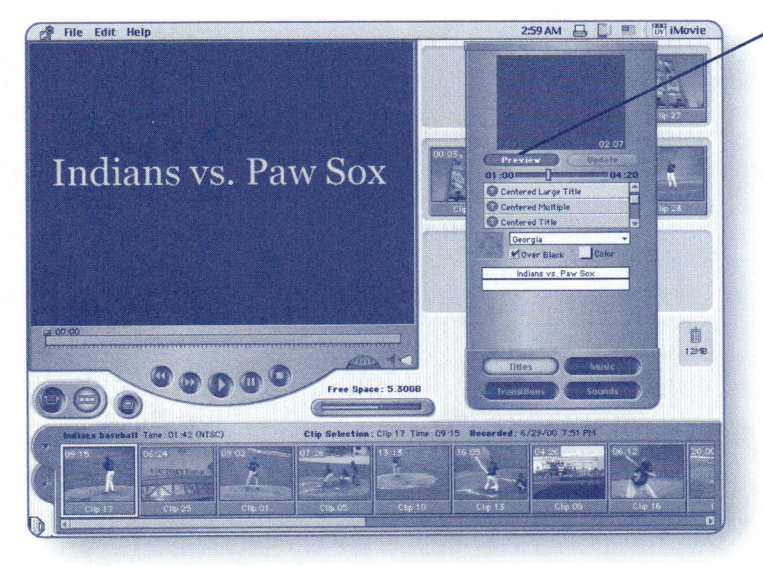

4. Click on the **Preview** button to see your selection in the Monitor window.

CHAPTER 7: TEXT IN iMOVIE: ROLLING TITLES, CREDITS, CAPTIONS

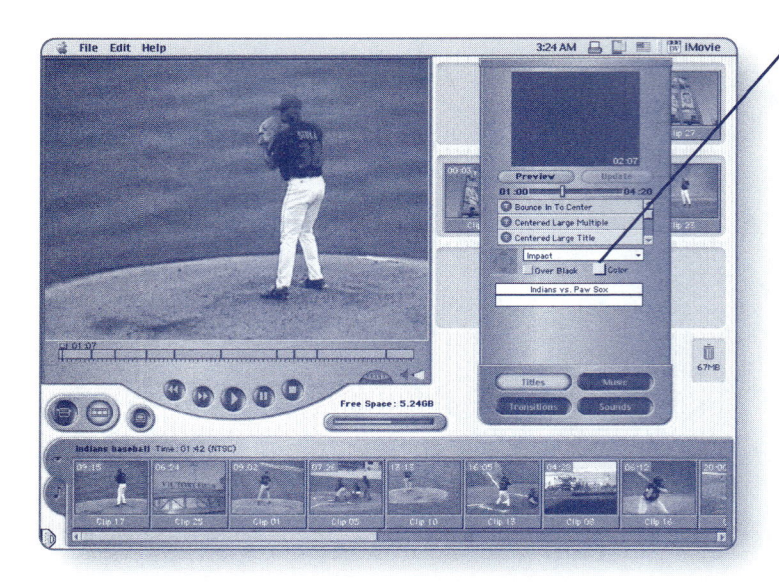

5. **Click** on the **color box**. A color palette will appear.

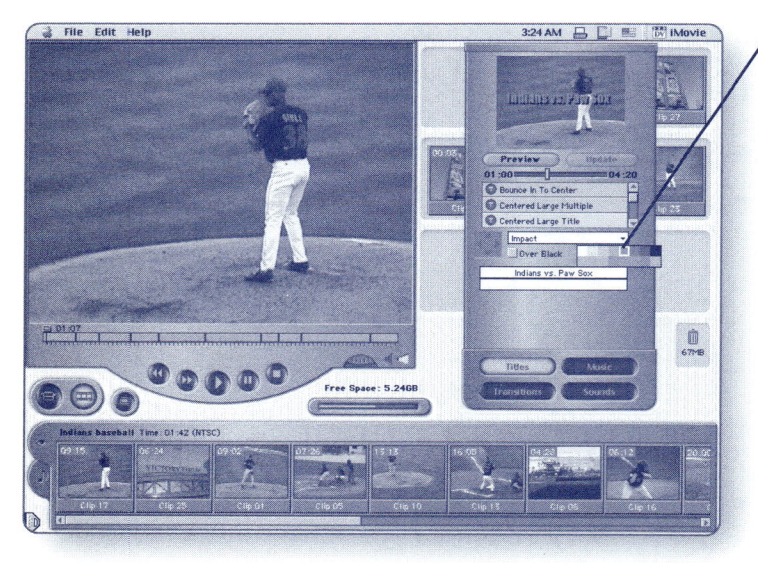

6. **Click** on a **color**. The color will be selected.

ADJUSTING THE DURATION OF YOUR TITLE 115

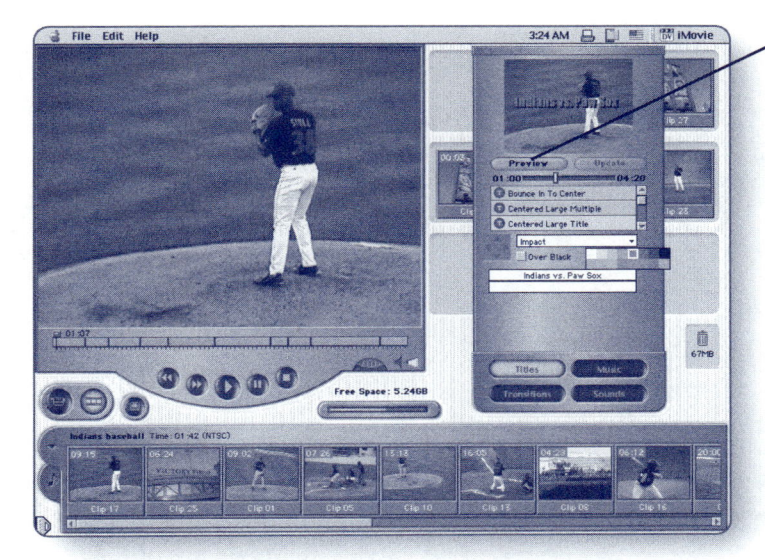

7. Click on the **Preview button** to preview your selection.

> **NOTE**
> Another thing to keep in mind when you select a font style is how you will show your movie to your audience. Although a thin, script-type font will look great on your computer monitor, it will probably look lousy in a QuickTime movie. It's usually best to use bolder, simpler fonts. The key is to make sure that any text in your movie will be readable in any format.

Adjusting the Duration of Your Title

You also need to adjust the duration of your title, which you will do in the Titles palette. Unless you want your title or credits to roll over more than one video clip, your title duration must be less than the duration of the clip in which you want the title to appear.

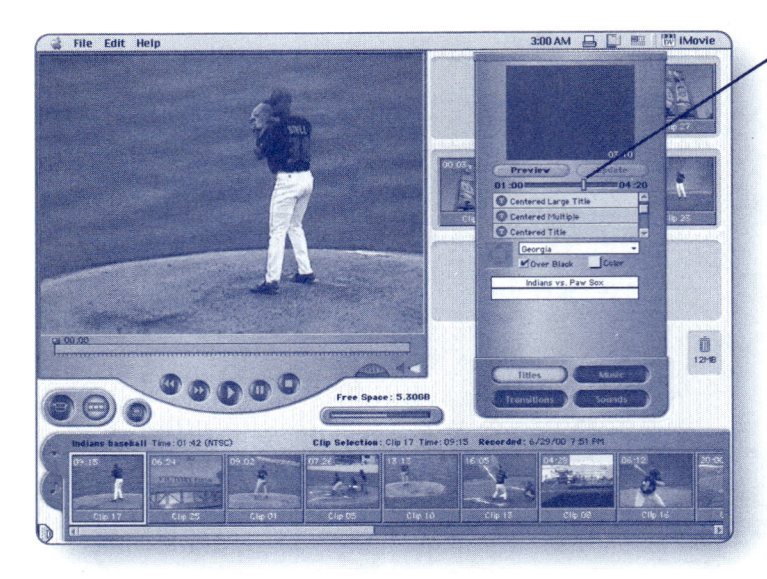

1. **Press and hold** the **mouse button** down on the duration slider and **drag** the **slider** left to decrease the duration or right to increase the duration of your title. The duration will change accordingly.

2. Release the **mouse button**. Your duration will be set.

NOTE
The durations of the title styles in iMovie are not all the same. As you click on title styles in the Titles palette, you'll notice that the numbers on the left and right ends of the duration slider bar change.

Positioning Your Title

There will be times when you want to position your title at a certain place and a certain point of time in your clip. However, certain title styles won't allow you to align text exactly where you want it. If you need to align your title in an area other than the center of a clip, make sure you choose a title style that allows you to do this. You will know that you can alter the alignment or scrolling direction of a certain title if, when you select the title, the alignment and scrolling arrows become active.

Specifying Alignment and Scrolling Direction

With some title styles, you can specify the alignment and scrolling direction of the title with the arrow buttons.

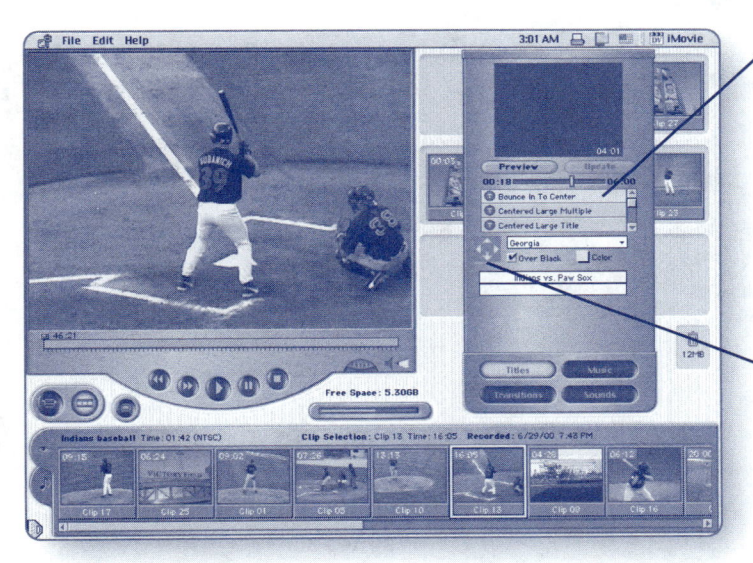

1. Click on a **title style** in the style box. If the arrows just below and to the left of the title style box become active, you can adjust the alignment or scrolling direction of that particular style. If they remain grayed out, you're out of luck.

2. Click on the **up, down, left, or right arrow**. The alignment or scrolling direction will adjust to your selection.

Setting the Exact Placement of Titles

What if you want the title to appear at a specific point within a clip—for example, exactly 10 seconds into the clip. Because iMovie only allows you to add a title to the beginning of a clip, you need to make that spot in the clip the beginning of a clip. You can do this by splitting the clip in two.

118 CHAPTER 7: TEXT IN iMOVIE: ROLLING TITLES, CREDITS, CAPTIONS

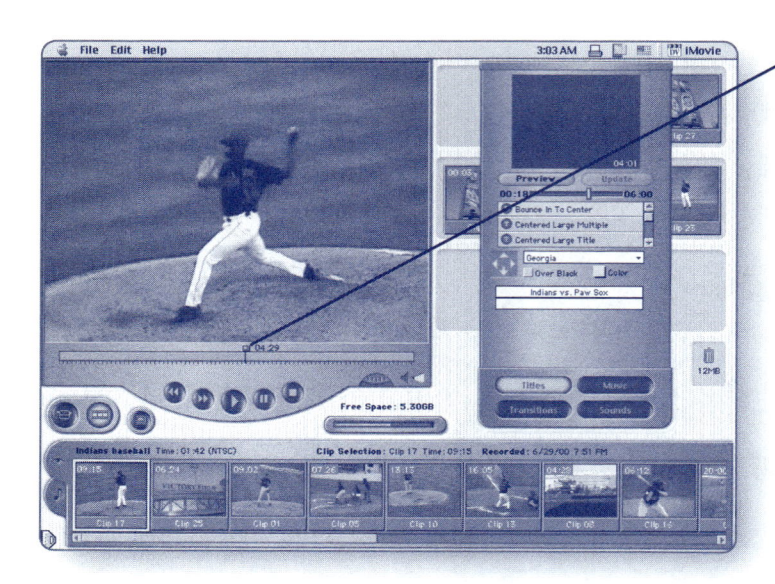

1. Press and hold the **mouse button** on the playhead in the Monitor window and **drag** the **playhead** to the time at which you want the title to appear.

2. Release the **mouse button**. The playhead will be placed where you released the mouse button.

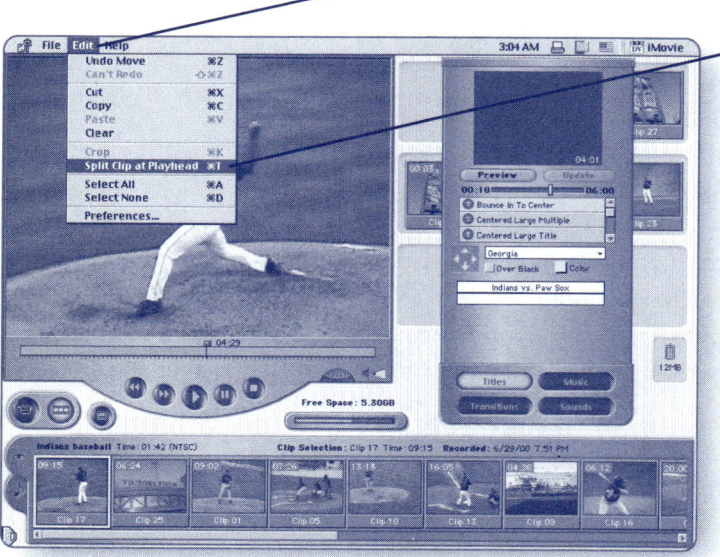

3. Click on **Edit**. The Edit menu will appear.

4. Click on **Split Clip at Playhead**.

ADDING THE TITLE TO YOUR MOVIE   **119**

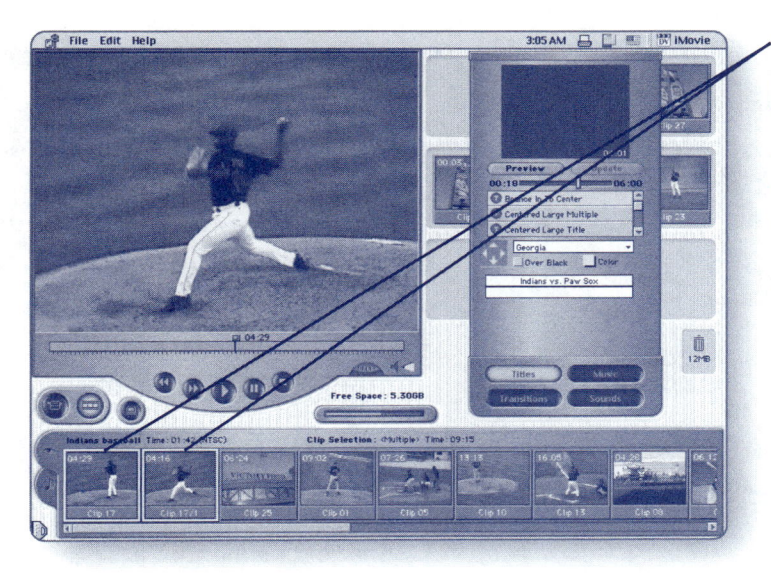

The clip will split in two and each clip will appear in the Viewer. The second clip is the exact point at which your title will begin, once you add it. You will learn how to add your title in the next section, "Adding the Title to Your Movie."

Adding the Title to Your Movie

After you have all of the specs for your titles and credits where you want them, you just need to add them to your production.

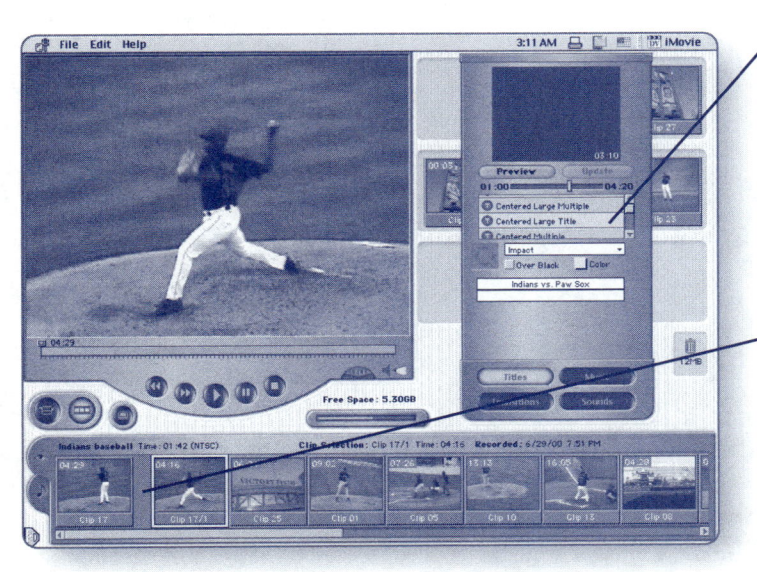

1. Press and hold the **mouse button** on your title selection in the Titles palette and **drag** the **title selection** to the clip in the Viewer to which you want to attach it. The clip will move slightly to the right.

2. Release the **mouse button**. The clip to which you attached the title will split in two. The portion of the clip with the title will become a new clip.

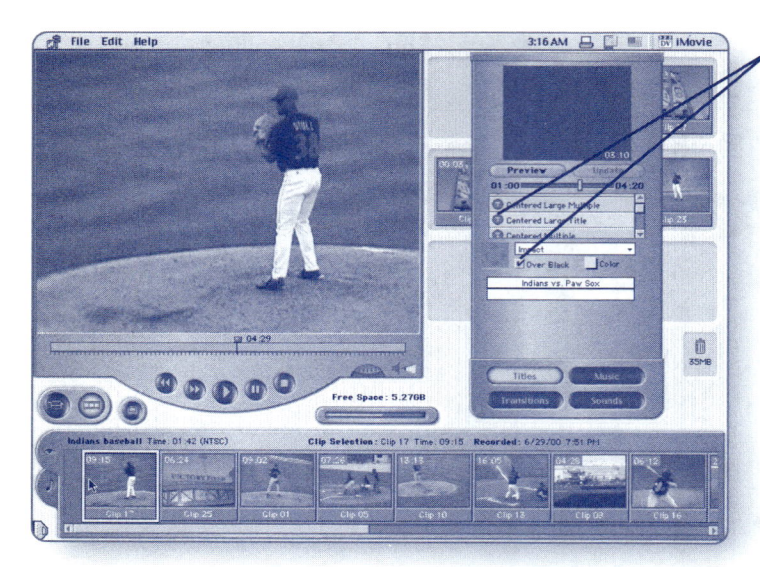

CHAPTER 7: TEXT IN iMOVIE: ROLLING TITLES, CREDITS, CAPTIONS

3. If you're placing a title over black, **press and hold** the **mouse button** on your title selection in the Titles palette and **drag** the **title selection** to the place in the Viewer where you want it to appear.

4. Release the **mouse button**. The title will begin rendering.

> **TIP**
>
> You can add more than one text element to a clip. After you add a Centered Large title to a clip, for example, add Subtitle text to the same clip, varying the font color, style, and duration for a different effect.

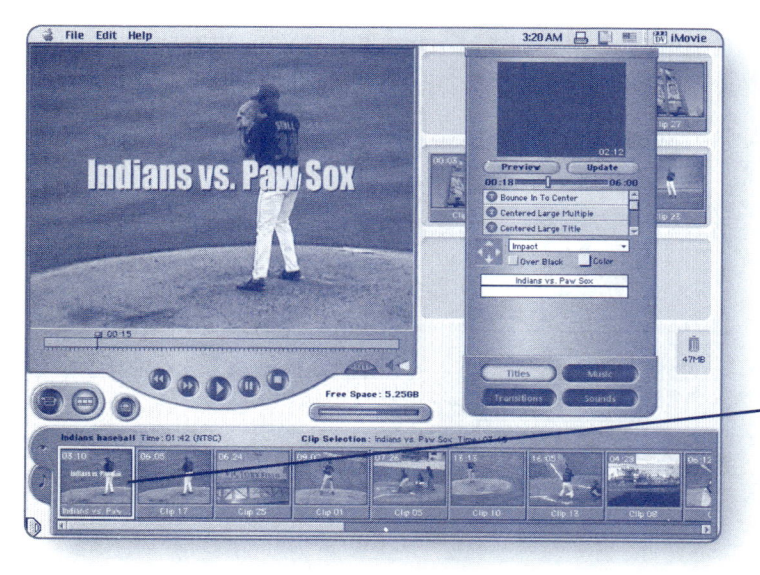

Changing Your Title

Perhaps you've created a title for your video and after looking at it, you decide you don't like what you see. Changing a title is a simple process.

1. Click on the **clip** that contains the title. The clip will be selected.

DELETING YOUR TITLE 121

2. Make any **changes** to the font style or color, title style or duration, and so on.

3. Click on the **Update** button. Your changes will take effect.

Deleting Your Title

Suppose after viewing your movie with its new title, you decide it's really not necessary and you want to get rid of it completely. You can just throw it in the trash.

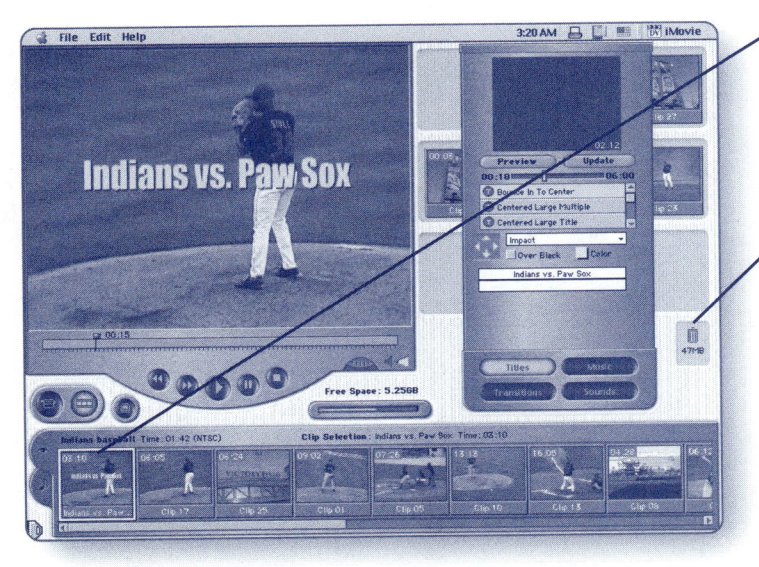

1. Press and hold the **mouse button** down on the clip that contains the title you want to discard and **drag** the **title** to the trashcan.

2. Release the **mouse button**. Your title will be deleted.

8

Audio: Adding Soundtracks, Scores, Sounds, and Narration

Musical scores or soundtracks set the mood for your movies, and adding sound effects and narration can also enhance your epic. The best movies have well-balanced audio effects to complement the visuals. Think of how different movies like "Goodfellas" and "Taxi Driver" would be without the voice-over narration, or how "Top Gun" and "Pulp Fiction" would be without the musical soundtracks. And how would "Star Wars" be without sound effects? Effective audio can change the whole complexion of your movies. In this chapter, you'll learn how to:

- Record music from a CD
- Add sound effects
- Add narration
- Crop, delete, and move audio tracks
- Adjust audio levels

CHAPTER 8: SOUNDTRACKS, SCORES, SOUNDS, AND NARRATION

Touring the Audio Viewer, Music Palette, and Sound Palette

The Audio Viewer is the tab with the musical note symbol, located behind the Clip Viewer you've been working with in previous chapters. This is the workspace in which you edit your iMovie's audio. The Music palette shows the various songs on a CD, and allows you to play, record, and add the individual songs. The Sounds palette houses a number of sound effects and allows you to record a narration.

1. Click on the **Audio Viewer tab**. The Audio Viewer will appear.

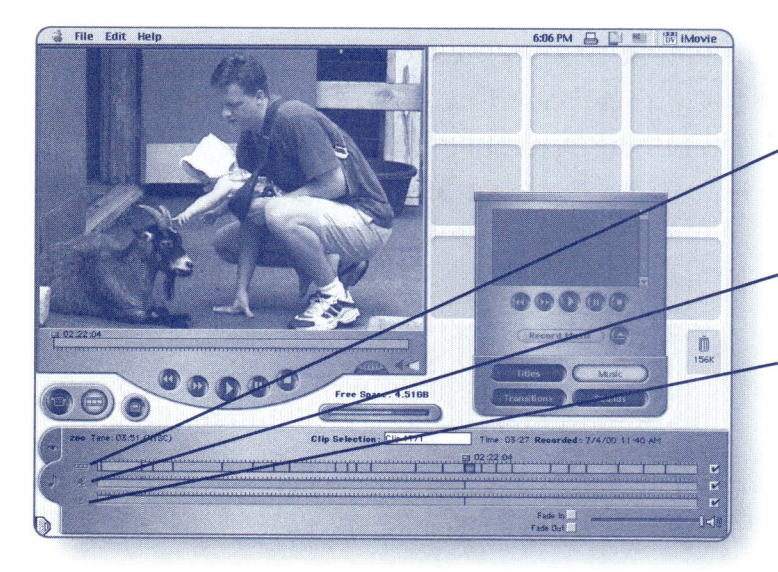

The Audio Viewer has three tracks:

- **Video camera soundtrack**. This track houses the sounds from your video footage.

- **Narration track**. This track is where you add narration.

- **Music track**. This track is where you add music.

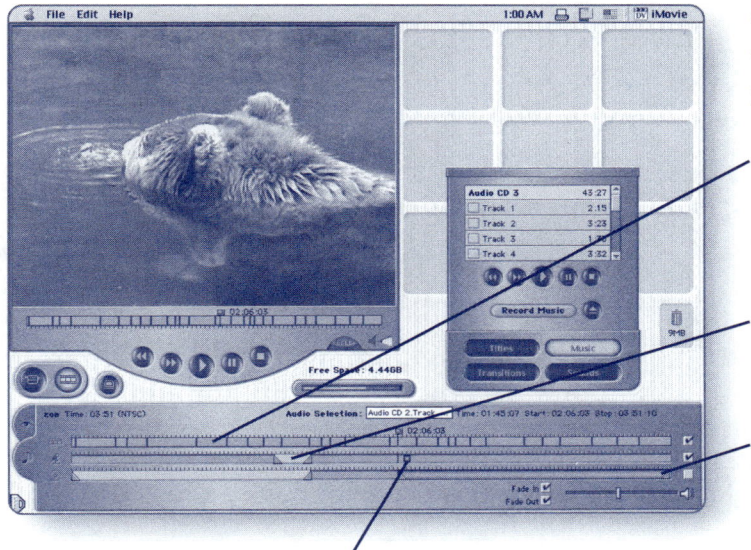

TOURING THE AUDIO VIEWER, MUSIC PALETTE, AND SOUND PALETTE   125

Other items in the Audio Viewer, which you'll learn more about as you read this chapter, include

- **Camera sound clip**. An individual audio clip from your camcorder, and its location in your movie.

- **Narration clip**. An individual narration clip that you add, and its location in your movie.

- **Music clip**. An individual music clip that you add, and its location in your movie.

- **Sound effect clip**. An individual sound effect clip that you add, and its location in your movie.

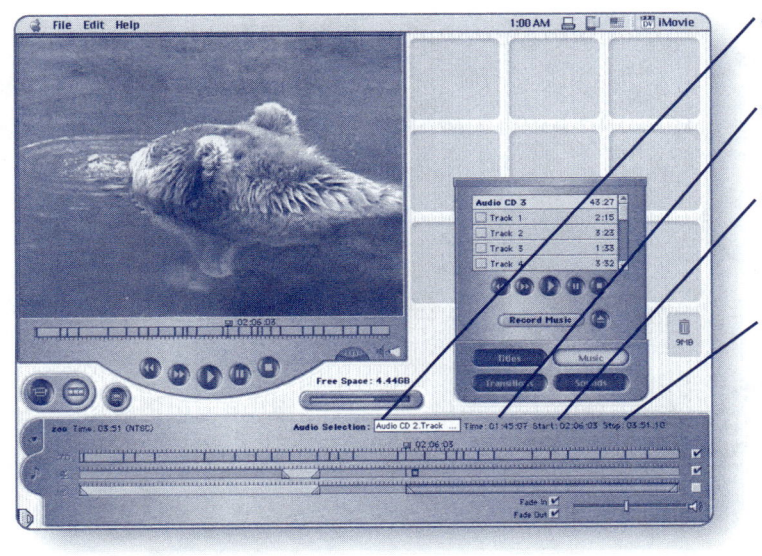

- **Name of clip**. The name of the selected audio clip.

- **Length of clip**. The length of the selected audio clip.

- **Start of clip**. The selected audio clip's start time in your movie.

- **End of clip**. The selected audio clip's stop time in your movie.

CHAPTER 8: SOUNDTRACKS, SCORES, SOUNDS, AND NARRATION

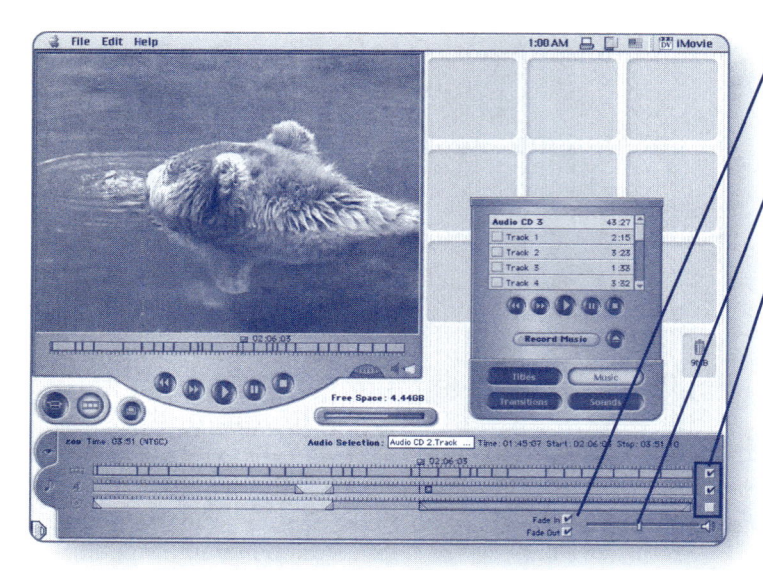

- **Fade In/Out check boxes**. Allow you to fade your audio clip in or out.

- **Volume slider**. Determines the volume level of clips.

- **Enable/Disable Track check boxes**. Allow you to enable or mute the video camera soundtrack, narration track, or music track.

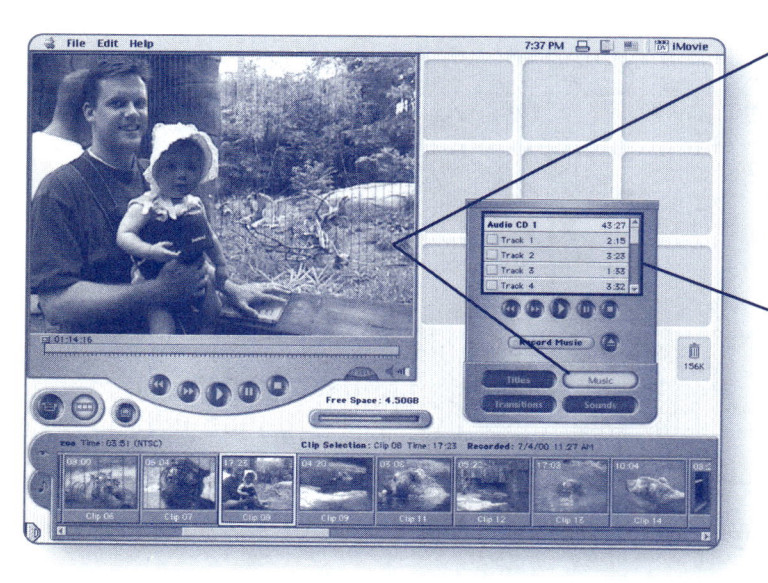

2. Click on the **Music button** in the Effects palette. The Music palette will appear.

The Music palette has the following features:

- **Soundtrack list box**. Lists all of the individual songs on your CD.

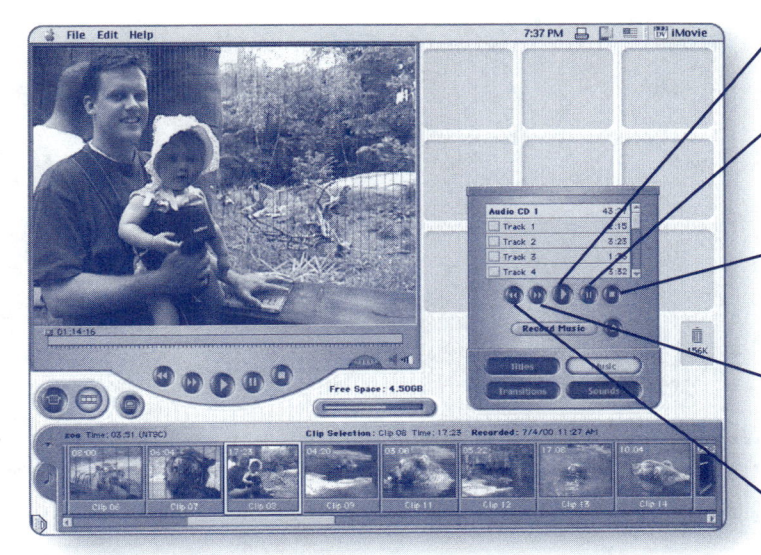

TOURING THE AUDIO VIEWER, MUSIC PALETTE, AND SOUND PALETTE   127

- **Play button**. Plays the selected song or songs.

- **Pause button**. Pauses the playback of the selected song or songs.

- **Stop button**. Stops the playback of the selected song or songs.

- **Next track button**. Finds the beginning of the next song on the CD.

- **Previous track button**. Finds the beginning of the previous song on the CD.

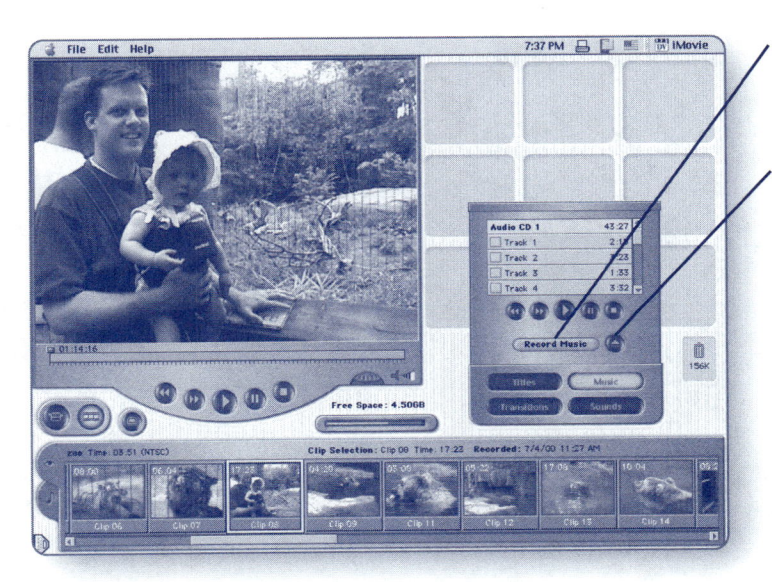

- **Record button**. Records song in the music track of the Audio Viewer.

- **Eject button**. Ejects your CD.

CHAPTER 8: SOUNDTRACKS, SCORES, SOUNDS, AND NARRATION

3. Click on the **Sounds button** in the Effects palette. The Sounds palette will appear.

The Sounds palette has the following features:

- **Sound effects list box**. Lists the sound effects available to you.

- **Record Voice button**. Records your voice for a narration effect.

ADDING MUSIC FROM AN AUDIO CD 129

Adding Music from an Audio CD

One of the simplest ways to include your favorite songs in your movies is to pop in a CD and record the song on the Audio Viewer. You can add entire songs or portions of your favorite hits.

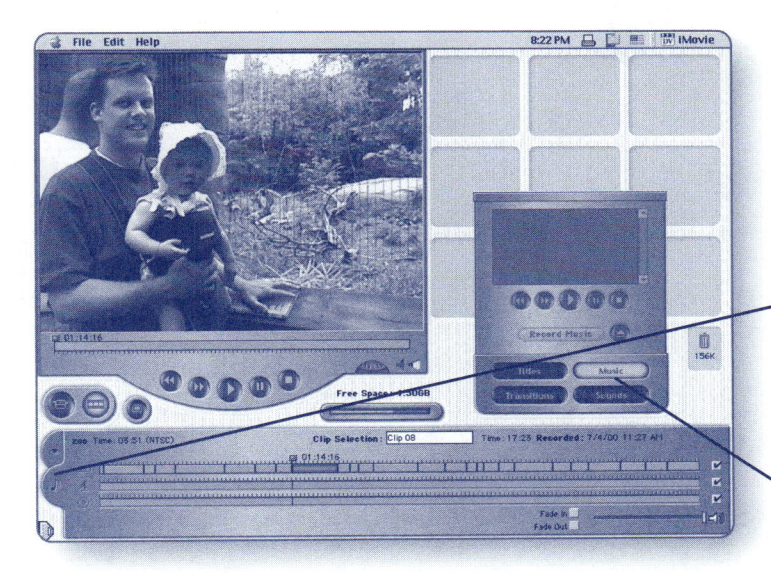

Adding a Song from a CD

Adding a song to your movie from a CD is a simple drag-and-drop procedure.

1. Click on the **Audio tab** in the Viewer, if you haven't already done so. The Audio Viewer will appear.

2. Click on the **Music button**. The Music palette will appear.

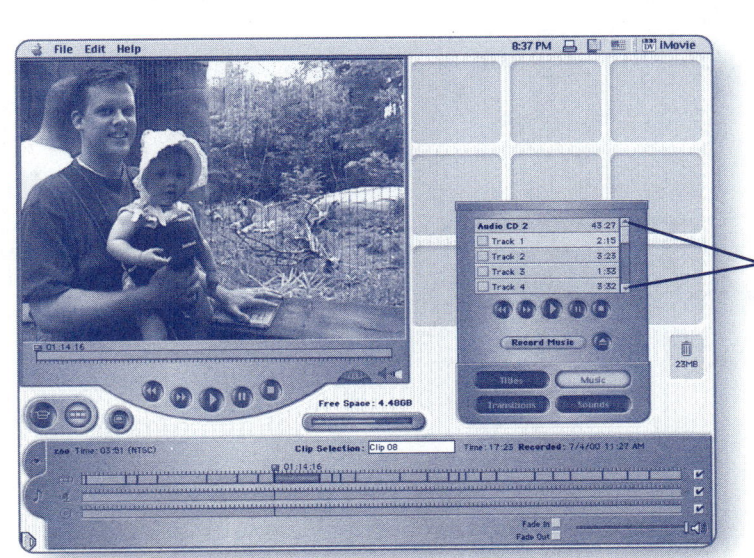

3. Insert your **CD** into the CD-ROM drive. The songs will appear in the list box Soundtrack after a few seconds.

4. Click on the **up and down arrows** in the scroll box to search for your song.

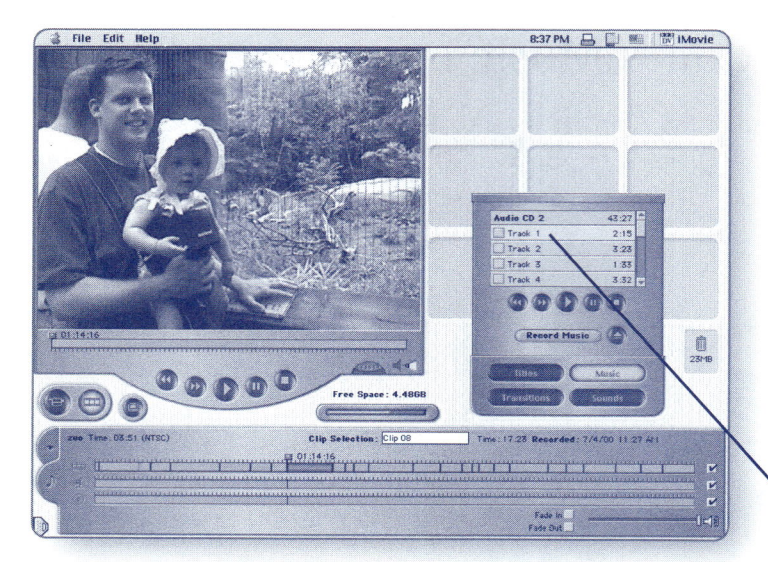

CHAPTER 8: SOUNDTRACKS, SCORES, SOUNDS, AND NARRATION

> **NOTE**
> iMovie doesn't reveal the actual names of the songs on your CD. If you can't figure out which song is which, just click on a track and then click on the Play button. The song will play, and you will know what track it is.

5. Press and hold the **mouse button** on the song you want to add and **drag it** to the music track in the Audio Viewer.

6. Release the **mouse button**. The song will import from the CD and appear in the music track after a few seconds.

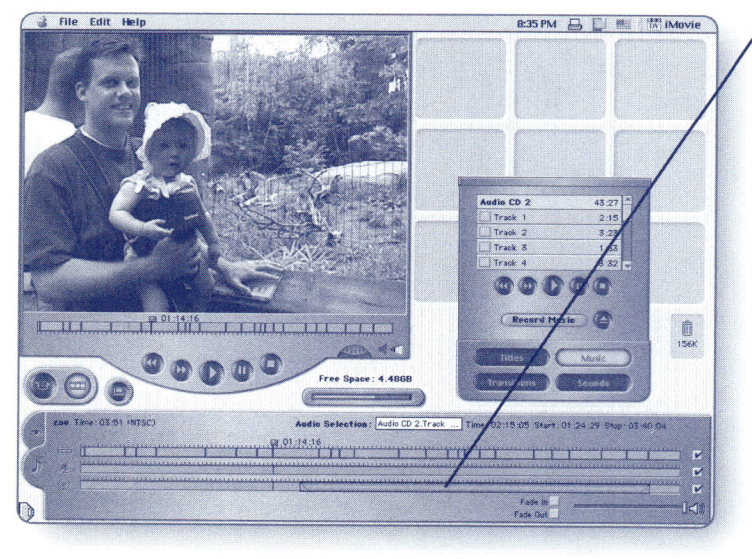

ADDING MUSIC FROM AN AUDIO CD 131

> **NOTE**
> There are copyright law issues to keep in mind when recording audio from CDs. As long as you are not selling or commercially releasing your movie, you are free to use audio without permissions. You can also pick up some royalty-free music, or buyout music, by searching for *royalty-free music* or *buyout music* in your browser. You'll be directed to some Web sites in which you can pay a one-time fee for tunes and not have to worry about getting into any trouble from using copyrighted music.

Adding a Portion of a Song

You have the freedom to record exactly what you want from your CD—you aren't limited to adding an entire song. Use the Record Music button to record just a portion of a song for your movie.

1. Repeat steps 1 through 4 in the previous section, "Adding a Song from a CD."

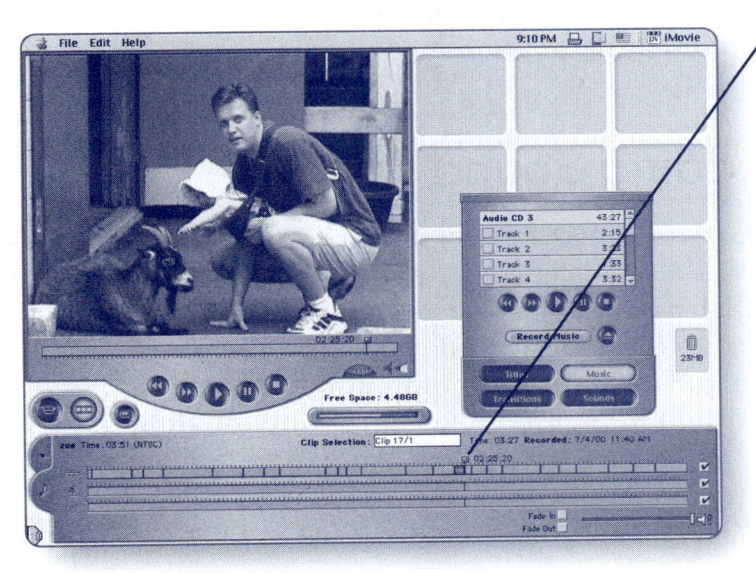

2. Press and hold your **mouse button** on the playhead and **drag** the **playhead** to the point in the Audio Viewer where you want the music to begin recording.

3. Release the **mouse button**. This is the point where your music will start recording.

> **TIP**
> Press the Home key on your keyboard to immediately move to the beginning of your clips.

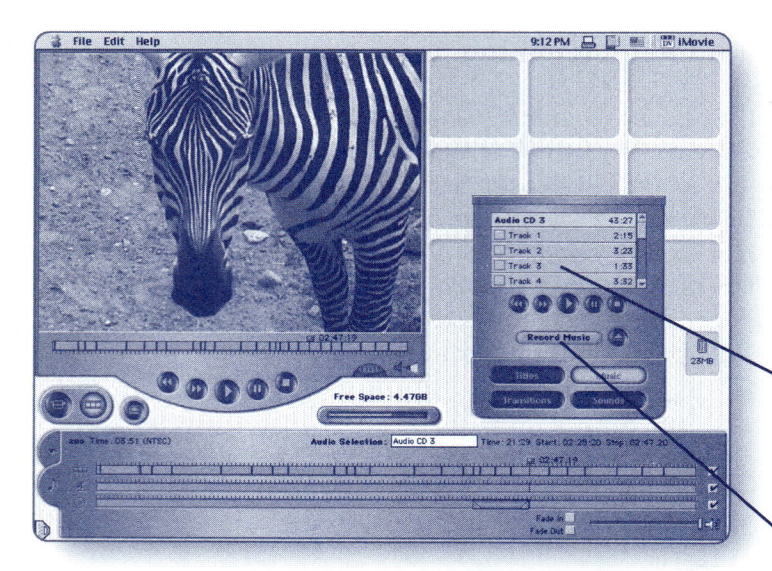

CHAPTER 8: SOUNDTRACKS, SCORES, SOUNDS, AND NARRATION

> **NOTE**
> You'll learn more about editing your audio clips later in this chapter. For now, you'll just focus on adding the music to your movie.

4. **Click** on the **track** you want to insert into your movie. The track will be selected.

5. **Click** on the **Record Music button**. The track will begin playing and recording in the music track in the Audio Viewer. The video footage will also play in the Monitor window as the song records. The Record Music button will become a Stop button.

6. **Click** on the **Stop button** to stop recording. The track will cease recording.

Adding Sound Effects

iMovie contains a handful of sound effects in its Effects palette. You can become the post-production sound effect artist for your movie by introducing footsteps, broken glass, rain falling, and other sounds. Add sound effects in either the narration track or the music track.

ADDING SOUND EFFECTS   133

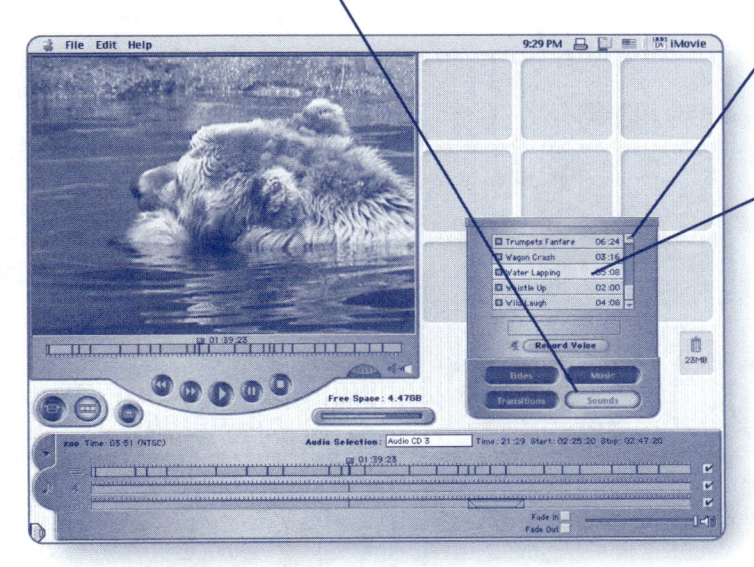

1. Click on the **Sounds button** in the Effects palette. The Sounds palette will appear.

2. Click on the **up and down arrows** to scroll through the list of effects.

3. Click on a **sound effect**. A sampling of the sound effect will play.

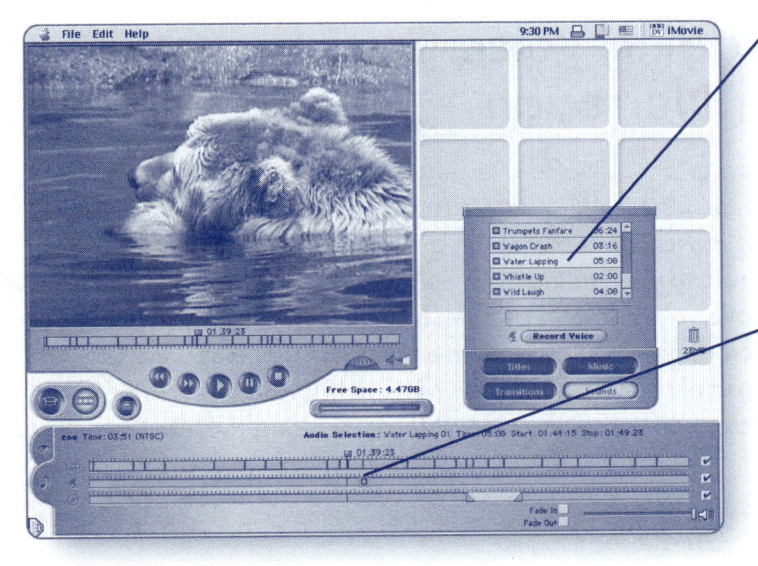

4. Press and hold the **mouse button** on the sound and **drag** the **sound** down to your desired location on either the narration track or the music track in the Audio Viewer. An outline of the sound will appear as you drag it.

5. Release the **mouse button**. The sound effect will be represented by a pink square in the Audio Viewer.

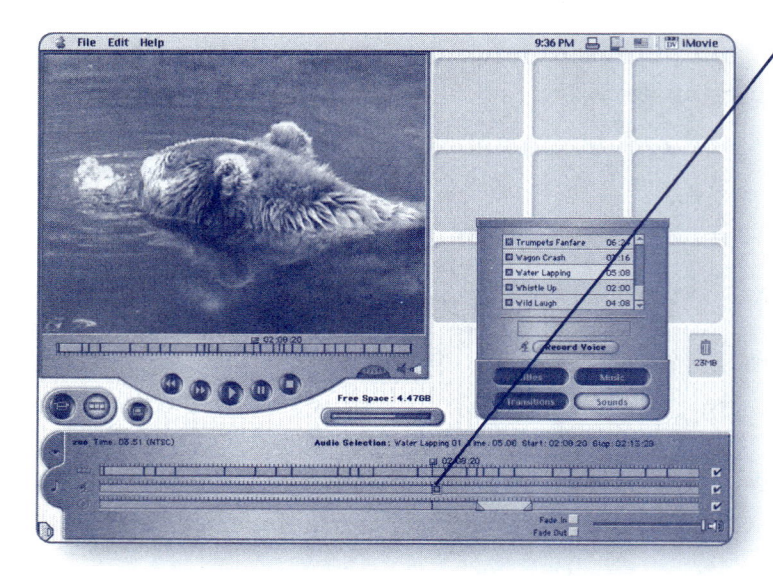

CHAPTER 8: SOUNDTRACKS, SCORES, SOUNDS, AND NARRATION

6. **Click and hold** the **mouse button** on the pink square and **drag it** left or right to the position where you want the sound effect.

7. **Release** the **mouse button**. The sound effect will be placed in the desired position.

> **TIP**
>
> To precisely locate the sound effect, click on the pink square to select it, and then press the left and right arrow keys on your keyboard to move left or right, frame-by-frame.

Adding Voice-Over or Narration

Narrate or add voice-over to tell the story of your movie or reveal behind-the-scenes information to your audience. iMacs and PowerBooks have built-in microphones, which you'll need to record your voice. Ever wonder what that little oval hole above your computer screen is? That's the internal microphone. You can also use an external microphone to accomplish this task. Power Macs come with an external microphone. This section will focus on using the internal mike.

ADDING VOICE-OVER OR NARRATION 135

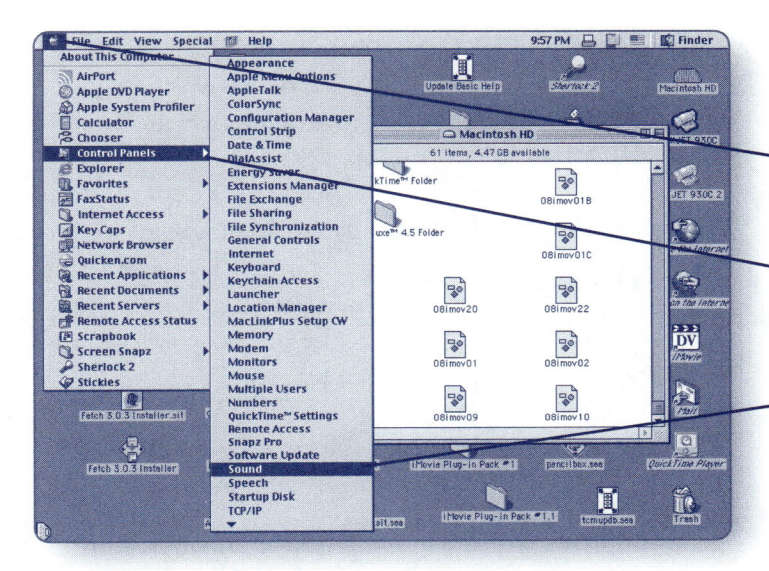

1. Quit iMovie, if you have it open. iMovie will close.

2. Click on the **apple icon**. The apple menu will appear.

3. Move the **mouse pointer** down to Control Panels. The Control Panels menu will appear.

4. Click on **Sound**. The Sound dialog box will open.

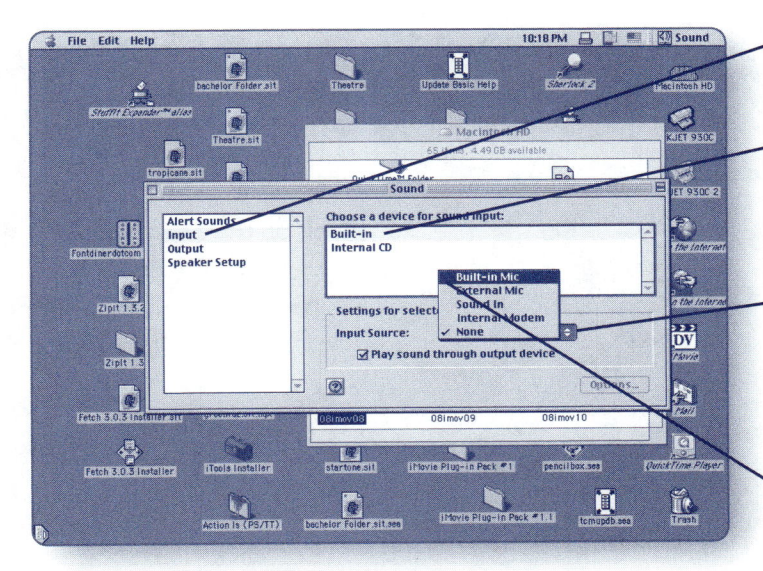

5. Click on **Input** in the left list box. Input will be selected.

6. Click on **Built-in** in the Choose a device for sound input list box. Built-in will be selected.

7. Click on the **up-and-down arrows** to the right of the Input Source list box. A pop-up list of input options will appear.

8. Click on **Built-in Mic**. Built-in Mic will be selected.

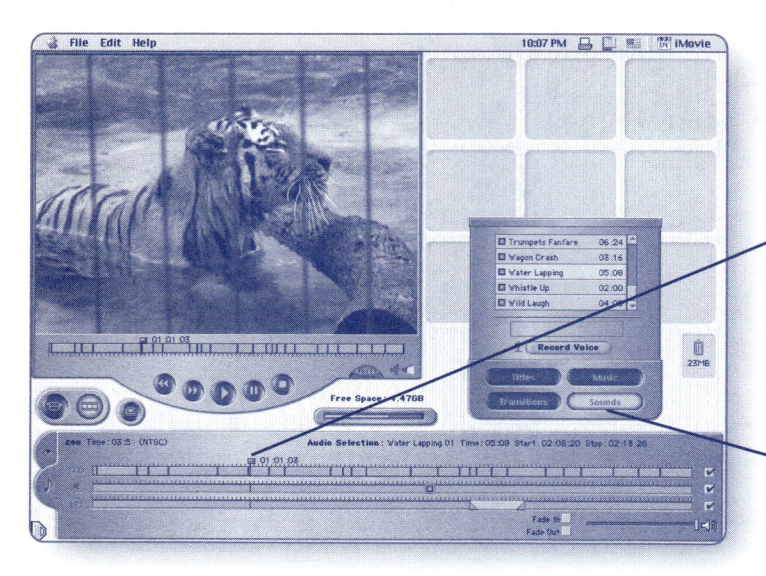

136 CHAPTER 8: SOUNDTRACKS, SCORES, SOUNDS, AND NARRATION

9. **Open iMovie** and **open** the movie **project** to which you want to add your voice. The project will open.

10. Drag the **playhead** to the point in the Audio Viewer where you want your narration to begin. The playhead will be positioned.

11. Click on the **Sounds button**. The Sounds palette will appear.

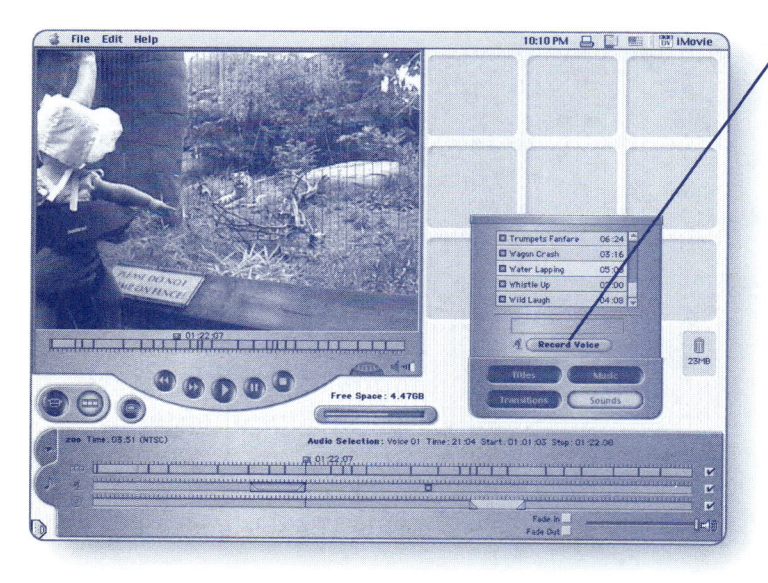

12. Click on the **Record Voice button** and **speak** into the **microphone**. Your narration will be recorded.

13. Click on the **Stop button** when you are done recording. The recording will stop.

Sound Bytes: Cropping Audio Clips

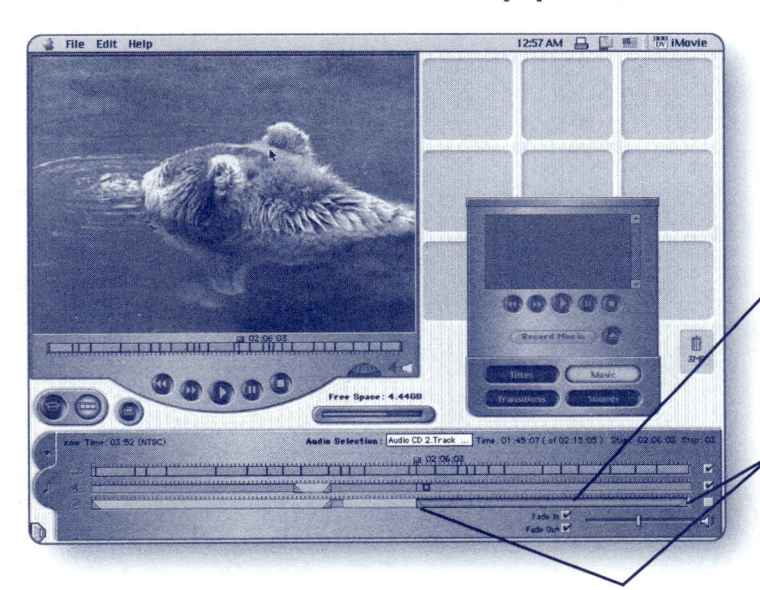

If you want to position a song to play over a certain portion or duration of your movie, you can crop the music exactly at the desired location and then fade it in and out to polish it up.

1. Click on **music clip** in the music track on the Audio Viewer. The music clip will be selected.

2. One at a time, **press and hold** the **mouse button** on the left and right crop markers and **drag** the **markers** to the desired locations.

3. Release the **mouse button**. The crop markers will be positioned.

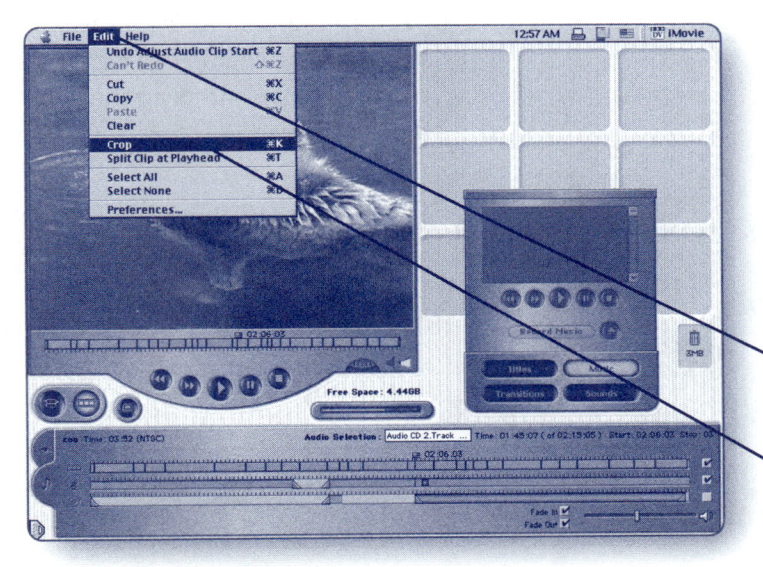

TIP

For more precise cropping, click on the beginning or end crop marker and press the left and right arrow keys to move a single frame at a time.

4. Click on **Edit**. The Edit menu will appear.

5. Click on **Crop**. The music clip will be cropped where you indicated.

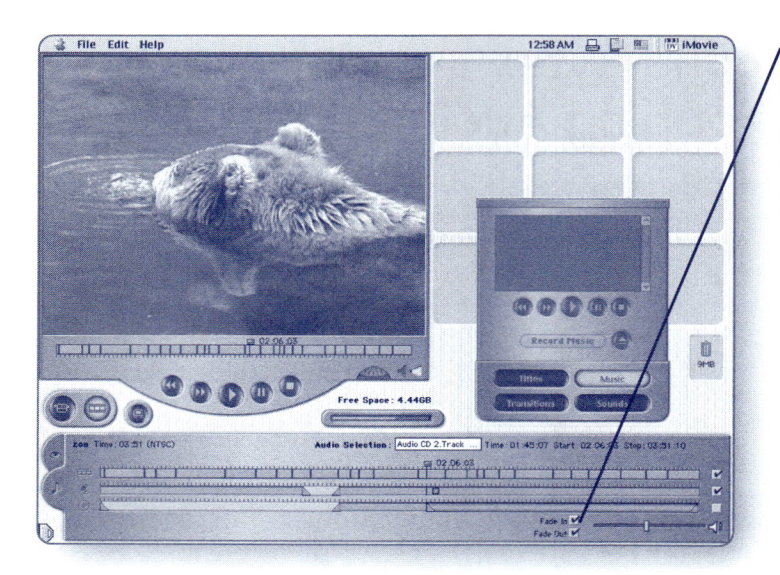

6. Click on the **Fade In and Fade Out check boxes** to insert check marks. The music clip will fade in at the beginning and fade out at the end.

Moving an Audio Clip

You can move narration, music, and sound effect clips to different places in the Audio Viewer. These audio clips can even overlap, and iMovie will play all of the sounds simultaneously.

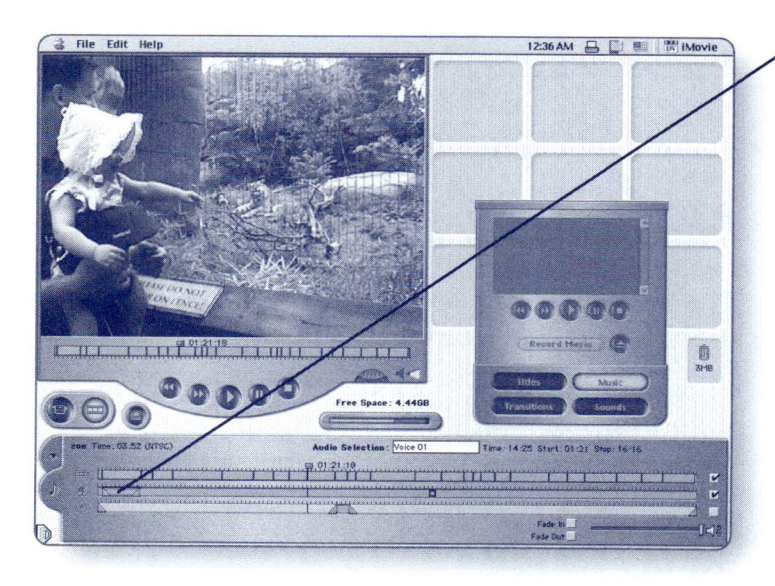

1. Press and hold the **mouse button** on an audio clip that you want to move and **drag** the **clip** to the desired position.

RENAMING AN AUDIO CLIP 139

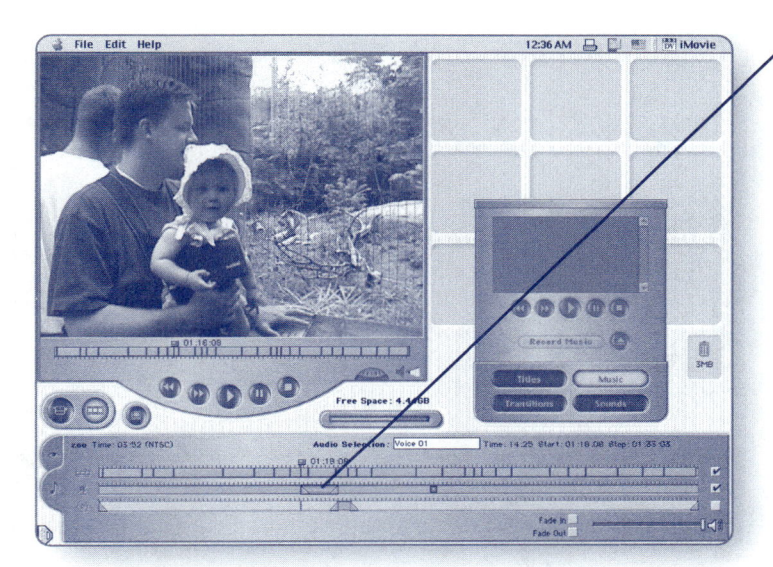

2. Release the **mouse button**. The audio clip will now be in its new position.

> **TIP**
> Remember, you can use the left and right arrow keys on the keyboard for more precise positioning.

Renaming an Audio Clip

Give your audio clips distinguishable names so you can easily remember what they are.

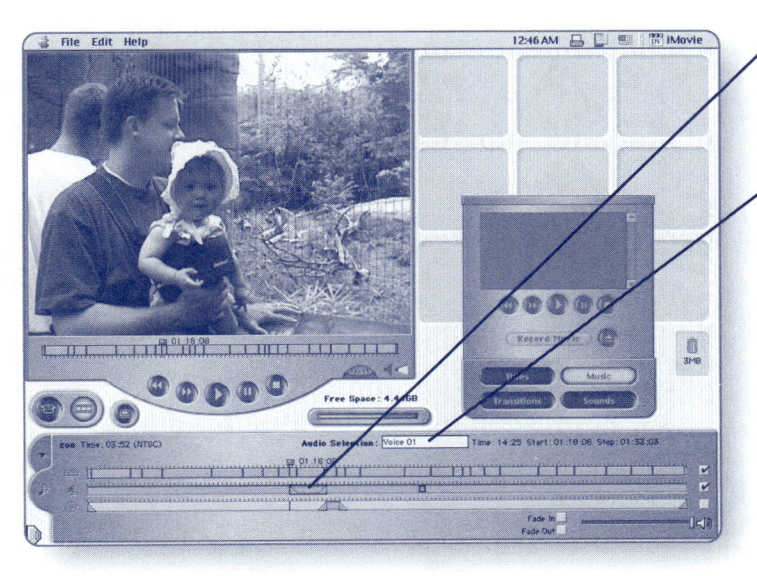

1. Click on an **audio clip** you want to rename. The audio clip will be selected.

2. Click and drag the **mouse pointer** on the current clip name in the Audio Selection text box. The name will be selected.

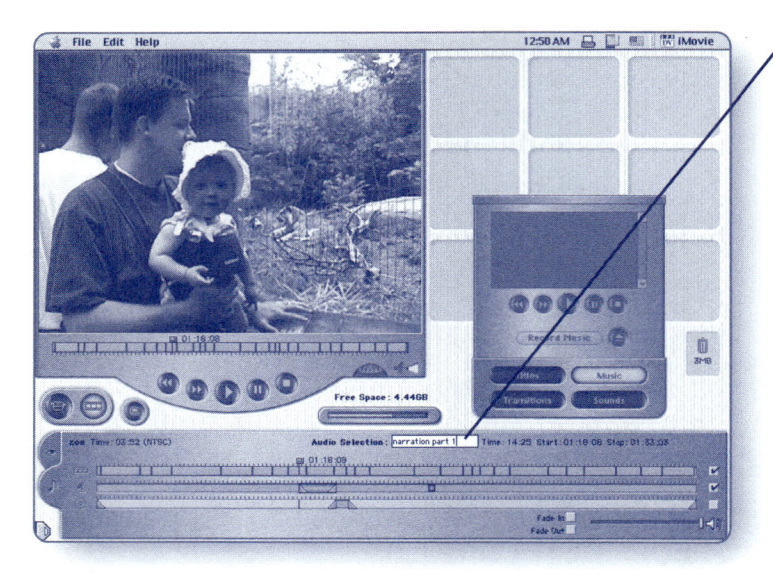

CHAPTER 8: SOUNDTRACKS, SCORES, SOUNDS, AND NARRATION

3. Type a **new name** for the clip. The new name will appear in the text box.

4. Press the **Enter key**. The clip will be renamed.

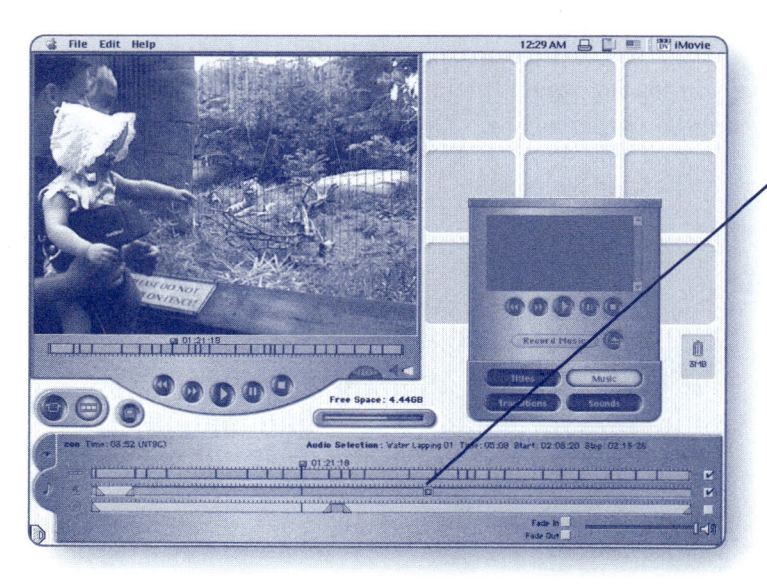

Deleting an Audio Track

1. Click on the **music track, sound effect, or narration clip** in the audio timeline. The audio track will be selected.

2. Press the **Delete key**. The audio track will be deleted.

Adjusting Audio Levels

Now that you know how to import your music, you need to make some adjustments. You can adjust the levels of sound in your video footage to a mere hum of background noise while your musical soundtrack plays, or you can reduce your musical soundtrack to a low harmony while the noise from your video footage dominates the scene. You can also mute the sound from your video footage altogether, and even fade your musical score in and out.

Adjusting the Volume of a Clip or Clips

You can adjust your computer's volume level for audio playback, and you can also adjust the volume of individual video camera sound clips, music clips, or narration sound clips.

TIP
Drag the slider all the way to the left to mute the sound of your selected audio clip (or clips).

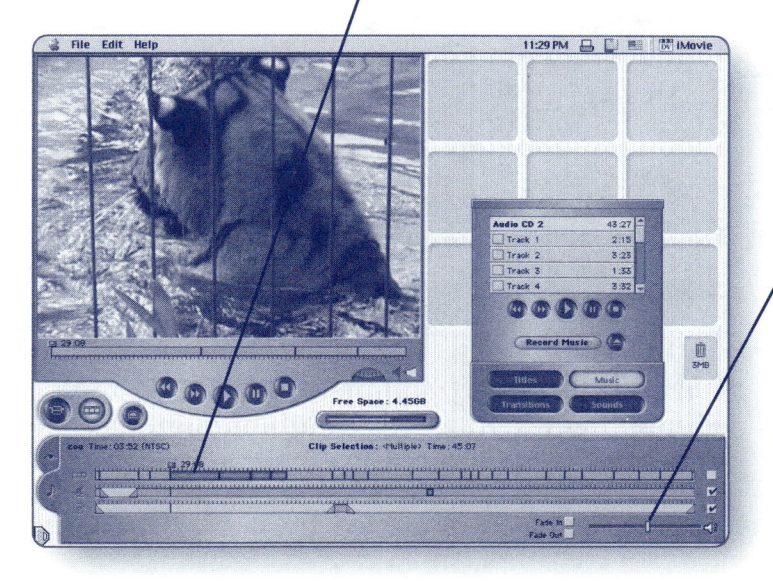

1. **Click** on an **audio clip or series of audio clips** in the Audio Viewer. The clip or clips will be selected. Audio clips in the video camera soundtrack will turn dark blue when selected. Audio clips in the narration and music tracks will turn dark yellow when selected.

NOTE
To select multiple clips, press and hold the Shift key as you click on clips.

2. **Press and hold** the **mouse button** on the volume slider and **drag** the **slider** left to decrease the volume or right to increase the volume. This will adjust the volume of the audio track or tracks you selected.

Adjusting the Volume within a Single Clip

Is there an annoying sound within a single clip that you want to reduce? To control the volume level within a single clip, you need to split the clip at the point where you want the sound level to vary, and then adjust the volume at that point.

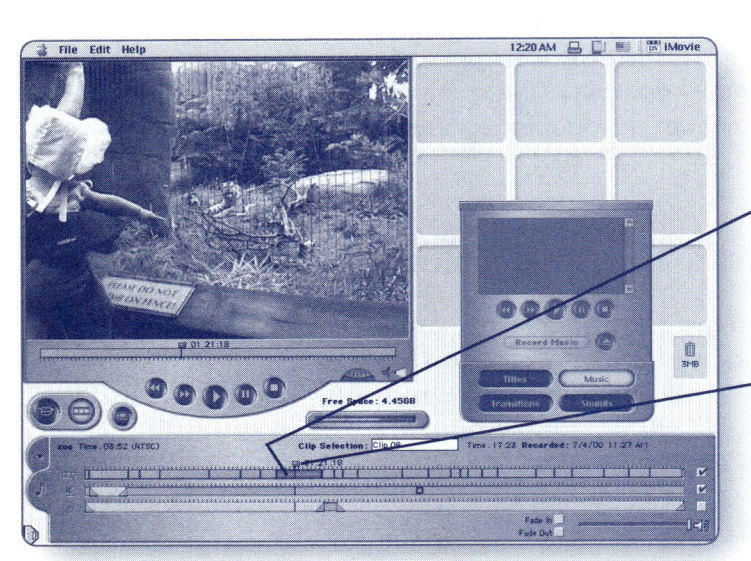

1. **Click** on the **audio clip** for which you want to adjust the volume. The audio clip will be selected.

2. Press and hold the **mouse button** on the playhead and **drag** the **playhead** to the point where you want to adjust the volume.

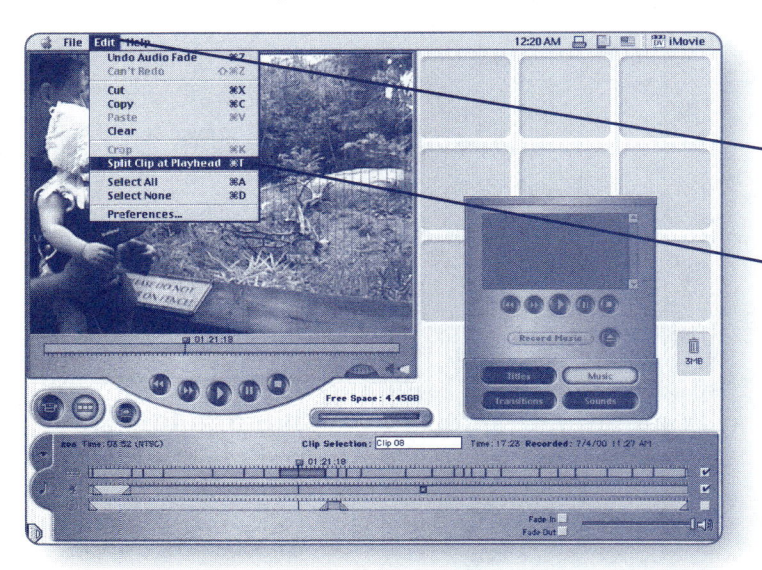

3. Release the **mouse button**. The playhead will be positioned.

4. Click on **Edit**. The Edit menu will appear.

5. Click on **Split Clip at Playhead**. The clip will be split into two new clips.

ADJUSTING AUDIO LEVELS 143

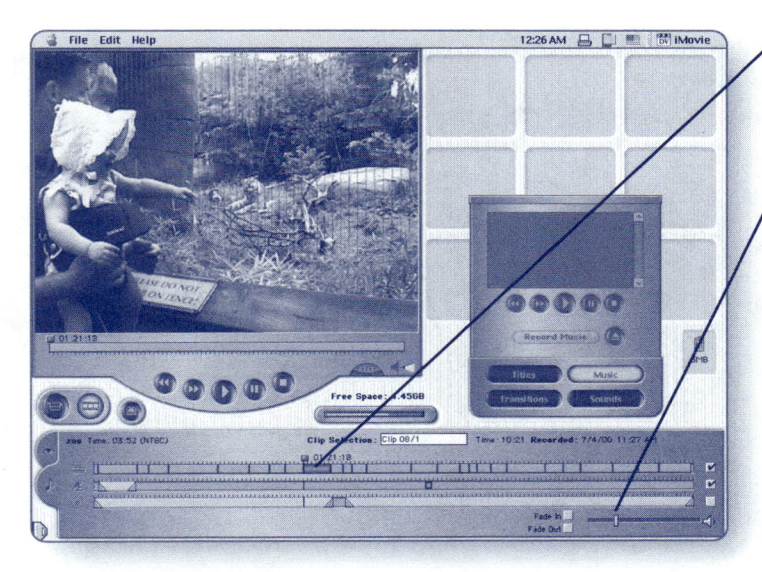

6. **Click** on the **second** of the two new clips. The clip will be selected.

7. **Press and hold** the **mouse button** on the volume slider and **drag** the **slider** left to reduce the sound level.

8. **Release** the **mouse button**. The sound level will be adjusted.

Muting Audio Tracks

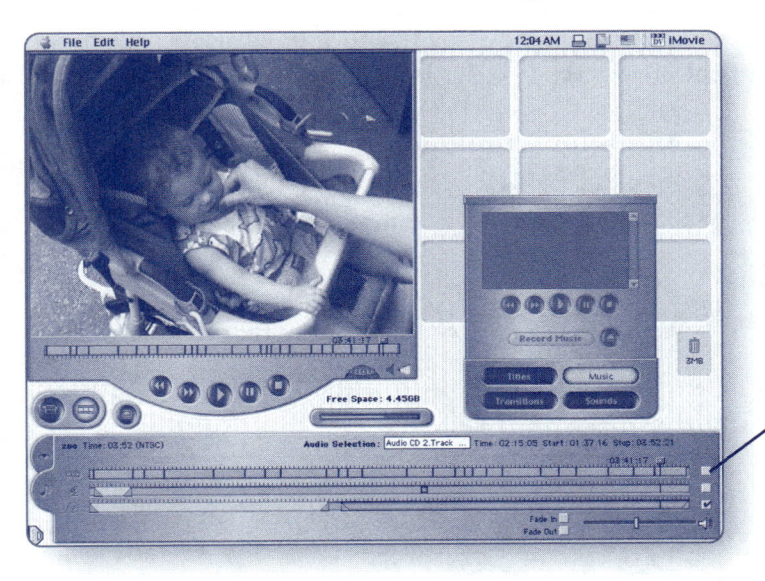

You can get rid of your video footage's background sounds altogether. You can also completely mute your recordings in the narration track and/or the music track.

1. **Click** on one or more of the following **options** to remove a checkmark:

- Removing the checkmark in the check box to the right of the video camera soundtrack will mute the video camera's sound.

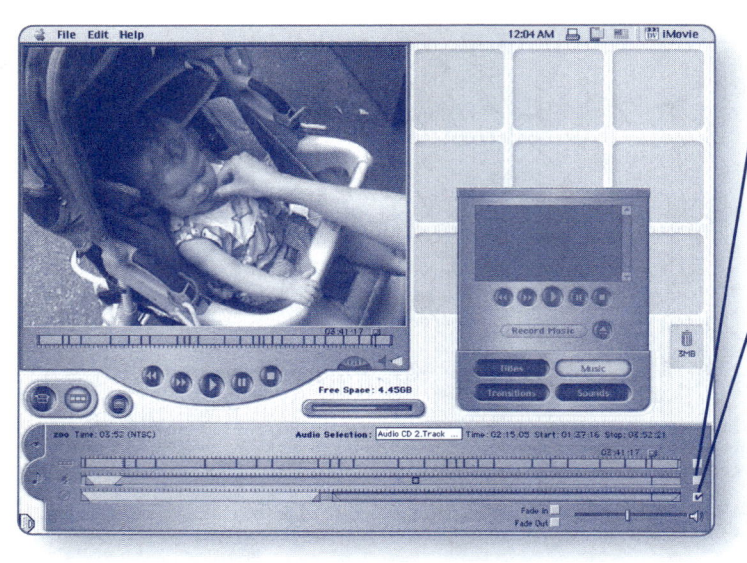

CHAPTER 8: SOUNDTRACKS, SCORES, SOUNDS, AND NARRATION

- Removing the checkmark in the check box to the right of the narration track will mute the narration and sound effects clips in the narration track.

- Removing the checkmark in the check box to the right of the music track will mute the music and sound effects clips in the music track.

Fading Your Recording In and Out

You can polish your movie by fading your music recordings in and out of your scenes. This is especially helpful when you are using only part of a song in a single clip or series of clips, or if your song is longer than your movie.

1. Click on an **audio clip** that you want to fade in and/or out. The clip will be selected.

2. Click on the **Fade In and Fade Out check boxes** to insert check marks. The sound in the clip you selected will fade in and out.

Expanding Your Sound Effect and Looping Music Library

You can add more sound effects and looping music files to your iMovie arsenal by inserting them into the Sound Effects folder, which can be found in the Resources folder within the iMovie folder on your hard drive. Apple's Web site has a nice collection of sound effects and looping music.

1. Go to **Apple's iMovie page**. The iMovie page will appear.

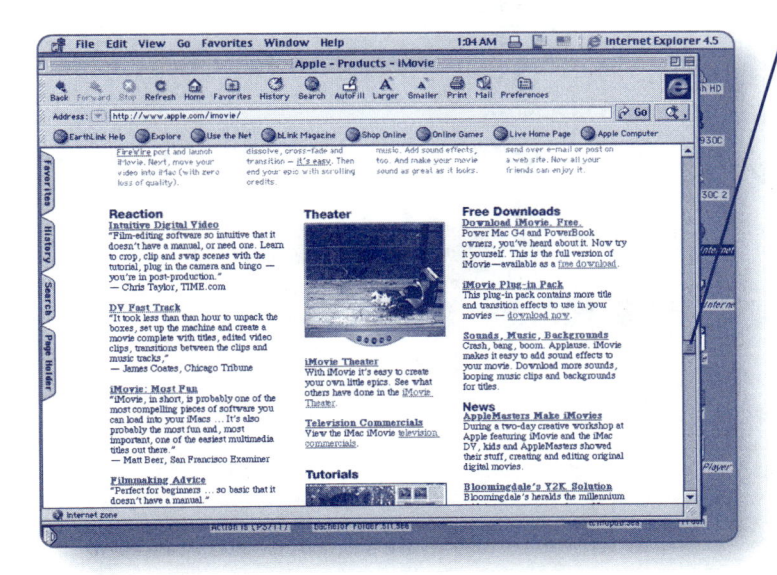

2. Scroll down to Sounds, Music, Backgrounds.

CHAPTER 8: SOUNDTRACKS, SCORES, SOUNDS, AND NARRATION

3. Click on **Sounds, Music, Backgrounds**. The library of backgrounds, sound effects, and looping music page will appear.

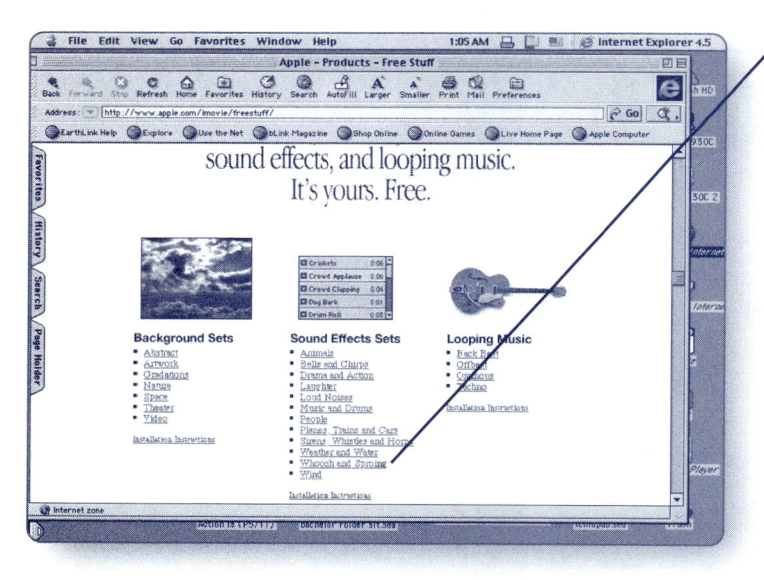

4. Click on a **Sound Effects Set or Looping Music sample**. The download page will appear.

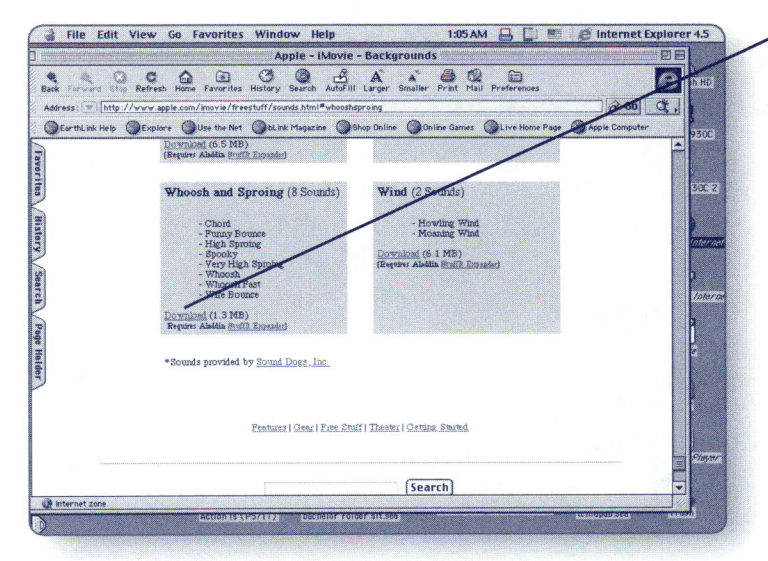

EXPANDING YOUR SOUND EFFECT AND LOOPING MUSIC LIBRARY 147

5. Click on **download** for the sample you want. The sample will download, and will appear on your desktop when finished.

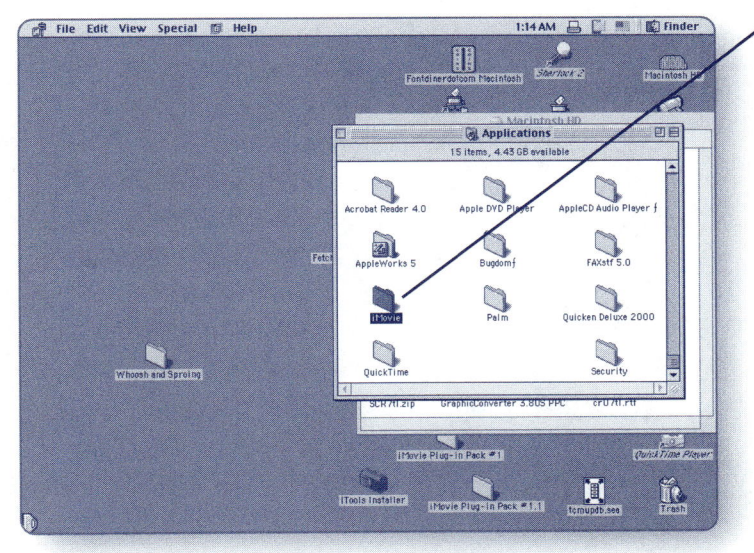

6. Double-click on the **iMovie folder** in the Applications dialog box. The iMovie folder will open.

CHAPTER 8: SOUNDTRACKS, SCORES, SOUNDS, AND NARRATION

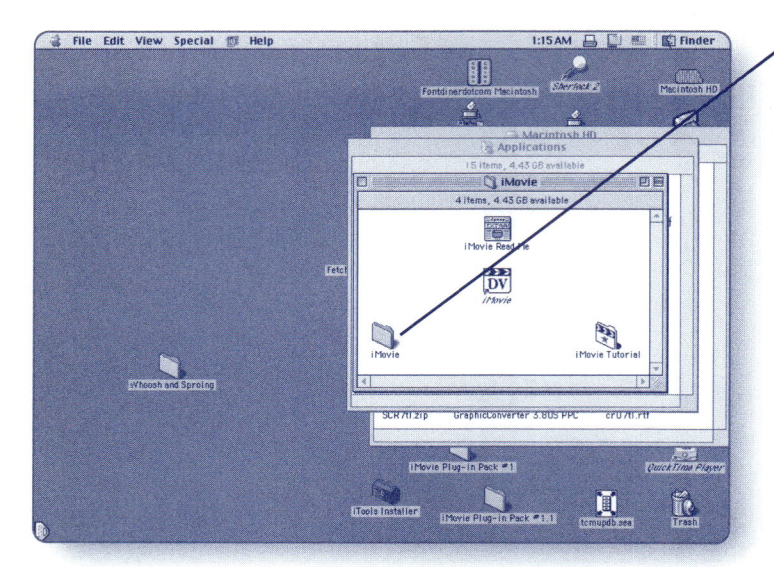

7. Double-click on the **second iMovie folder**. The second iMovie folder will open.

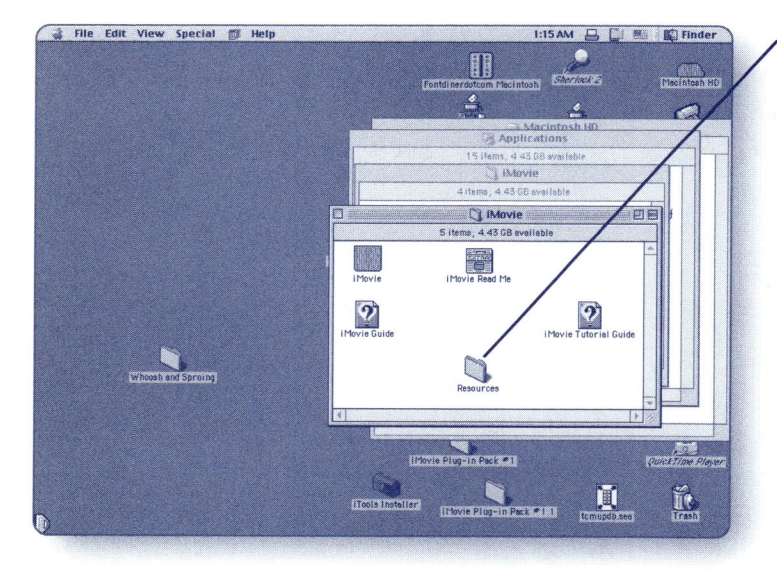

8. Double-click on the **Resources folder**. The Resources folder will open.

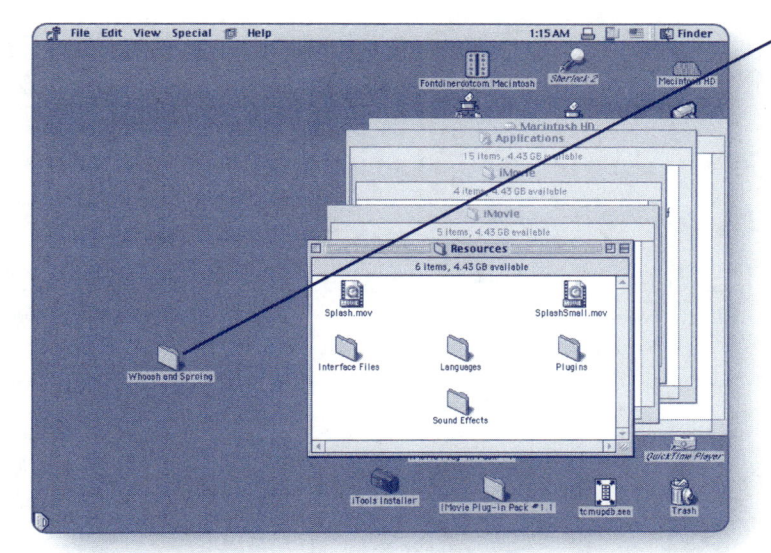

EXPANDING YOUR SOUND EFFECT AND LOOPING MUSIC LIBRARY   149

9. Double-click on the **sample folder** that you downloaded to your desktop. The folder will open.

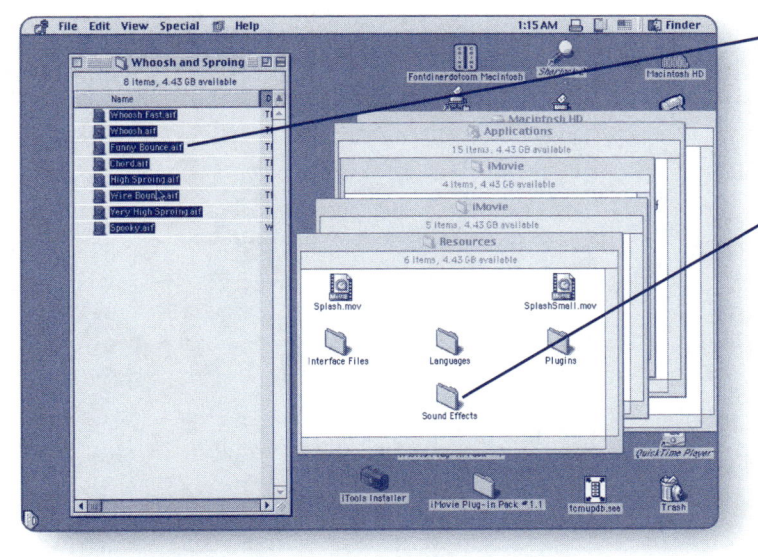

10. Hold down the **Shift key** and **click** on all of the **sounds** in the folder. The sounds will be selected.

11. Press and hold the **mouse button** down on the selected sounds and **drag** the **sounds** to the Sound Effects folder. The Sound Effects folder will be highlighted.

12. Release the **mouse button**. Your sounds will be added to iMovie.

9

iMovie and Still Images

Adding a still shot or series of still shots to your movie can add documentary-style impact. With iMovie, you also have the ability to create a slideshow or storyboard by using a series of still images, or to juxtapose stationary shots with your video clips to create an interesting montage of movement and still life. iMovie allows you to import PICT, GIF, JPEG, BMP, and Photoshop files into your movies. It also allows you to create still images from your video footage to add to your movies or your collection of photographs taken with your traditional camera. You can even e-mail your still images to friends and relatives. In this chapter, you'll learn how to:

- Extract a still image from your video
- Add a still image to your video
- Set the frame rate or vary the duration of stills
- Add transitions to slideshows
- Add titles to slideshows

Extracting Still Images from Your Videos

There are many ways to obtain still images to import into your movies. If you have existing photographs, you can scan them and save them in PICT, GIF, JPEG, BMP, or Photoshop format. Or, you might already have stills on your hard drive in these formats. With iMovie, you can even create your own stills by pulling them from scenes in your videos.

1. Click on the **video clip** from which you want to extract the still image. The clip will appear in the Monitor window.

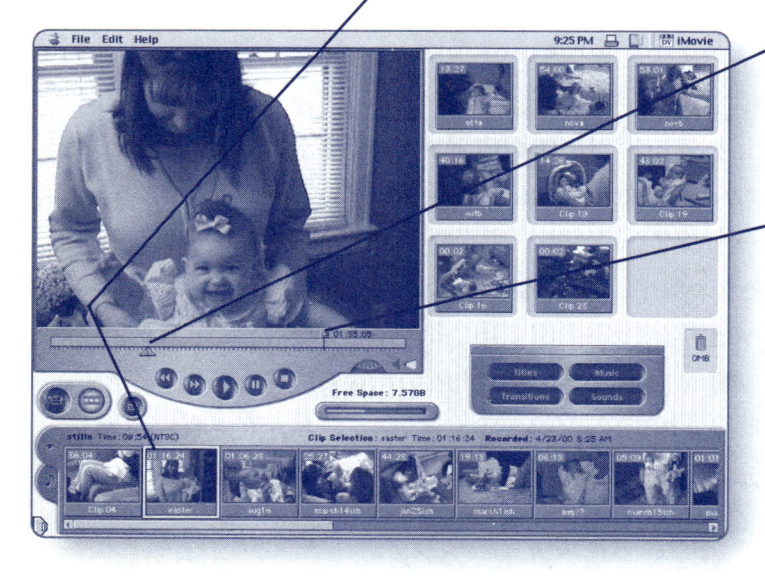

2. Click on the **Scrubber bar** below the Monitor window. The crop marks and playhead will appear.

3. Press and hold the **mouse button** down on the playhead and **drag** the **playhead** left or right to locate the frame that you want to extract. The playhead will move in the direction you drag it.

4. Release the **mouse button**. The frame to extract will appear in the Monitor window.

TIP
To move one frame at a time, use the right and left arrow keys on your keyboard. This will make it easier for you to find the exact frame that you want.

EXTRACTING STILL IMAGES FROM YOUR VIDEOS   153

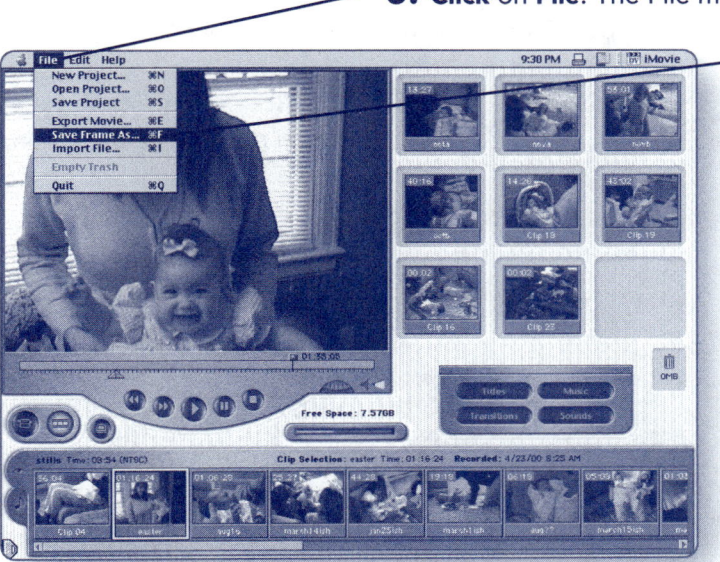

5. Click on **File**. The File menu will appear.

6. Click on **Save Frame As**. The Save Frame As Image dialog box will open.

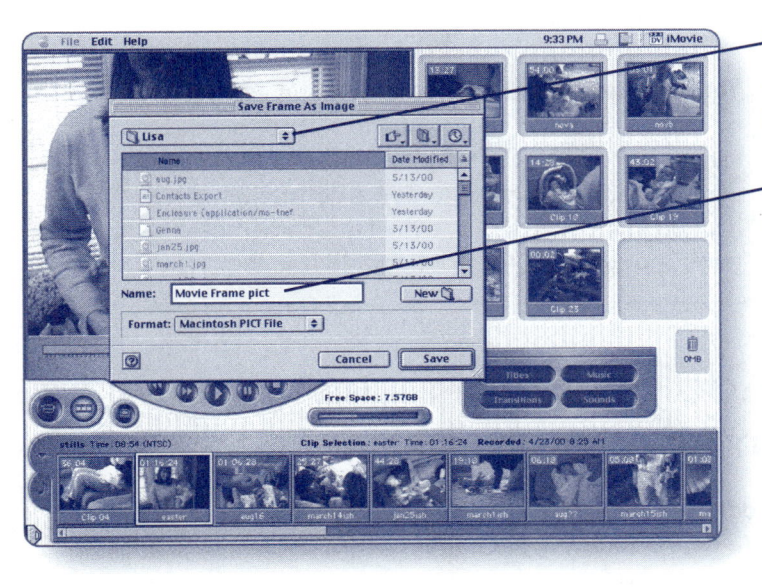

7. Click on a **folder** in which to save the image. The folder will be selected.

8. Type a **name** for the still image in the Name text box.

9. Click on the **up and down arrows** to the right of the Format list box. Two image formats will appear.

10a. Click on **Macintosh PICT File** if you plan to use the still in an iMovie. The format will be selected.

OR

10b. Click on **JPEG** if you plan to use this image to e-mail to friends. The format will be selected.

11. Click on **Save**. The image will be saved in the folder you designated.

NOTE
You may notice that your stills sometimes have a grainy or jagged effect to them. iMovie will not produce the same high quality digital stills as new digital still cameras do. But, they should be good enough to include in movies and as e-mail attachments—they just might not suitable for printing and framing.

Adding a Still Image to an iMovie

Adding stills to your movies adds another interesting effect. Whether you want to create an entire slideshow of stills or intersperse them here and there within your video clips to create stop-action effects, you need to know how to import stills into your iMovie project.

ADDING A STILL IMAGE TO AN iMOVIE 155

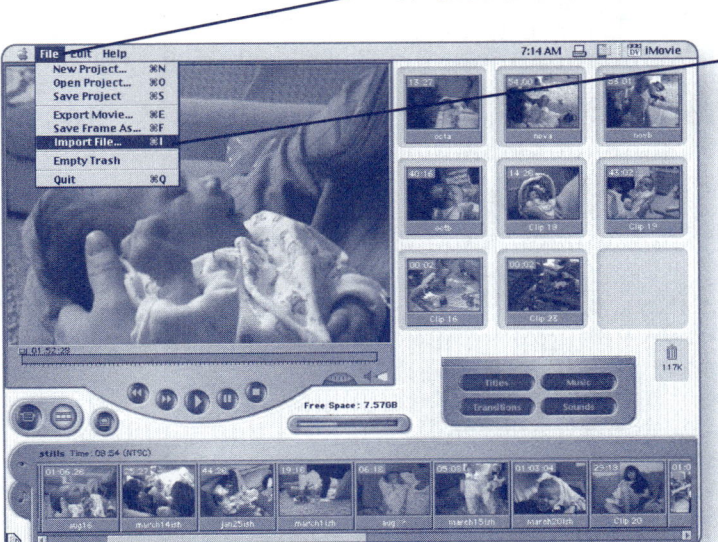

1. Click on **File**. The File menu will appear.

2. Click on **Import File**. The Import File dialog box will open.

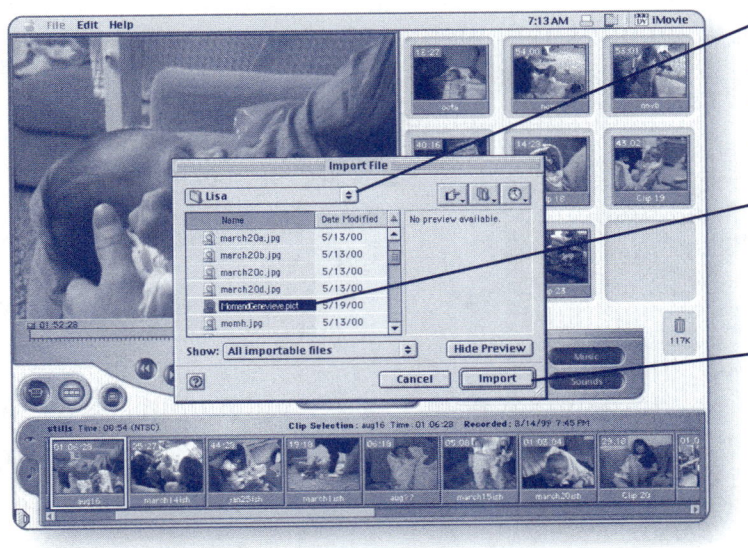

3. Click on the **folder** that contains the still image you want to import. The folder will open, revealing the images it contains.

4. Click on the **file name** of the still image you want to import. The image will be selected.

5. Click on **Import**.

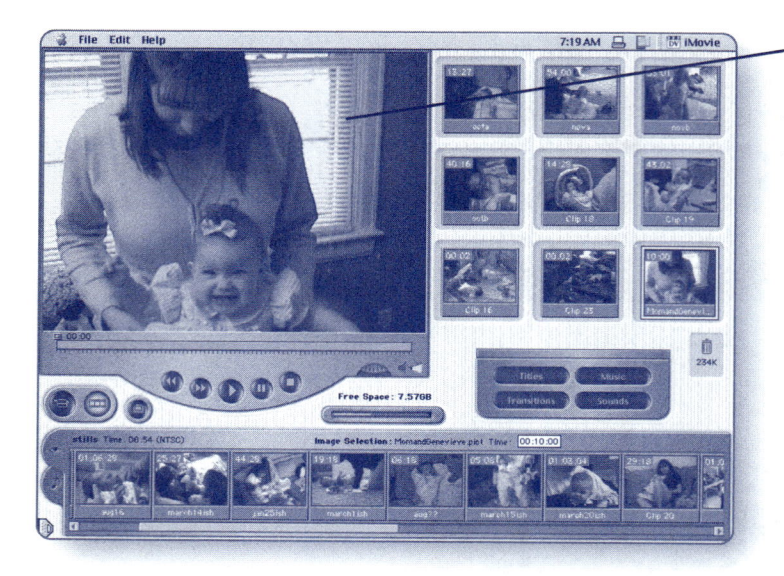

The image will be imported to your iMovie and will appear in the Shelf and in the Monitor window.

Creating a Slideshow

One of the coolest things you can do in iMovie is to create a slideshow by using a series of stills. To produce a new slideshow, open a new project.

1. Click on **File**. The File menu will appear.

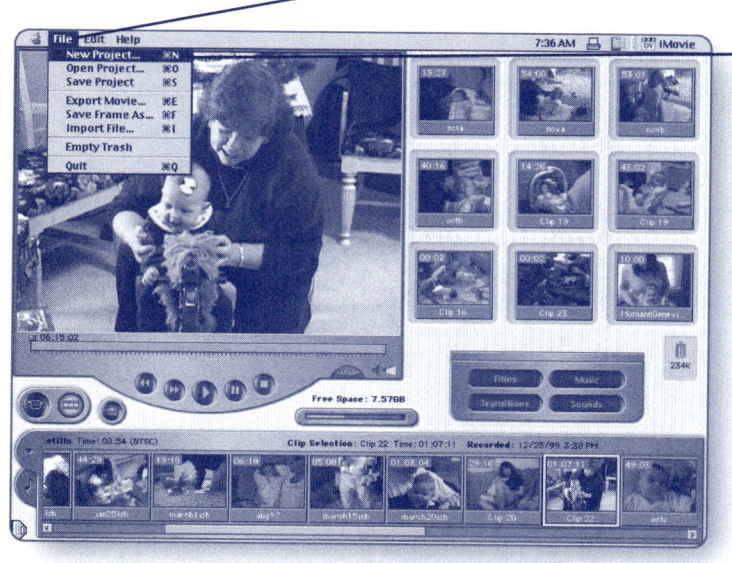

2. Click on **New Project**. The Create New Project dialog box will open.

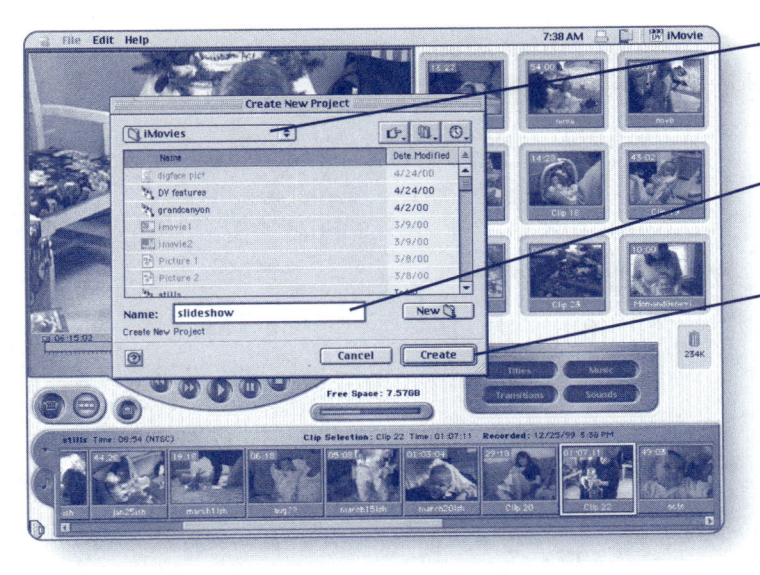

CREATING A SLIDESHOW 157

3. **Click** on a **folder** in which to store your movie. The folder will be selected.

4. **Type** a **name** for your presentation in the Name field.

5. **Click** on **Create**. A new, blank canvas will appear for you to start your slideshow.

Adding Stills to Your Shelf and Timeline

Now that you have your blank canvas, you need to put something on it. Gather up your slides. If you already have created them or scanned them in, you're ready to go. Otherwise, scan in your photos or extract a number of still images from your videos, as you learned earlier in the section, "Extracting Still Images from Your Videos."

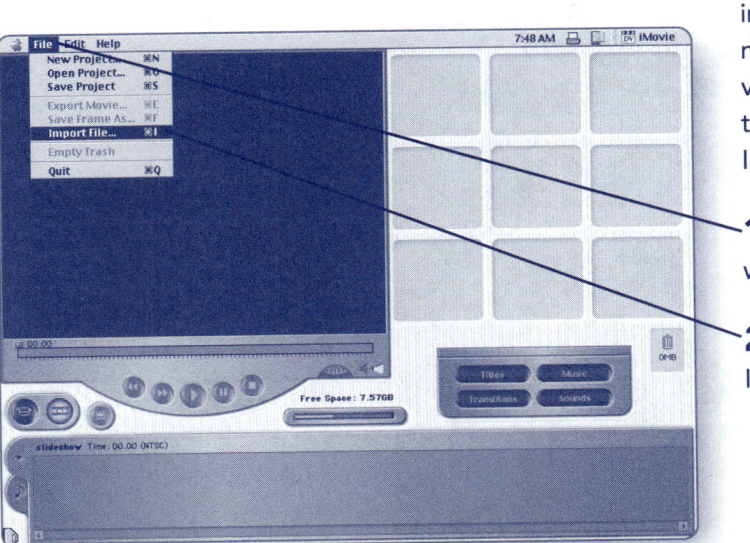

1. **Click** on **File**. The File menu will appear.

2. **Click** on **Import File**. The Import File dialog box will open.

3. Click on the **folder** where your still images are stored. The folder will open, revealing the images it contains.

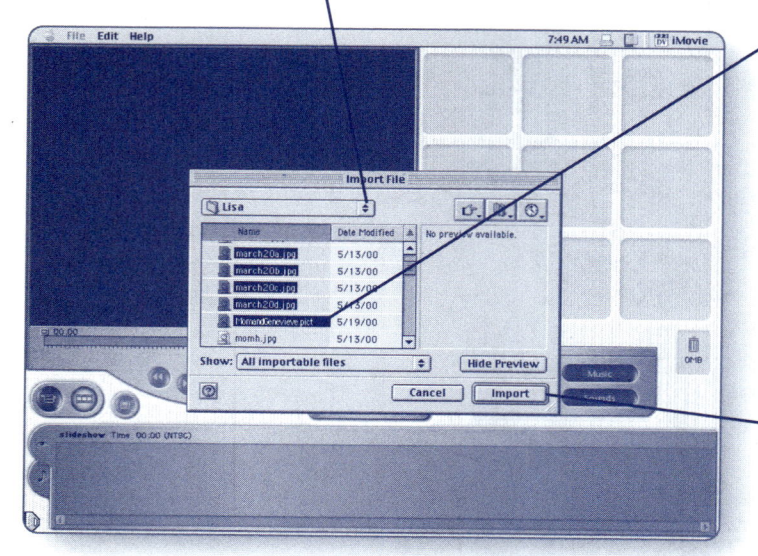

4. Click on a **file** to select it. The file name will be highlighted.

TIP
To select multiple files, hold down the Shift key as you click on image files.

5. Click on **Import**. The file or files will be imported to your project.

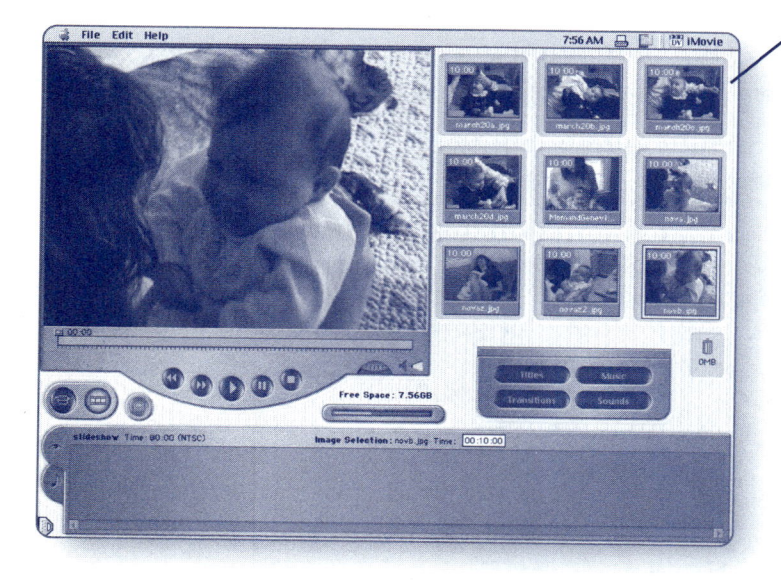

6. Repeat these **steps** until you have imported all the slides you want into your project.

CREATING A SLIDESHOW 159

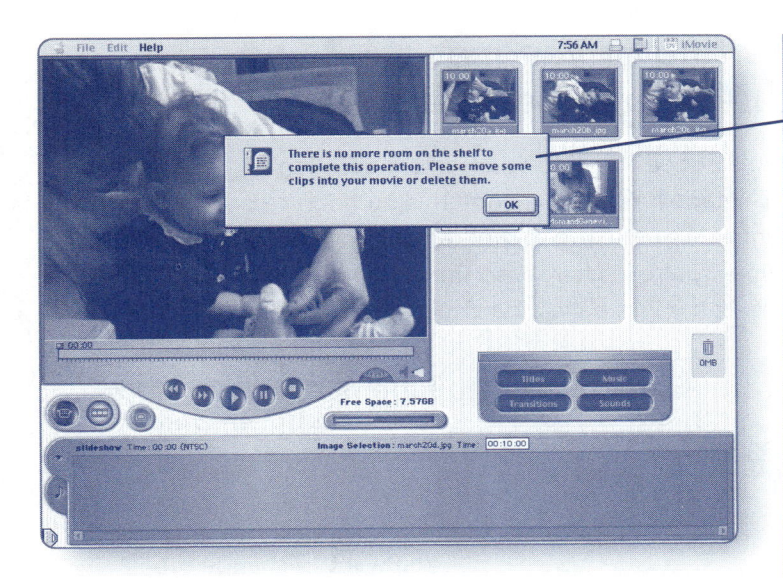

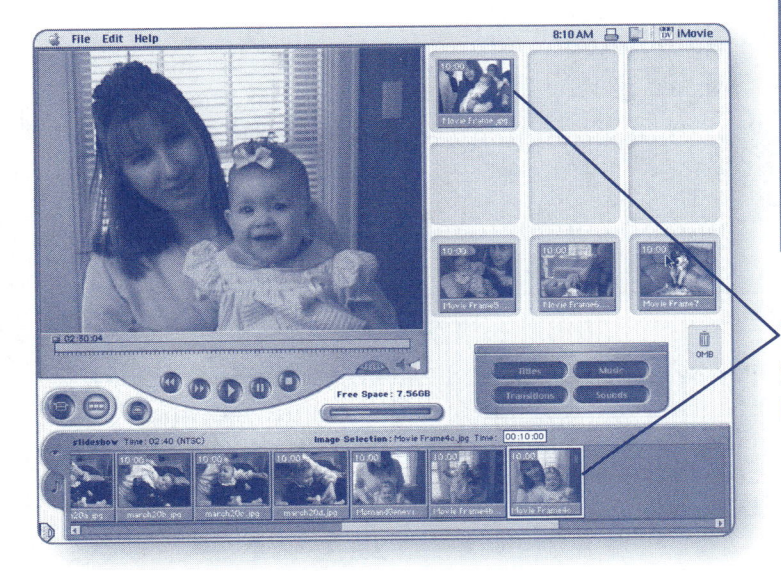

NOTE
Because the images you import go directly to the Shelf by default, if you try to import more still images than the Shelf will hold, you will get an error message. You can only import nine at a time (or 12, whichever your Shelf is set to hold) and then drag them from the Shelf to the Clip Viewer. Or, you can set your importing preference to import to the Viewer instead of to the Shelf. When you import to the Viewer, you can import an unlimited number of clips. You learned how to set this preference in Chapter 4, "Beginning the Importing and Editing Process."

7. Drag and arrange your **images** in the Viewer until you have them in the desired order.

Setting or Varying the Duration of the Stills

You'll notice that iMovie assigns a duration of 10 seconds to still images. You can change this duration to be shorter in some stills and longer in others, or you can keep them all the same. You're in charge, so there's no right or wrong way to do this. You might have a particularly striking image that you want on the screen for 10 seconds and another image that works better as a three-second clip.

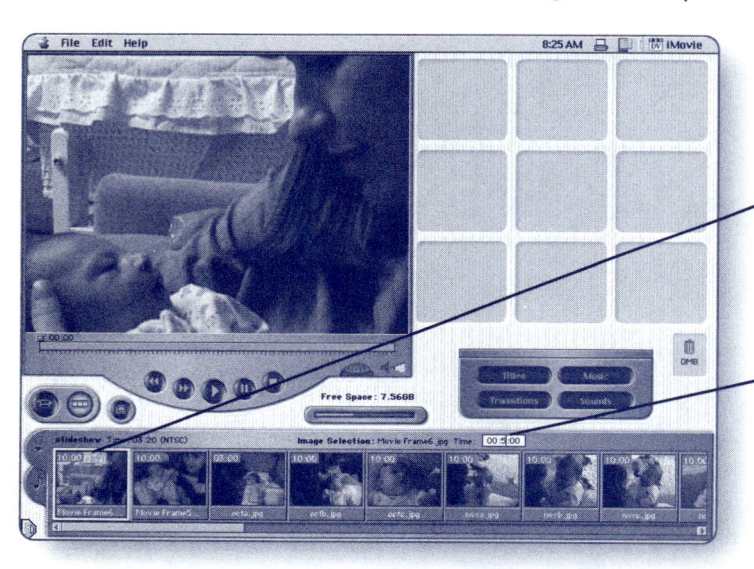

1. Click on the **clip** for which you want to change the duration. The clip will be selected.

2. Click in the **duration box** in the Clip Viewer. The cursor will appear in the duration box.

> **TIP**
> iMovie assigns a default duration of 10 seconds to a still that you have imported. That can be an eternity in an iMovie. It's best to keep the duration under 5 seconds—just enough time to study the picture, but not long enough to bore the audience.

3. Type a new **duration**.

4. Press the **Enter key**. The new duration will take effect.

5. Repeat these **steps** to set the duration for all of your slides.

Transition Hints for the Slideshow

You can use any transition in your slideshow, but I've found that the Push Right transition gives your project an authentic slideshow look. Refer to Chapter 6, "Adding Stylish Transitions," if you need a refresher on transition styles and how to use them.

1. Click on **Transitions** in the Effects palette. The Transitions palette will appear.

2. Click on a **transition type** in the palette. The transition type will be selected.

3. Drag the **duration slider** to your desired duration. The new duration will be set.

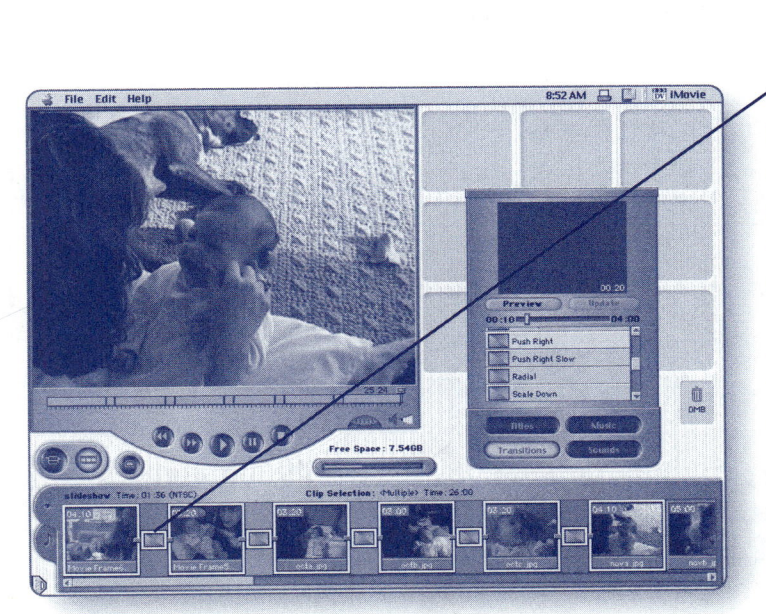

4. Click and hold the **mouse button** on the transition and **drag** the **transition** into place between your slides. The slides will move over a tad to make room for the transition.

5. Release the **mouse button**. The transition will appear and render between the slides.

6. Repeat steps 1 through 5 to add transitions to all your slides.

Title Hints for the Slideshow

Adding small titles to individual slides is something that can be very effective for your slideshow. For example, say you went on a family vacation, Clark W. Griswald-style, and wanted to document all the different places you went and monuments you saw. You could add titles to your slides of the Grand Canyon, the world's largest ball of twine, Wally World, and so on.

Refer to Chapter 7, "Text in iMovie: Rolling Titles, Credits, and Captions," if you need a refresher course on any elements of creating and adding titles.

1. Click on **Titles** in the Effects palette. The Titles palette will appear.

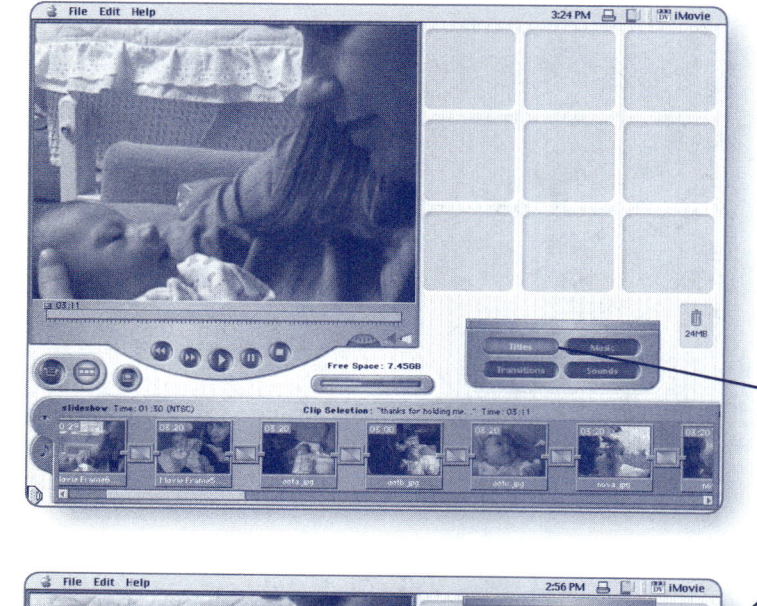

2. Click on a **title style** in the palette. The style will be selected.

3. Click on a **font style**. The font will be selected.

4. Click on a **font color**. The font color will be selected.

5. Type the **title** of your slide in the title text box.

CREATING A SLIDESHOW   163

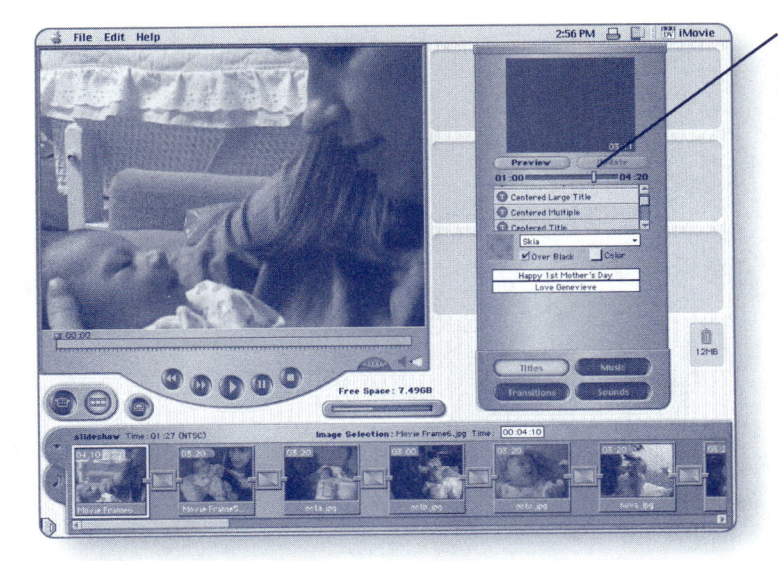

6. Drag the **duration slider** to your desired length. The duration will be set.

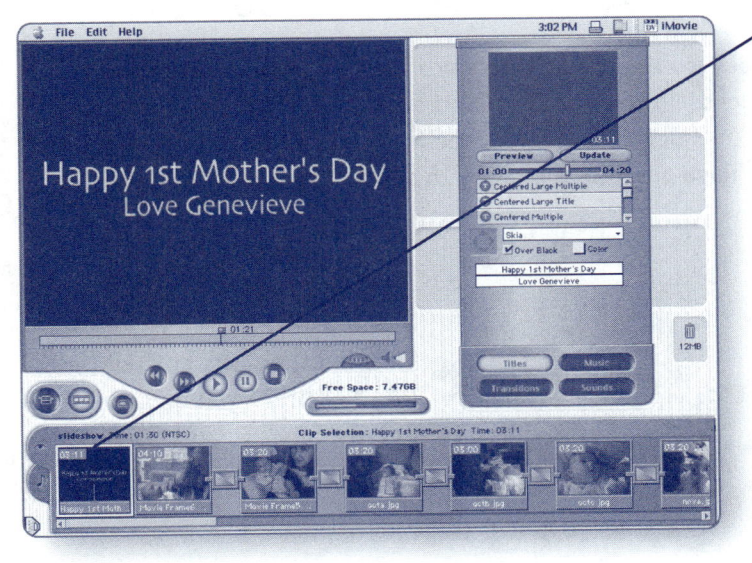

7. Drag your **finished title** to the beginning of your clips in the Viewer.

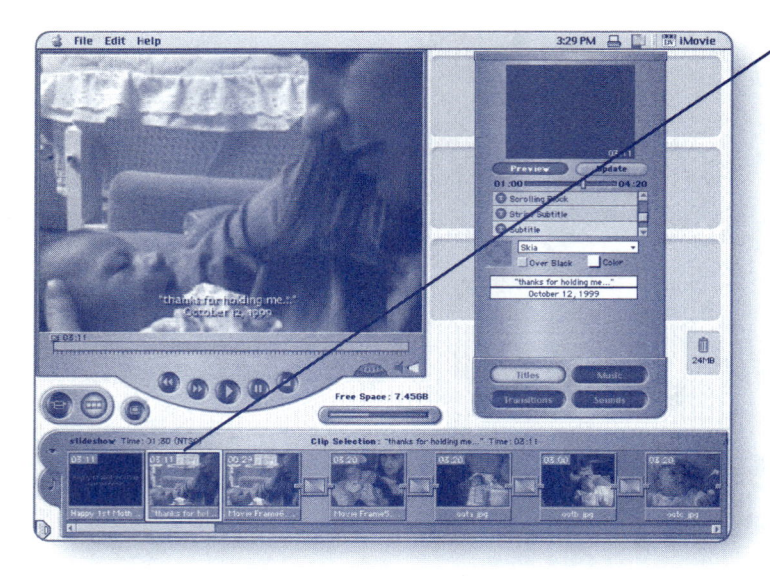

8. Add any other **small titles**, such as dates or quotes, to your slides. The Subtitle style works great for this type of effect.

Sound Advice for Your Slideshow

Because there won't be any sound with your stills, it's almost necessary to add some kind of soundtrack or narration to your slideshow. Think of the mood that you want your project to have and add a melody to set the tone of the slideshow.

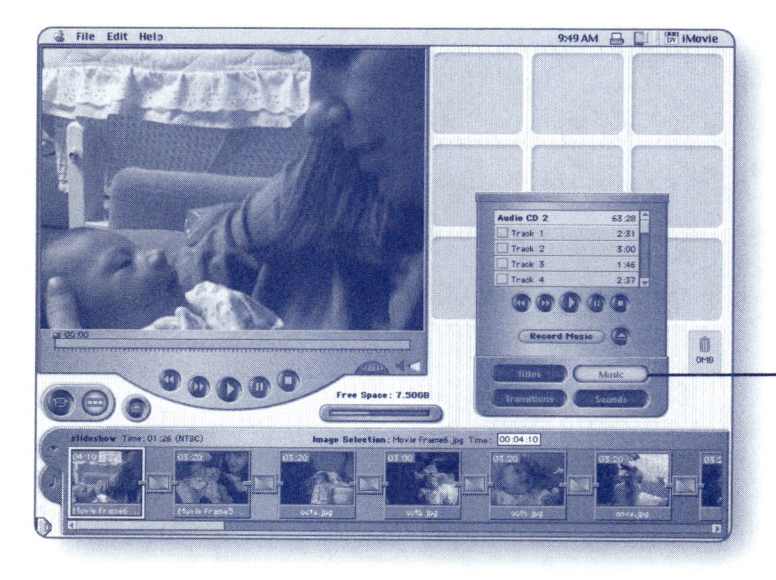

1. Insert the **CD** that has the song you want or **import** an **audio file** from your hard drive. Take another look at Chapter 8, "Audio: Adding Soundtracks, Scores, Sounds, and Narration," if you need to review how to do this.

2. Click on **Music** in the Effects palette. The Music palette will appear.

CREATING A SLIDESHOW   **165**

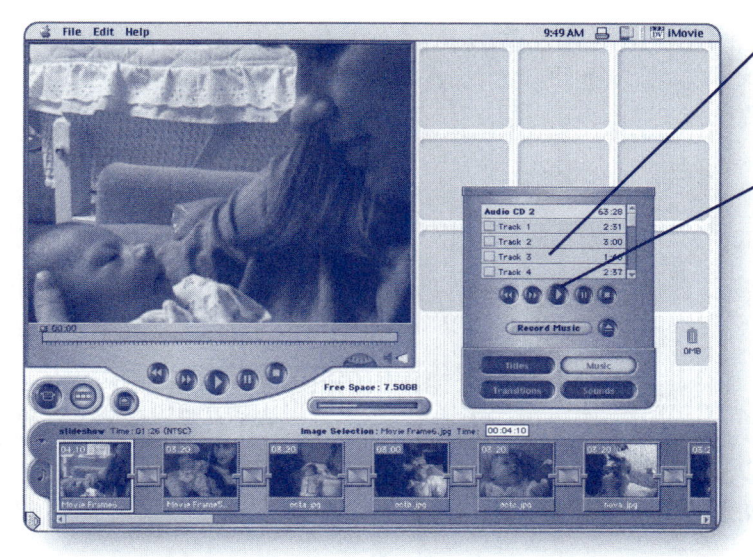

3. Click on the **track** you want to use. The track will be selected.

4. Click on the **Play button**. The audio track will play.

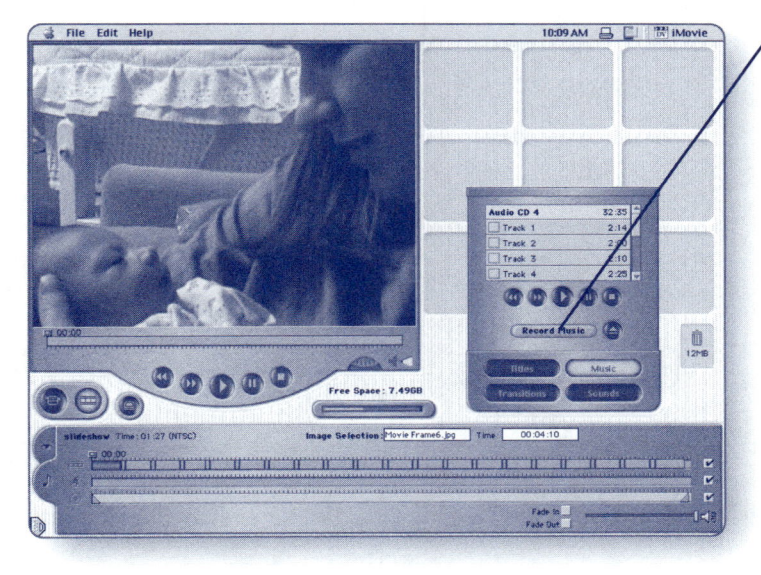

5. Click on **Record Music**. The music will start recording.

6. Click on **Stop Recording** when you want the recording to cease.

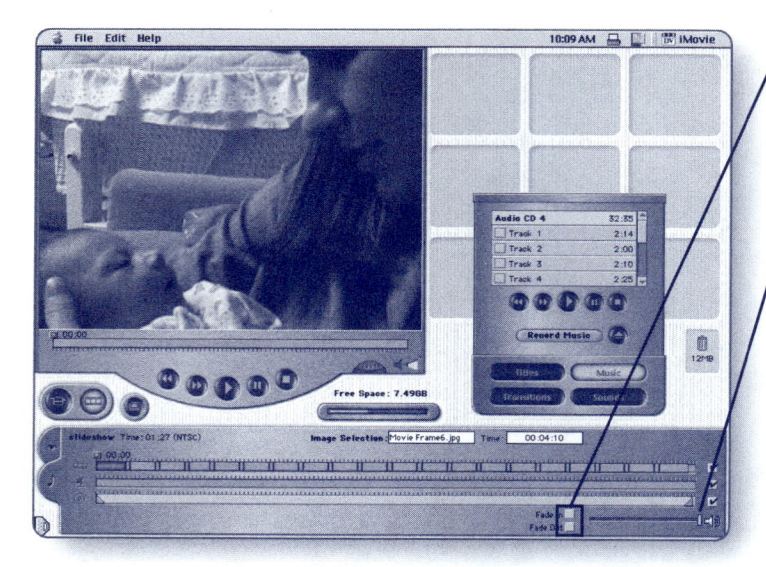

7. Click on the **Fade In and Fade Out check boxes** in the Audio Viewer to fade your music in and out at the beginning and end of your slideshow.

8. Drag the **sound slider** to adjust the volume on your recording.

> **NOTE**
>
> Review Chapter 8, "Audio: Adding Soundtracks, Scores, Sounds, and Narration," to refresh your memory on the many soundtrack techniques available in iMovie.

10

Compressing and Exporting Your Movies

Now that you've finished your masterpiece, you need to prepare it for presentation. After all, if your movie is not in a format that your audience can view, what good is it? Perhaps you want to put it on videotape, send it as an e-mail attachment, place it on a Web site, or burn it onto a CD. To utilize these formats, you need to know how to compress and export your movies. In this chapter, you'll learn how to:

- Save your iMovie
- Make a copy of your iMovie
- Export your movie to your camera
- Make a copy of your movie on VHS tape
- Export your movie to QuickTime

Saving Your iMovie

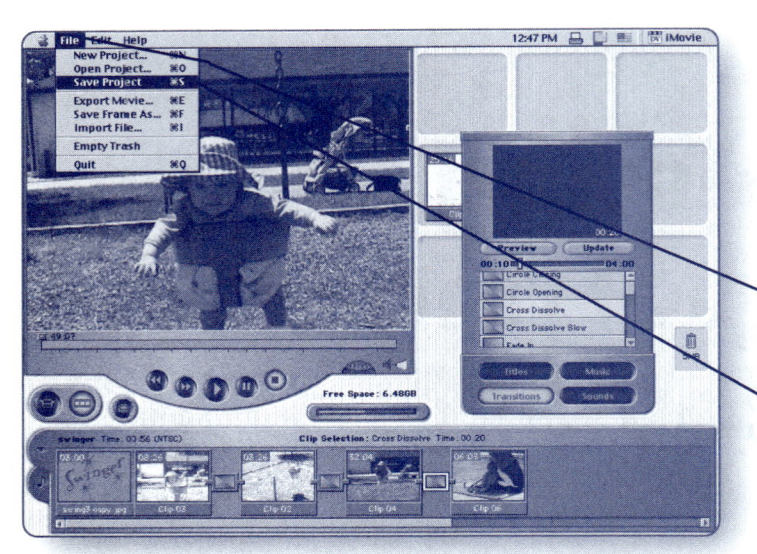

Before you export your movie, you need to save it. In case a problem occurs during the exporting process, you don't want to lose any of your hard work.

1. Click on **File**. The File menu will appear.

2. Click on **Save Project**. The movie will be saved.

> **NOTE**
> You already gave your project a name and saved it to a particular folder, so you won't be asked to name your movie or save it to a folder again. You are simply making the final save of all the edits and special effects you have recently applied to your project. See the following section, "Making a Copy of Your iMovie," to learn about saving another version of the same movie.

Making a Copy of Your iMovie

Because iMovie does not have a traditional Save As command, you need to take a different approach to save a copy of your movie project. If you want to make changes to a movie project while keeping a copy of the original version, make a copy of the project file on your hard drive and then make your edits to the duplicate version of the movie.

MAKING A COPY OF YOUR iMOVIE 169

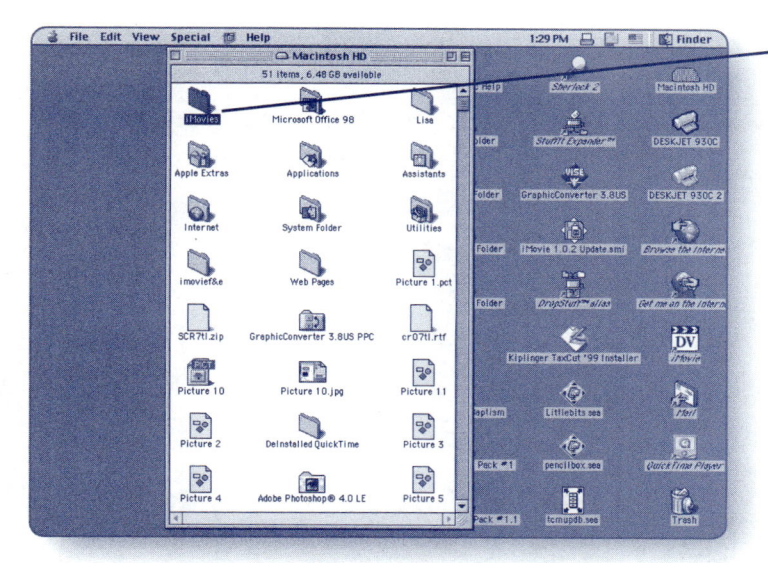

1. Double-click on the **folder** that contains the movie you want to copy. The folder will open.

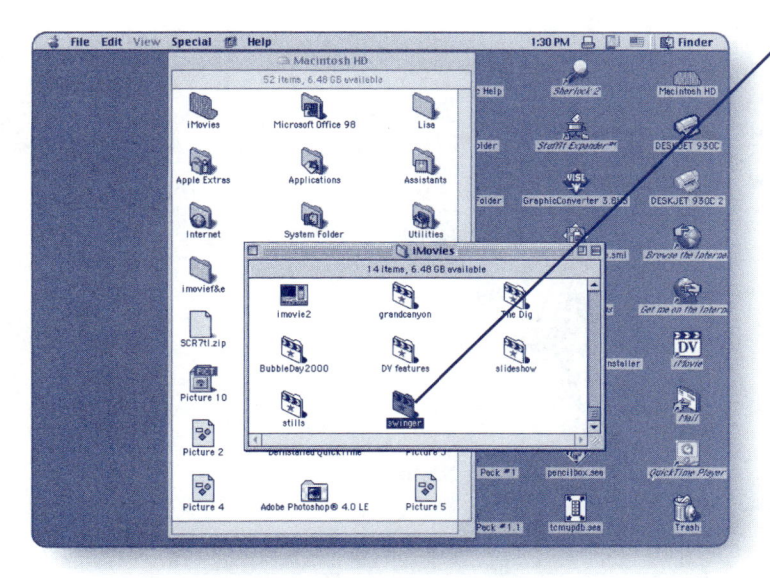

2. Click on the **movie** you want to copy. The movie will be selected.

170   **CHAPTER 10: COMPRESSING AND EXPORTING YOUR MOVIES**

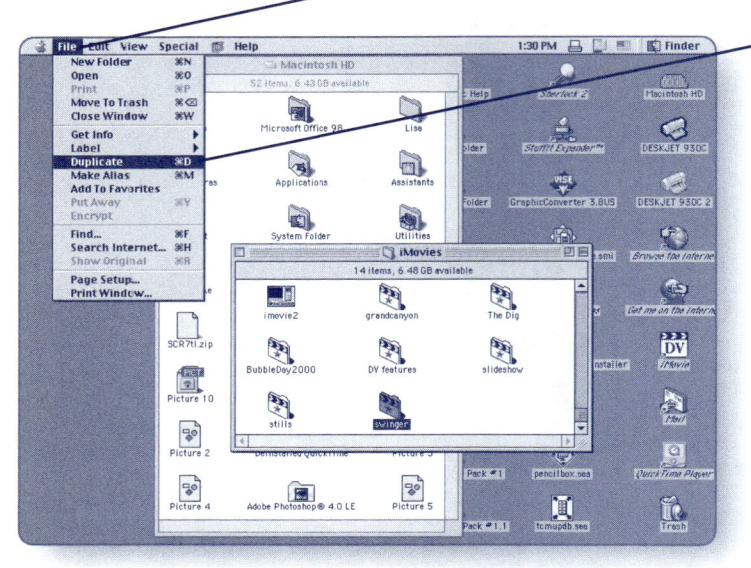

3. Click on **File**. The File menu will appear.

4. Click on **Duplicate**. Your movie files will begin to duplicate.

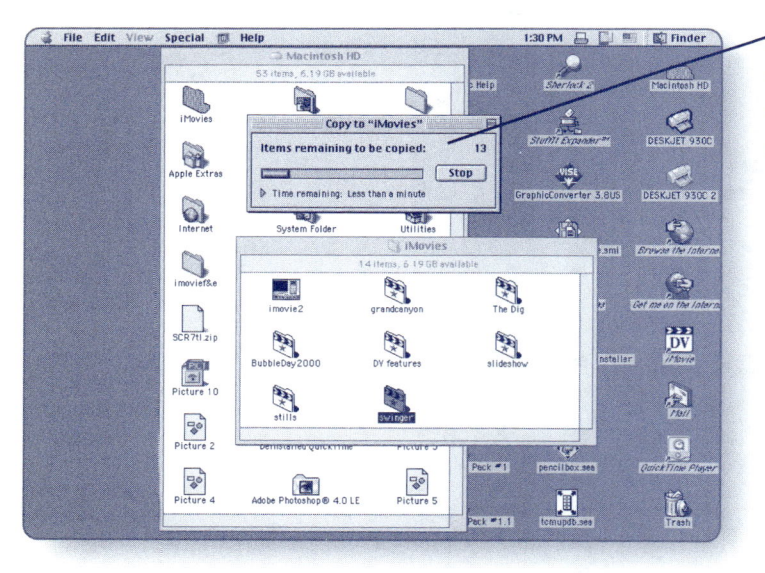

After the duplication process is complete, a copy of the movie will appear next to the original movie file.

MAKING A COPY OF YOUR iMOVIE **171**

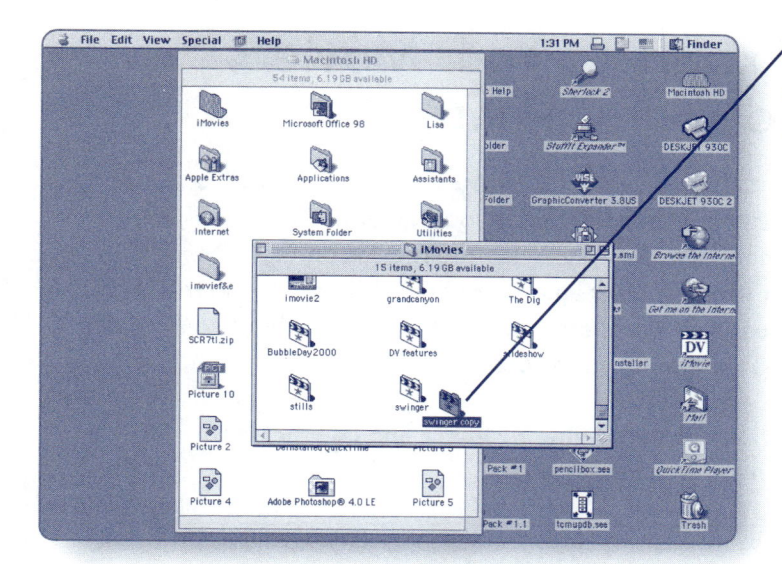

5. Click on the **name** of the copy. The name will be highlighted.

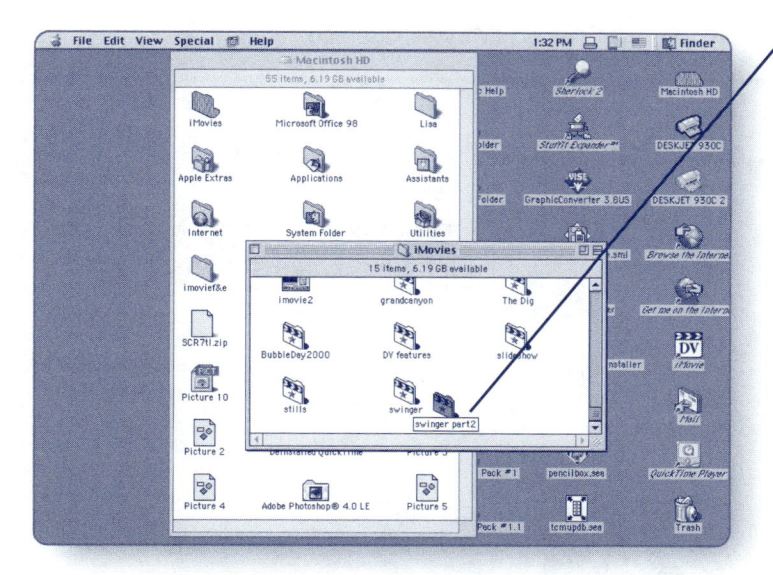

6. Type a **new name** for the copied version.

Exporting Your Movie to Your Camera

You are now ready to export your finished product. One method of exportation is your DV tape. This allows you to create a library of your edited movies on tape. iMovies take up a tremendous amount of hard drive space, so this is a great way to collect your masterpieces without soaking up your computer's precious space.

1. Turn on your **video camera** and **connect it** to your computer via the FireWire.

> **TIP**
> Make sure your DV tape is cued to where you want your finished movie to be. Using a tape dedicated only to your finished iMovies is a nice touch.

2. Click on **File**. The File menu will appear.

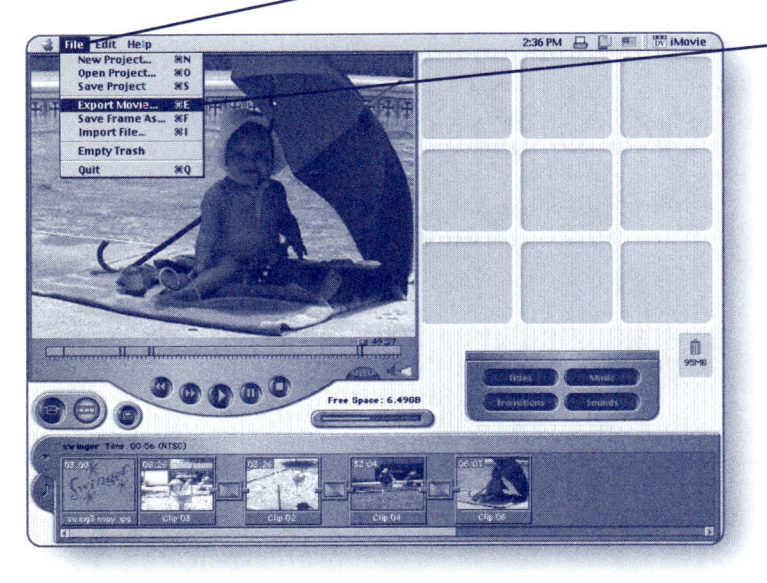

3. Click on **Export Movie**. The Export Movie dialog box will open.

EXPORTING YOUR MOVIE TO YOUR CAMERA   173

4. Click on the **up and down arrows** to the right of the Export to box. Two export options will appear.

5. Click on **Camera**, if it isn't already selected. The export option will be set to Camera.

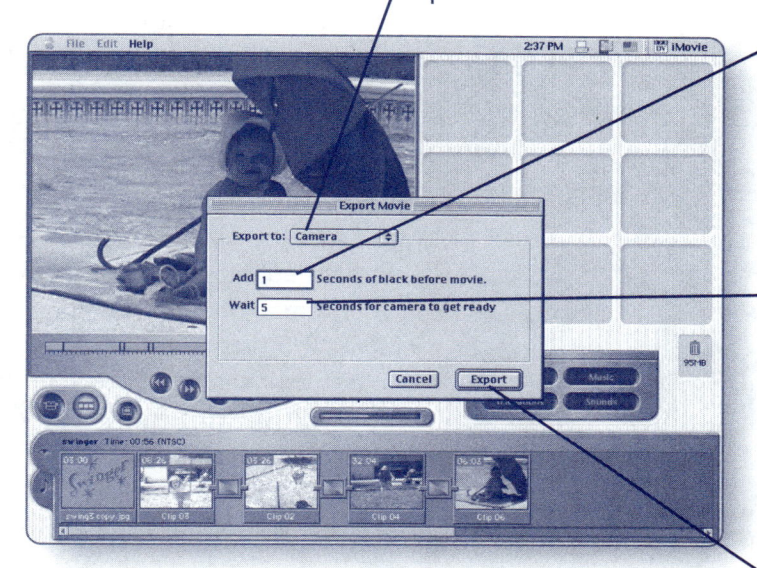

6. Type the **duration** of black space you want added to the beginning of your movie. This gives you a buffer, so that your movies don't begin abruptly when they are played.

7. Type in the **amount of time** in seconds you want to allow your camera to get ready for the export. This gives your camera the time it needs to be ready before iMovie starts exporting your movie.

8. Click on the **Export button**. Your movie will play in the Monitor window as it exports to your camera.

NOTE

The footage might appear grainy as it plays in the Monitor window during exportation. It will not appear this way on your DV tape.

9. Rewind the **tape** in your video camera and play back your masterpiece.

174   **CHAPTER 10: COMPRESSING AND EXPORTING YOUR MOVIES**

Making a Copy on VHS Tape

Your friends and relatives might not have entered the digital video age yet. For these folks, you need to copy this footage onto a traditional VHS tape. Unfortunately, you cannot export your iMovie from your Mac straight to a VHS tape. But you can export your iMovie to DV tape and then copy the DV tape to VHS tape.

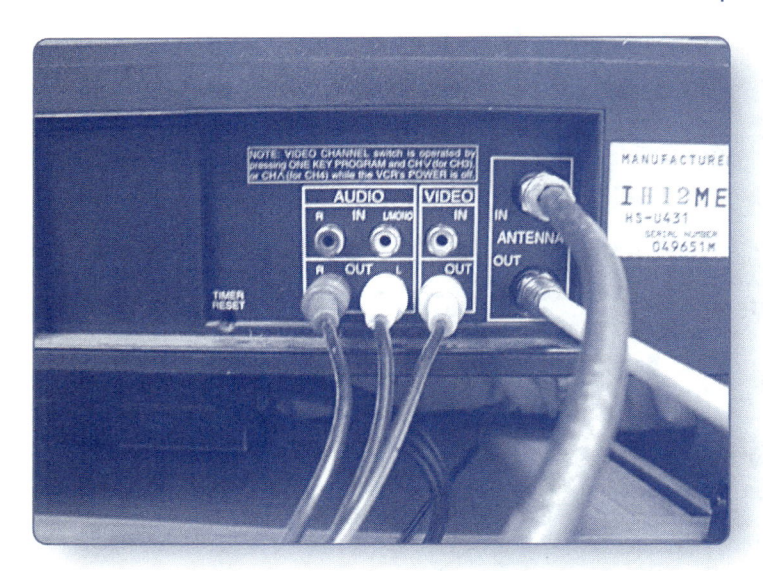

Make sure the DV tape with your finished iMovie is cued up in your camcorder and you have a blank VHS tape in your VCR. Connect your camcorder to your VCR with A/V connecting cables. These cables usually come with your camcorder. Make sure you connect the A/V cable to the Line In input on your VCR. Check with your camcorder manual if you have trouble connecting your camcorder to your VCR.

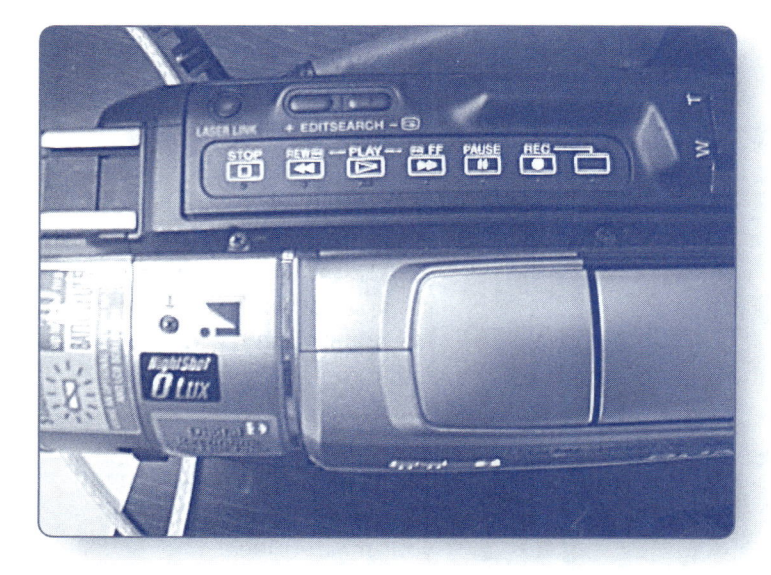

Set the VCR/TV selector to VCR. Press the Play button on your camcorder and at the same time, press the record button on your VCR. Press the Stop button when you are finished recording.

Exporting Your Movie to QuickTime

The QuickTime setting allows you to export your video into QuickTime's player, which compresses the iMovie file to ready it for e-mail, Web, or CD-ROM formats.

1. Click on **File**. The File menu will appear.

2. Click on **Export Movie**. The Export Movie dialog box will open.

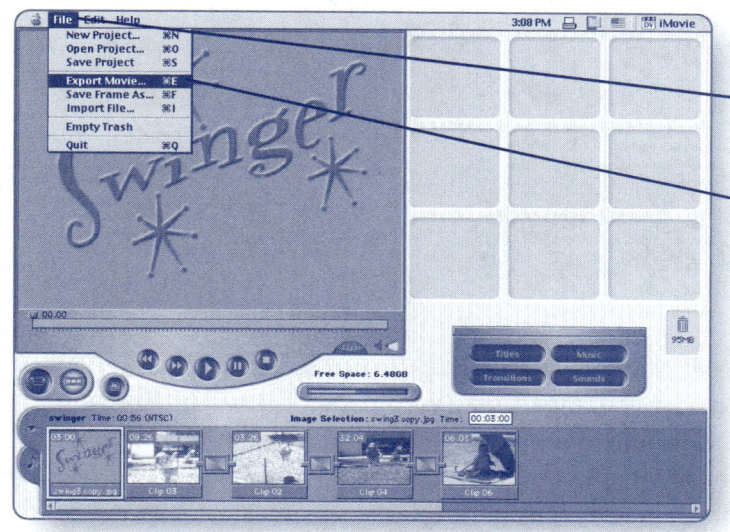

3. Click on the **up and down arrows** to the right of the Export to box. A pop-up list will appear.

4. Click on **QuickTime**. The QuickTime settings will appear in the lower half of the dialog box.

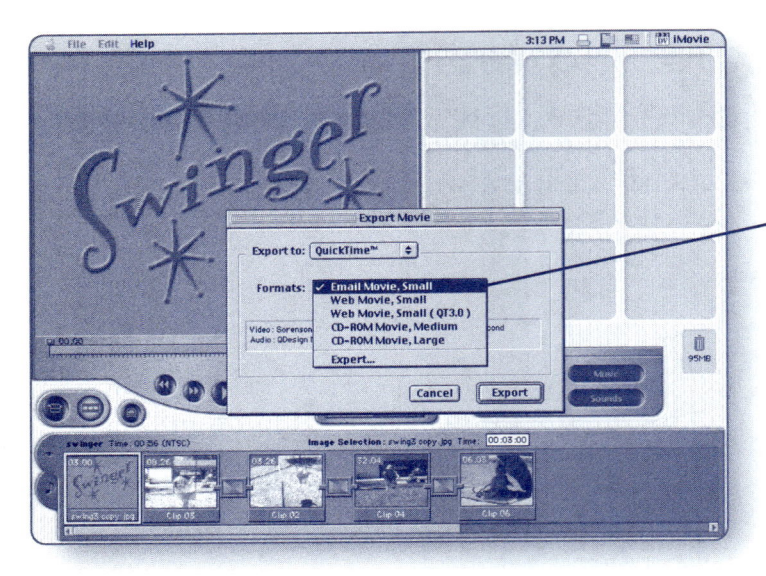

5. Click on the **up and down arrows** to the right of the Formats box. A pop-up list will appear.

6. Click on a **QuickTime movie format**. Your choices are the following:

- **Email Movie, Small**. This is the option you select if you plan to send your movie as an e-mail attachment. Your iMovie is compressed into a relatively compact QuickTime movie.

- **Web Movie, Small**. This is the option you select if you plan to post your movie on a Web page. The size of the QuickTime movie is bigger and the frame rate is higher than in the Email Movie, Small option, therefore it is a better quality movie for the viewer. You still may want to use the Email Movie, Small option for posting on the Web because a movie this big may be difficult for many people to download unless they have a high-speed Internet connection.

- **Web Movie, Small (QT3.0).** This is the same option as Web Movie, Small, except that anyone still using QuickTime version 3.0 will be able to play your movie.

- **CD-ROM Movie, Medium.** This is the option you select if you plan to record your movie onto a CD-ROM, or if you plan to create a QuickTime movie to store and play on your hard drive.

- **CD-ROM Movie, Large.** You will probably never use this option—it creates a massive file. So, unless you're a pro, skip this option.

EXPORTING YOUR MOVIE TO QUICKTIME 177

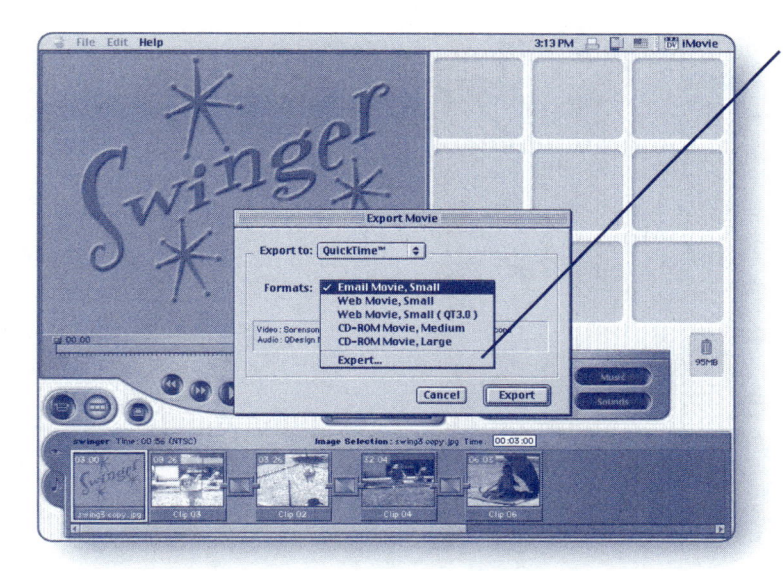

- **Expert.** The Expert settings are reserved for when you become a seasoned video-compression guru. The iMovie creators have designed this software with all the compression settings the casual user should ever need, and therefore you should not have to change them. Using the Expert settings goes beyond the scope of this book.

> **NOTE**
>
> Notice that when you select a format, the video and audio compression specifications appear at the bottom of the Export Movie dialog box. This will give you an idea just how much your video needs to be compressed for these particular formats. For example, the video for a small QuickTime movie that you would attach to an e-mail compresses from 30 to 10 frames per second. You definitely will lose a bit of playback quality in the QuickTime viewer, but it is necessary to compress your movie to send it over the Internet or post it on a Web page.

> **NOTE**
>
> There are a few things to consider when you send a QuickTime movie in an e-mail message. Even though iMovie compresses the file down in size, it is still a big file to send over the Internet as an e-mail attachment. For example, a 60-second movie will compress to approximately a 3-MB file, which is still fairly large. With that in mind, you need to make sure that the recipient of this file knows that you are sending it and can clear several minutes for the download.

CHAPTER 10: COMPRESSING AND EXPORTING YOUR MOVIES

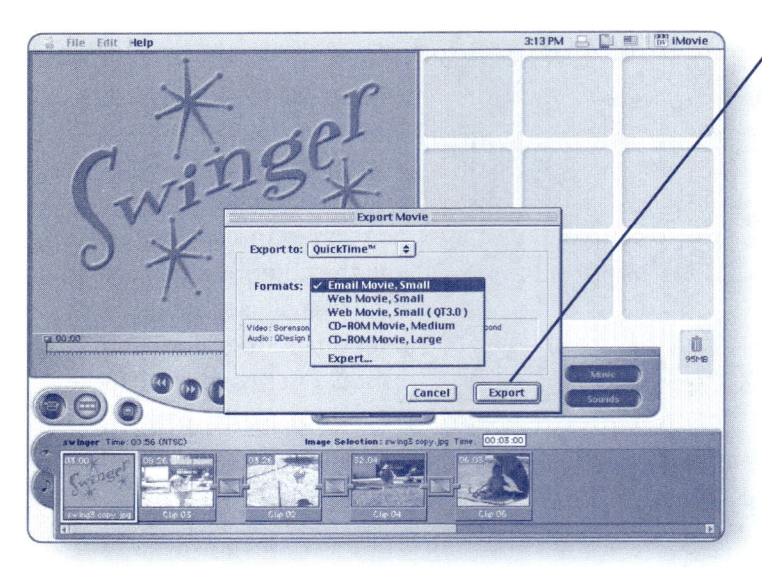

7. Click on the **Export button**. The Export QuickTime Movie dialog box will open.

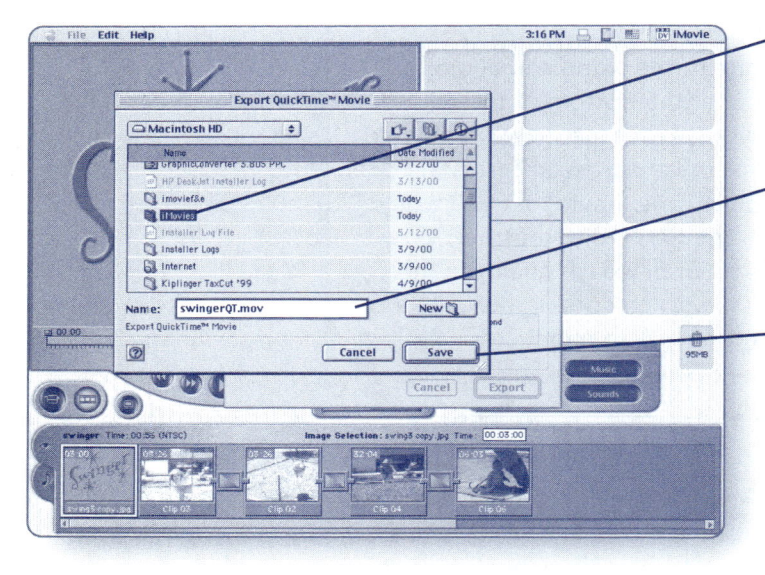

8. Click on the **folder** in which you want to save your movie. The folder will be selected.

9. Type a **title** for your QuickTime movie in the Name text box.

10. Click on **Save**. iMovie will begin to export your movie into a QuickTime file.

EXPORTING YOUR MOVIE TO QUICKTIME 179

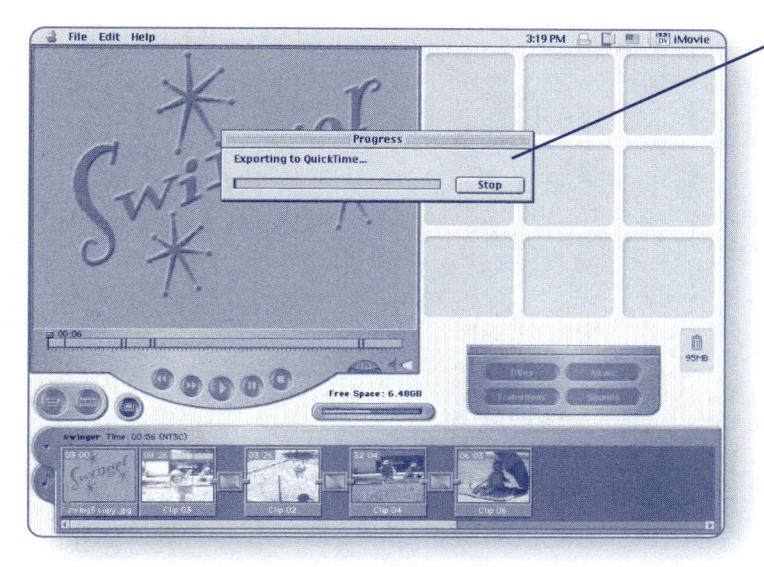

The Progress Bar will show your movie exporting to QuickTime. Depending on the size of your movie, this could take several minutes. So, leave the computer, grab a cannoli, and relax for a bit.

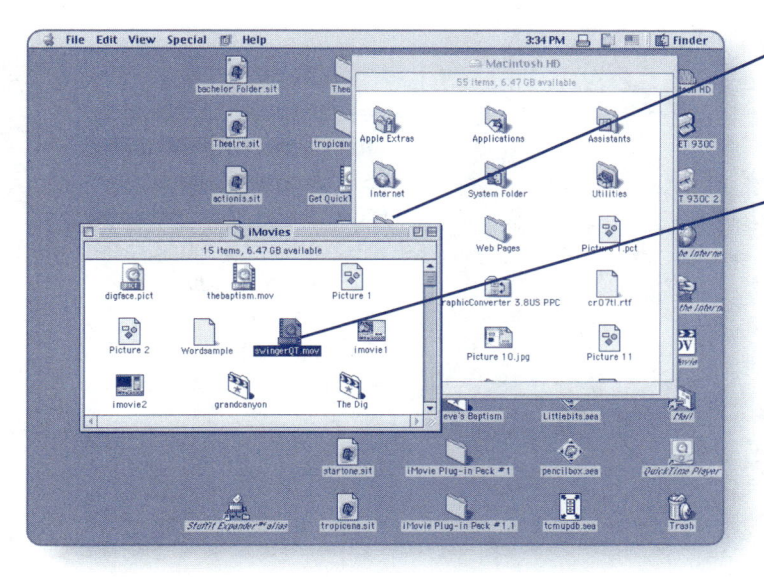

11. **Double-click** on the **folder** where you saved the QuickTime file. The folder will open.

12. **Double-click** on the **QuickTime movie file**. The QuickTime Player will open with your movie in it.

180   **CHAPTER 10: COMPRESSING AND EXPORTING YOUR MOVIES**

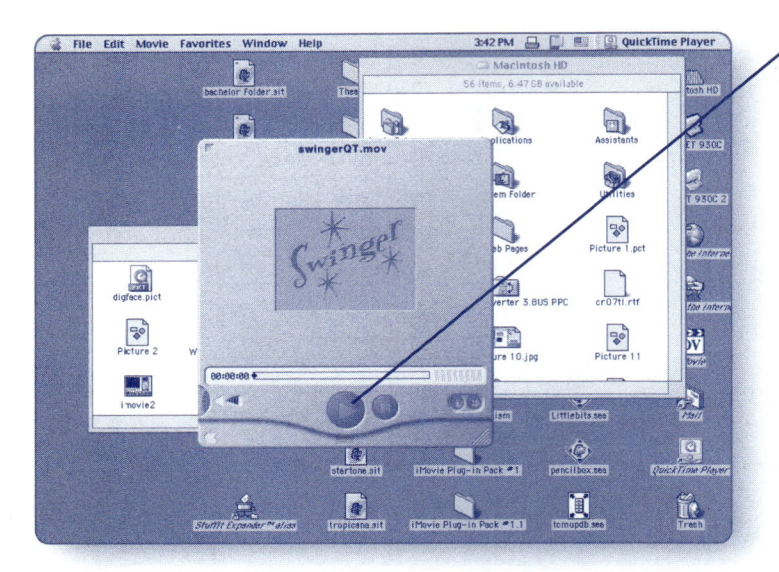

13. Click on the **Play button**.
The QuickTime movie will play.

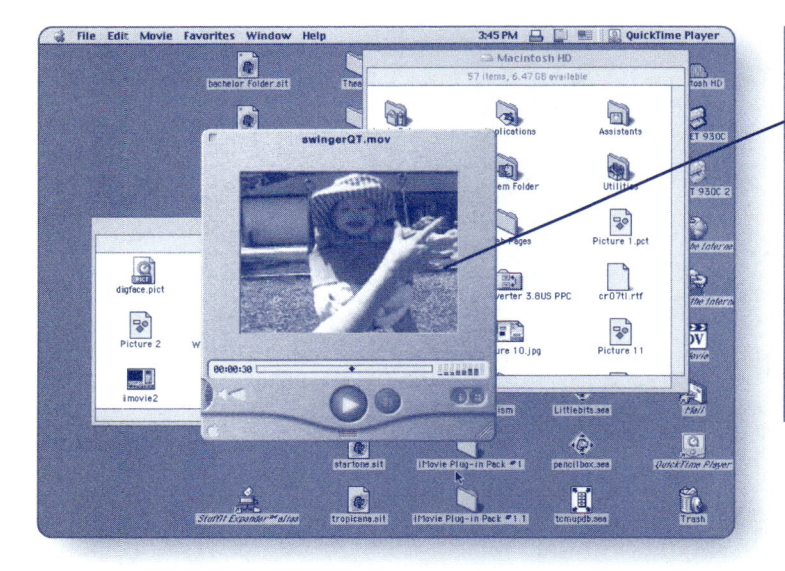

NOTE

See Chapter 12, "Using QuickTime with iMovie," to learn more about QuickTime Pro, and how, with this simple upgrade, you can take advantage of more unique features of this program to enhance your iMovies.

Part III Review Questions

1. How do you establish the length of a transition? *See Setting Transition Speed in Chapter 6*

2. What is rendering? *See Adding the Transition in Chapter 6*

3. How can you add a title over a black background instead of over your video? *See Selecting a Title Background in Chapter 7*

4. Can you make a title align or scroll in a certain direction? *See Specifying Alignment and Scrolling Direction in Chapter 7*

5. How do you position a song to play precisely over a certain portion of your movie? *See Sound Bytes: Cropping Audio Clips in Chapter 8*

6. How do you add polish to the beginning and end of your recording? *See Fading Your Recording In and Out in Chapter 8*

7. What still image file formats are compatible with iMovie? *See Extracting Still Images from Your Videos in Chapter 9*

8. How do you import a photo into your iMovie project? *See Adding a Still Image to an iMovie in Chapter 9*

9. Why would you want to make a copy of your iMovie? *See Making a Copy of Your iMovie in Chapter 10*

10. Why would you export your movie into a QuickTime file? *See Exporting Your Movie to QuickTime in Chapter 10*

PART IV

Outside iMoviemaking

Chapter 11
　　Tricks with Text **185**

Chapter 12
　　Using QuickTime with iMovie **229**

Chapter 13
　　Getting Your iMovie on the Web **263**

11

Tricks with Text

Is iMovie's Titles palette stopping the flow of your creative juices? You can give the text in your titles and credits more pizzazz by taking advantage of other photo manipulation and paint programs outside of iMovie and importing the finished files into iMovie. Photoshop, PhotoDeluxe, and even AppleWorks' paint program allow you to go a few steps further with text, images, patterns, gradients, filters, and so on. Take the ideas used in this chapter and adapt them to fit your needs in your own movies. In this chapter, you'll learn how to:

- Create opening film countdowns
- Add more exciting titles
- Insert silent film dialog placards
- Add silent film sound effects

Creating an Opening Film Countdown

I like most of my movies to have a silent-film or film noir feel to them. To help accomplish this, I film a lot in black and white or with sepia filters. Remember the old films that had the numbers counting down before the film began? Duplicating effects like this, as well as the others you'll create in this chapter, can help give your movie a "Touch of Evil." Begin by opening whatever photo manipulation or paint program you have. I use Photoshop 4.0, but the techniques I show you should be similar to other programs, and I'll point out differences here and there.

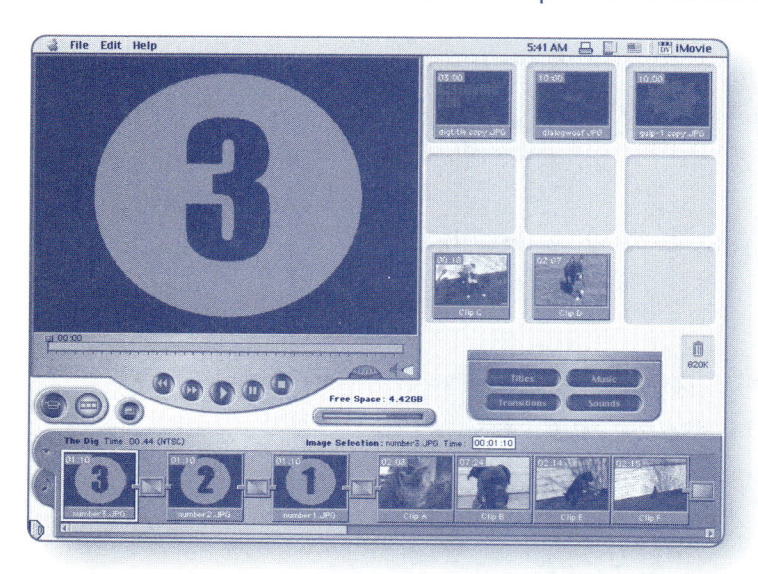

Preparing Your Canvas

Before you create the number sequence, you need to ready your canvas. This canvas will be used as the starting point for all of your numbers in this effect.

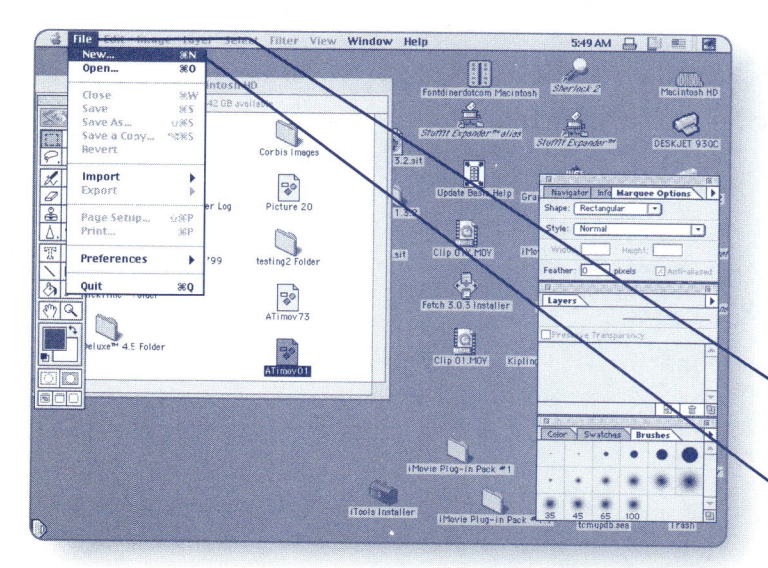

1. Open your **photo manipulation or paint program**.

2. Click on **File**. The File menu will appear.

3. Click on **New**. The New dialog box will open.

CREATING AN OPENING FILM COUNTDOWN   187

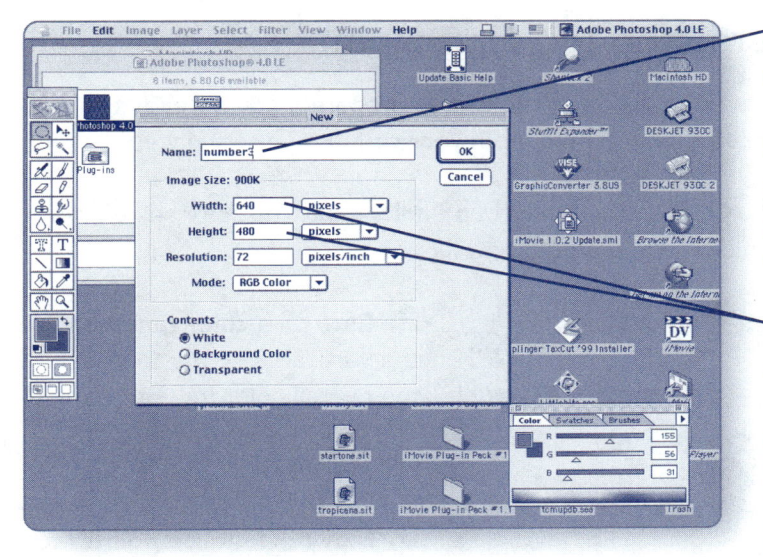

4. In the Name field, **type** a **name** for the file.

5. If your program asks you to, **set** all the **margins** to 0. Some programs do not have this option.

6. Set the **size** of the image to 640 pixels by 480 pixels.

NOTE
640 by 480 pixels is the size of the frame that will fit in iMovie without any cropping or additions of a border, so it is important to make this the dimension of your images.

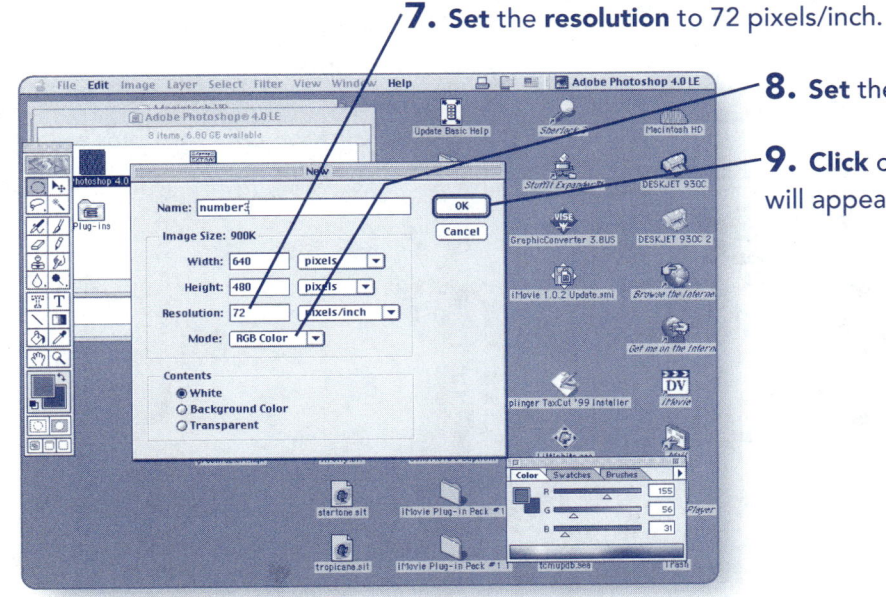

7. Set the **resolution** to 72 pixels/inch.

8. Set the **Mode** to RGB Color.

9. Click on **OK**. A blank canvas will appear.

Creating the First Number

Now that you have the canvas prepared, you're ready to create the first number in your countdown sequence.

1. Click on the **foreground color box**. The color selector or Color Picker dialog box will open.

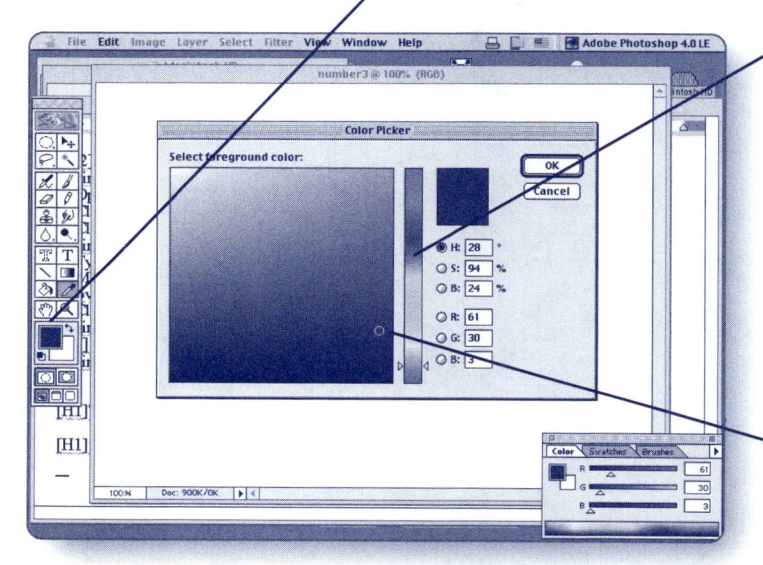

2. Click on a **color range** on the vertical color bar to select the overall color for your canvas. The color range you selected will appear.

3. Move the **mouse pointer** to the large box to the left of the vertical color bar. The mouse pointer will change to a circle.

4. Click on a **color**. Select a color that has some black tones in it, because you want this to have an older, slightly black-and-white look.

5. Click on **OK**. The color will be selected.

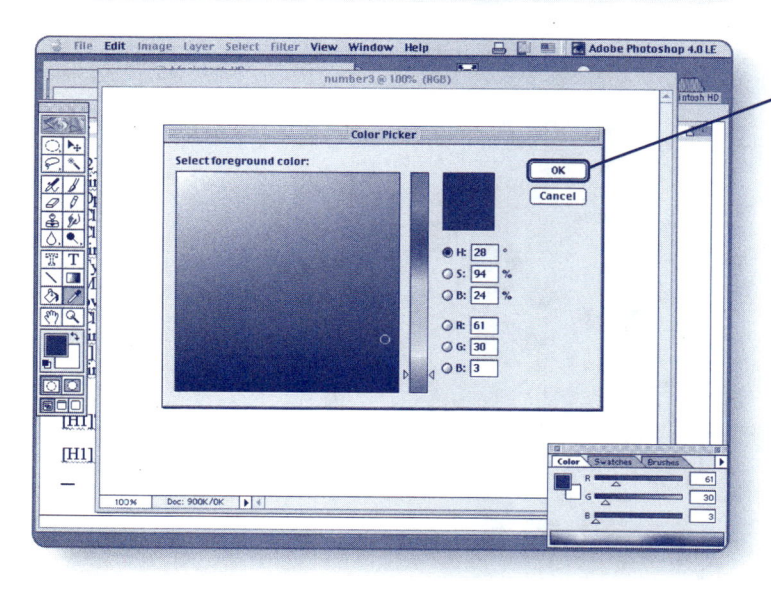

CREATING AN OPENING FILM COUNTDOWN 189

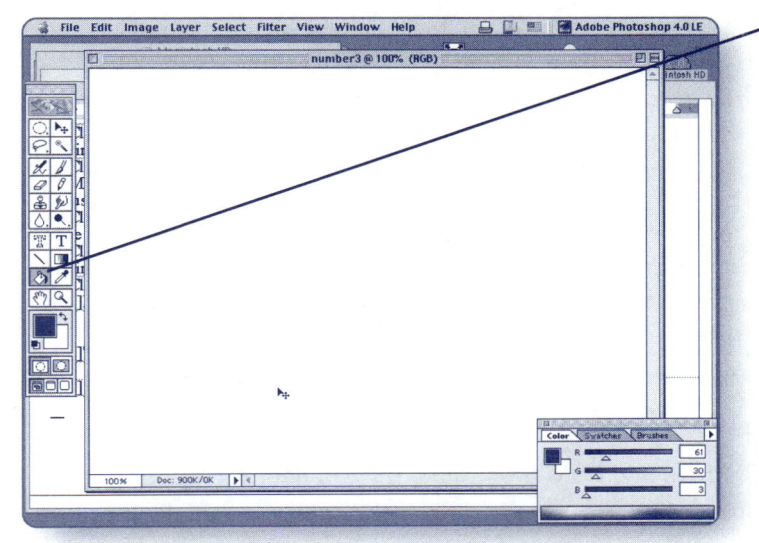

6. Click on the **Fill or Paint Bucket tool**. The tool will be selected, and the mouse pointer will change to a paint bucket icon.

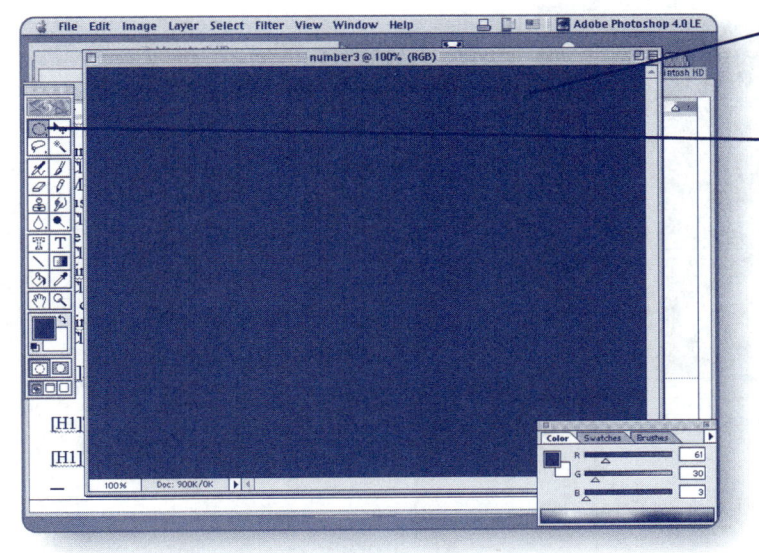

7. Click on the **canvas**. The color will fill up the canvas.

8. Click on the **Oval marquee tool**. The tool will be selected, and the mouse pointer will change to a crosshair.

CHAPTER 11: TRICKS WITH TEXT

> **NOTE**
>
> If the toolbox is showing a dotted-line rectangle, or Rectangular marquee tool, you have to change it to the dotted-line circle, or Oval marquee tool. Just press and hold the mouse button on the Rectangle marquee tool until a pop-up menu appears. Then, move the mouse pointer to the dotted-line oval icon and release the mouse button. The tool will change to the Oval marquee tool.

9. **Press and hold** the **mouse button** near the upper-left corner of your canvas and **drag** the **mouse** to the lower-right corner of the canvas to form a circle. A dotted-line circle will appear as you drag.

10. **Release** the **mouse button**. The circle will appear, and your mouse pointer will change to a Move tool.

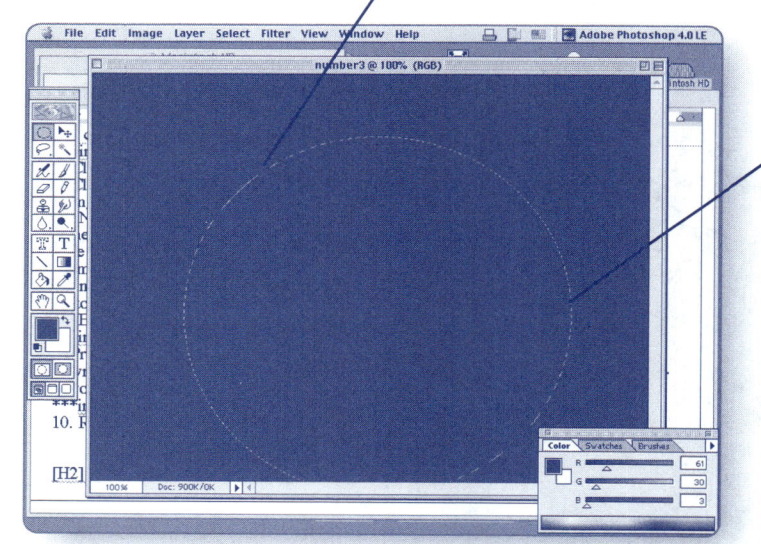

> **NOTE**
>
> Depending on the program you are using, the mouse pointer may or may not automatically change to a Move tool. If it doesn't, just select the Move tool from your program's toolbar. Most programs' Move tools will look like an arrow icon.

CREATING AN OPENING FILM COUNTDOWN 191

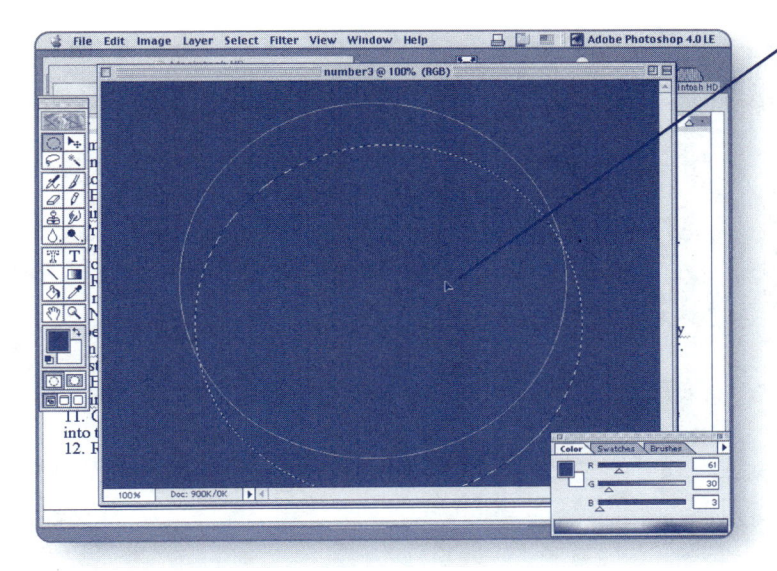

11. **Click and hold** the **mouse button** in the circle you just created and **drag** the **circle** into the center of the canvas.

12. **Release** the **mouse button**. The circle will now be located in the center of the canvas.

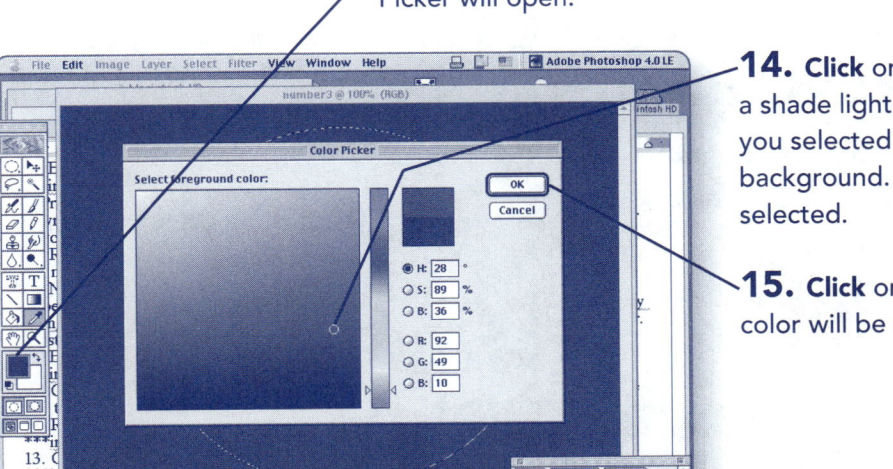

13. **Click** on the **foreground color square** again. The Color Picker will open.

14. **Click** on a **color** that is just a shade lighter than the color you selected for your background. The color will be selected.

15. **Click** on **OK**. The new color will be selected.

192 CHAPTER 11: TRICKS WITH TEXT

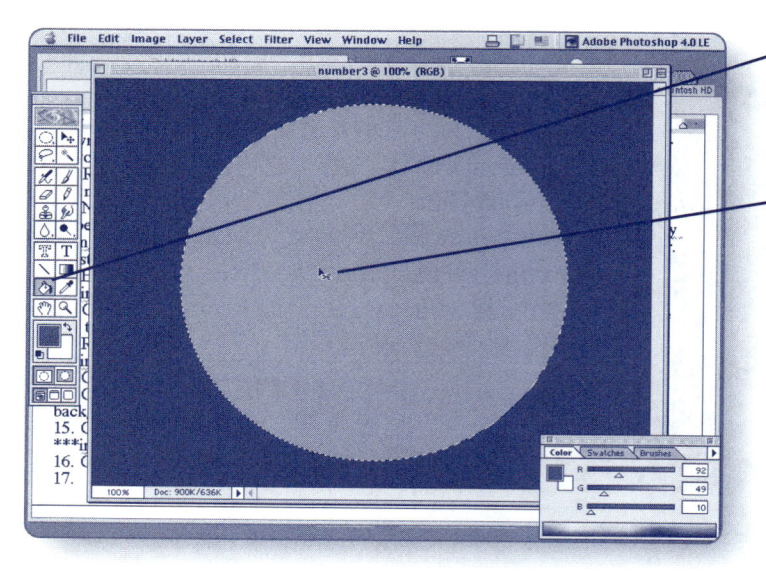

16. **Click** on the **Fill or Paint Bucket tool**. The tool will be selected.

17. **Click** inside the **circle** you made. The circle will be filled with your new color.

18. **Click** on the **foreground color square** again. The Color Picker will open.

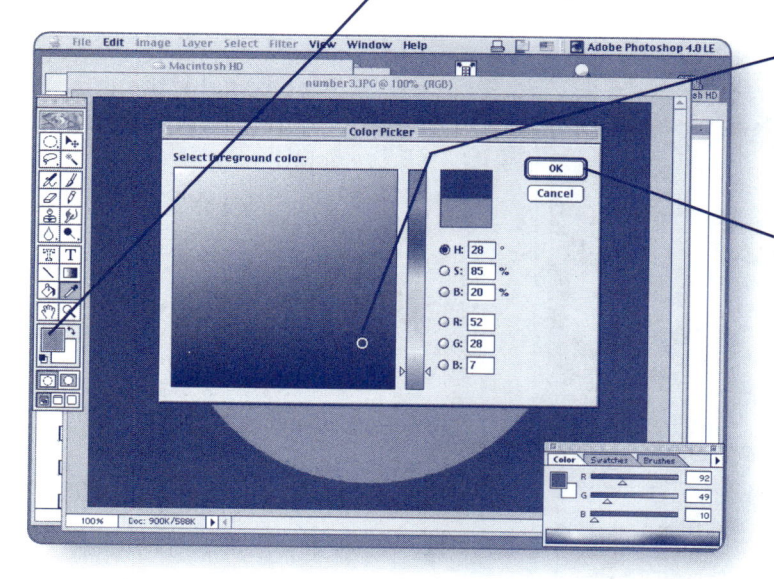

19. **Select** a **slightly darker shade** of the previous color tone you selected. The color will be selected.

20. **Click** on **OK**. The Color Picker will close.

CREATING AN OPENING FILM COUNTDOWN   193

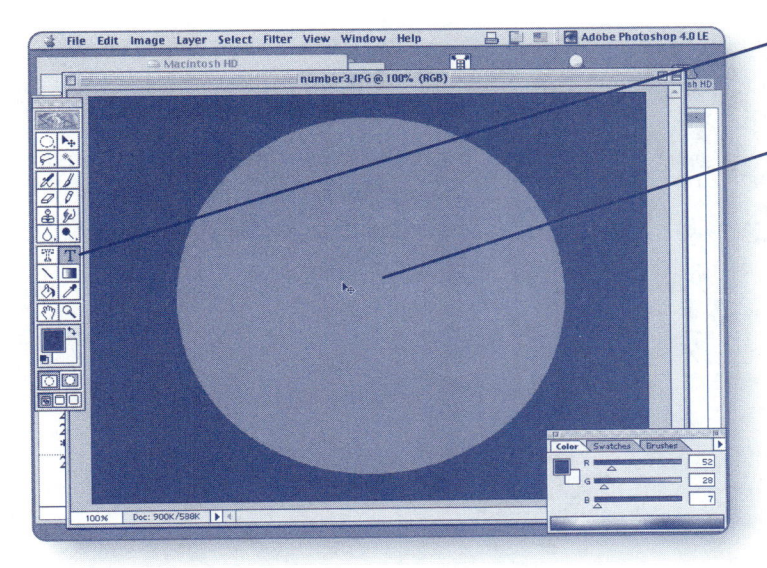

21. **Click** on the **Type tool**. The Type tool will be selected.

22. **Click** in the **center** of the circle. The Type Tool dialog box will open.

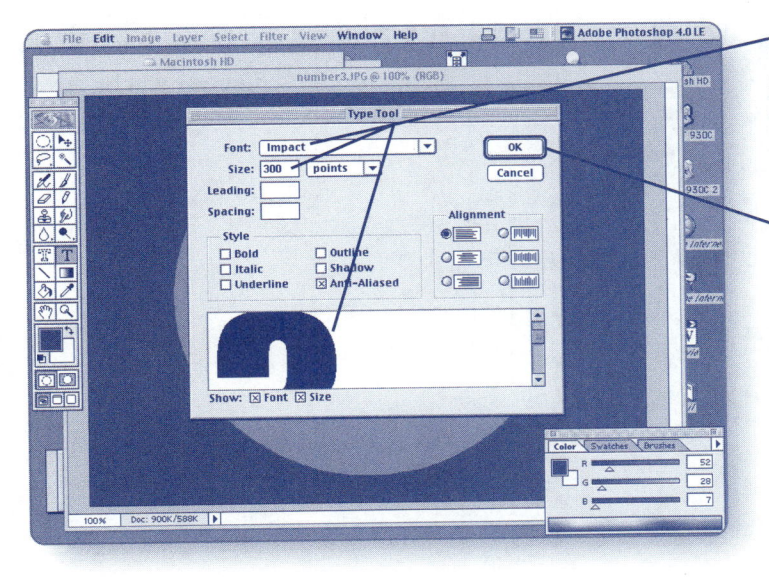

23. **Select** a **font style and size** and **type** the number **3** in the text box that appears at the bottom of the dialog box.

24. **Click** on **OK**. The number 3 will appear on your canvas.

CHAPTER 11: TRICKS WITH TEXT

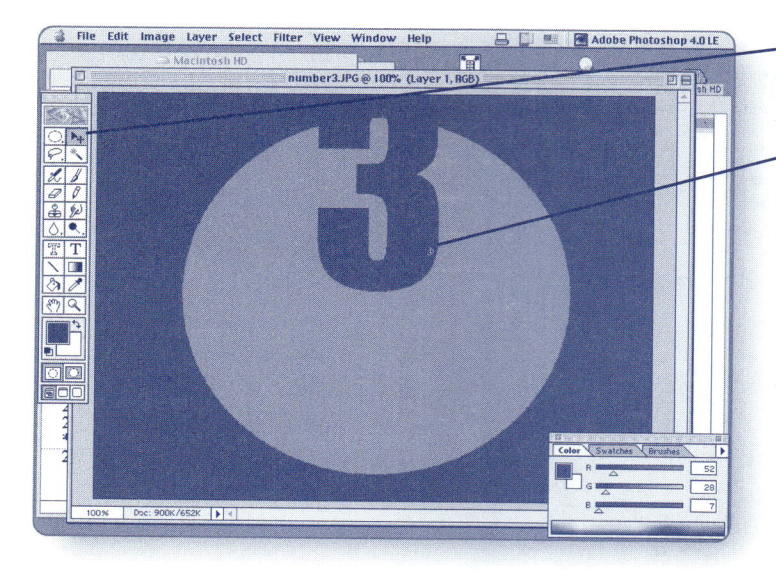

25. **Click** on the **Move tool**. The Move tool will be selected.

26. **Press and hold** the **mouse button** on the number 3 and **drag it** to center the number in your circle.

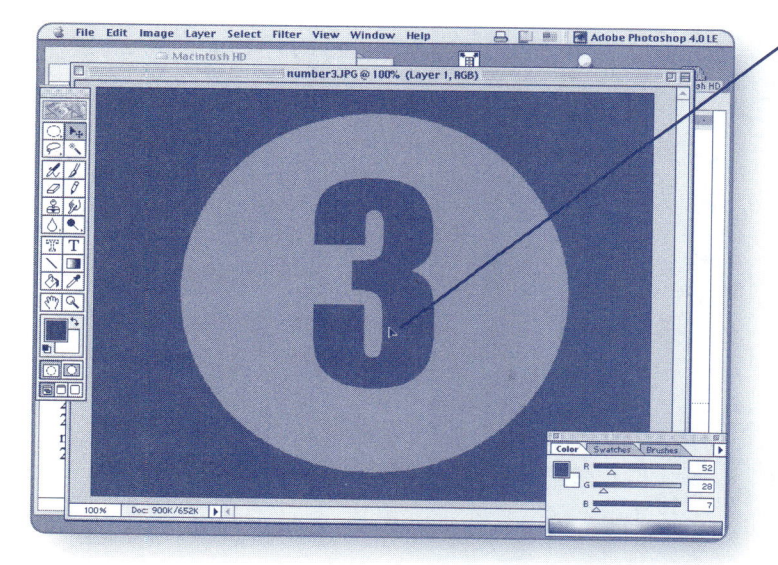

27. **Release** the **mouse button**. The number will be centered.

CREATING AN OPENING FILM COUNTDOWN 195

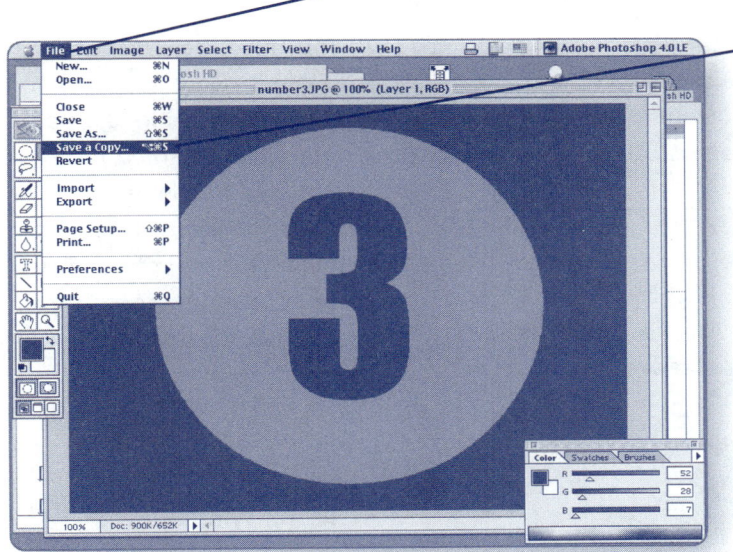

28. **Click** on **File**. The File menu will appear.

29. **Click** on **Save a Copy**. The Save dialog box will open.

> **NOTE**
> You want to save a copy of the file because you will be using this file again to make more numbers.

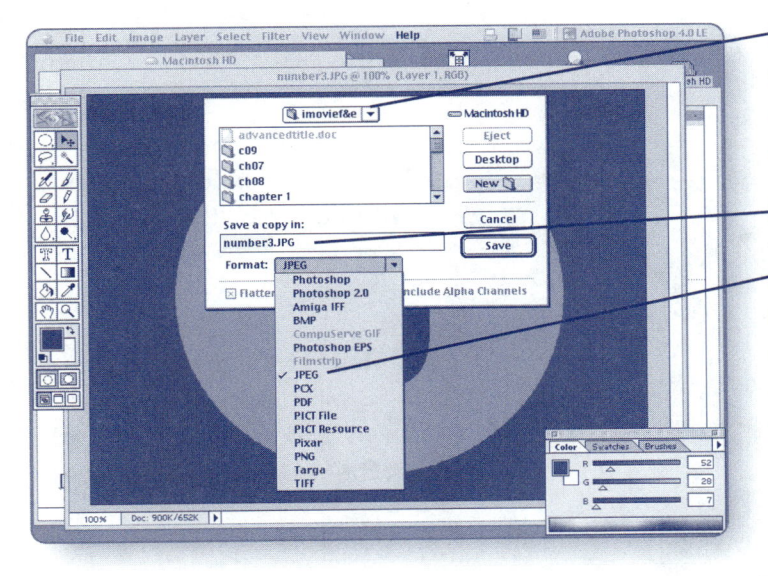

30. **Click** on the **down arrow** to select a folder in which to save your file. The folder will be selected.

31. **Type** a **name** for your file.

32. **Click** on **JPEG** in the Format drop-down list. A check mark will appear next to JPEG, and your file will be saved in this format.

You have finished your first number image. Make sure you keep this file open, because in the next section you will use this to create the other number images for your effect.

Creating the Other Numbers

Depending on the image program you are using, you can easily convert the file you created in the previous section into your other number images. Photoshop, for example, uses a process called layers, where each different element you create in a single file becomes a separate layer that you can manipulate, move, edit, and so on. If your program doesn't use layers, you can just start over and repeat the previous section's steps. Here, you will use the layers process.

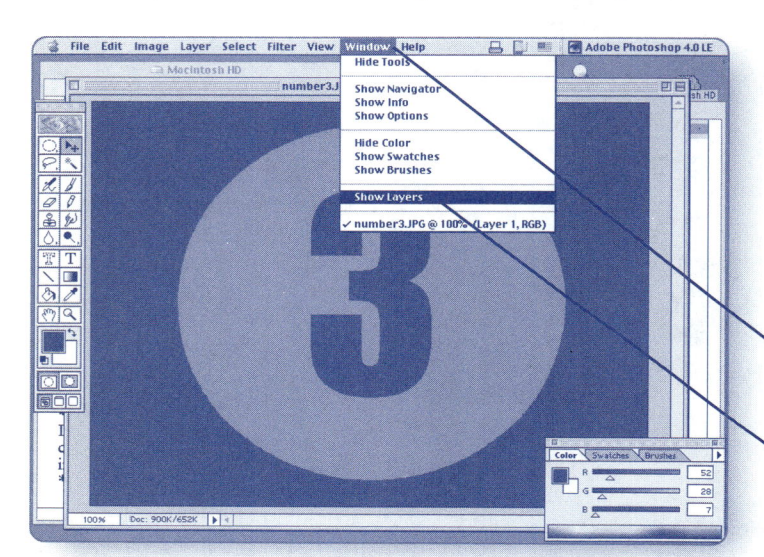

1. Click on **Window**. The Window menu will appear.

2. Click on **Show Layers**. The Layers dialog box will open.

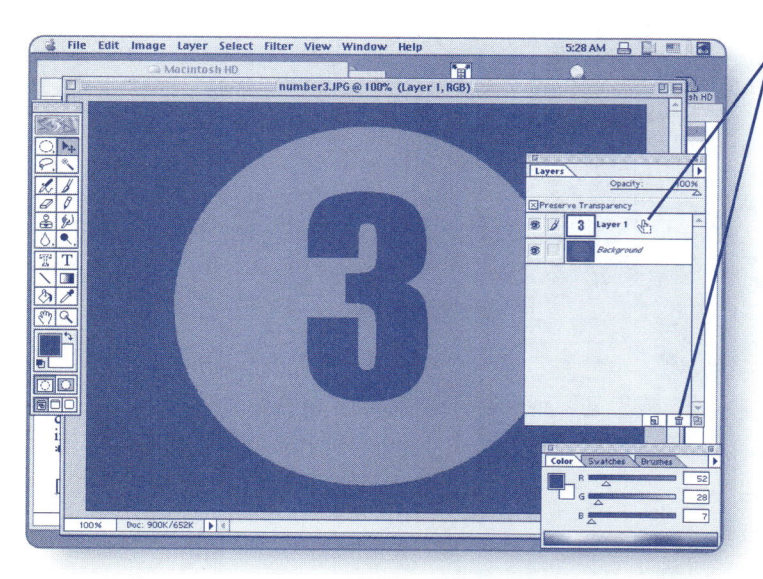

3. Press and hold the **mouse button** down on the layer with the number 3 and **drag it** to the trash can.

4. Release the **mouse button**. The 3 will disappear from your canvas, and you will be left with just the background and circle.

CREATING AN OPENING FILM COUNTDOWN 197

> **NOTE**
> If the program you are using does not use the layer process, click on Edit, Undo until you undo the number 3. You should just have the canvas with the circle in the middle and no number. Then, save a copy of this file (of the canvas and the circle with no number) and use it for the next number you create.

5. Click on the **Type tool**. The Type tool will be selected.

6. Click in the **center** of the circle. The Type Tool dialog box will open.

7. Select the **same font style and size** as you did for the first number.

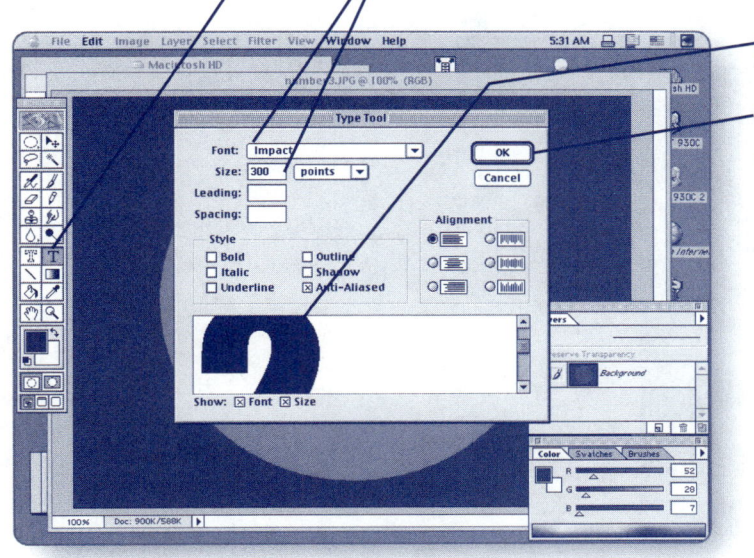

8. Type 2 in the text box.

9. Click on **OK**. The number 2 will appear on your canvas.

198 CHAPTER 11: TRICKS WITH TEXT

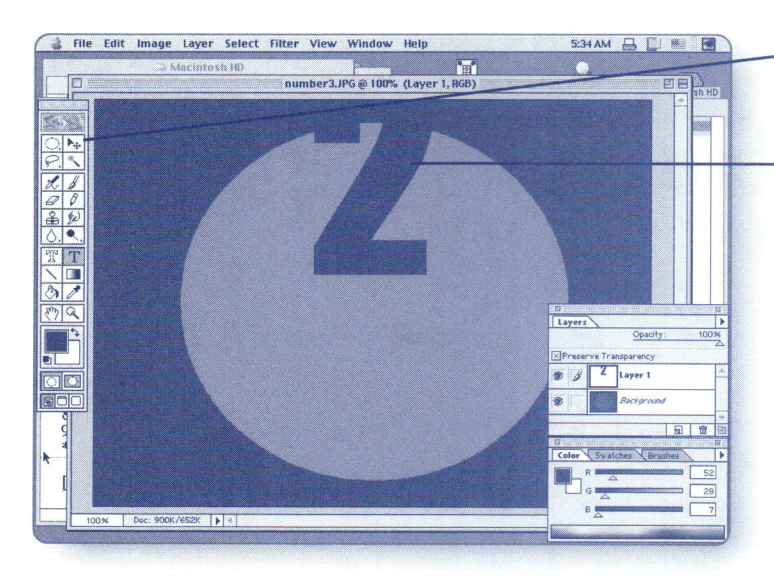

10. Click on the **Move tool**. The Move tool will be selected.

11. Press and hold the **mouse button** on the number 2 and **drag it** to the center of the circle.

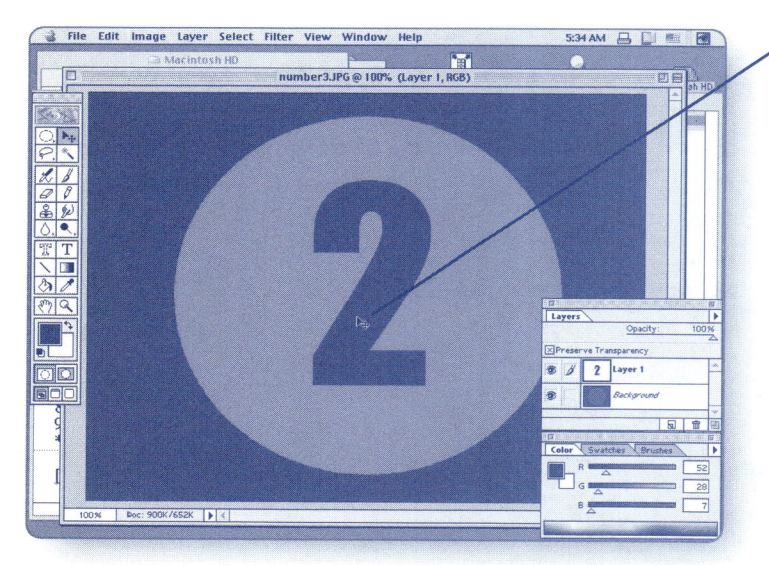

12. Release the **mouse button**. The number 2 will be centered.

CREATING AN OPENING FILM COUNTDOWN   199

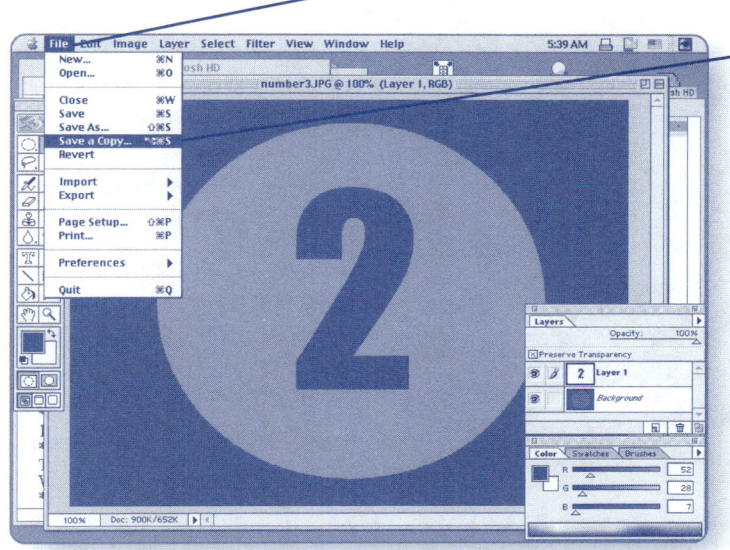

13. Click on **File**. The File menu will appear.

14. Click on **Save a Copy**. The Save dialog box will open.

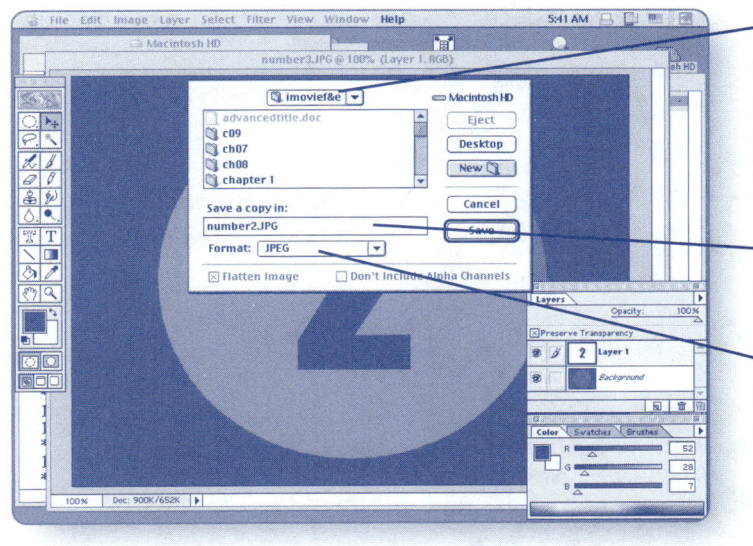

15. Click on the **down arrow** to select a folder in which to save your number 2. Save it in the same folder as your number 3.

16. Type a **name** for your number 2 file.

17. Click on **JPEG** from the Format drop-down list. JPEG will be selected.

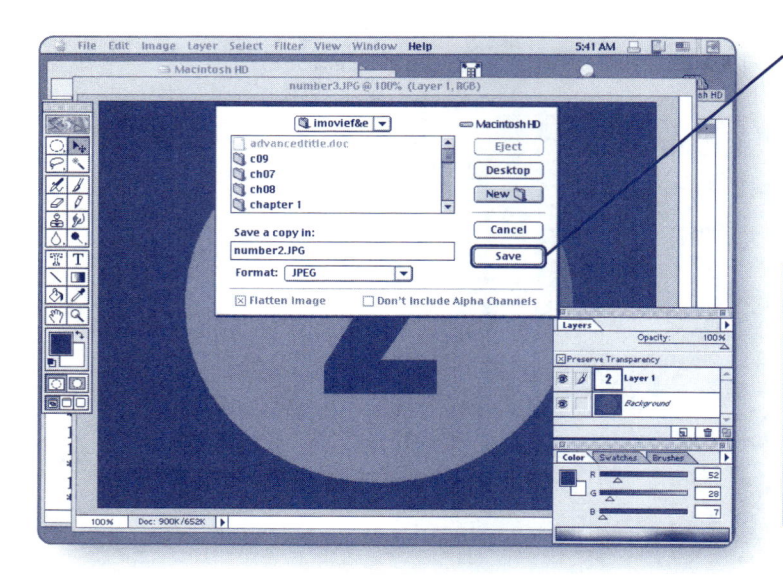

18. Click on **Save**. Your number 2 will be saved.

19. Repeat steps 3 through 12 to create a number 1.

> **NOTE**
>
> The Layers dialog box should still be open, unless you closed it. If it is not open, click on Window and then click on Show Layers.

Adding the Images to iMovie

Now that you've created your images, you need to add them to your iMovie production.

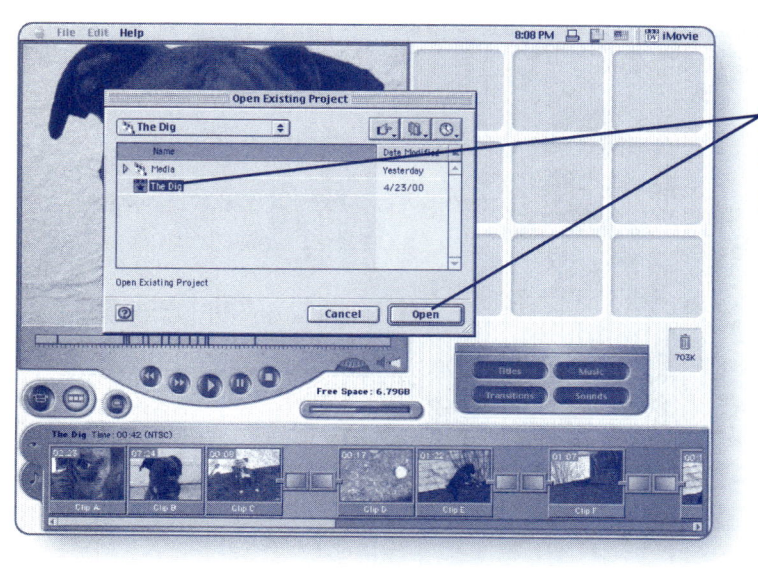

1. Open iMovie.

2. Open the **iMovie project** into which you want to import your newly created files.

CREATING AN OPENING FILM COUNTDOWN 201

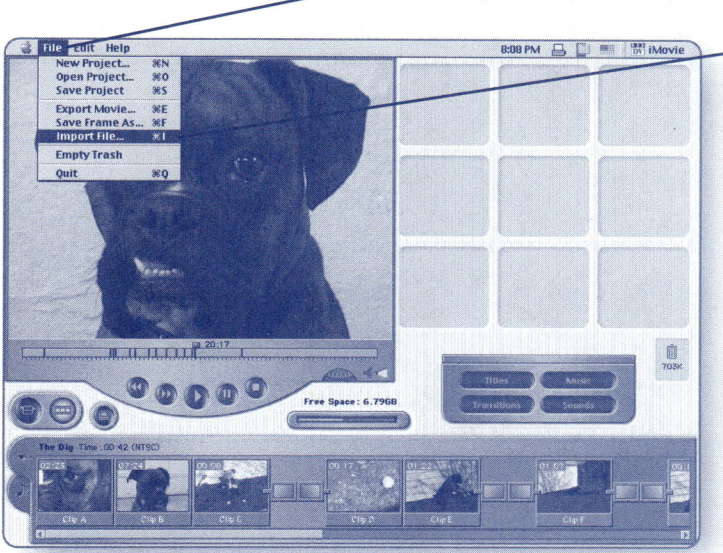

3. Click on **File**. The File menu will appear.

4. Click on **Import File**. The Import File dialog box will open.

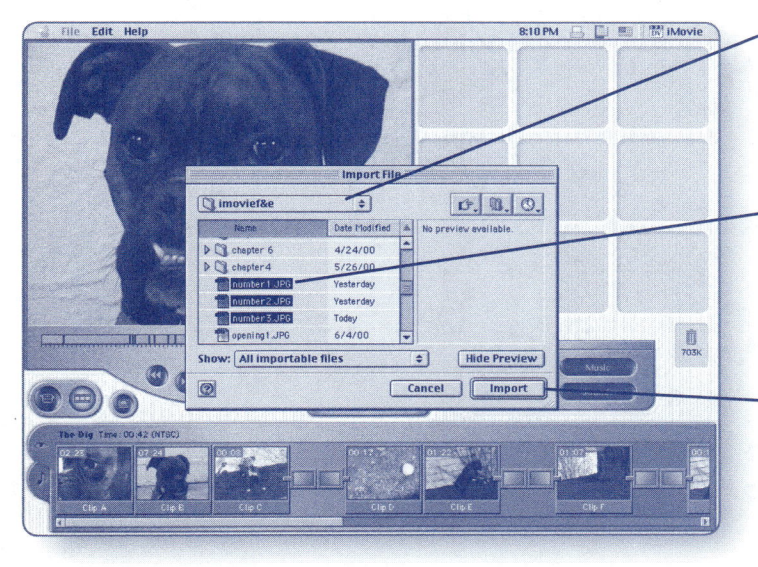

5. Click on the **folder** in which your images reside. The folder will open and reveal your images.

6. Press the **Shift key** and **click** on the three **images** that you created. The images will be selected.

7. Click on the **Import button**. The files will be imported to the Shelf in your iMovie project.

202 CHAPTER 11: TRICKS WITH TEXT

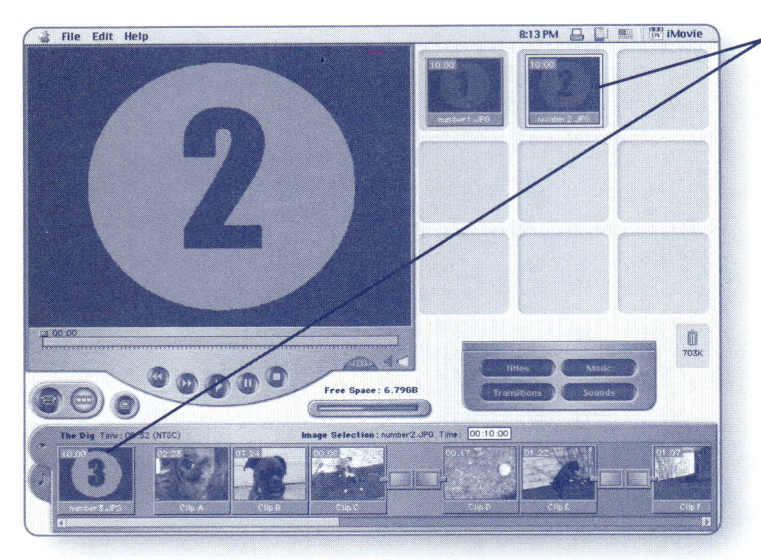

8. Drag the **images** from the Shelf and **drop them** in the Clip Viewer. The clips will appear in the Clip Viewer.

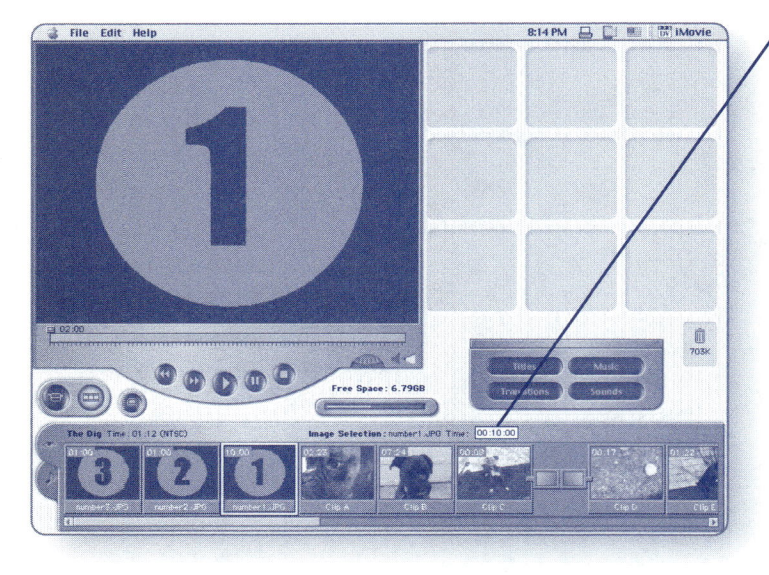

9. Click in the **duration box** and **type** a **duration** for the clips. Approximately 2 seconds each is a good duration for this effect.

10. Press the **Enter key**. The new duration will be set.

CREATING AN OPENING FILM COUNTDOWN 203

Adding Transitions

If you want, add a transition between the images you just created. You can get that old, numbered countdown effect without any transition, but it looks even better with the Radial transition.

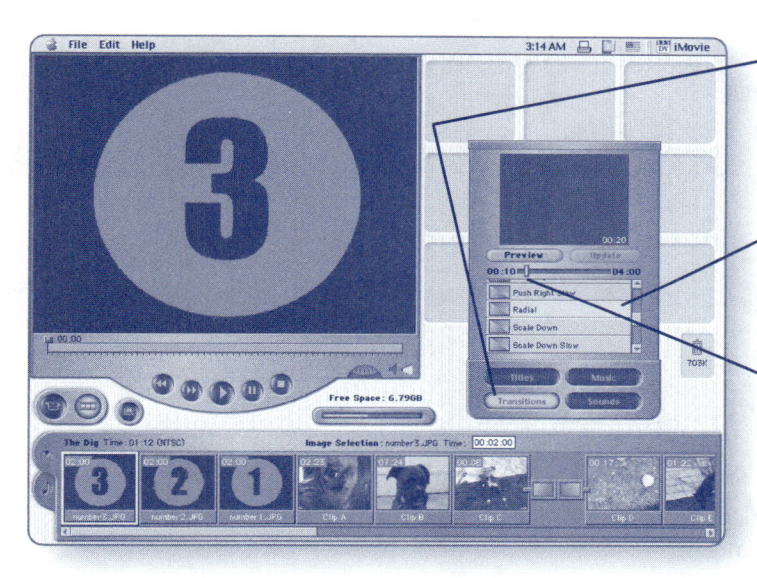

1. Click on the **Transitions button** in the Effects palette. The Transitions palette will open.

2. Click on the **Radial effect**. The Radial transition will be selected.

3. Drag the **duration slider** to about 2 seconds. The transition duration will be set.

4. Drag and drop the **transition** between the 3 and the 2 and between the 2 and the 1. The transitions will appear between the numbers and will begin to render.

CHAPTER 11: TRICKS WITH TEXT

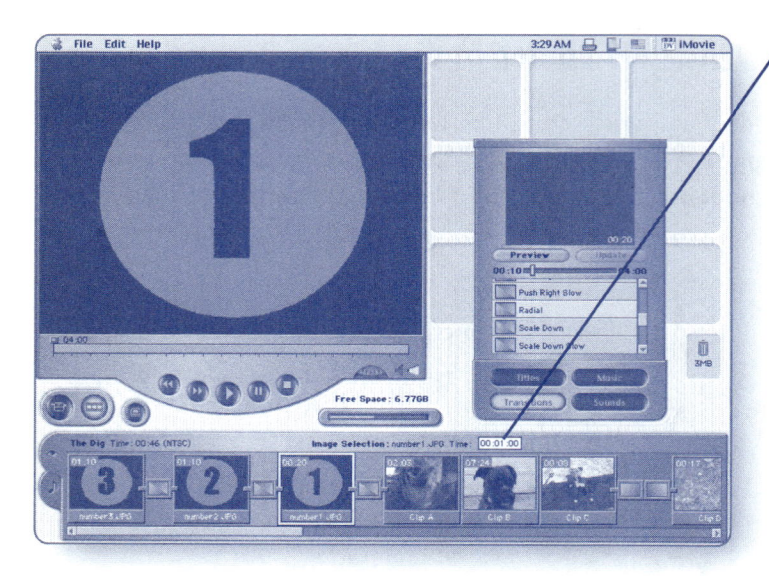

5. If you want to change the duration of the clips, **select** each of your **number clips** and **change** the **duration time** to equal lengths in the duration text box.

Playing Your Effect

To see if everything is the way you want it, you can play back just those clips you worked on and then make any desired changes.

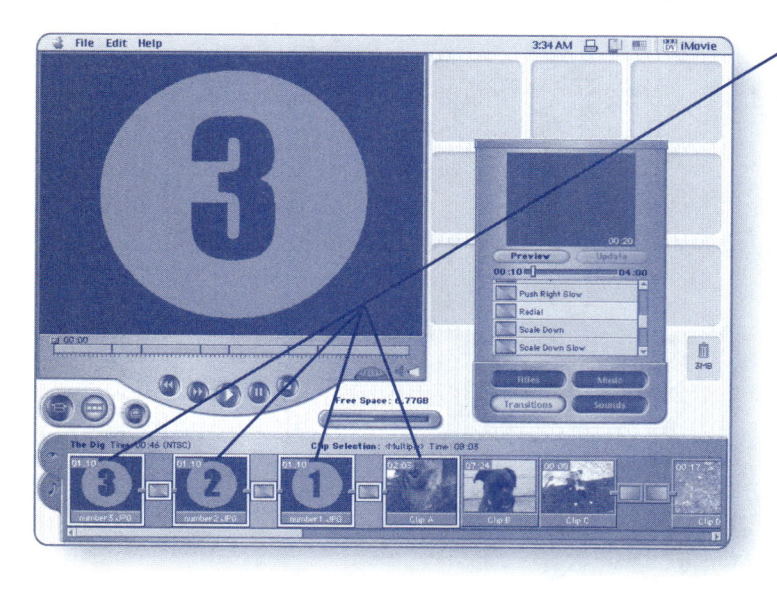

1. Press the **Shift button** and **click** on all the **clips** you want to play back. The clips, and the transitions between them, will be selected.

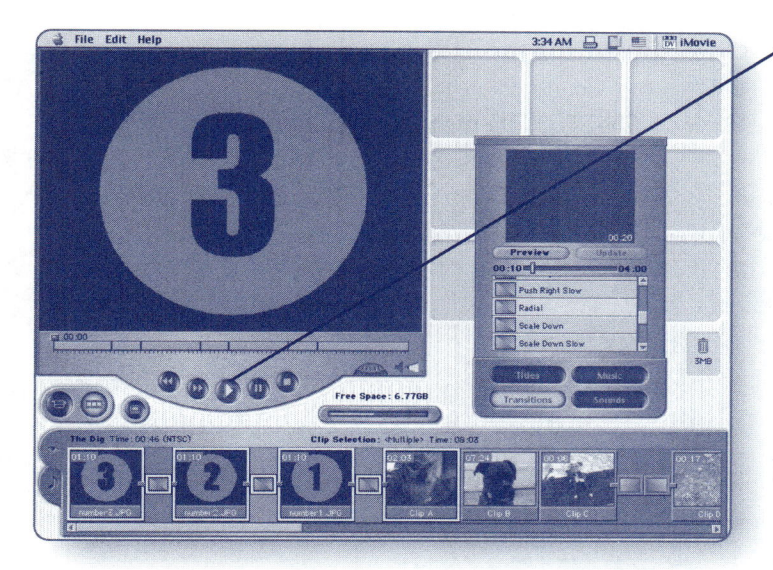

2. Click on the **Play button** in the Monitor window. The selected clips will play back in the Monitor window.

3. Make any desired **adjustments** to the effect you created.

Inserting More Exciting Titles

Using another program, you can get more creative with your titles in iMovie. You have more freedom with text size, position, color, and style using programs outside of iMovie to create titles. Let's add a title that complements the numbered countdown effects you created in the previous section.

Preparing Your Canvas

You need to ready your canvas for your title in the same manner as you did with the number sequence.

CHAPTER 11: TRICKS WITH TEXT

1. Open your **image manipulation program**.

2. Click on **File**. The File menu will appear.

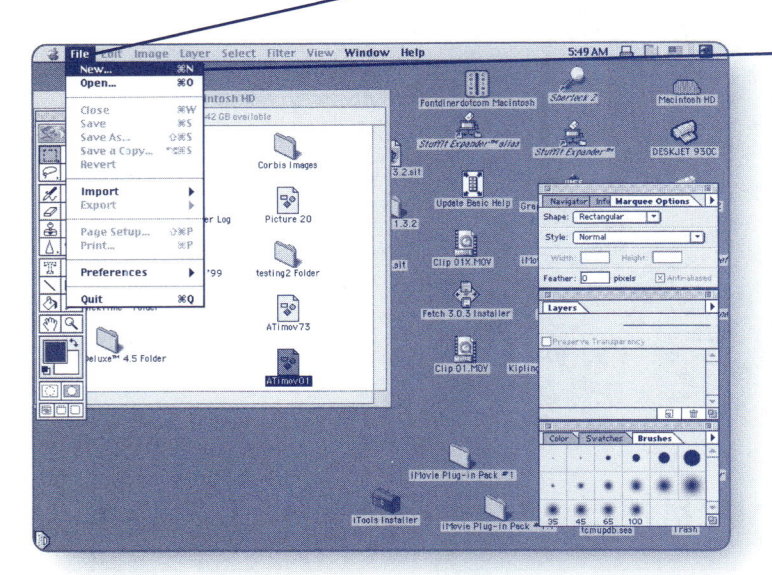

3. Click on **New**. The New dialog box will open.

4. Type a **new name** for the file.

5. Set all **margins** to 0, if your program asks you to. The margins will be set.

6. Set the **dimensions** for the image size to 640 by 480 pixels. The dimensions will be set.

7. Set the **resolution** to 72 pixels/inch. The resolution will be set.

8. Set the **Mode** to RGB Color. The mode will be set.

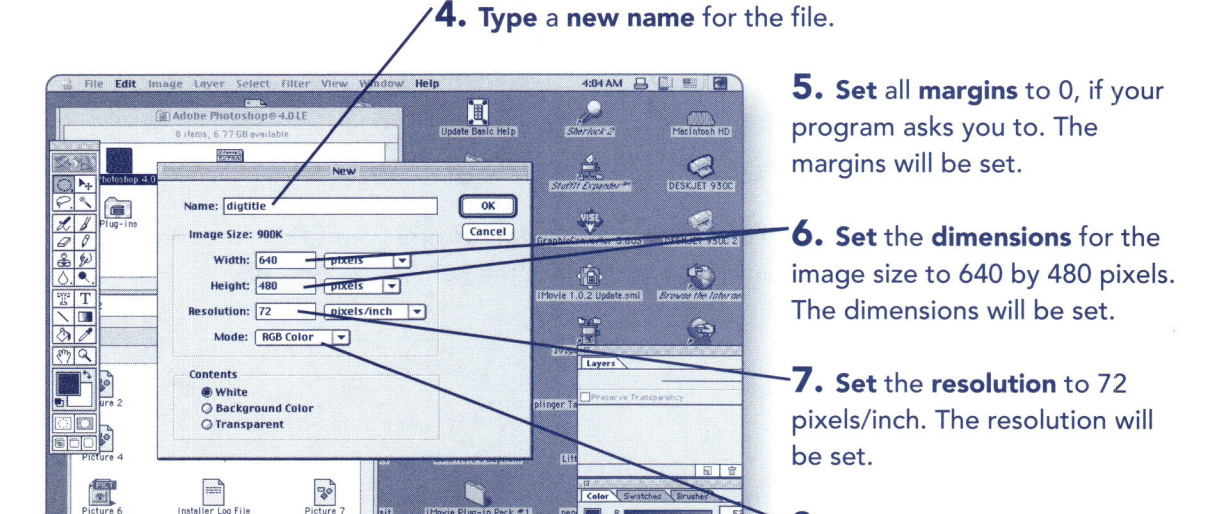

INSERTING MORE EXCITING TITLES   207

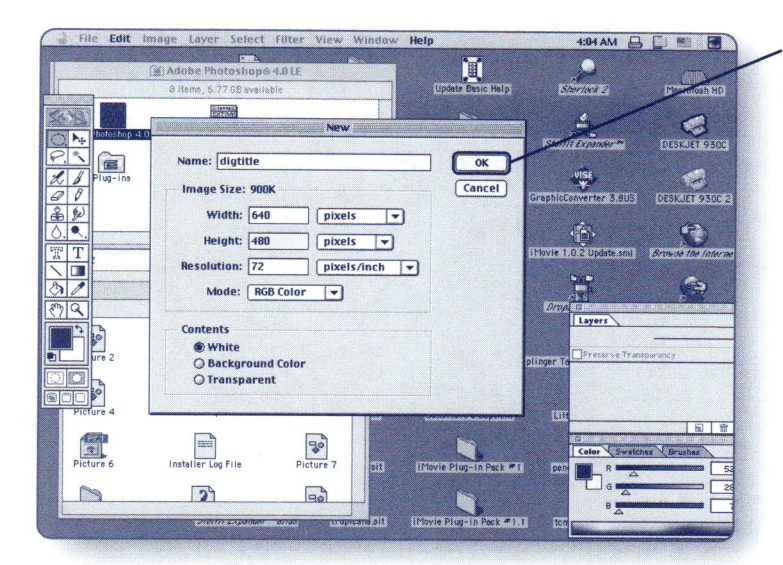

9. Click on **OK**. Your blank canvas will appear.

Creating the Title

Now it's time to start creating your title. Remember, you want it to look similar to your number sequence.

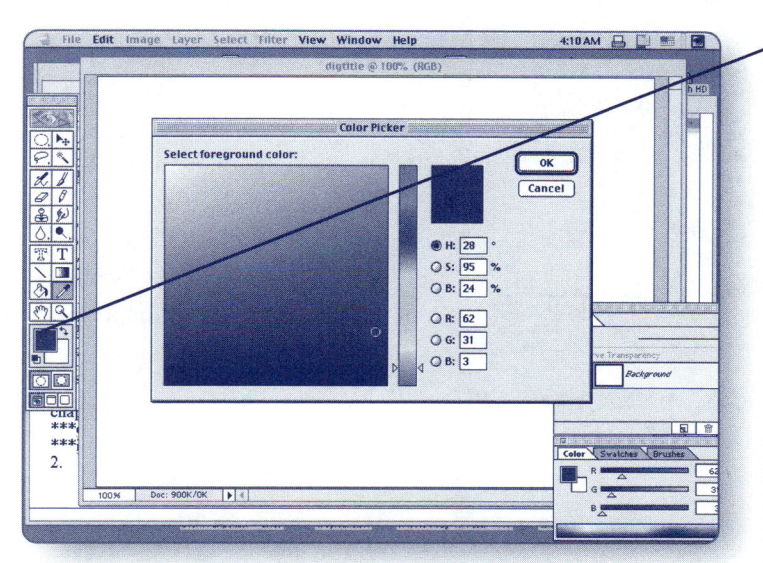

1. Click on the **foreground color square**. The color selector or Color Picker will open.

NOTE

This will be the color of your entire canvas. It is a good idea to use the same color (or a complementary color) as you used for the number effect you created in the first section of this chapter, in order to create a similar look and feel for the whole movie.

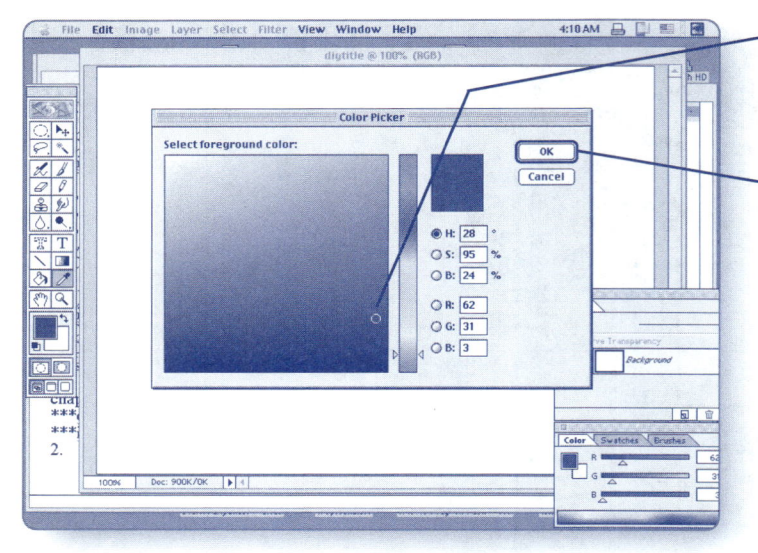

2. Choose a **color** in the Color Picker. The color will be selected.

3. Click on **OK**. The Color Picker dialog box will close, and you will be returned to your canvas.

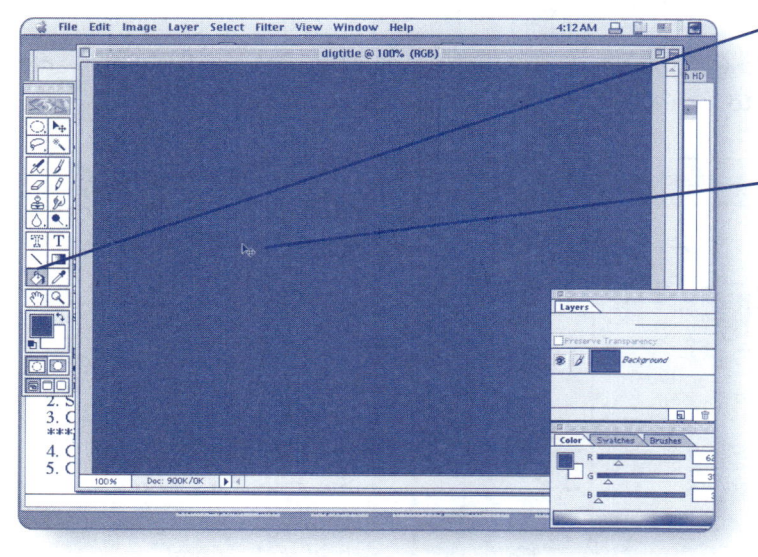

4. Click on the **Fill or Paint Bucket tool**. The tool will be selected.

5. Click on your **canvas**. The color will fill the canvas.

6. Repeat steps 1 through 3 to change your foreground color. This will be the color of your text, so you might want to match it with the text used in the numbered countdown effect.

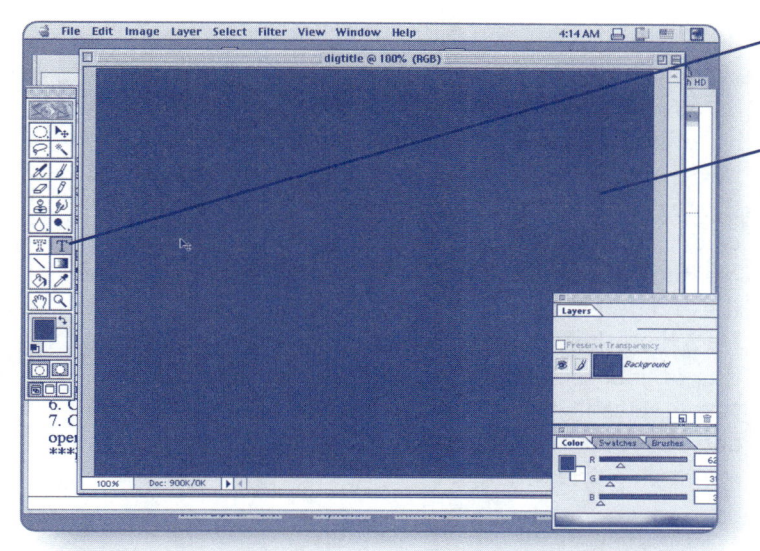

INSERTING MORE EXCITING TITLES 209

7. Click on the **Type tool**. The tool will be selected.

8. Click on the **canvas** at the approximate place where you want the title. The Type Tool dialog box will open.

9. Set the **font style and size**. You should keep the same font settings as those you used in the numbered countdown effect.

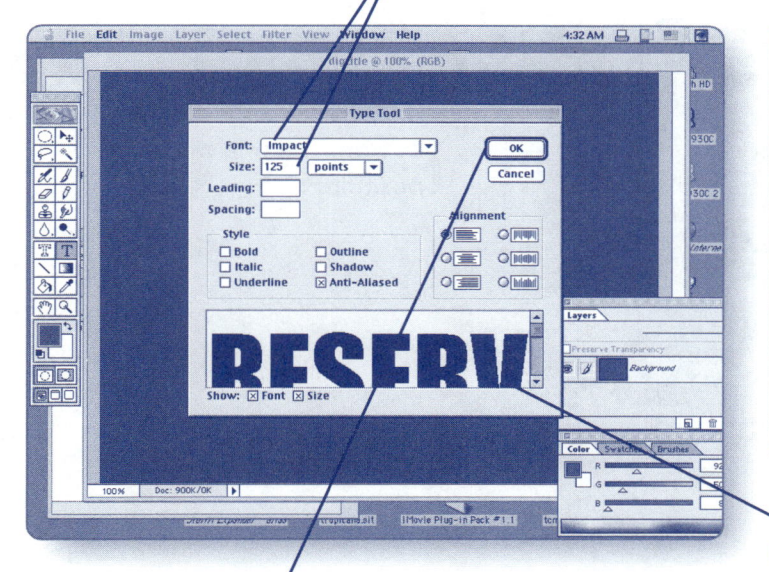

TIP

For titles, remember that it is always best to use thicker, bolder fonts because they will eventually appear on televisions, QuickTime videos, and so on. Thinner fonts and script-type fonts tend to be difficult to read in these formats.

10. Type your **title** in the text box.

11. Click on **OK**. Your title will appear on the canvas.

CHAPTER 11: TRICKS WITH TEXT

> **NOTE**
>
> If you want several stacked lines or a block of text hovering over your movie title—for example, "A Film by *So and So*"—repeat steps 7 through 11 and adjust the text accordingly. You might want to use different colors or font sizes for these other text elements, to create a nice effect. You also have the freedom to move these different text elements around the page separate from the other text elements. Or, if you don't want the title of your movie on the same page as your block of text, you can always create completely separate images and insert them among your video clips for an equally interesting title scheme.

12. Click on the **Move tool**. The Move tool will be selected.

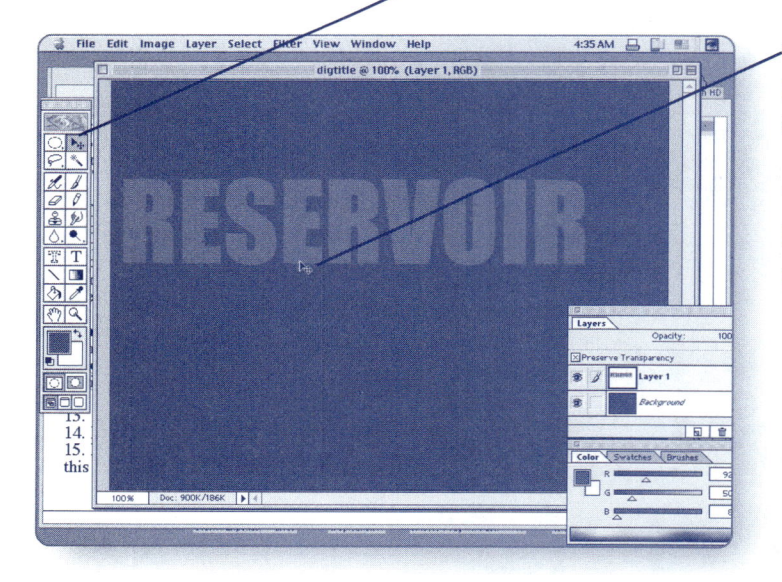

13. Click and hold the **mouse button** on the title and **drag** the **title** to your desired location.

14. Release the **mouse button**. The title will be in position.

INSERTING MORE EXCITING TITLES 211

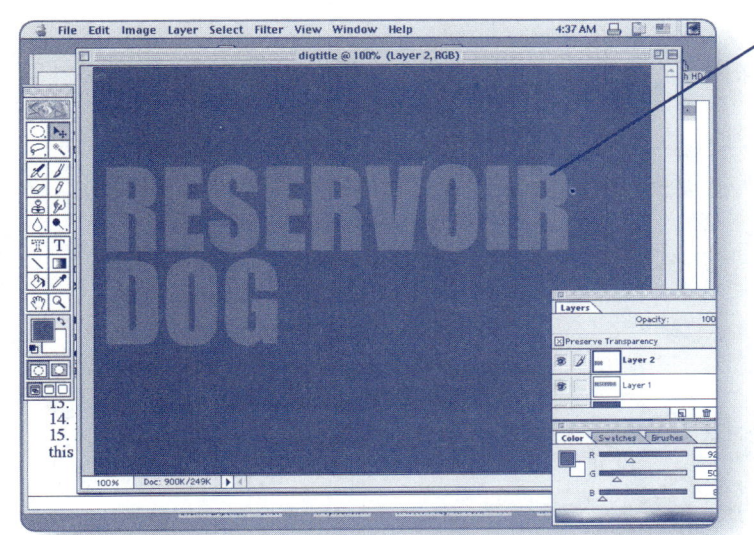

15. **Repeat steps 7 through 14** for any other part of your title or any other text you want to insert on this page.

> **NOTE**
>
> In many image programs, you can add interesting effects to your text, such as drop shadows, beveling and embossing, and so on. Feel free to take advantage of these effects. See your program's help files to learn how to utilize these effects.

16. **Click** on **File**. The File menu will appear.

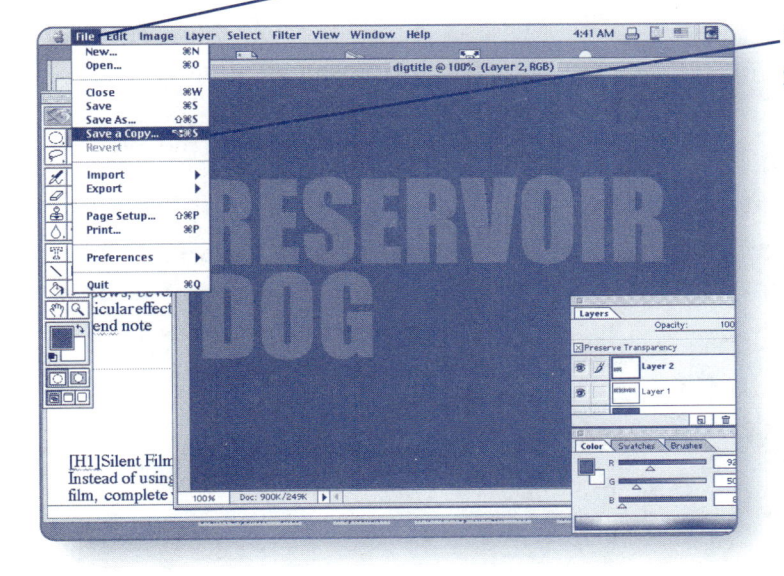

17. **Click** on **Save a Copy**. The Save dialog box will open.

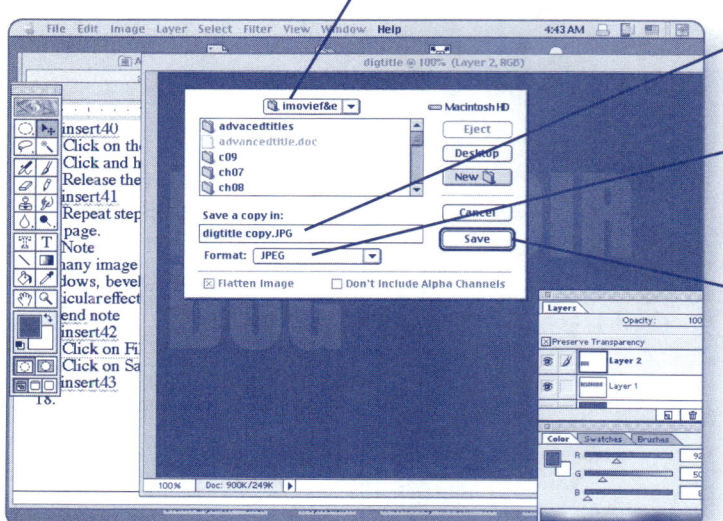

212 CHAPTER 11: TRICKS WITH TEXT

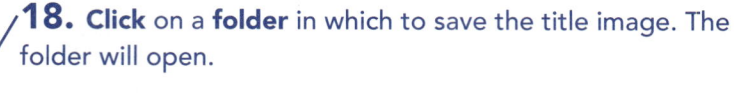

18. Click on a **folder** in which to save the title image. The folder will open.

19. Type a **name** for the image.

20. Click on **JPEG** in the Format drop-down list. JPEG will be selected.

21. Click on **Save**. The image will be saved in JPEG format.

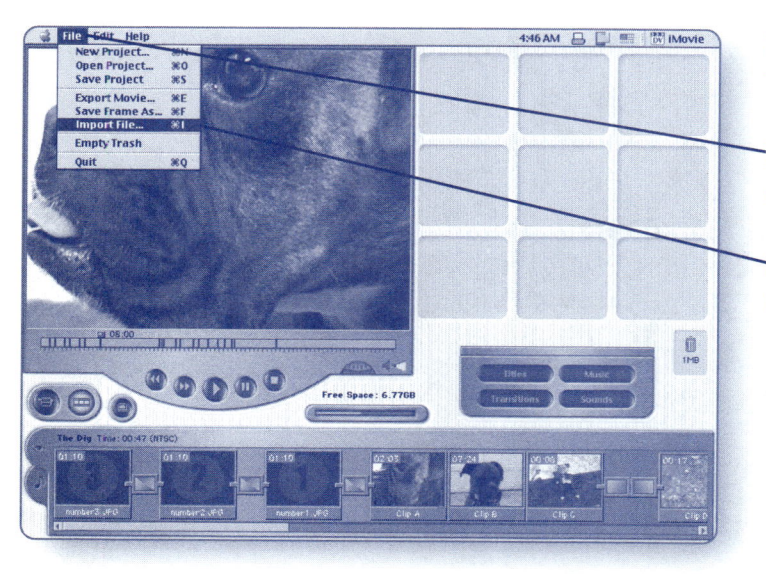

22. Open your **iMovie project**. The project will open.

23. Click on **File**. The File menu will appear.

24. Click on **Import File**. The Import File dialog box will open.

INSERTING MORE EXCITING TITLES   213

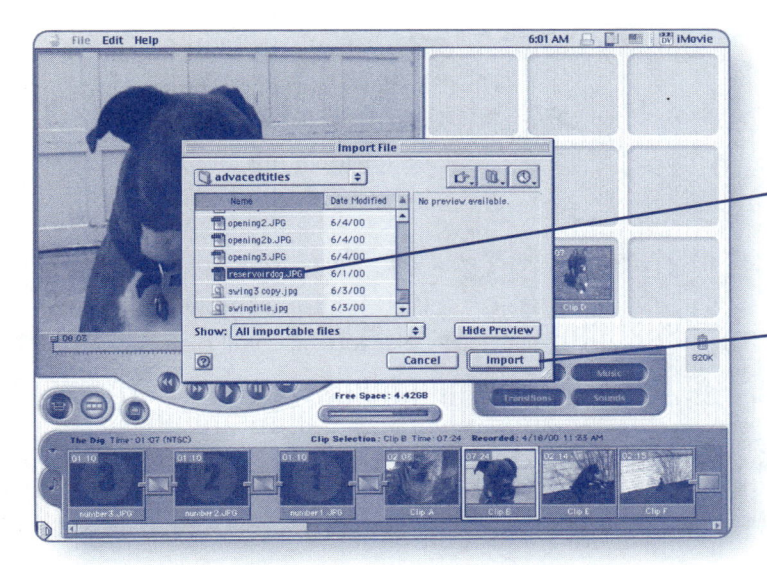

25. **Click** on the **folder** in which your image is saved. The folder will open.

26. **Click** on the **title image** you just created. The image will be selected.

27. **Click** on **Import**. The image will be imported to the iMovie Shelf.

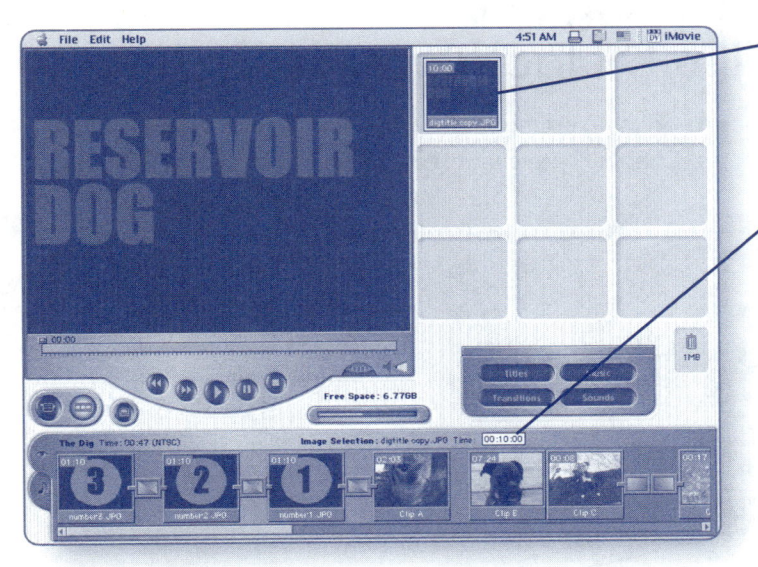

28. **Drag** the **image** from the Shelf and drop it on the Clip Viewer. The image will appear in the Clip Viewer.

29. **Set** the **duration** of your title. The duration will be set.

CHAPTER 11: TRICKS WITH TEXT

30. Press the **Shift key** and click on a **group of clips** that surround the title and countdown effects. The clips will be selected.

31. Click on the **Play button** in the Monitor window. The selected clips will play.

Inserting Silent Film Dialog Placards

Instead of using sound in this movie, let's try making this a Charlie Chaplain-like silent film, complete with those dialog placards they used to insert between the moving picture frames.

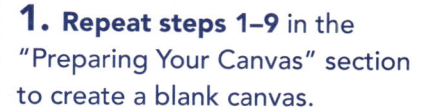

1. Repeat steps 1–9 in the "Preparing Your Canvas" section to create a blank canvas.

2. Click on the **foreground color square**. The Color Picker will open.

3. Click on a **color**. Remember to select the same (or a complementary) color as you used for the other text effects you created in this chapter.

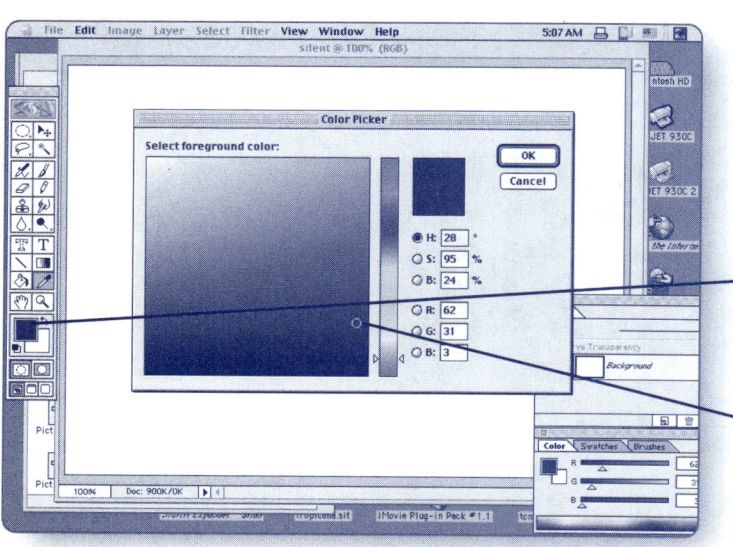

INSERTING SILENT FILM DIALOG PLACARDS 215

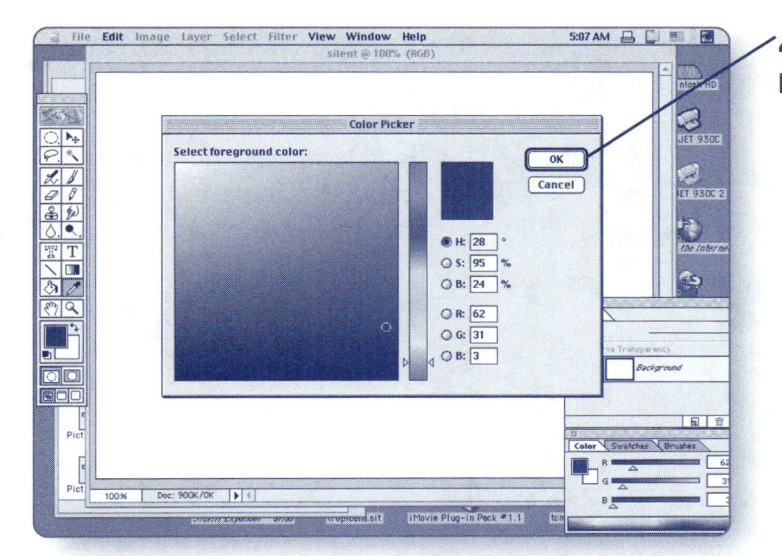

4. Click on **OK**. The color will be selected.

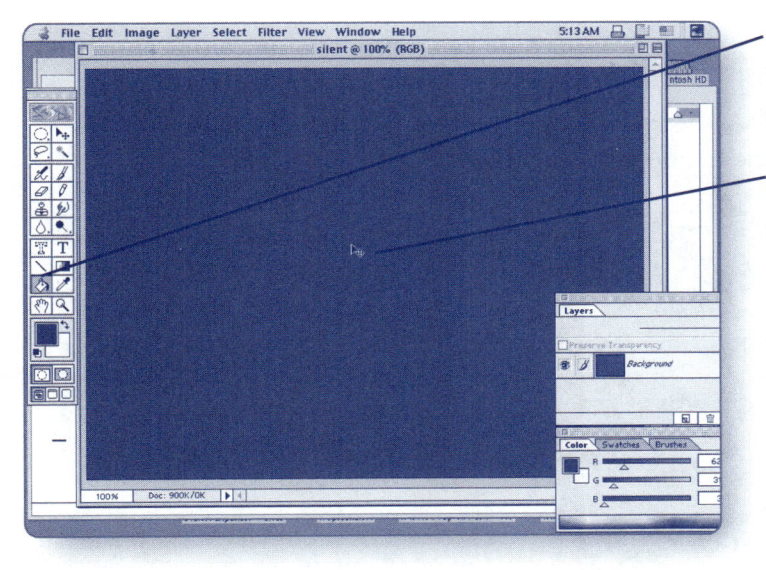

5. Click on the **Fill or Paint Bucket tool**. The tool will be selected.

6. Click on the **canvas**. The color will fill the canvas.

7. **Click** on the **foreground color square** again. The Color Picker will open.

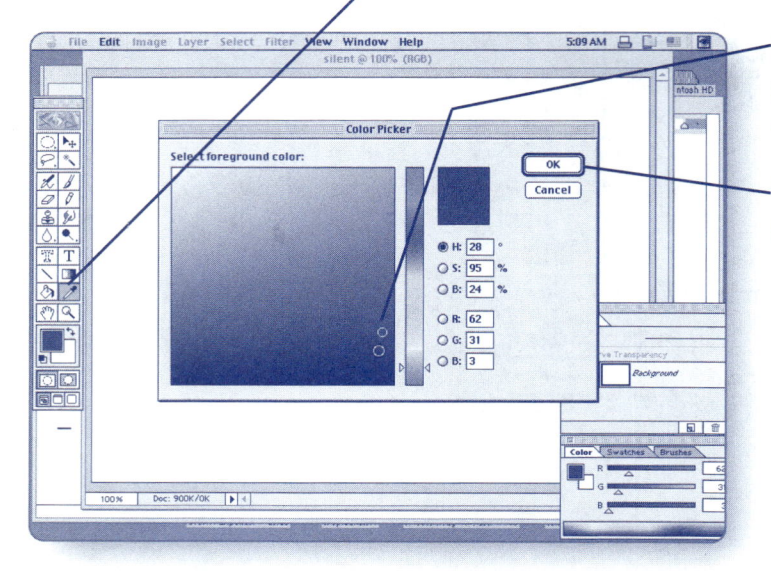

8. **Select** the **same color** as you used in the text effects you created earlier in this chapter.

9. **Click** on **OK**. The color will be selected.

10. **Click** on the **Marquee or Rectangular selection tool**. The Marquee tool's options palette will open.

11. Click and hold the **mouse pointer** in the upper-left corner of your canvas and **drag** the **mouse** down to the lower-right corner of your canvas to form a rectangle just inside the outer edge of your canvas.

12. Release the **mouse button**. A marching ants square will appear.

INSERTING SILENT FILM DIALOG PLACARDS   217

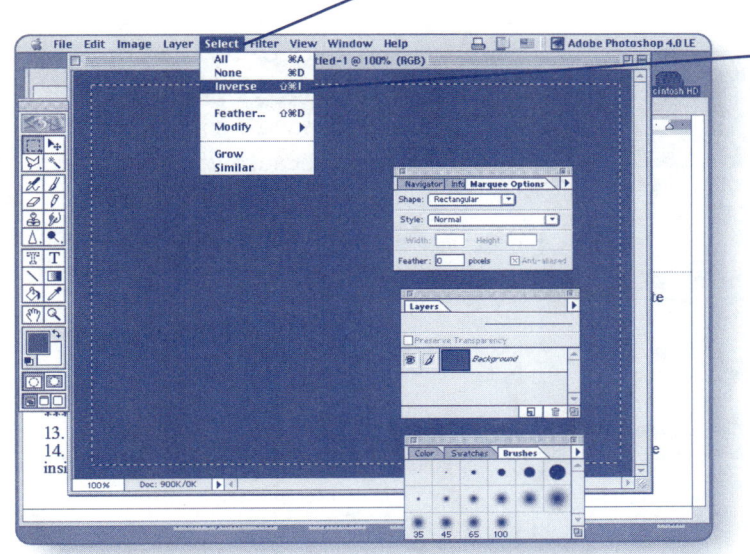

13. **Click** on **Select**. The Select menu will appear.

14. **Click** on **Inverse**. The area outside of the marching ants will be selected, instead of the inside.

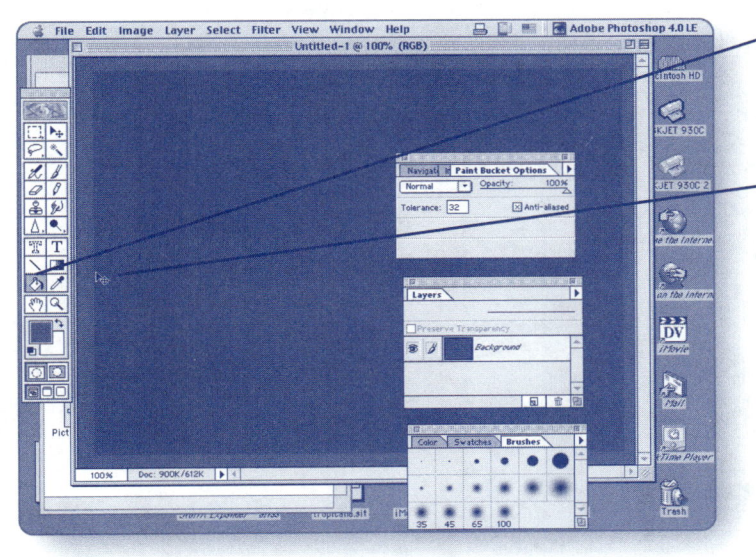

15. **Click** on the **Paint Bucket or Fill tool**. The tool will be selected.

16. **Click** in your **canvas**. The border will be filled with the color you selected.

CHAPTER 11: TRICKS WITH TEXT

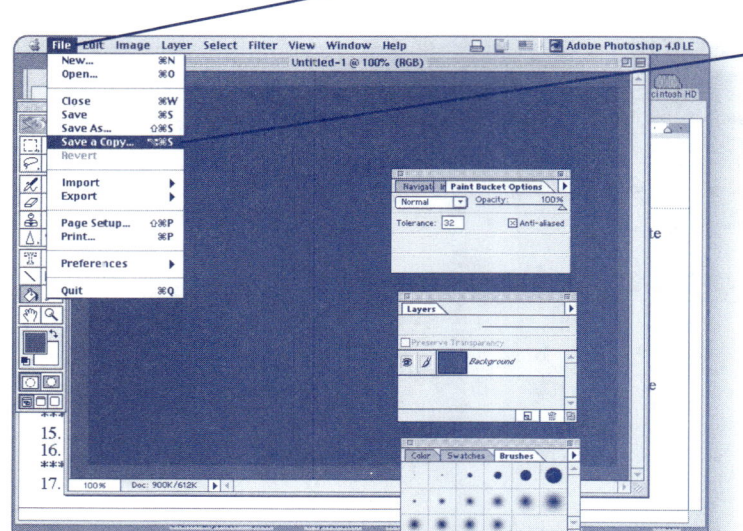

17. Click on **File**. The File menu will appear.

18. Click on **Save a Copy**. The Save dialog box will open. You want to save a copy of this image because you are going to reuse it with different sets of dialog throughout your movie.

19. Click on a **folder** in which to save your image. The folder will be selected.

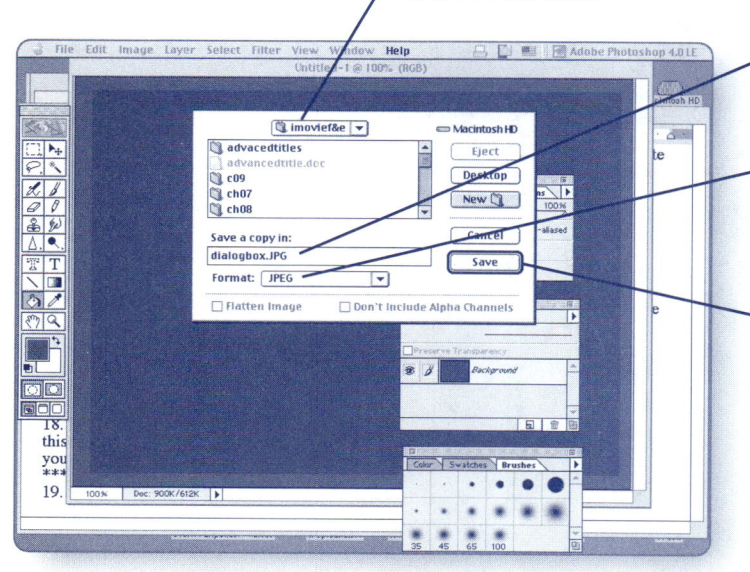

20. Type a **name** for your image.

21. Click on **JPEG** from the Format drop-down list. JPEG will be selected.

22. Click on **Save**. The file will be saved.

INSERTING SILENT FILM DIALOG PLACARDS

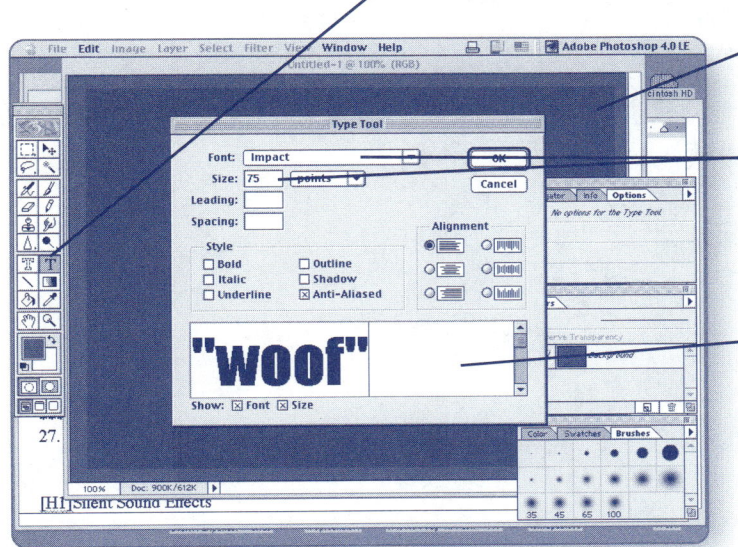

23. **Click** on the **Type tool**. The Type tool will be selected.

24. **Click** on the **canvas**. The Type Tool dialog box will open.

25. **Select** a **font style and size**. Remember to keep it the same as or complementary to your previous text.

26. **Type** your **dialog** in the text box at the bottom of the Type Tool dialog box.

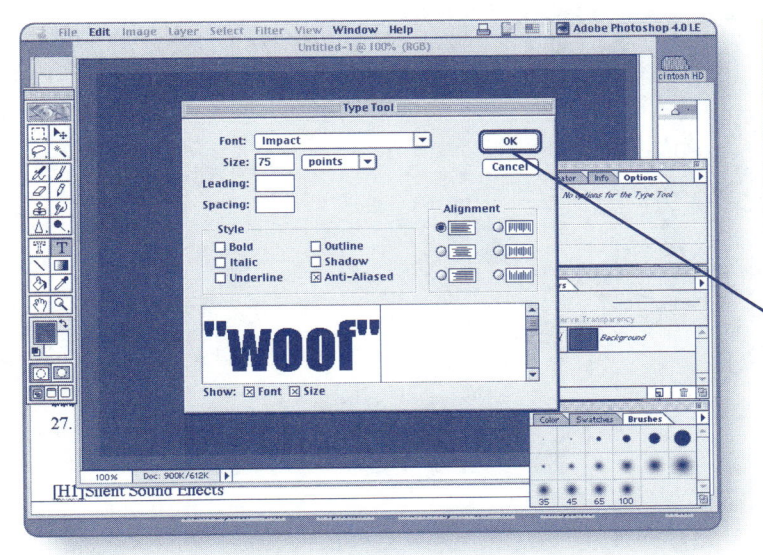

TIP
Be sure to add quotes around your text if it is the dialog of one of your actors.

27. **Click** on **OK**. The text will appear in your canvas.

220 CHAPTER 11: TRICKS WITH TEXT

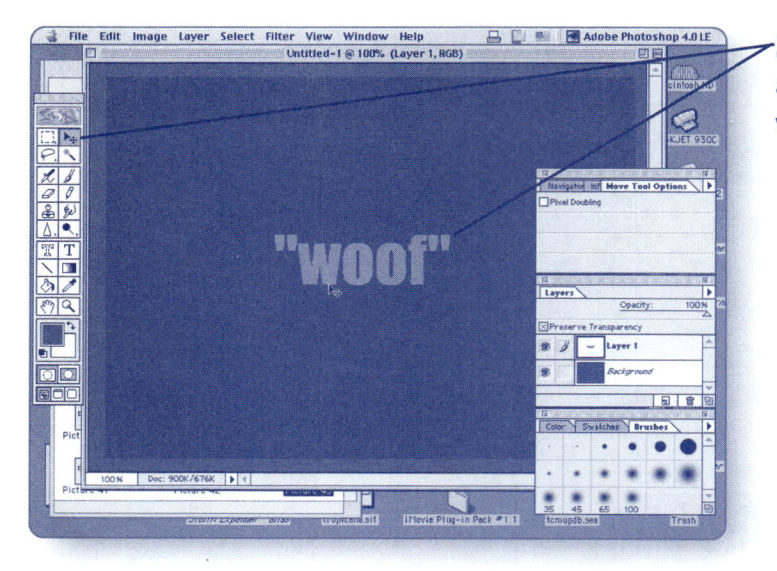

28. **Click** on the **Move tool** and **center** your **text**. The text will be centered.

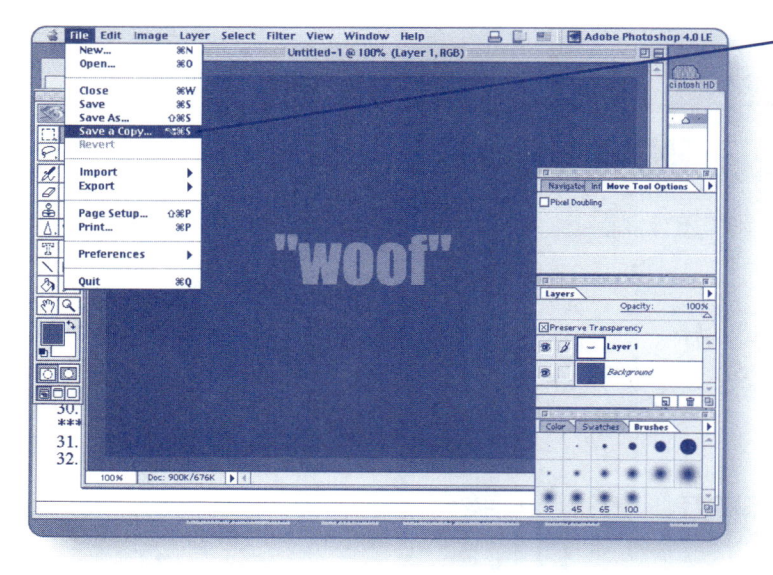

29. **Save** your **file**.

30. **Repeat** this **process** to create other silent dialog placards.

INSERTING SILENT FILM DIALOG PLACARDS   221

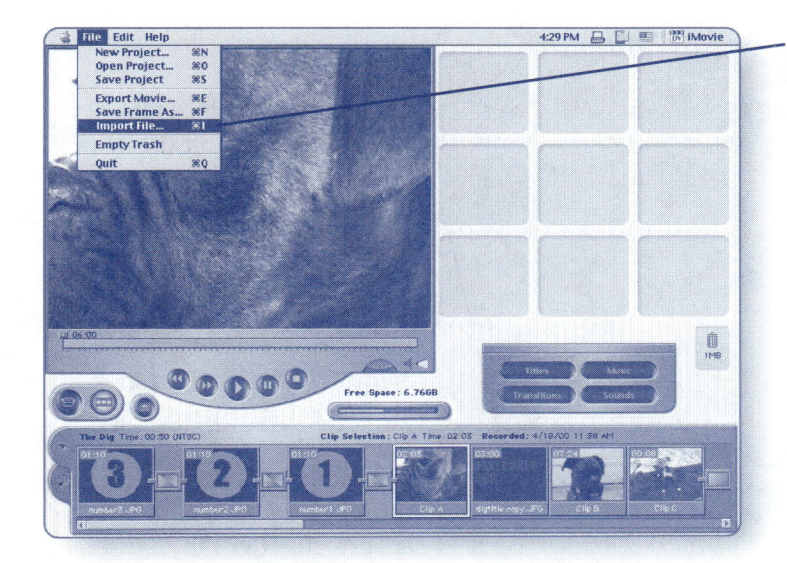

31. **Open iMovie** and **import** the **files** you created. The files will be imported.

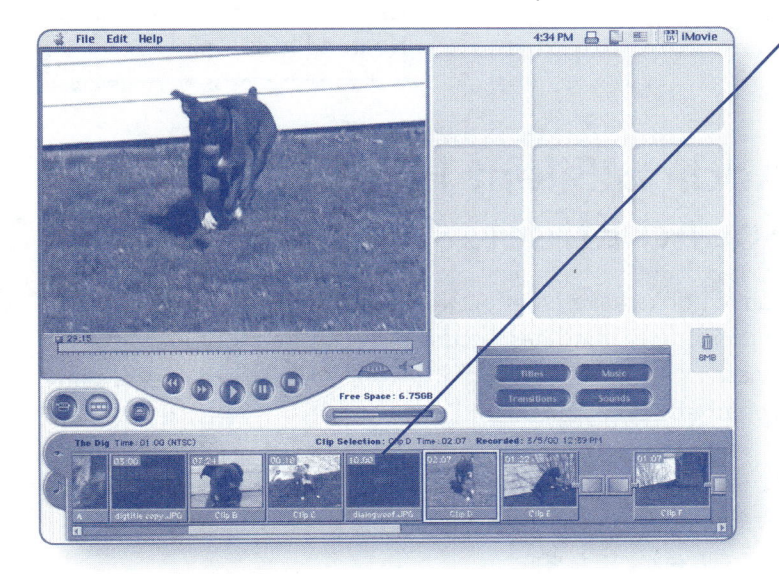

32. Move the **images** into place in your movie. The images will be positioned where you place them.

33. Adjust the **duration** of your clips. The new durations will be set.

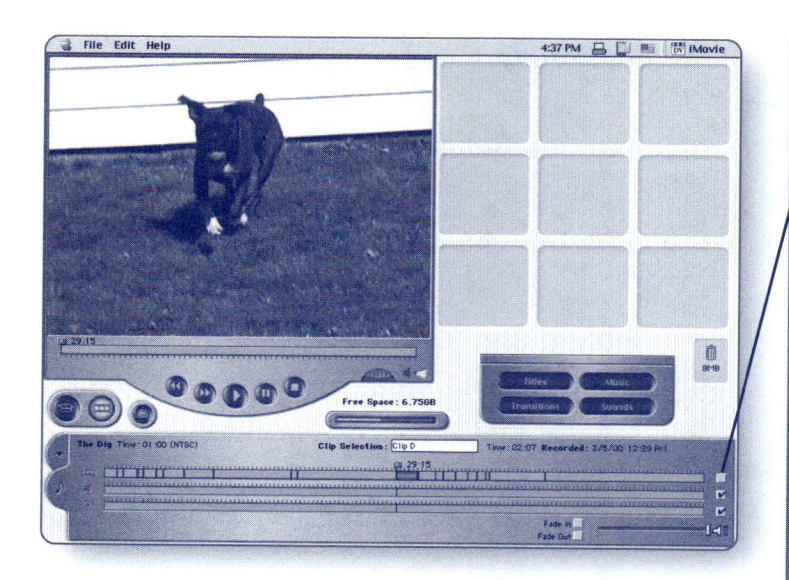

TIP

To have a true silent film, you should turn off the audio in the Audio Viewer, which you learned to do in Chapter 8, "Audio: Adding Soundtracks, Scores, Sound Effects, and Narration." Click on the Audio Viewer tab and then click to remove the check mark at the right end of the Audio bar. Also, adding a soundtrack to silent films is very effective. Try using that crazy, rapid-pace music from those old Charlie Chaplain or Buster Keaton films.

Adding Silent Film Sound Effects

Comic books have an effective way of telling the reader that an important sound has occurred. An entire storyboard frame encases the word "Pow!" or "Crash!" You can create the same type of effect in your silent iMovie.

1. Repeat steps 1 through 9 in the "Preparing Your Canvas" section, and steps 2 through 9 of the previous section to fill your canvas with color.

ADDING SILENT FILM SOUND EFFECTS 223

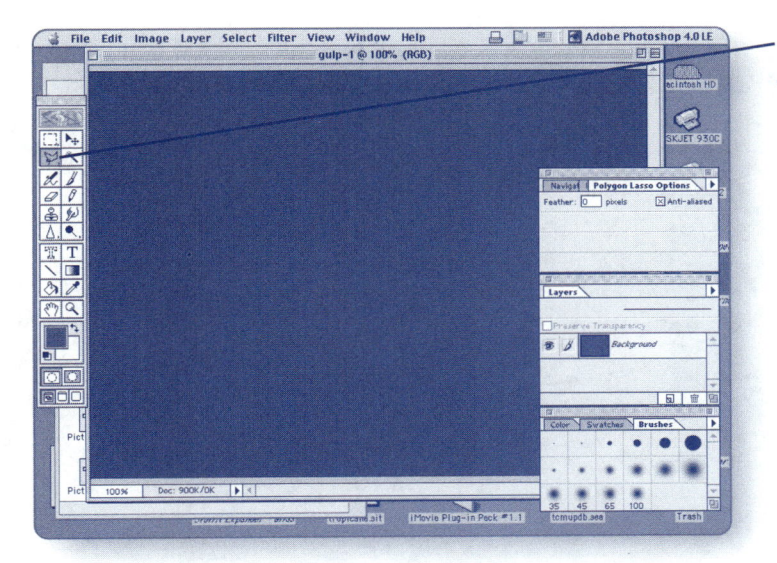

2. Click on the **Polygon Lasso tool**. The tool will be selected.

3. Click on the **canvas**. The selection line will be anchored.

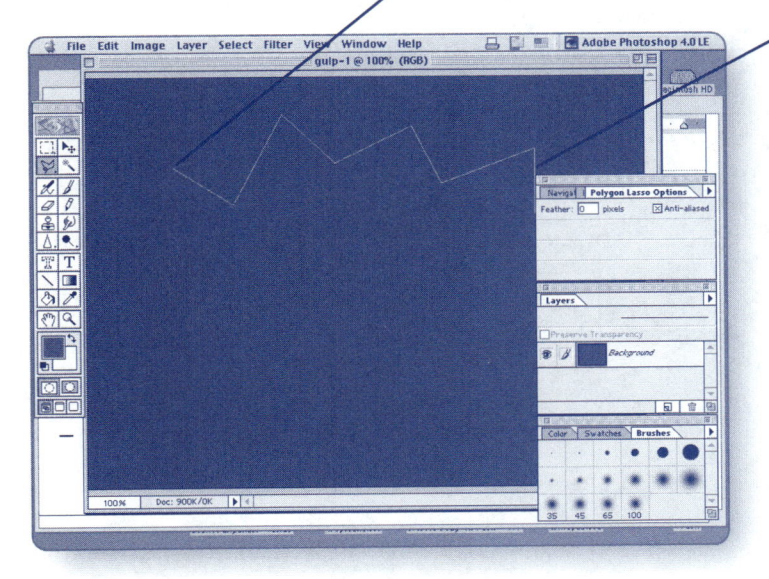

4. Move the **mouse pointer** to draw a line and **click** the **mouse** again to end the line. Continue in this fashion until you have a starburst-type shape.

CHAPTER 11: TRICKS WITH TEXT

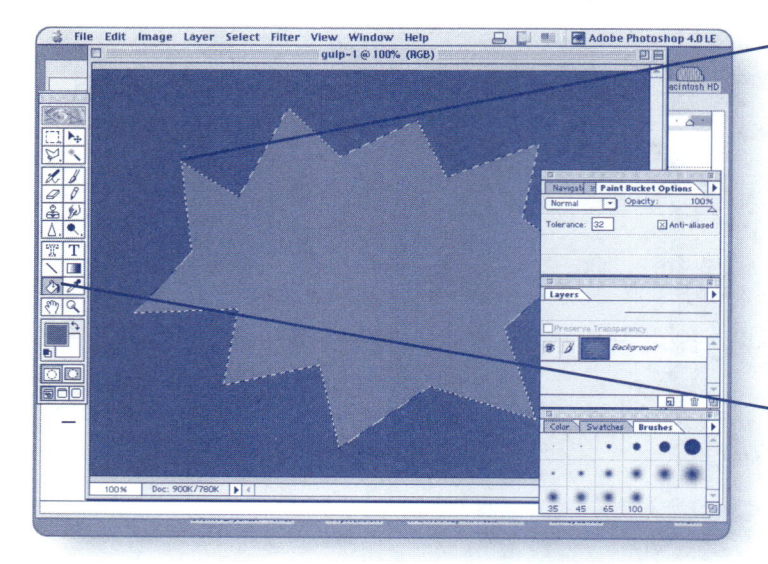

5. Connect the **final line** with the starting line. The selection will be complete and marching ants will appear to indicate your selection.

6. Select a new **color** to fill your burst shape. The color will be selected.

7. Click on the **Fill or Paint Bucket tool**. The tool will be selected.

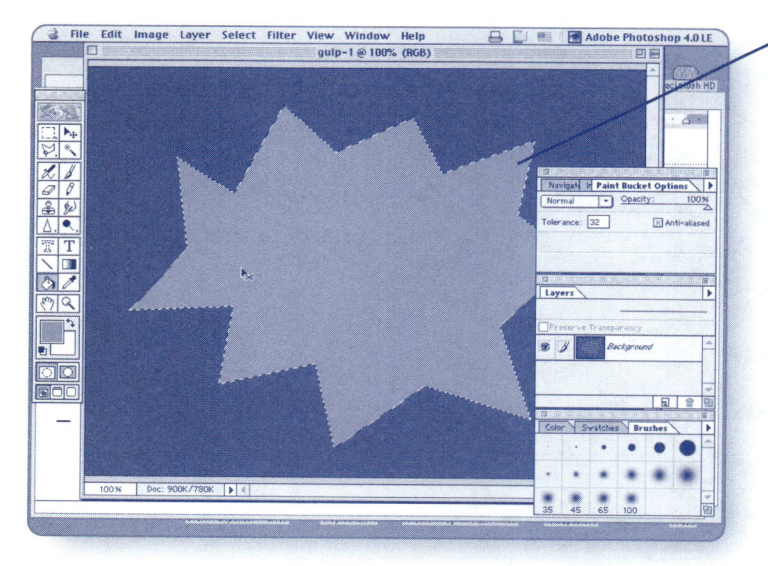

8. Click in the **burst**. The burst will fill with the new color.

ADDING SILENT FILM SOUND EFFECTS 225

9. Click on the **Type tool**. The tool will be selected.

10. Click in the **burst**. The Type Tool dialog box will open.

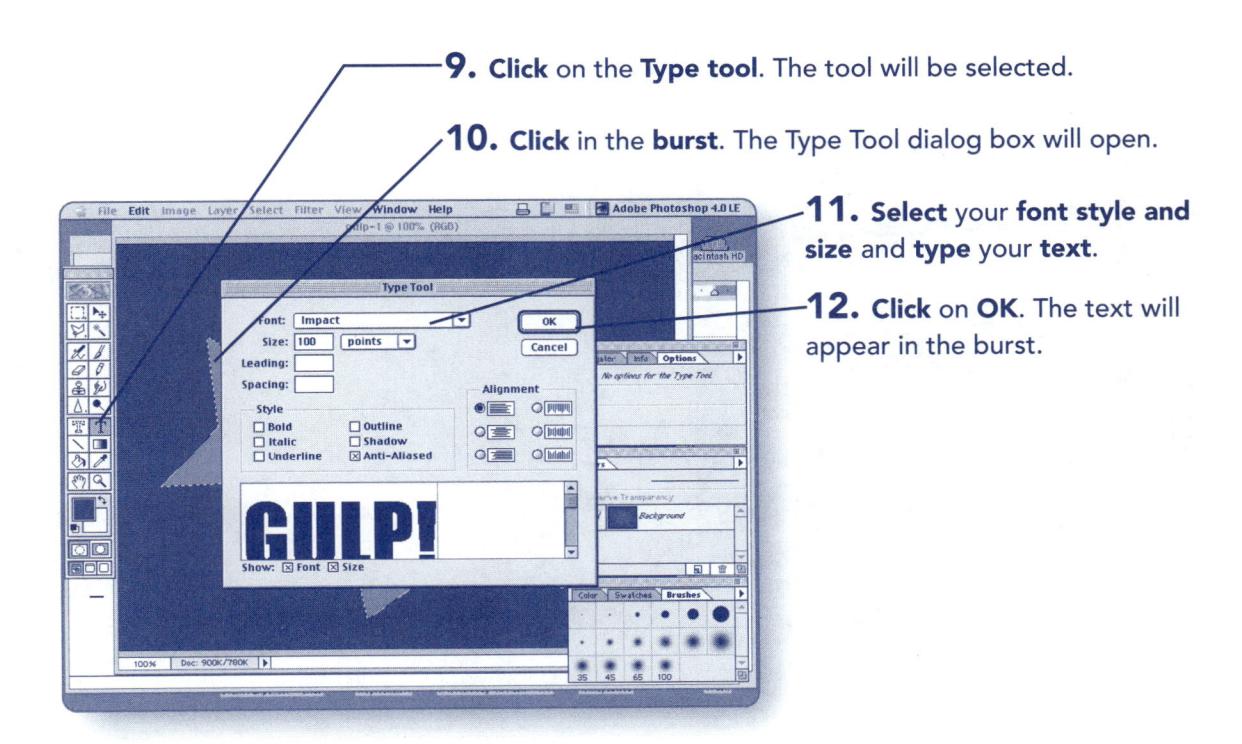

11. Select your **font style and size** and **type** your **text**.

12. Click on **OK**. The text will appear in the burst.

13. Click on the **Move tool**. The Move tool will be selected.

14. Click on the **text** and **drag it** to the center of your canvas. The text will move into place.

CHAPTER 11: TRICKS WITH TEXT

15. Click on **Layer**. The Layer menu will appear.

16. Click on **Transform**. The Transform submenu will appear.

17. Click on **Rotate**. Sizing handles will appear around your text.

18. Press and hold the **mouse button** on one of the sizing handles and **drag it** up or down. The text will move accordingly.

19. Release the **mouse button**. The text will rotate.

ADDING SILENT FILM SOUND EFFECTS   227

20. Save your **file**.

21. Repeat this **process** to create other silent film sound effect images.

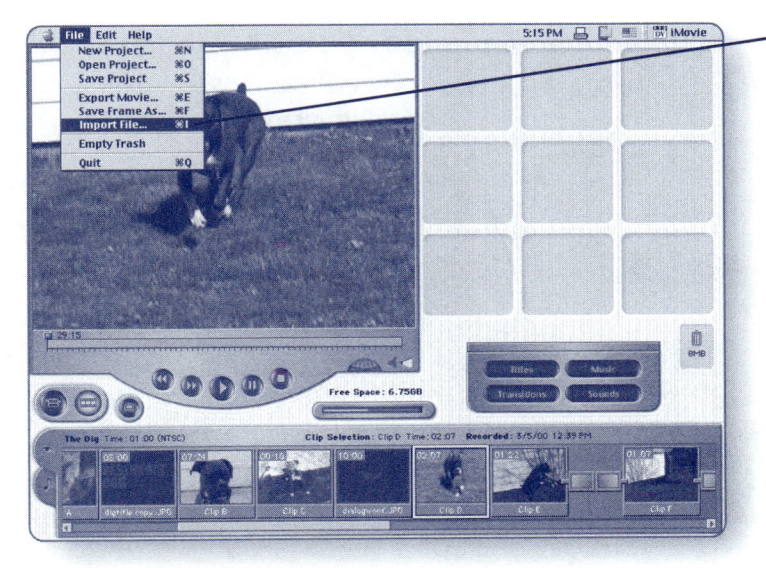

22. Open iMovie and **import** the **files** you created. The files will be imported into your iMovie project.

228 CHAPTER 11: TRICKS WITH TEXT

23. **Drag and drop** the **files** into place in the Clip Viewer. The files will appear in the Clip Viewer.

24. **Adjust** the **duration** of your clips. The new durations will be set.

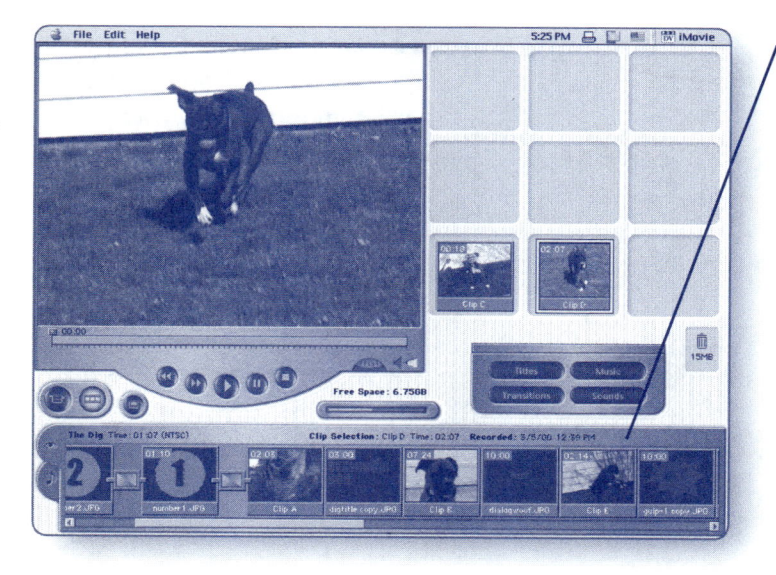

25. **Select all of your clips** and view your entire silent film masterpiece!

12

Using QuickTime with iMovie

QuickTime is the vehicle iMovie uses to view your compressed movies. When you export your movies for use in e-mail, on the Web, or on a CD-ROM, as you learned in Chapter 10, "Compressing and Exporting Your Movies," iMovie converts your project into a compressed QuickTime movie. Usually, the QuickTime program is already installed on your Mac. A simple, inexpensive upgrade to QuickTime Pro can unleash more creative effects for your iMovies. In this chapter, you'll learn how to:

- Upgrade to QuickTime Pro
- Open a QuickTime movie
- Use the QuickTime Player
- Edit QuickTime clips
- Import QuickTime clips into your iMovies
- Add special QuickTime video effects

Upgrading to QuickTime Pro

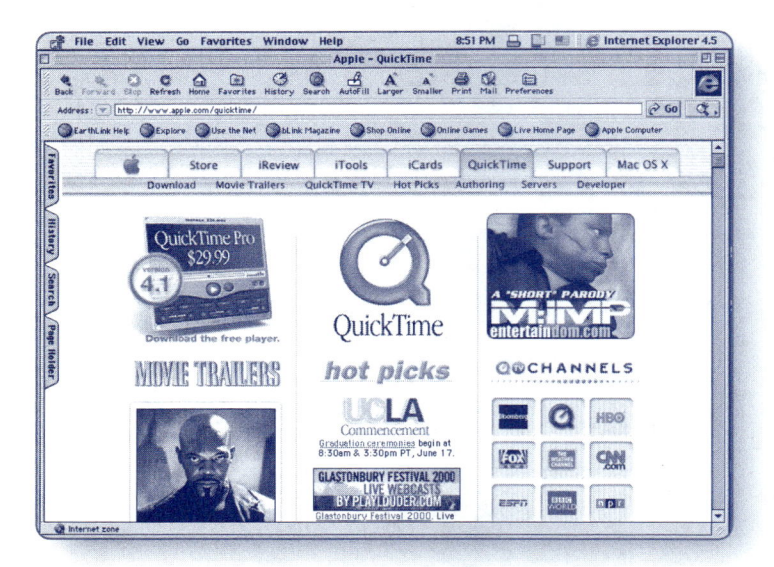

Although some of the features described in this chapter are available with the free version of QuickTime that you probably already have, I focus on features that are available with the QuickTime Pro upgrade. I highly recommend that you make this upgrade, which can be done easily. At this time it's only $30, and it's available at Apple's Web site (http://www.apple.com).

After you purchase the Pro upgrade, you will receive a key number that will unlock the hidden features in your QuickTime program.

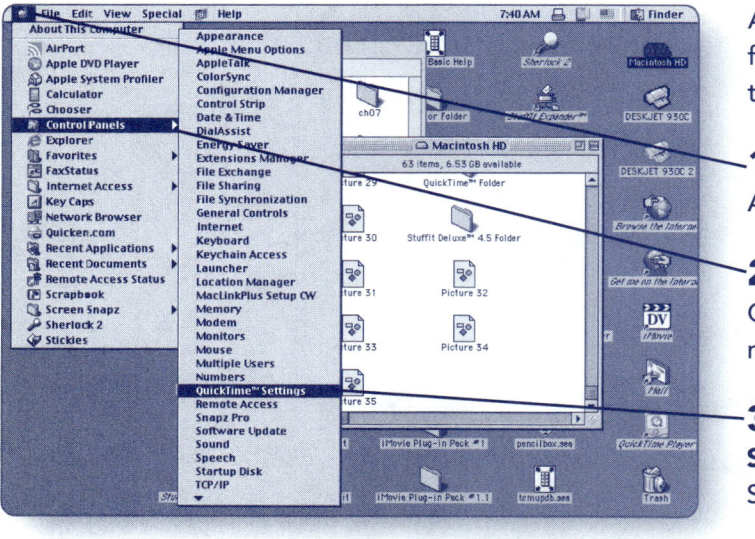

After receiving the key number, follow these steps to unleash the bonus features:

1. Click on the **Apple icon**. The Apple menu will appear.

2. Hold the **mouse** over Control Panels. A cascading menu will appear.

3. Click on **QuickTime Settings**. The QuickTime Settings dialog box will open.

OPENING A QUICKTIME MOVIE   **231**

4. Select Registration in the QuickTime Settings box, if it isn't already selected.

5. Click on the **Enter Registration button**. A text box will open.

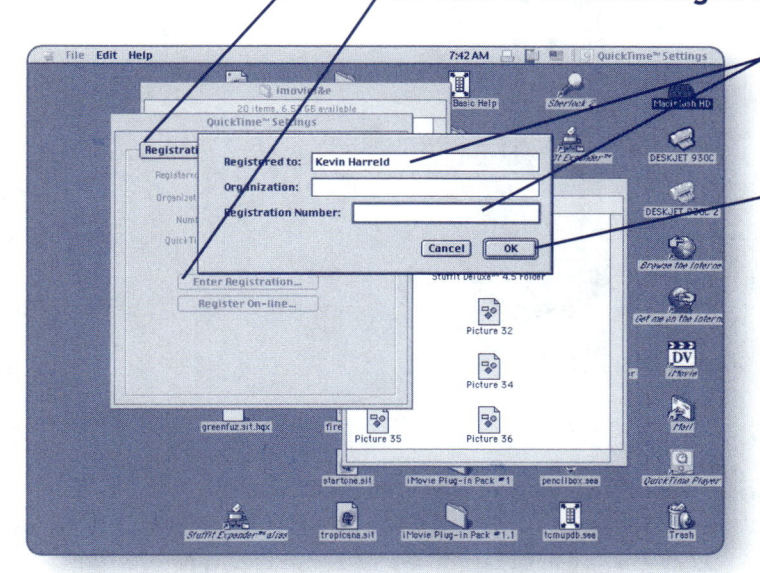

6. Enter your **name and key number** exactly the way you received it.

7. Click on **OK**. You will now be able to unlock the great features of QuickTime Pro.

Opening a QuickTime Movie

If you have exported one of your iMovies to the QuickTime setting, as you learned in Chapter 10, "Compressing and Exporting Your Movies," iMovie has created a QuickTime movie for you. There are two ways to open a QuickTime movie.

1. Navigate to the **folder** in which you saved your QuickTime movie.

2. Double-click on the **movie**. The movie will open in the QuickTime Player.

You can also open a QuickTime movie through the desktop icon and menu commands.

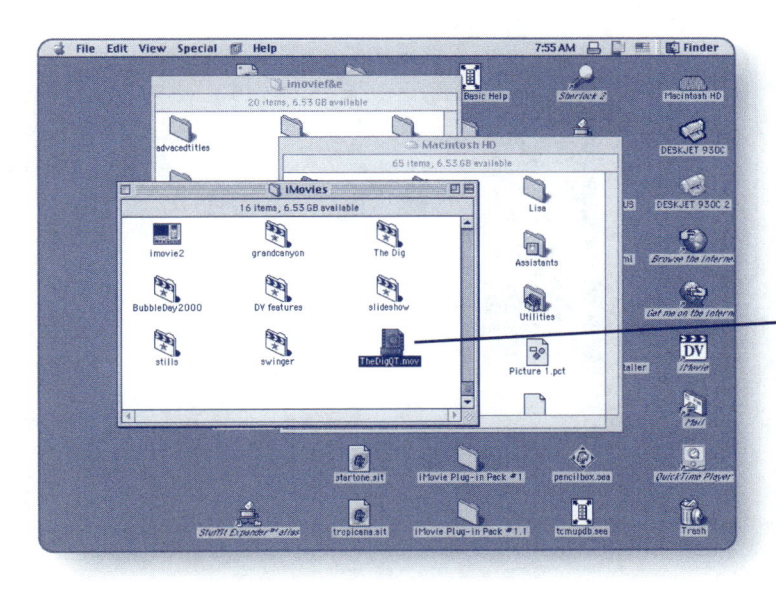

232 CHAPTER 12: USING QUICKTIME WITH iMOVIE

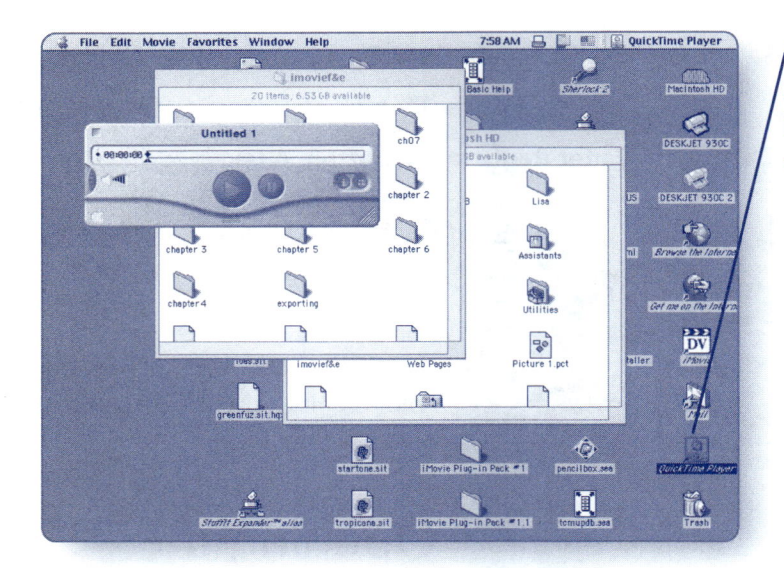

1. Double-click on the **QuickTime Player desktop icon**. The QuickTime Player will open.

2. Click on **File**. The File menu will appear.

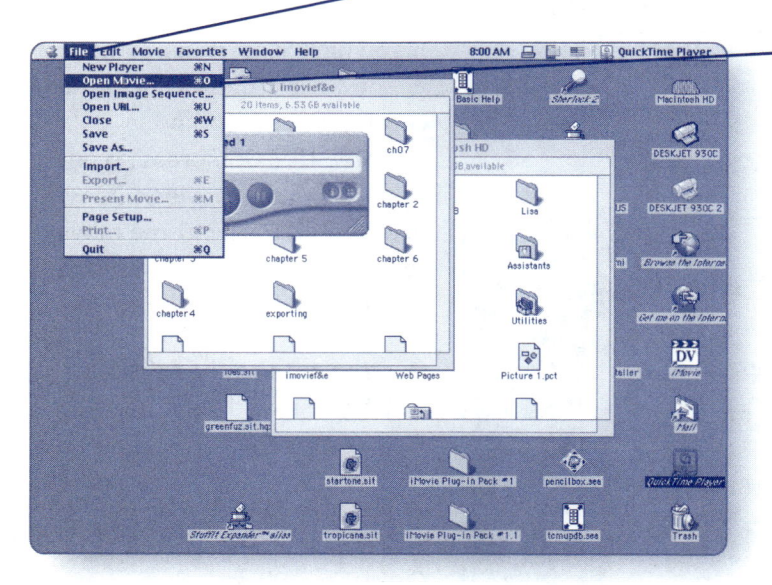

3. Click on **Open Movie**. An Open dialog box will open.

OPENING A QUICKTIME MOVIE 233

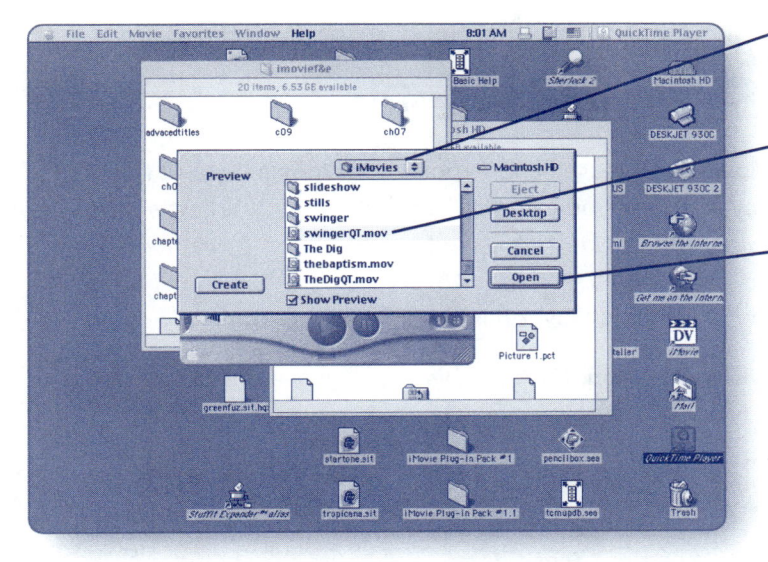

4. Navigate to the **folder** that contains your QuickTime movie.

5. Click on the **movie**. The movie will be highlighted

6. Click on **Open**.

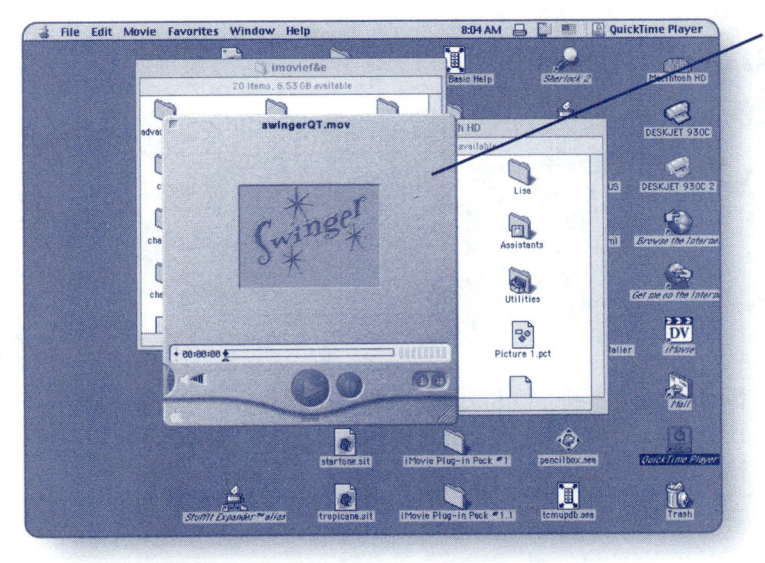

The movie will open in the QuickTime player.

Understanding the QuickTime Player

iMovie compresses and exports your movies into QuickTime's Player. There, you can play back your movie, adjust sound levels, and so on.

The QuickTime Player has the following features:

- **Close button**. Click on this box to close the QuickTime Monitor window.

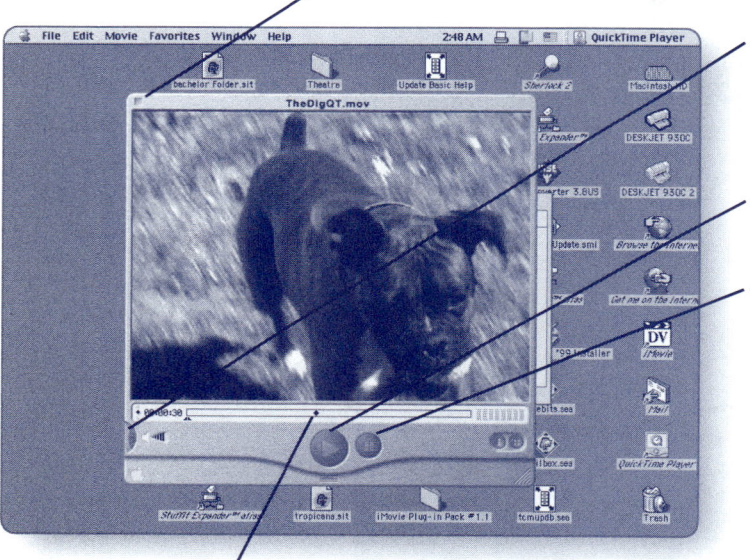

- **Volume wheel**. Press and hold the mouse button on this and drag up or down to control volume.

- **Play button**. Click on this button to play the movie.

- **Pause/Stop button**. Click on this button to stop playback of the movie.

- **Scroll bar**. Press and hold the mouse button on the black diamond and drag it left or right to move forward or backward quickly in your movie.

UNDERSTANDING THE QUICKTIME PLAYER 235

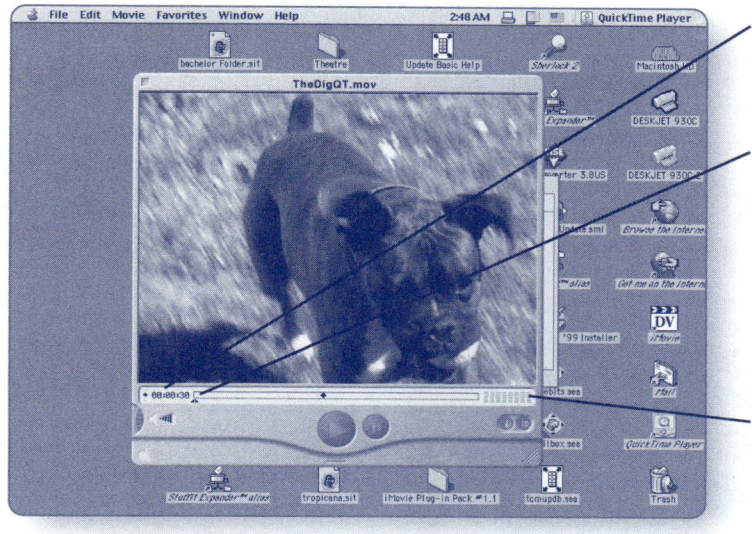

- **Counter**. Indicates, in hours, minutes, and seconds, where you are in the movie.

- **Selection handles**. Press and hold the mouse button on these black triangles and drag them to select a portion of your movie. This feature is only available in the QuickTime Pro update.

- **Audio levels**. Indicates the audio frequencies.

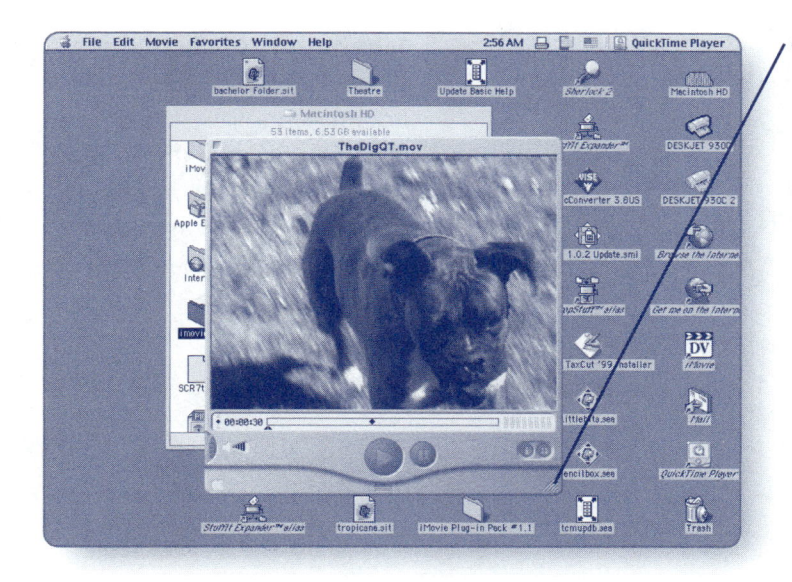

- **Resize handle**. Press and hold the mouse button on these slanted grooves and drag down and to the right to expand the Player, or up and to the left to shrink the Player.

CHAPTER 12: USING QUICKTIME WITH iMOVIE

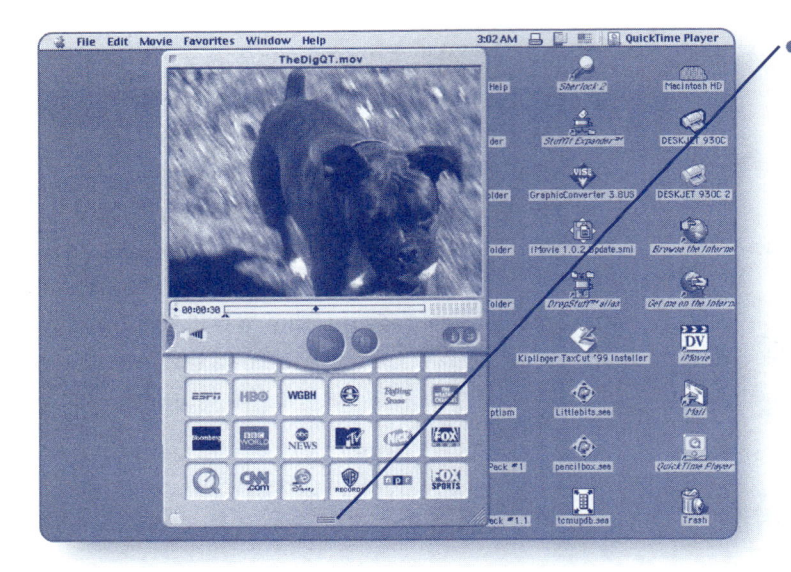

- **Favorites drawer**. Press and hold the mouse button on these horizontal grooves and drag down to reveal the Favorites panel. Here, you add icons of your movies.

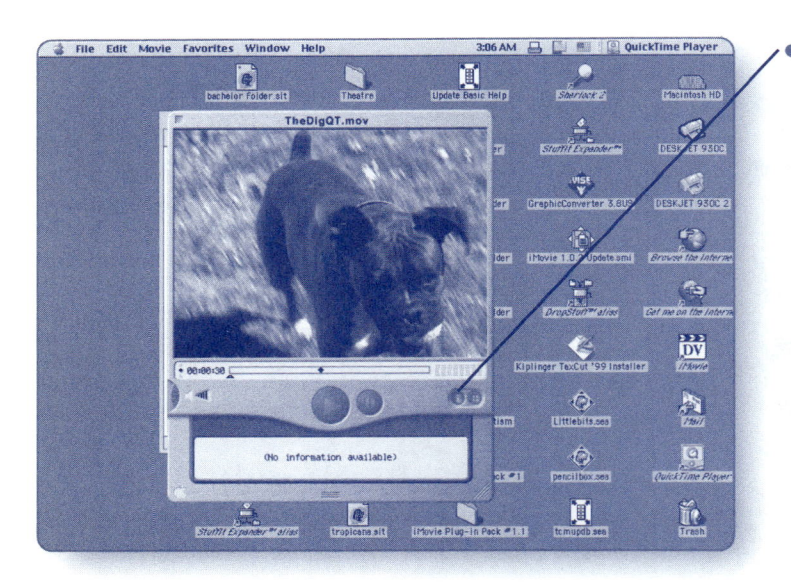

- **Info button**. Click on this button to reveal information about the movie you are viewing. Click it again to hide it. Usually this will only house information, such as copyright info, for movies that you download from the Web.

SIZING AND PLAYBACK WITH MENU COMMANDS 237

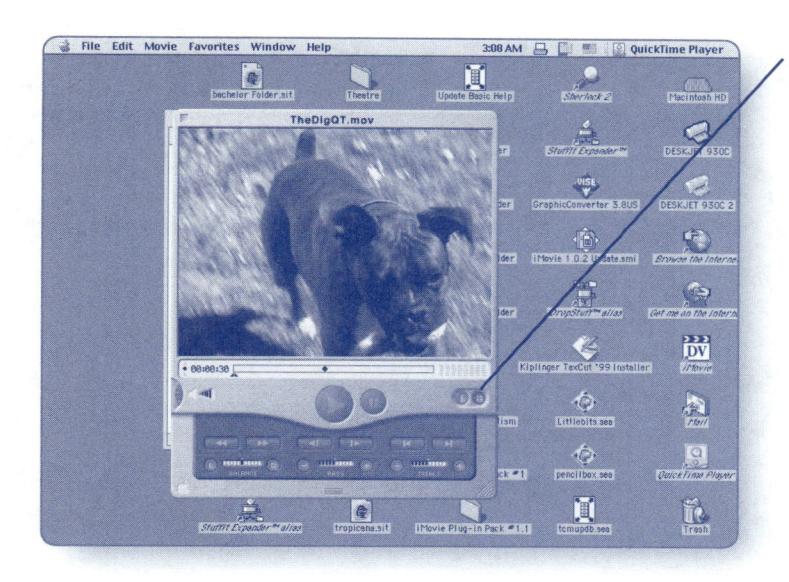

- **Shirt button**. Click on this button to open more precise navigation and sound controls. Click the Shirt button again to close the pop-up menu.

Sizing and Playback with Menu Commands

QuickTime Pro has a few menu commands that allow you to resize the QuickTime player and screen. It also has some different ways that you can play back your movies in QuickTime.

1. Click on **Movie**. The Movie menu will appear.

2. Click on one of the following **sizing options**.

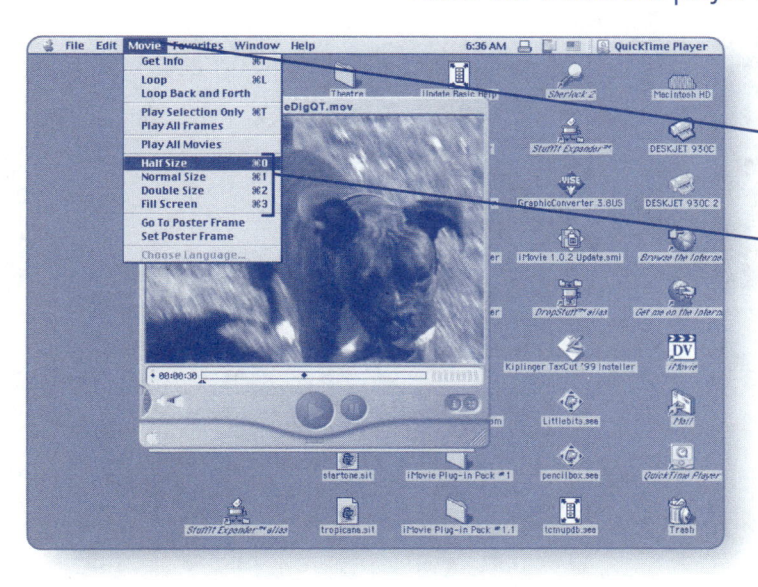

238 CHAPTER 12: USING QUICKTIME WITH iMOVIE

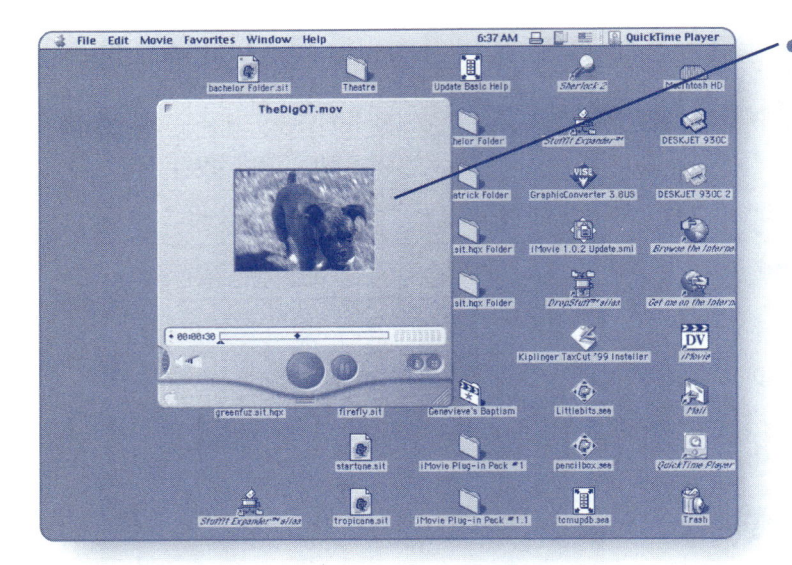

- **Half Size**. Your movie screen will shrink to half the normal size.

- **Double Size**. Your movie will expand to double its normal size.

SIZING AND PLAYBACK WITH MENU COMMANDS 239

- **Fill Screen**. Your movie will expand to fit nicely on your computer screen.

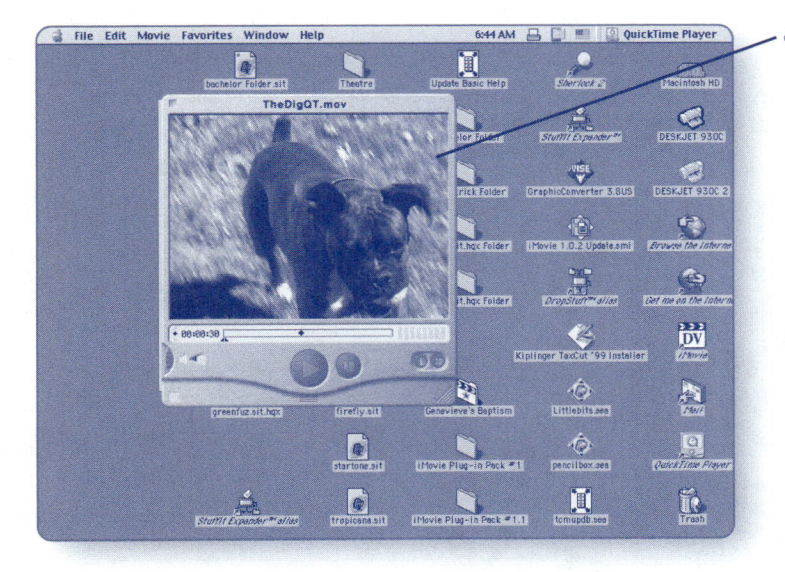

- **Normal Size**. Your movie will revert to its normal size.

CHAPTER 12: USING QUICKTIME WITH iMOVIE

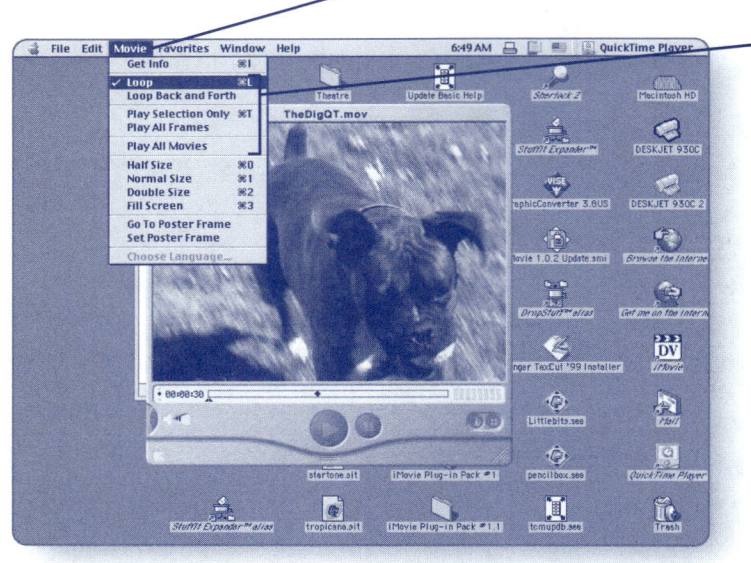

3. Click on **Movie**. The Movie menu will appear again.

4. Click on one of the following **playback options**:

- **Loop**. When you click on the Play button, the movie will continue to play over and over until you click on Stop.

- **Loop Back and Forth**. When you click on the Play button, the movie will continue to play forward and then backward, if you can believe that, over and over again until you click Stop.

- **Play All Frames**. When you click on the Play button, QuickTime will play every frame of the movie, instead of a lesser amount of frames, in order to reduce the file size.

- **Play Selection Only**. If you have moved the selection handles to highlight only a portion of your movie, only that portion of the movie will play when you click on the Play button.

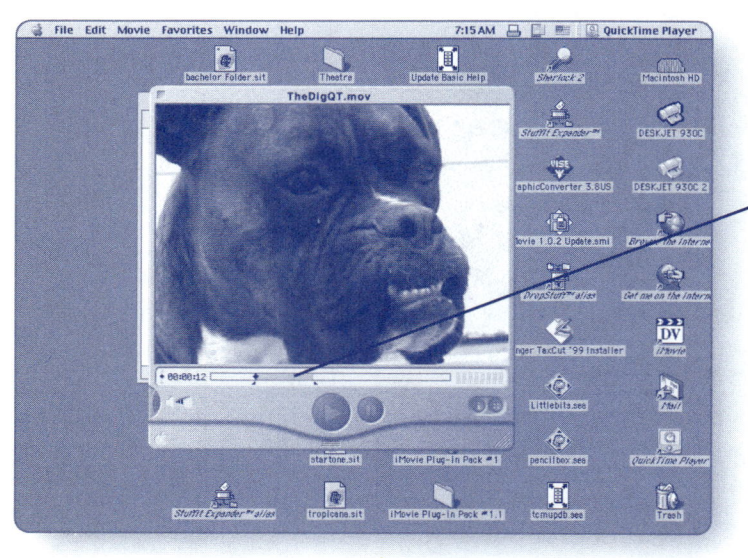

SHOWING YOUR MOVIE ON YOUR COMPUTER SCREEN   241

- **Play All Movies**. If you have two or more QuickTime movies open, click on this option and all your movies will begin playing at once.

Showing Your Movie on Your Computer Screen

Perhaps you want to see your QuickTime movie on your computer screen, but you're distracted by all the other stuff on your desktop. You can play your movie minus all the icons, toolbars, and so on, so that all the attention is on your masterpiece.

1. Open your **QuickTime movie**. The movie will open.

2. Click on **File**. The File menu will appear.

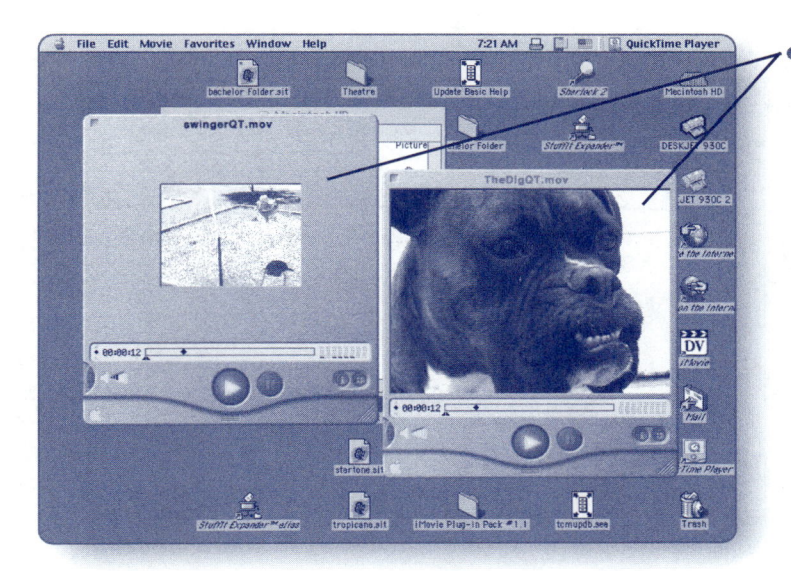

3. Click on **Present Movie**. The Present Movie dialog box will open.

CHAPTER 12: USING QUICKTIME WITH iMOVIE

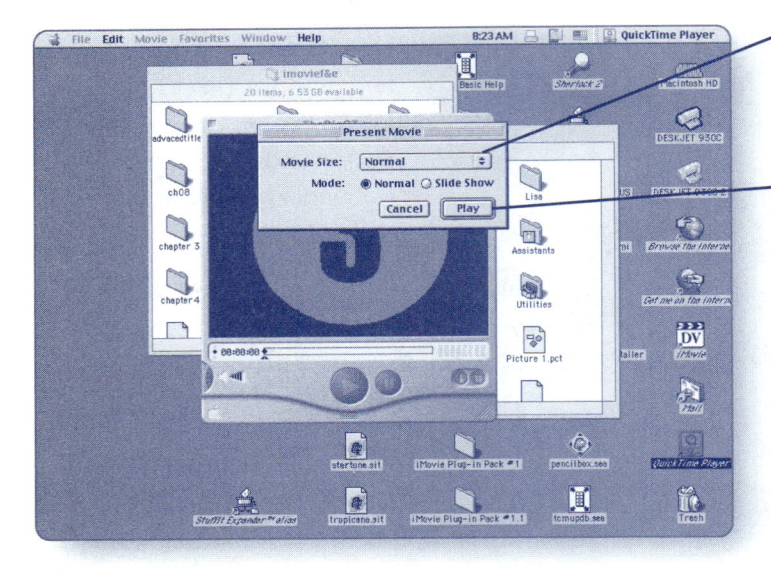

4. Click on the up and down **arrows** to the right of the Movie Size box and **select** a **size**.

5. Click on **Play**. The movie will play on your screen with a black background.

Editing QuickTime Clips

Similar to iMovie, QuickTime allows you to edit your video and sound clips.

Cutting, Copying, and Pasting

You can cut, copy, and paste clips or portions of clips within a QuickTime movie or movies.

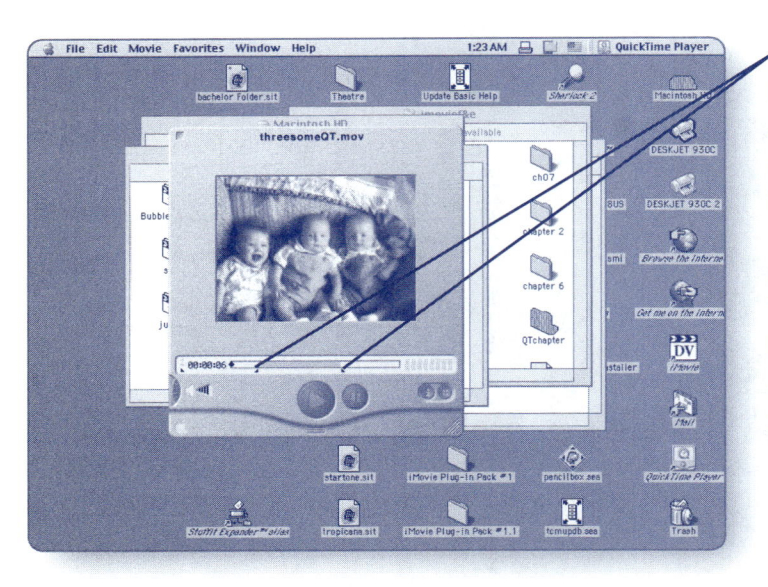

1. Press and hold the **mouse button** on the black triangles and **drag** the **triangles** left and right to select a portion of your movie.

2. Release the **mouse button**. That portion of your movie will be selected, indicated by the gray shaded area on the Scrubber bar.

EDITING QUICKTIME CLIPS 243

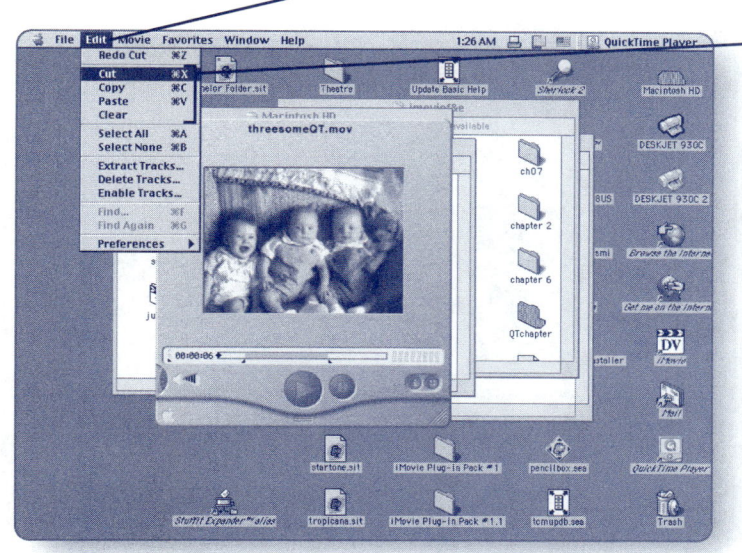

3. Click on **Edit**. The Edit menu will appear.

4. Click on **one** of the following options:

- **Cut**. This will cut your selected footage and hold it on your Clipboard. The gray shaded area (the selected area) on the Scrubber bar will disappear.

- **Copy**. This will copy your selected footage and hold it on your Clipboard.

- **Clear**. This will clear the selected footage altogether. The gray shaded area on the Scrubber bar will disappear.

- **Paste**. This will allow you to paste your cut or copied selections into a different place within the same QuickTime movie, or into another QuickTime movie.

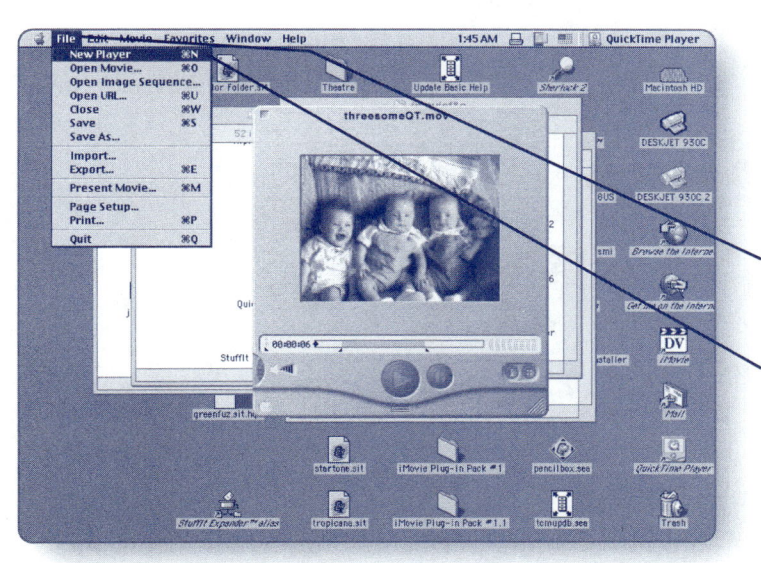

Now you have cut or copied footage on your Clipboard to paste in the movie you already have open or into another QuickTime movie.

5. Click on **File**. The File menu will appear.

6. Click on **New Player**. A new QuickTime Player will open.

244 CHAPTER 12: USING QUICKTIME WITH iMOVIE

7. Click on **File**. The File menu will appear.

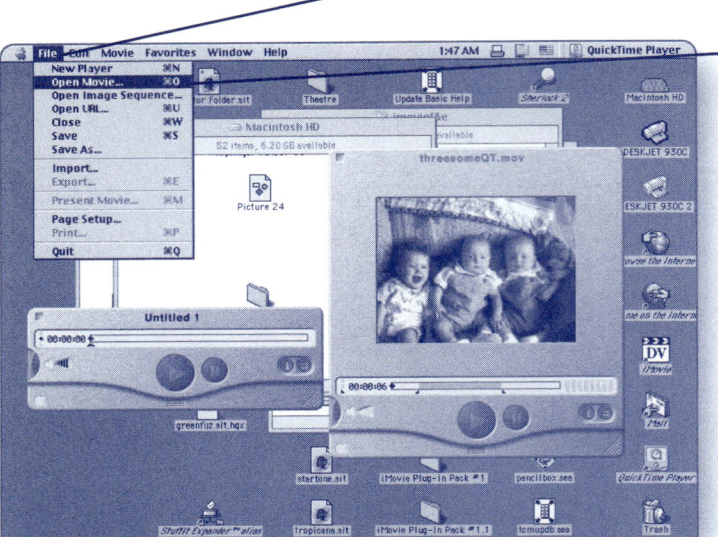

8. Click on **Open Movie**. An Open dialog box will open.

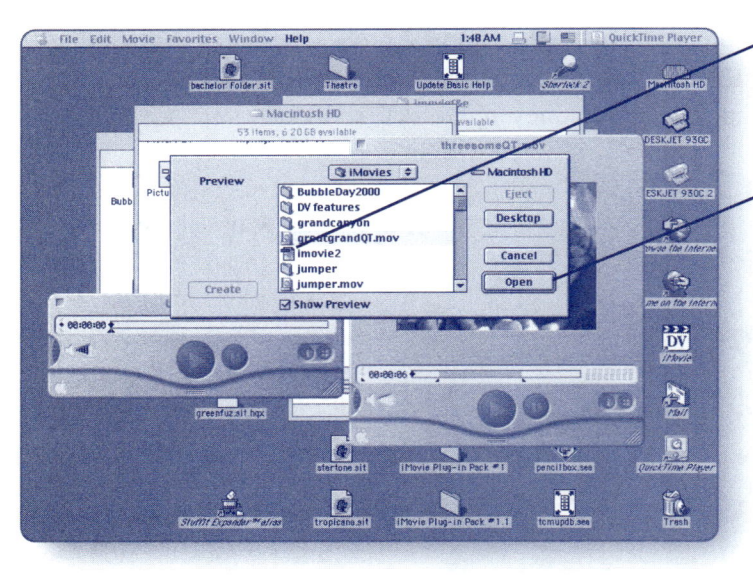

9. Click on the **QuickTime movie** to which you want to add your copied or cut footage.

10. Click on **Open**. The movie will open in the new QuickTime Player.

11. **Press and hold** the **mouse button** on the black diamond and **drag** the **diamond** to where you want to add the copied or cut footage from your other QuickTime movie.

12. **Click** on **Edit**. The Edit menu will appear.

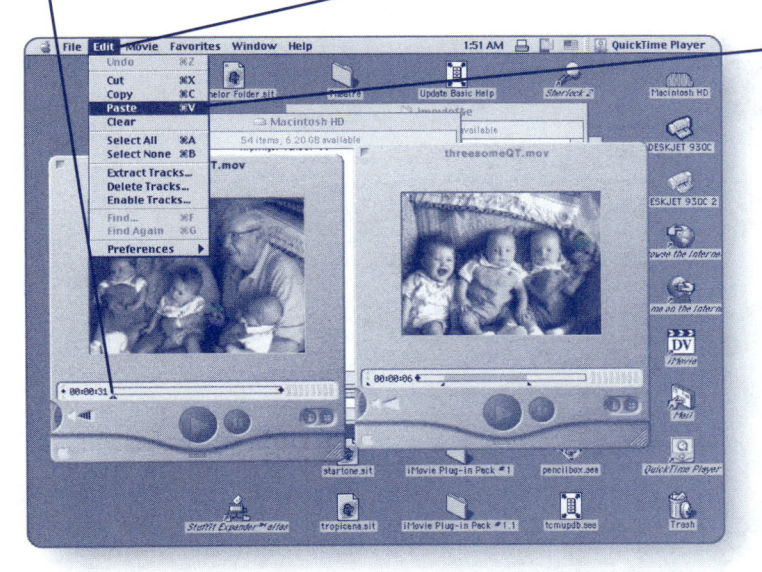

13. **Click** on **Paste**. The copied or cut footage will appear in the new QuickTime movie.

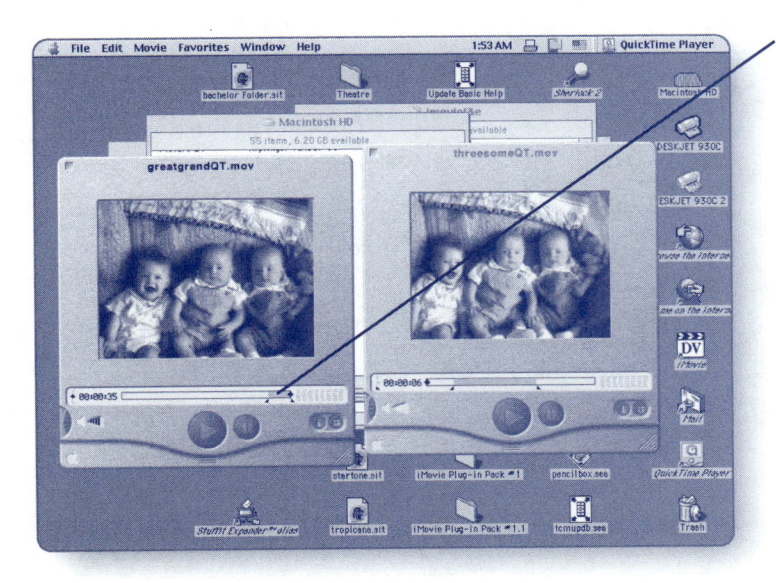

Now, you can save a version of your QuickTime movie with the added footage without disturbing the original movie.

CHAPTER 12: USING QUICKTIME WITH iMOVIE

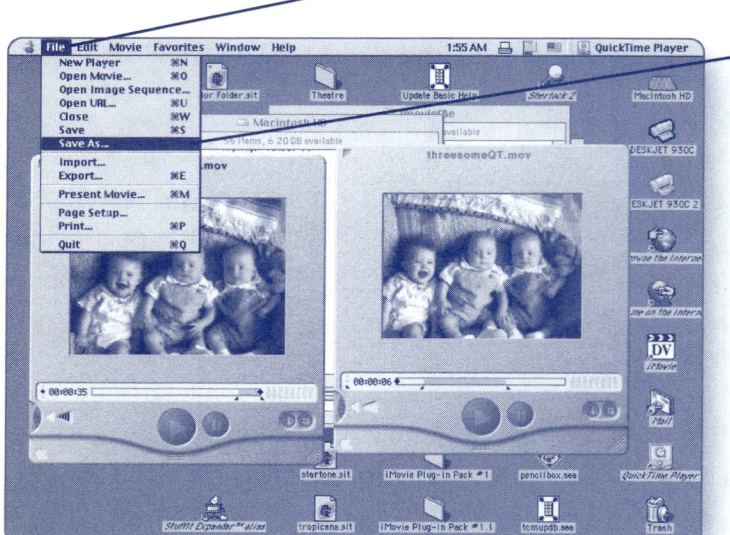

14. Click on **File**. The File menu will appear.

15. Click on **Save As**. The Save As dialog box will open.

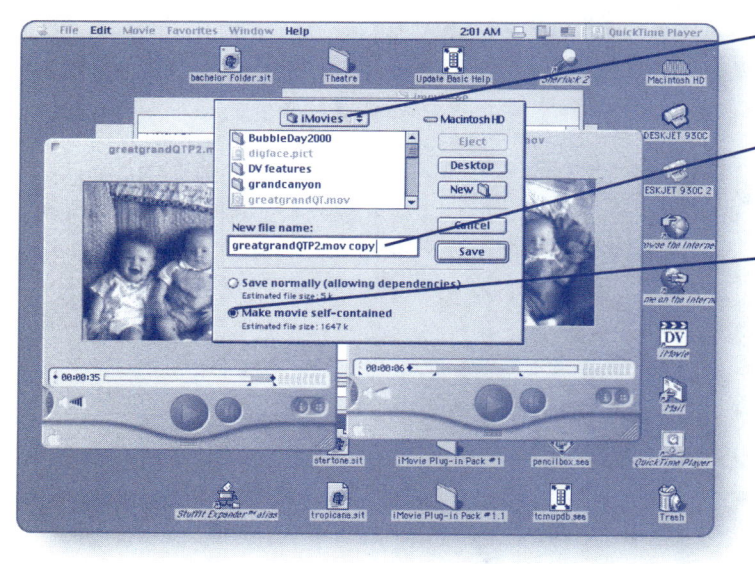

16. Select a **folder** in which to save your new movie.

17. Type a **new name** for the new movie.

18. Click on **Make movie self-contained**. QuickTime will create an edited copy of your movie.

EDITING QUICKTIME CLIPS 247

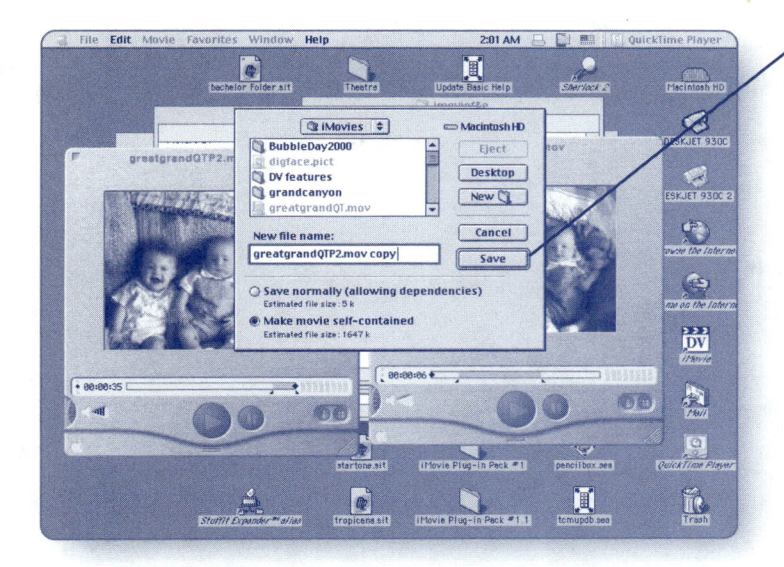

19. **Click** on **Save**. The new movie will be saved.

Extracting, Enabling, and Deleting

You can also turn on or off, extract, or delete the video clips and sound tracks in a QuickTime movie. Start by opening a QuickTime movie that you want to manipulate.

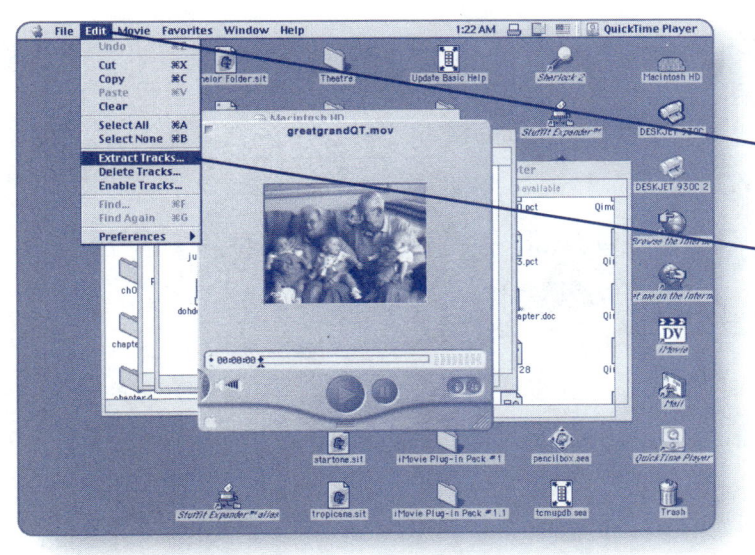

Extracting Video and Sound Tracks

1. **Click** on **Edit**. The Edit menu will appear.

2. **Click** on **Extract Tracks**. The Extract Tracks dialog box will open.

CHAPTER 12: USING QUICKTIME WITH iMOVIE

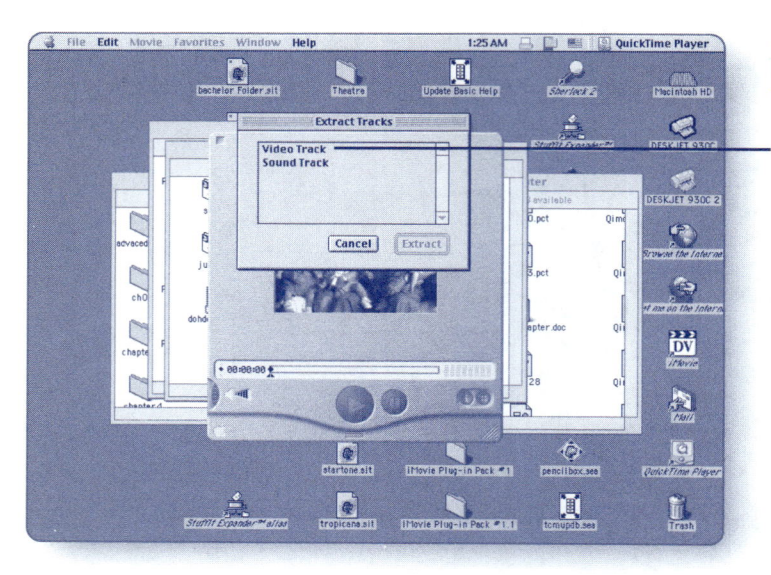

3. **Click** on one or more of the following **options**:

- **Video Track**.

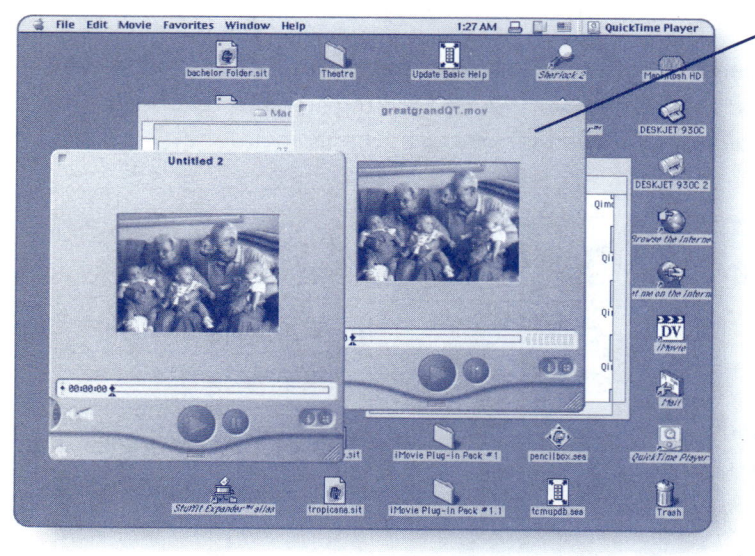

This will extract a copy of the video track and insert it into a new QuickTime Player.

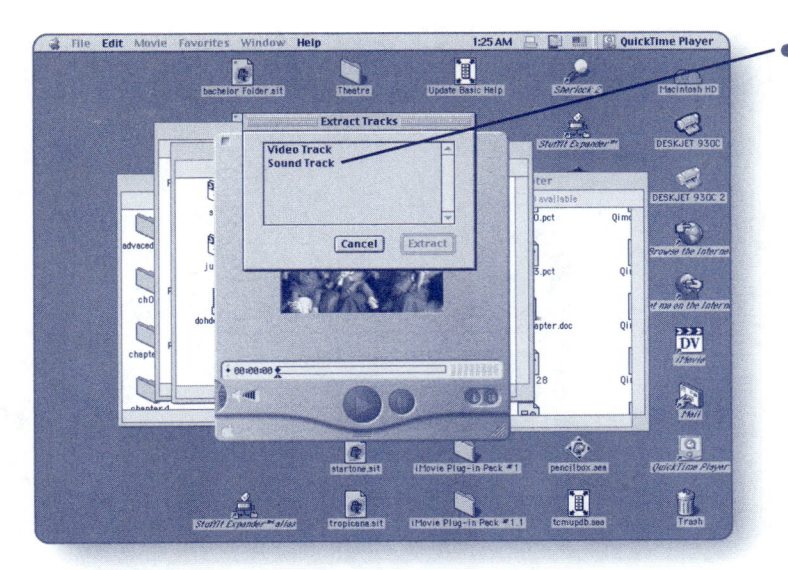

EDITING QUICKTIME CLIPS 249

• **Sound Track**.

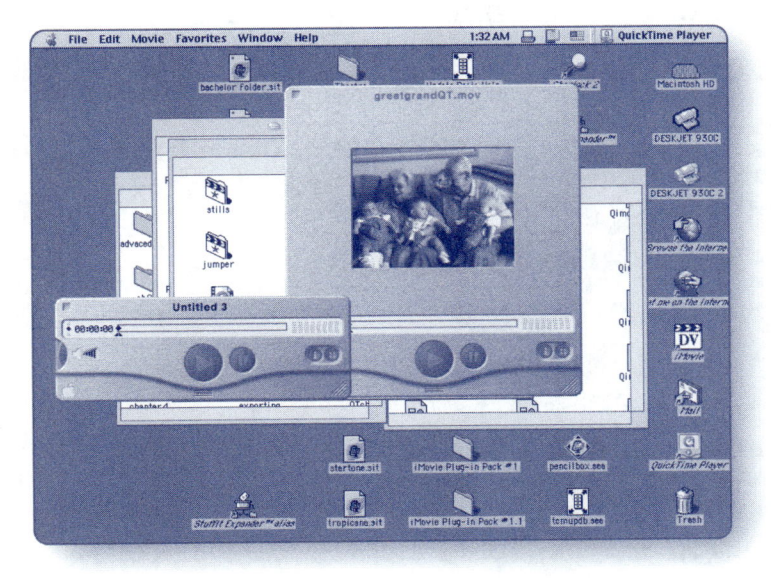

This will extract a copy of the sound track and insert it into a new QuickTime Player.

NOTE

Some movies will have multiple sound tracks and/or video tracks. If that is the case, click on the particular sound track or video track that you want to extract from the movie.

CHAPTER 12: USING QUICKTIME WITH iMOVIE

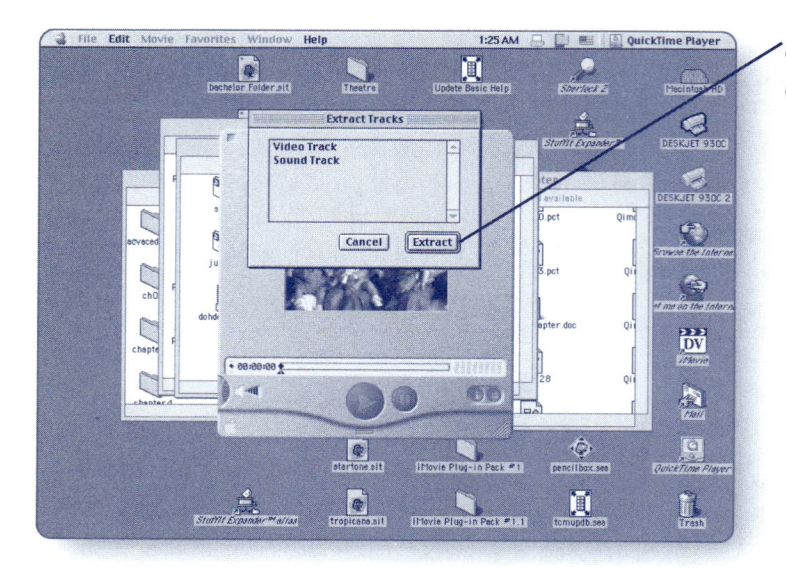

4. Click on **Extract**. The extracting will take effect.

Deleting Video and Sound Tracks

1. Click on **Edit**. The Edit menu will appear.

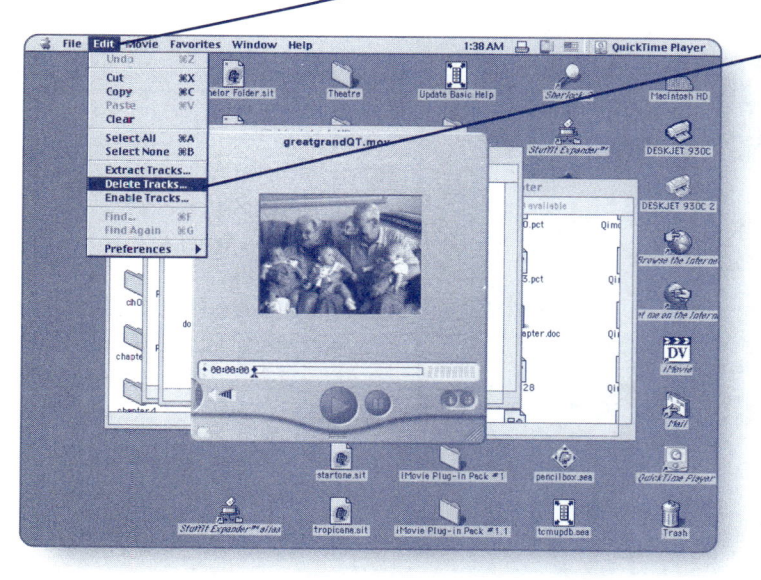

2. Click on **Delete Tracks**. The Delete Tracks dialog box will open.

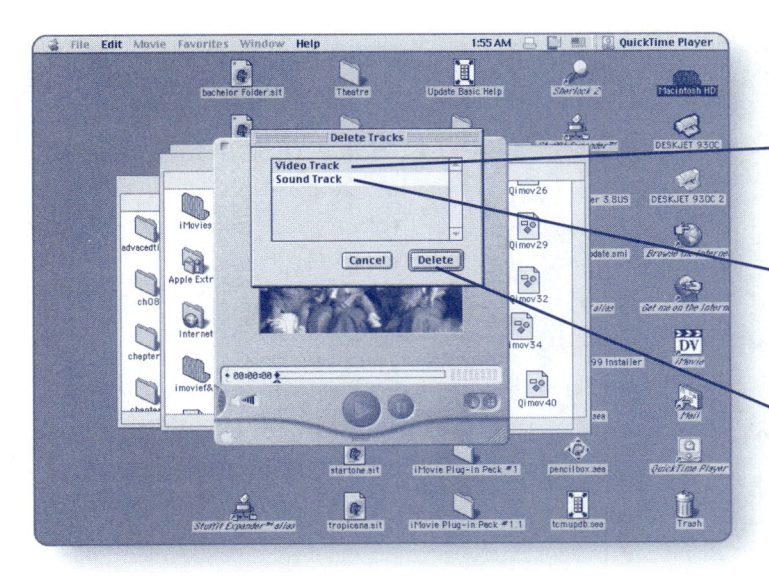

EDITING QUICKTIME CLIPS **251**

3. Click on one or more of the following **options**:

- **Video Track**. This will delete the selected video track from your QuickTime movie.

- **Sound Track**. This will delete the selected sound track from your QuickTime movie.

4. Click on **Delete**. The selected track will be deleted.

Enabling Video and Sound Tracks

1. Click on **Edit**. The Edit menu will appear.

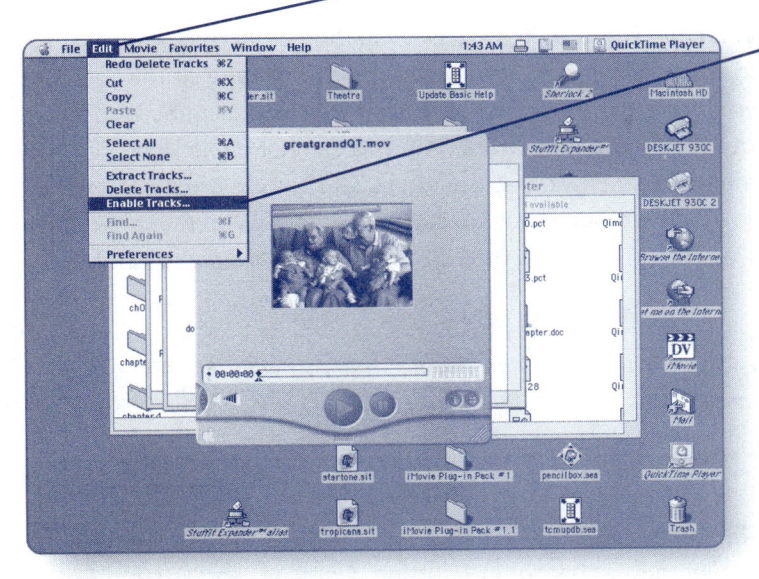

2. Click on **Enable Tracks**. The Enable Tracks dialog box will open.

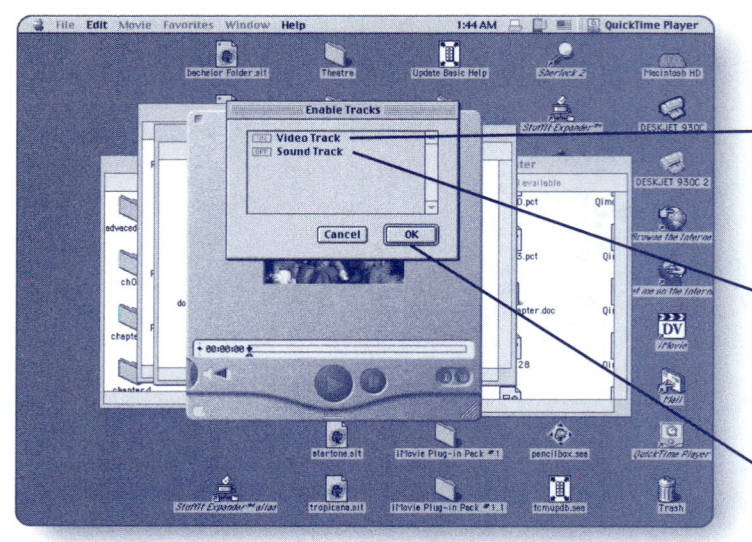

3. **Click** on **one or more** of the following options:

- **Video Track**. Setting the On or Off position will temporarily enable or disable the video track.

- **Sound Track**. Setting the On or Off position will temporarily enable or disable the selected sound track.

4. **Click** on **OK**. The track(s) will be enabled/disabled.

Importing QuickTime Clips into Your iMovies

If you have footage in a QuickTime movie file that you want to add to an iMovie, or if you want to add footage of the wedding scene from the Godfather into your sister's wedding footage, iMovie and QuickTime Pro can handle it. Just remember the laws that govern redistribution of copyrighted material. If you use that Godfather footage, you must keep it for your own personal use. Otherwise, you'll sleep with the fishes.

1. **Open** the **QuickTime movie** that you want to insert into iMovie.

TIP

Remember the QuickTime editing techniques you learned earlier in this chapter in "Cutting, Copying, and Pasting." If you want only part of this QuickTime movie to become a clip in iMovie, select that portion of the movie.

IMPORTING QUICKTIME CLIPS INTO YOUR iMOVIES

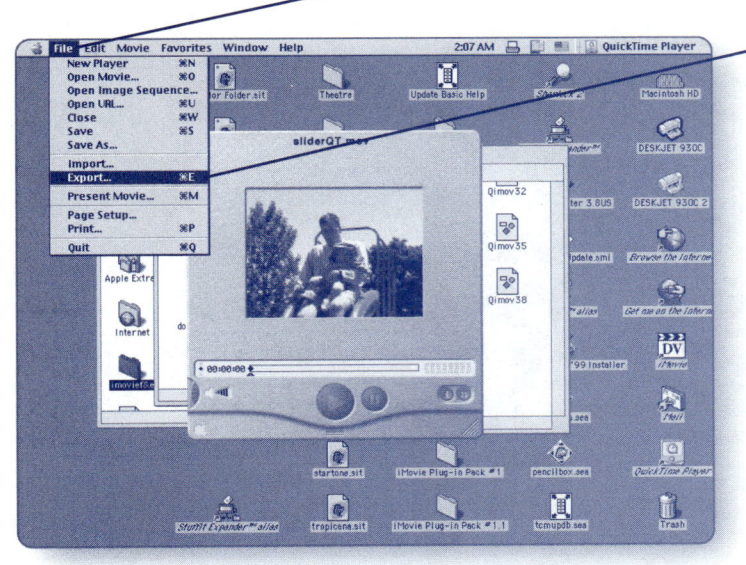

2. Click on **File**. The File menu will appear.

3. Click on **Export**. The Export dialog box will open.

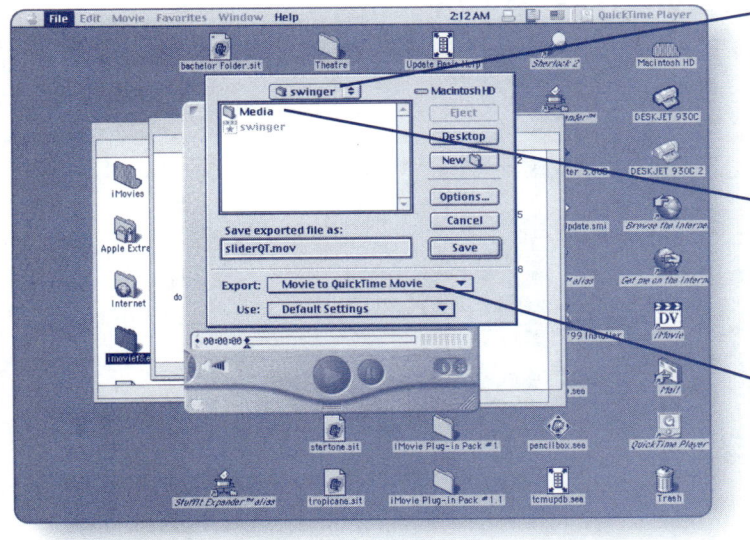

4. Click on the **folder** for the iMovie project into which you want to add the QuickTime clip. The folder will be selected.

5. Click on the **Media folder** for the iMovie project. This is where you will want to save the converted QuickTime clip.

6. Click on the **down arrow** to the right of the Export box. A pop-up menu will appear.

CHAPTER 12: USING QUICKTIME WITH iMOVIE

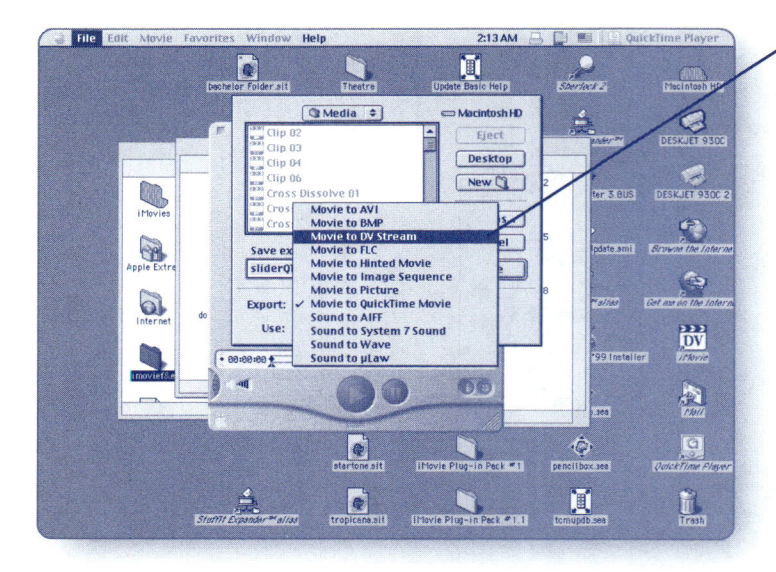

7. Click on **Movie to DV Stream**. The file extension on the clip name will change from .mov to .dv.

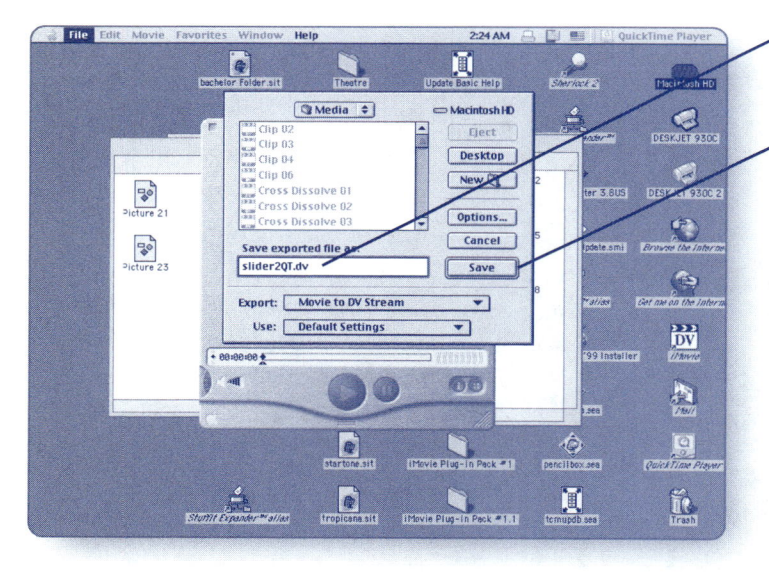

8. In the Save exported file as field, **type** a **name** for your clip.

9. Click on **Save**. The clip will convert to a file that is compatible with your iMovie files.

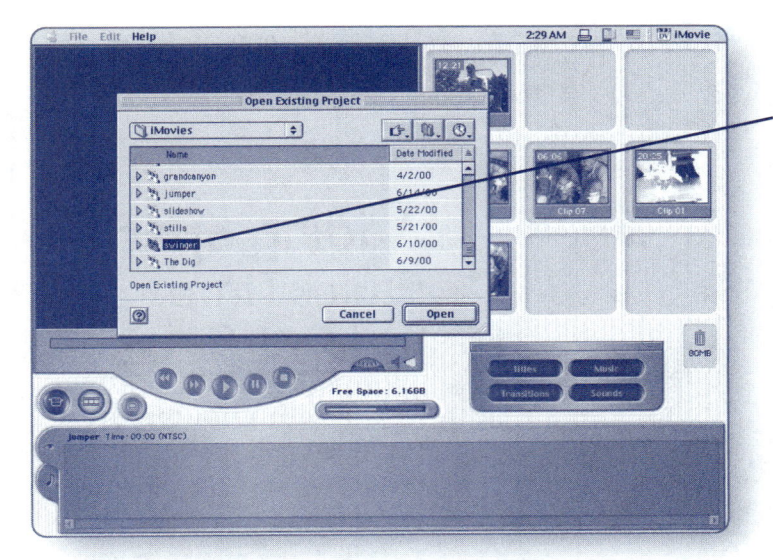

IMPORTING QUICKTIME CLIPS INTO YOUR iMOVIES   255

10. **Open iMovie**.

11. **Open** the **iMovie project** that contains the QuickTime clip that you just exported. iMovie will give you a message that says there was a stray clip in the project folder and that it will be loaded onto the Shelf.

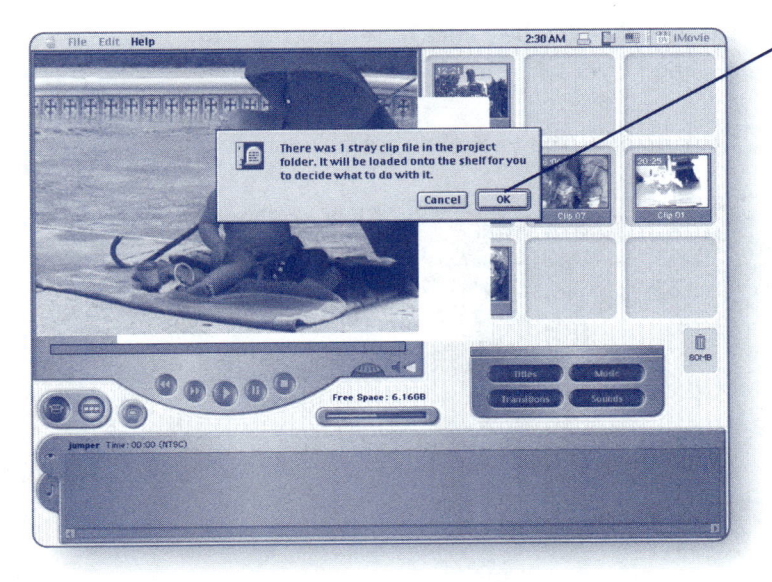

12. **Click** on **OK**.

CHAPTER 12: USING QUICKTIME WITH iMOVIE

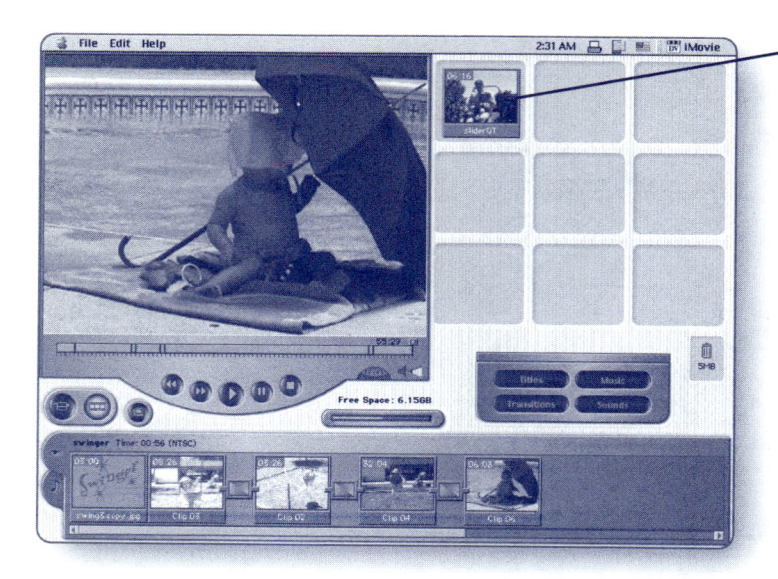

The clip will appear on the Shelf for you to add to your iMovie project.

Adding Special QuickTime Video Effects

QuickTime Pro includes several cool filters and special effects that iMovie doesn't offer. You can open the QuickTime player and add these effects to your iMovie clips.

1. Double-click on the **QuickTime desktop icon**. The QuickTime Player will open.

2. Click on **File**. The File menu will appear.

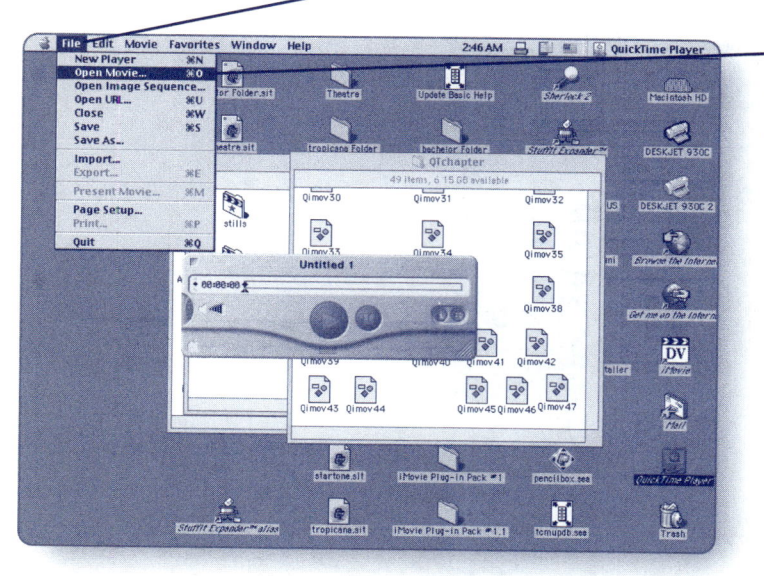

3. Click on **Open Movie**. The Open Movie dialog box will open.

ADDING SPECIAL QUICKTIME VIDEO EFFECTS

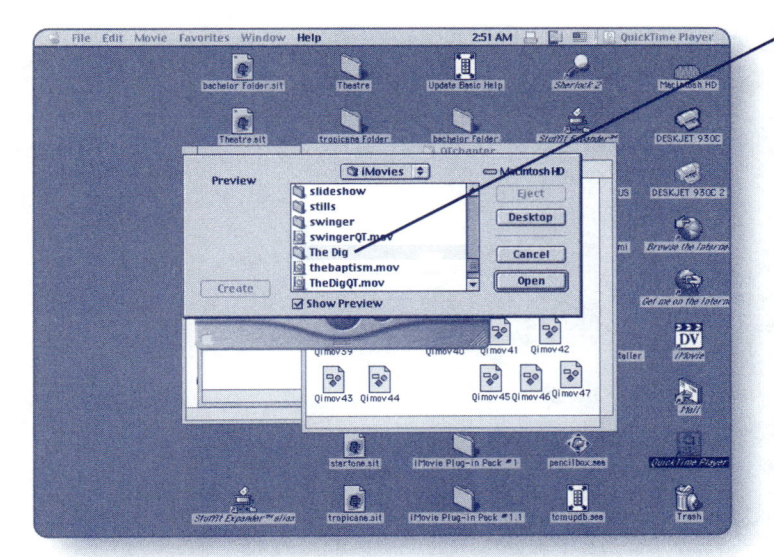

4. Double-click on the **folder** that contains the clip to which you want to add a special effect. The folder will open.

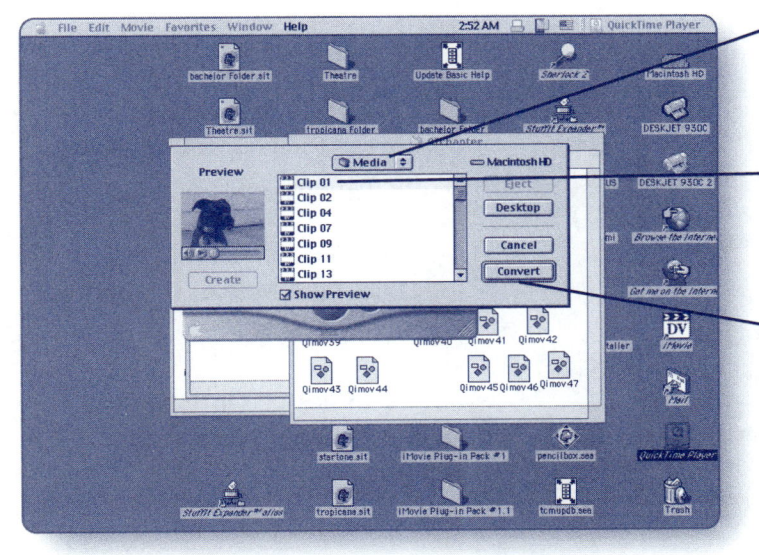

5. Click on the **Media folder** for the iMovie project. All of the clips in the movie will appear.

6. Click on a **clip (or clips)**. The clip(s) will appear in the preview window.

7. Click on **Convert**. The clip will appear in a large QuickTime Player window on your desktop.

258   **CHAPTER 12: USING QUICKTIME WITH iMOVIE**

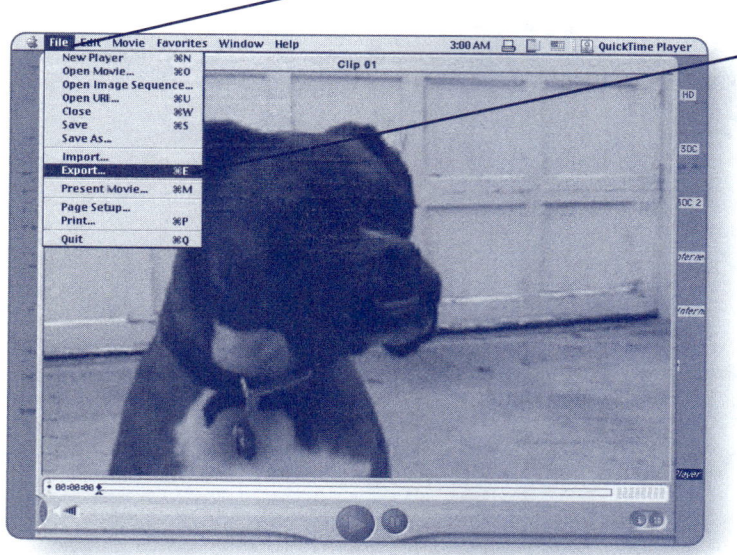

8. Click on **File**. The File menu will appear.

9. Click on **Export**. The Export dialog box will open.

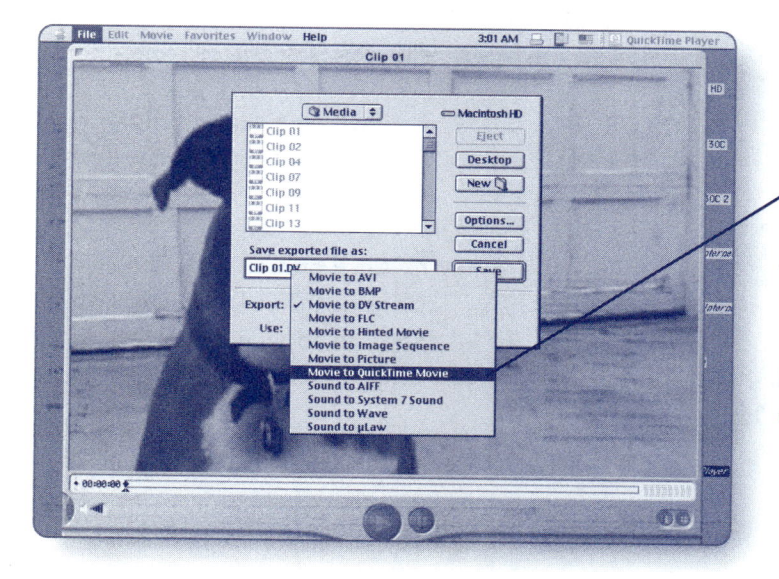

10. Click on the **down arrow** next to the Export box. A pop-up menu will appear.

11. Click on **Movie to QuickTime Movie**. The option will be selected.

12. Click on **Options**. The Movie Settings dialog box will open.

ADDING SPECIAL QUICKTIME VIDEO EFFECTS 259

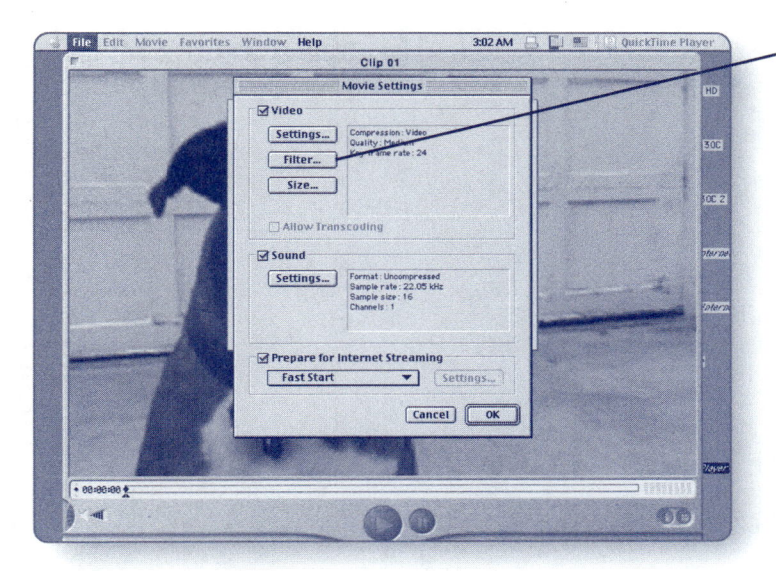

13. **Click** on **Filter**. The Choose Video Filter dialog box will open.

14. **Click** on a **filter** in the box on the left. The filter's effect will appear in the preview window below the list of filters.

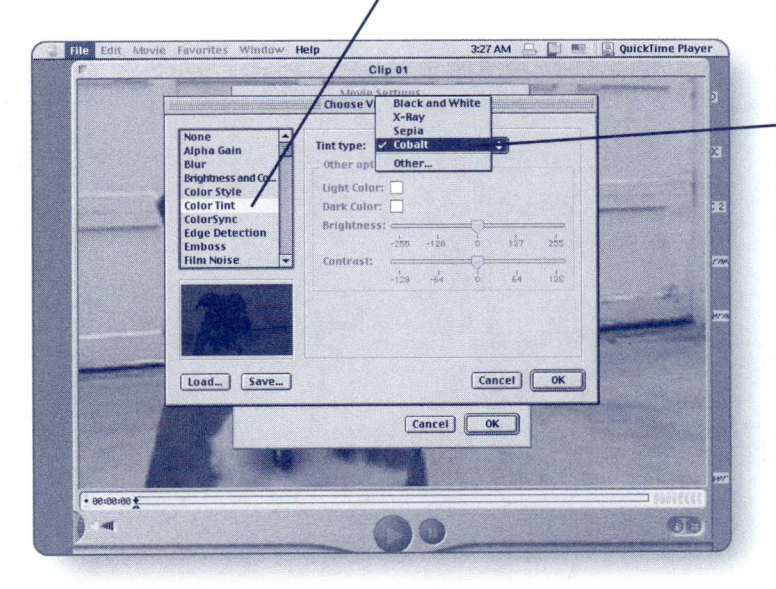

NOTE

Some of the filter effects have additional settings and more effects. Select a filter and see what appears in the right side of the dialog box. You might have to experiment to see what kind of effects you can utilize.

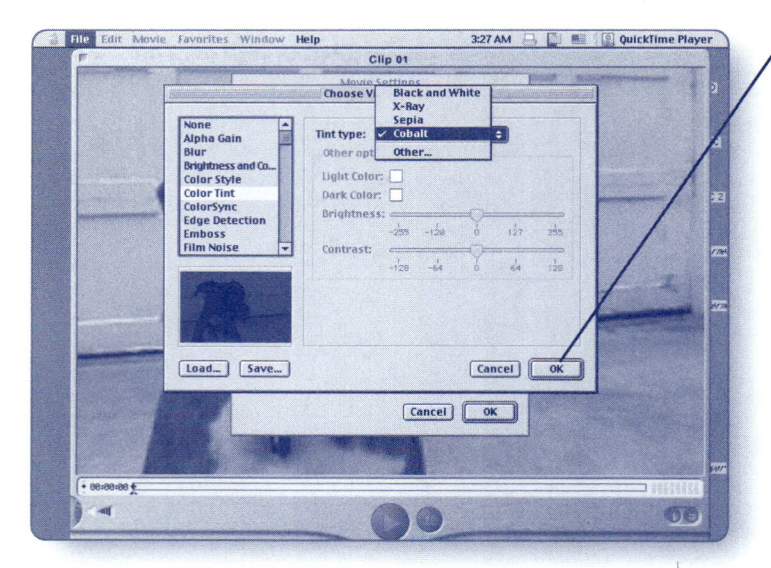

15. Click on **OK**. The Movie Settings dialog box will reappear.

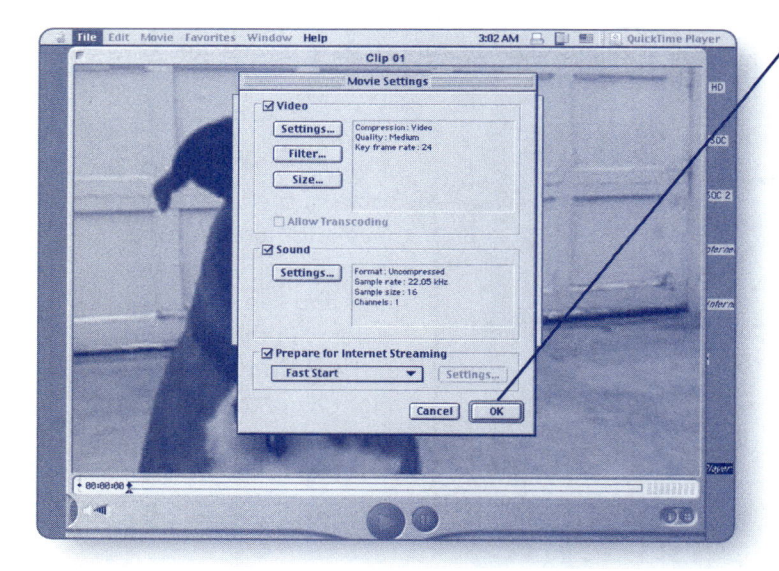

16. Click on **OK**. The Export dialog box will reappear.

ADDING SPECIAL QUICKTIME VIDEO EFFECTS   261

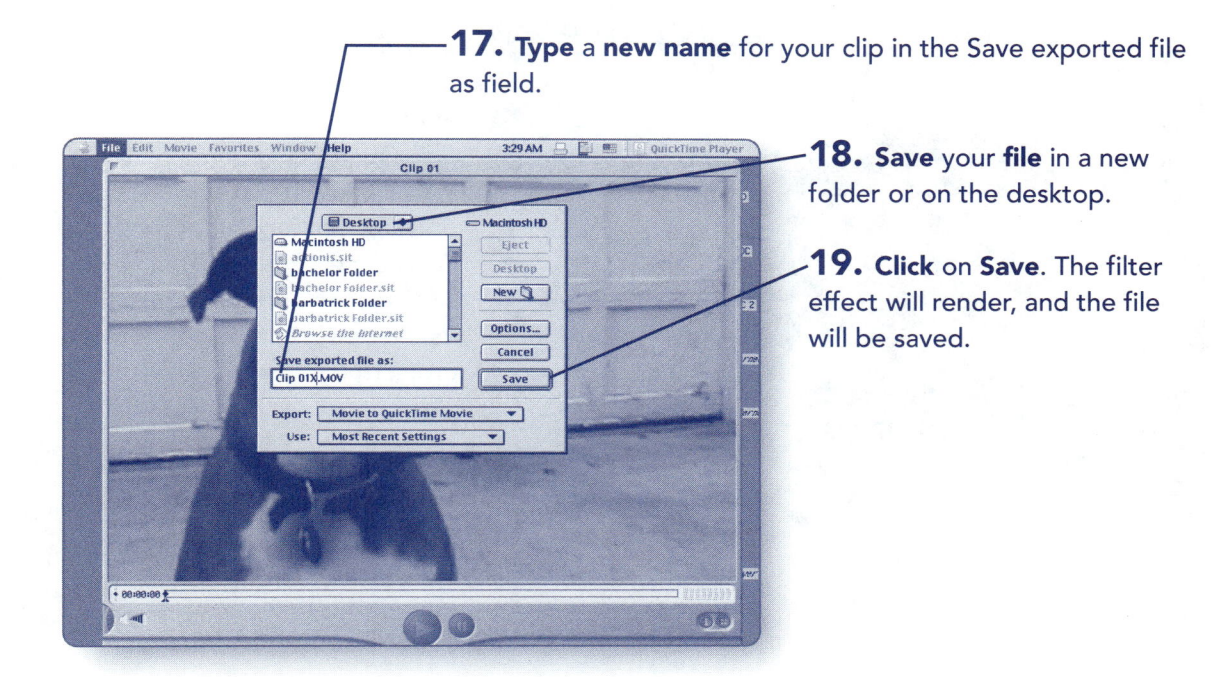

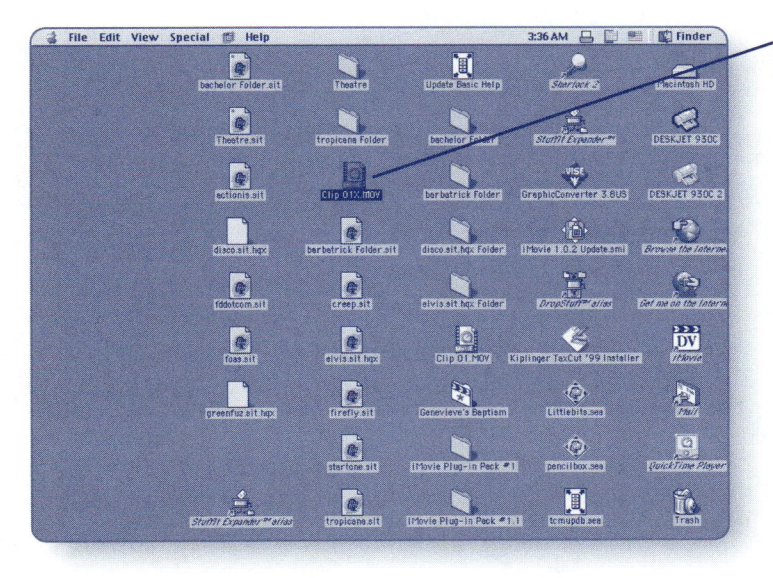

17. **Type** a **new name** for your clip in the Save exported file as field.

18. **Save** your **file** in a new folder or on the desktop.

19. **Click** on **Save**. The filter effect will render, and the file will be saved.

20. **Double-click** on the **file**. The file will open.

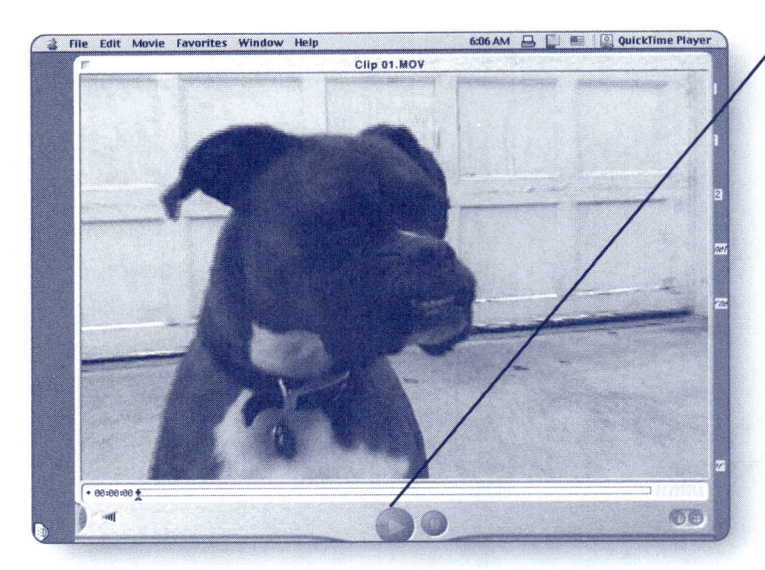

21. Click on the **Play button** to see your new cool effect. The effect will play.

22. Follow the **steps** in the previous section, "Importing QuickTime Clips into Your iMovies," to add this clip, with its filter effect, into your iMovie project.

13

Getting Your iMovie on the Web

A great way to premiere your movie is to post it on a Web site. This way, family and friends can go to your Web site and view your movie at their leisure. You don't jam up their e-mail with a huge attachment, and you don't spend time and money on videotapes and postage sending Junior's home run to everyone. Apple provides a nifty service especially for iMovie makers—you can create your own Web site and add a page to it that specifically showcases your iMovies. In this chapter, you'll learn how to:

- Set up an iTools account
- Access your iDisk
- Create and edit your home page
- Add your movie to your home page

Setting Up an iTools Account

The first step in creating a Web page to showcase your iMovies is to sign up for and open an Apple iTools account. iTools is a free Internet service provided by Apple for Macintosh users. It allows you to create an e-mail address, make the Internet safer for your kids, store files on Apple's Internet server, and create your own personal Web site.

1. Go to **Apple's Web site**. The Apple home page will appear.

2. Click on the **iTools tab**. The iTools page will appear.

3. Scroll down the **page** and **read** about **what you can do** with iTools.

SETTING UP AN iTOOLS ACCOUNT 265

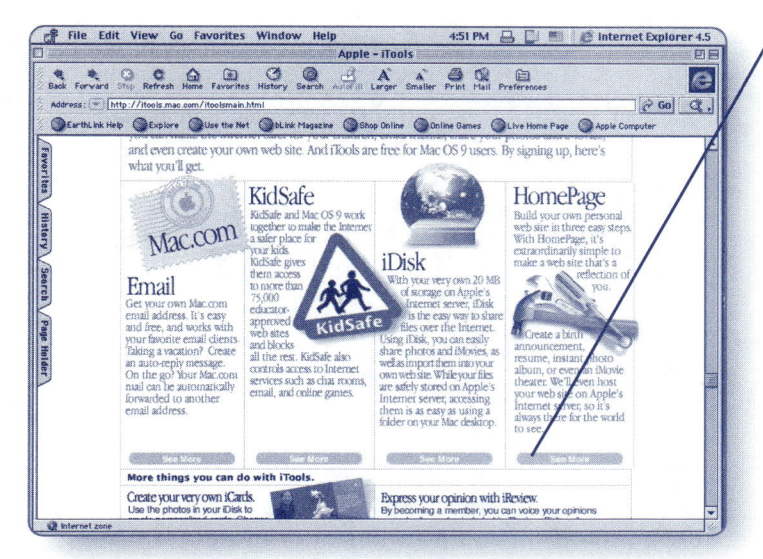

4. Click on the **See More button** under the HomePage section. A page will appear that explains the things you will be able to do with a home page from iTools.

TIP
Click on the See A Sample Web Site button if you want to see an example of what you can create.

5. Click on **Free Sign Up**. The iTools setup page will appear.

CHAPTER 13: GETTING YOUR iMOVIE ON THE WEB

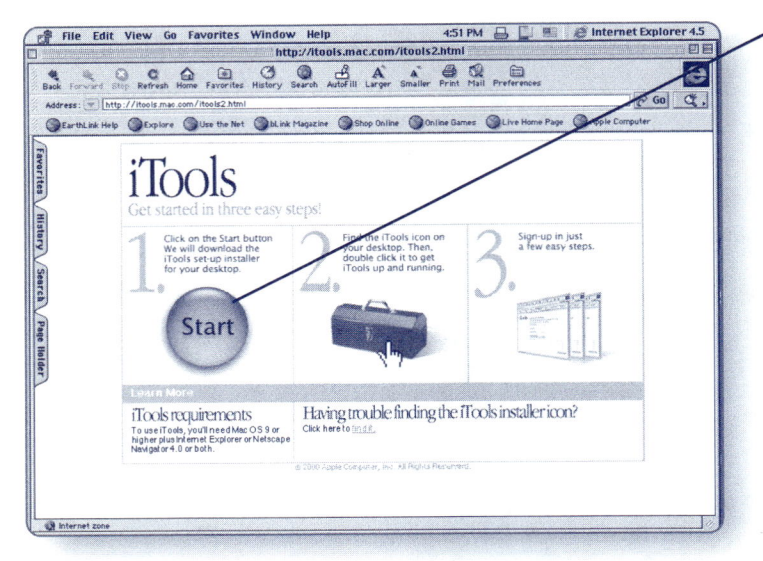

6. **Click** on the **Start button**. The iTools installer icon will download to your desktop.

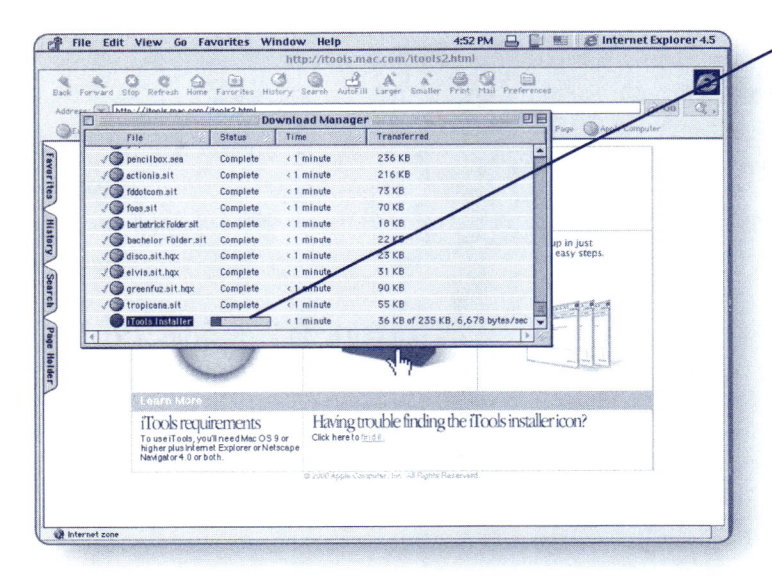

7. **Wait** for the **installer** to finish downloading. The iTools installer icon will appear on your desktop when it's finished downloading.

SETTING UP AN iTOOLS ACCOUNT **267**

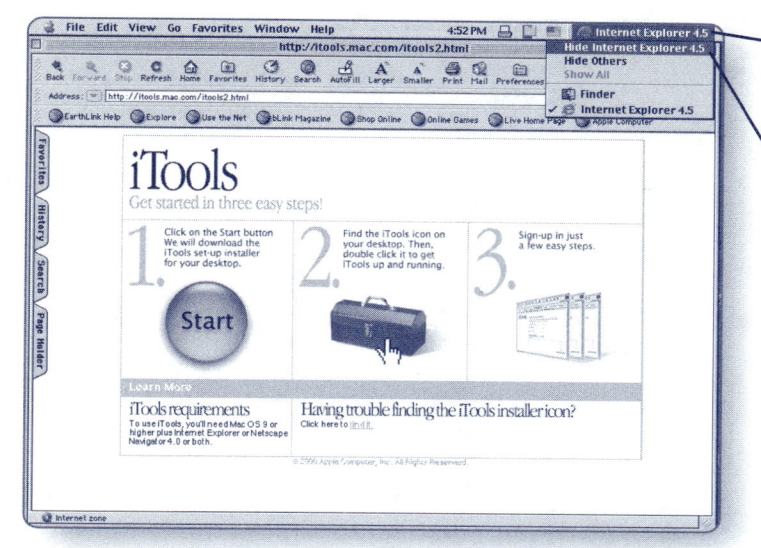

8. Click on the **Finder**. The Finder menu will appear.

9. Click on **Hide Internet Explorer 4.5** (or whatever your browser is). The page will be hidden.

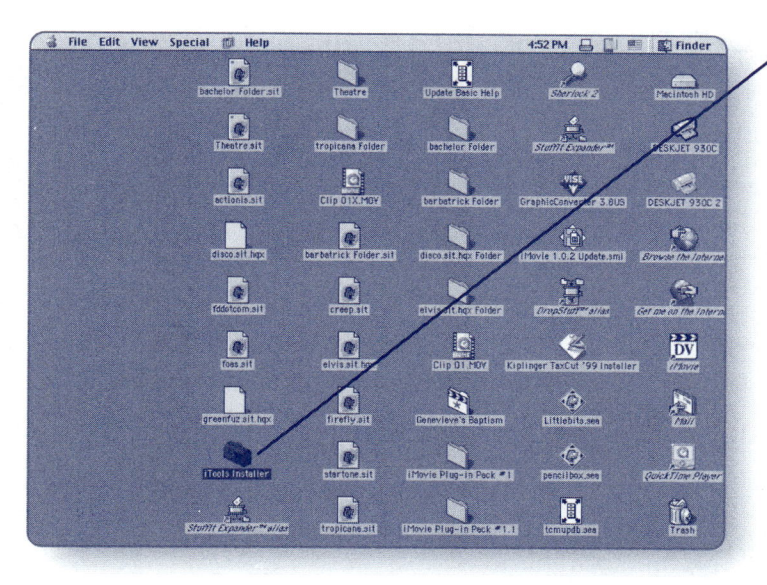

10. Locate and double-click on the **iTools Installer** (it looks like a red toolbox). The iTools New member sign up page will appear.

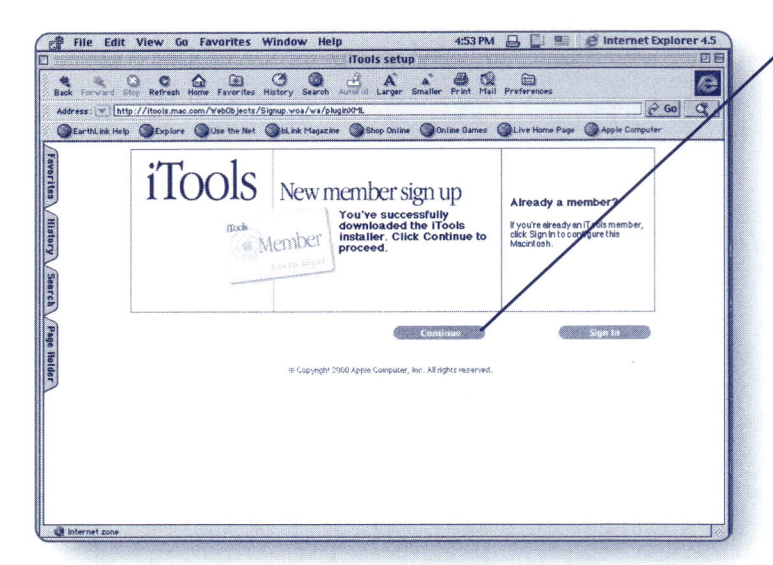

11. **Click** on the **Continue button**. The iTools Select your country page will appear.

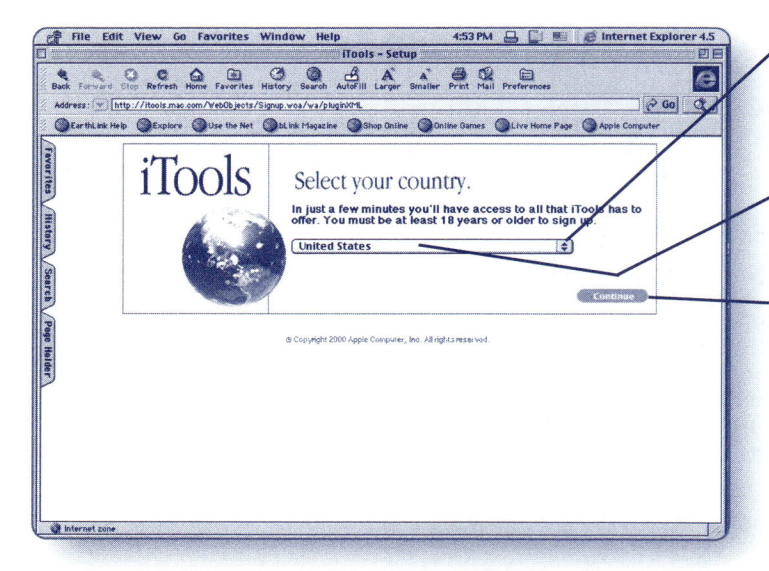

12. **Click** on the **up and down arrows** to the right of the list box. A pop-up list will appear.

13. **Click** on your **country**. Your country will be selected.

14. **Click** on the **Continue button**. The iTools Tell us about yourself page will appear.

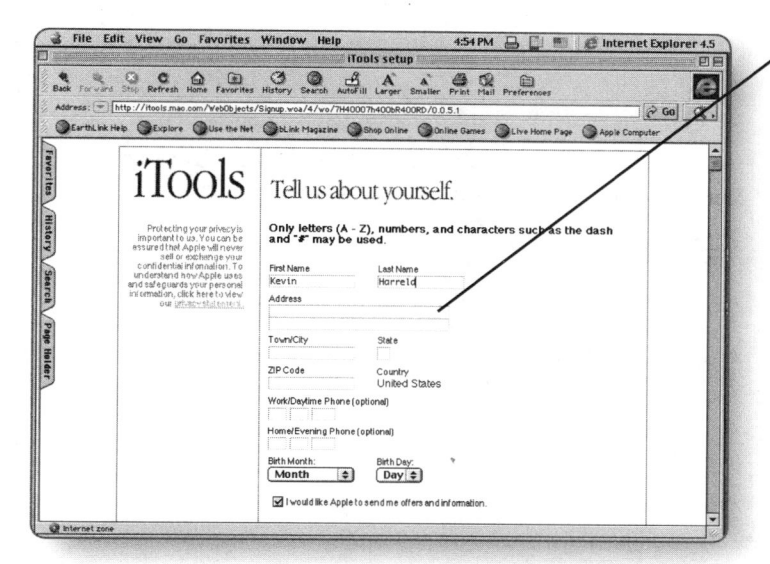

SETTING UP AN iTOOLS ACCOUNT   269

15. **Fill** in the **text boxes** with the appropriate information about yourself.

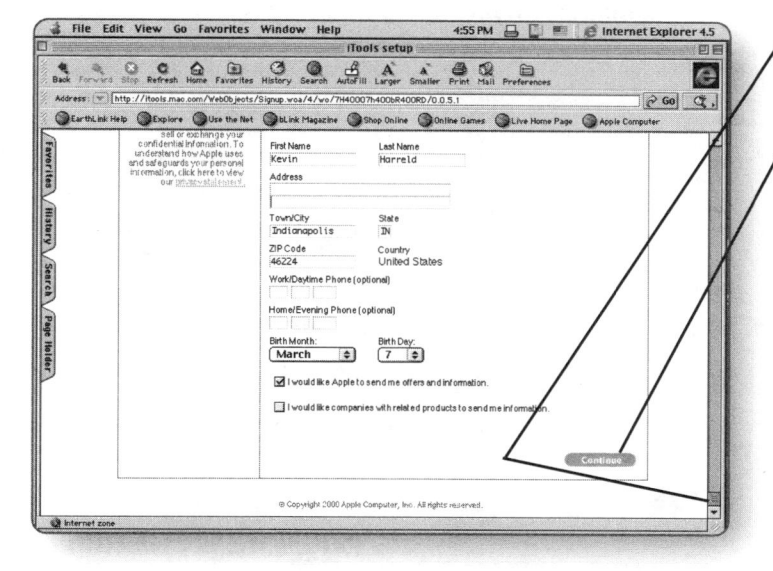

16. Scroll down to the **bottom** of the page.

17. Click on the **Continue button**. The Terms of Agreement page will appear.

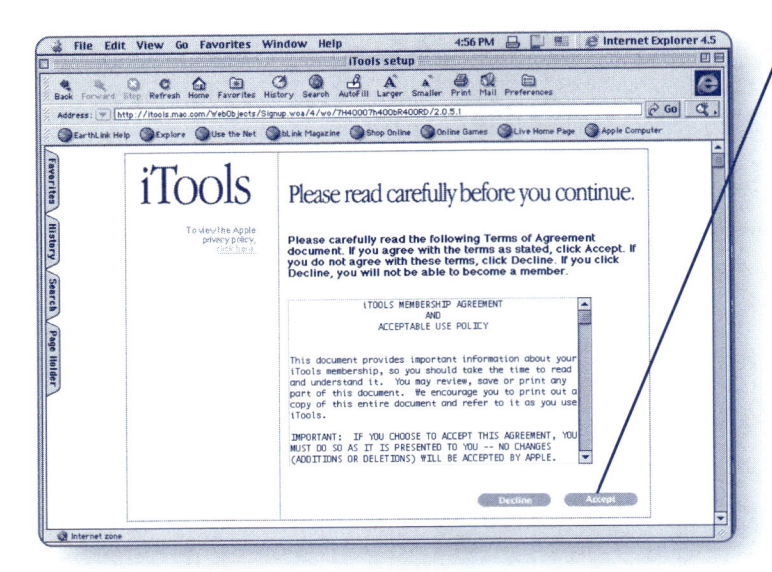

18. Read the **membership agreement terms** and **click** on the **Accept button**. The iTools Choose your member name and password page will appear.

19. Type a **member name** in the Member Name text box.

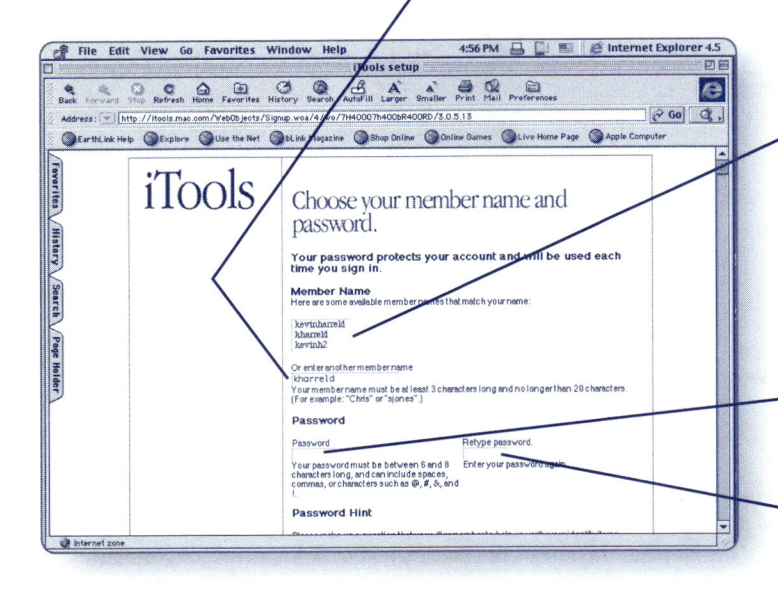

NOTE

iTools might provide some sample member names for you. If you like one of them, click on it and it will appear in the Member Name text box.

20. Type a **password** in the Password text box.

21. Retype the **password** in the Retype password text box.

SETTING UP AN iTOOLS ACCOUNT

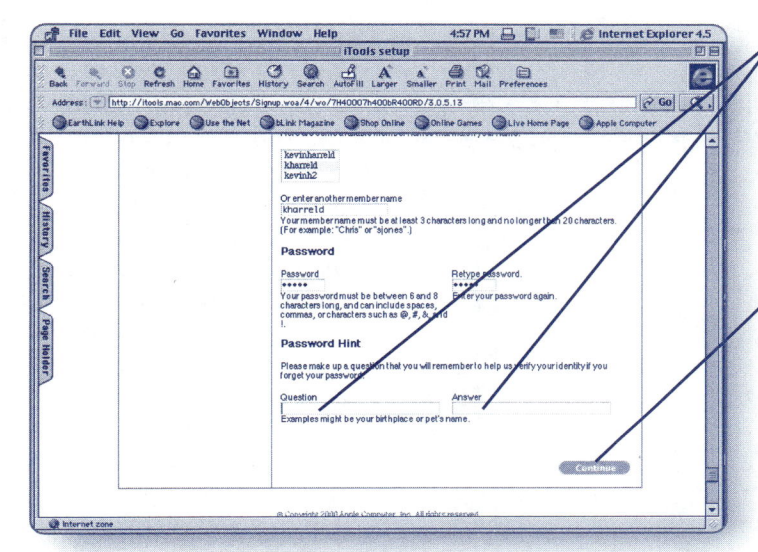

22. Type a **Question and Answer** in the Password Hint text boxes. This will help Apple identify you if you forget your password and need to be reminded of it.

23. Click on the **Continue button**. The iTools Save for your records page will appear.

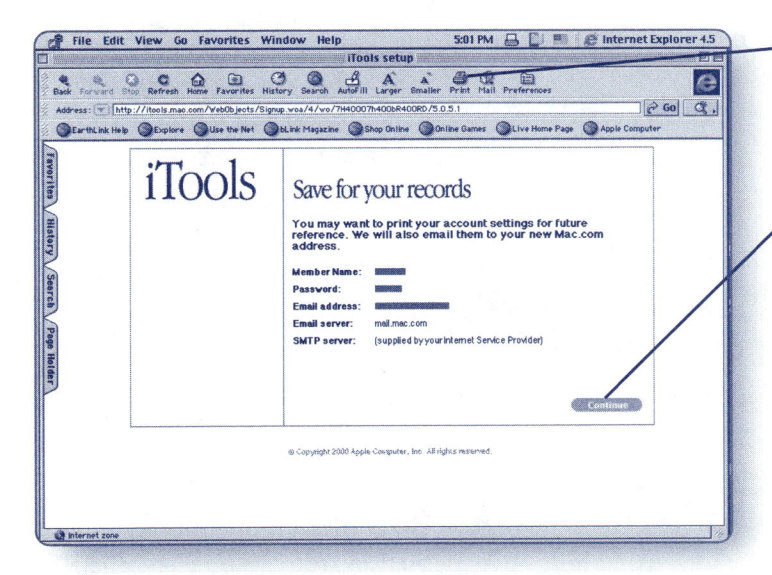

24. Click on the **Print button**. You will want to keep this information for your records, in case you ever need to access it.

25. Click on the **Continue button**. You will be taken to an Announce your new email address page.

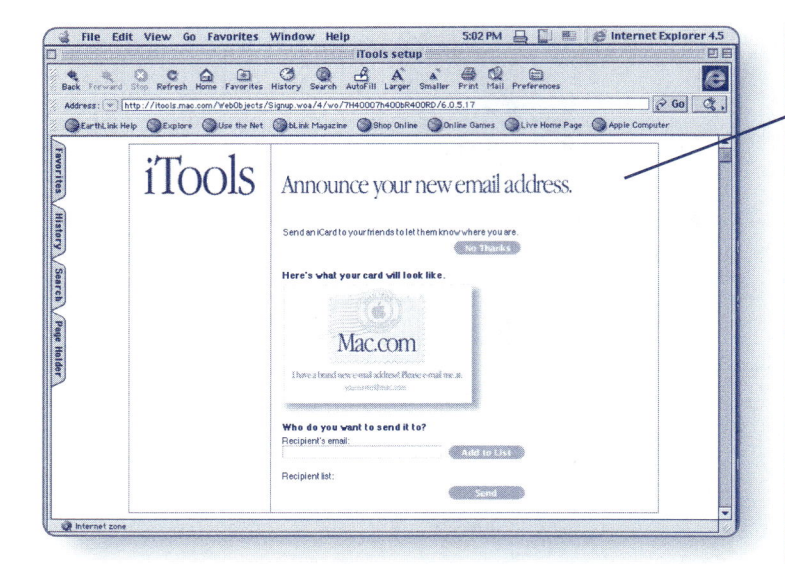

NOTE

iTools has created an e-mail address and user name for you. This allows Apple to create your home page address, and it also gives you a new e-mail address, if you want to use it. From here, you can send a card to your friends announcing this new address. If you would like to announce this, type the addresses of your friends and family in the text box and click on the Add to List button. When you are finished, click on the Send button. If you don't want to send this address out, click on the No Thanks button. You will then be taken to the Member sign in page.

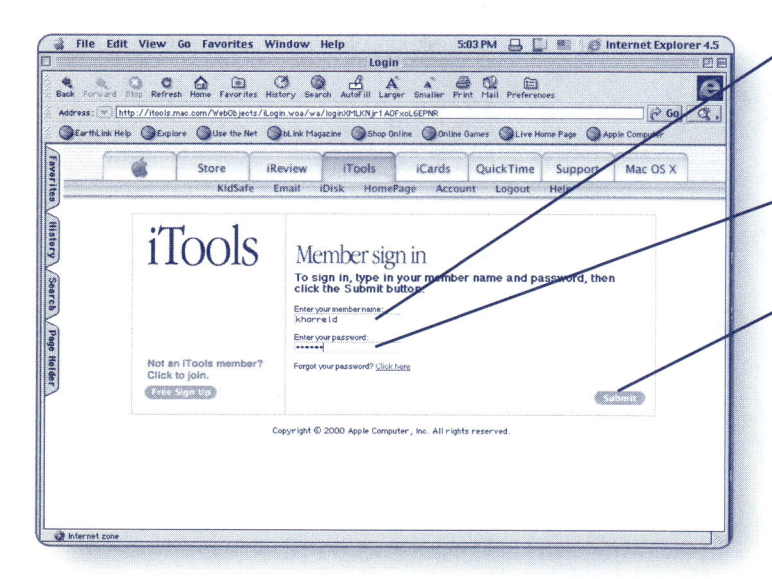

26. **Type** your **member name** in the Enter your member name text box.

27. **Type** your **password** in the Enter your password text box.

28. **Click** on the **Submit button**. You are now an official iTools member, with access to all of the perks.

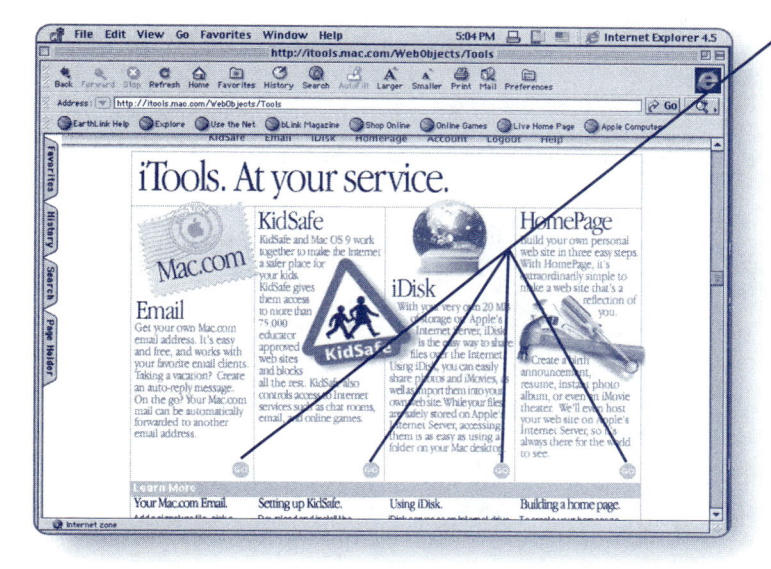

ACCESSING YOUR iDISK 273

When you sign in, notice that the iTools opening page includes Go buttons in the Email, KidSafe, iDisk, and HomePage categories. Now that you are a member, you can access all of these services by clicking on their respective Go buttons.

Accessing Your iDisk

Before you create your Web site to premiere your iMovies, you need to open iDisk. iDisk creates 20 MB of storage space for you on Apple's Internet server. It basically works as a backup disk of free and secure storage. It is also the avenue through which you import your iMovies (compressed into QuickTime movies, of course) into your soon-to-be created Web site. iTools will not allow you to post an iMovie on your Web site without first importing it into iDisk.

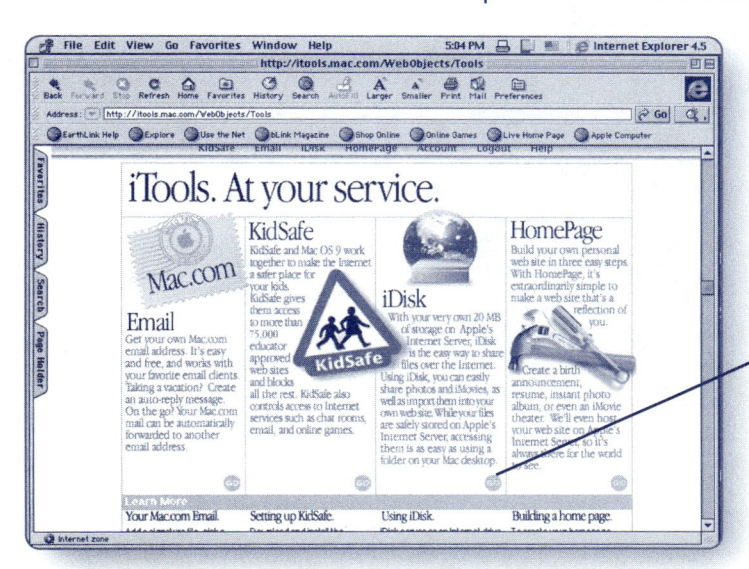

1. From the iTools opening page, **click** on the **Go button** at the bottom of the iDisk section. The iDisk page will appear.

CHAPTER 13: GETTING YOUR iMOVIE ON THE WEB

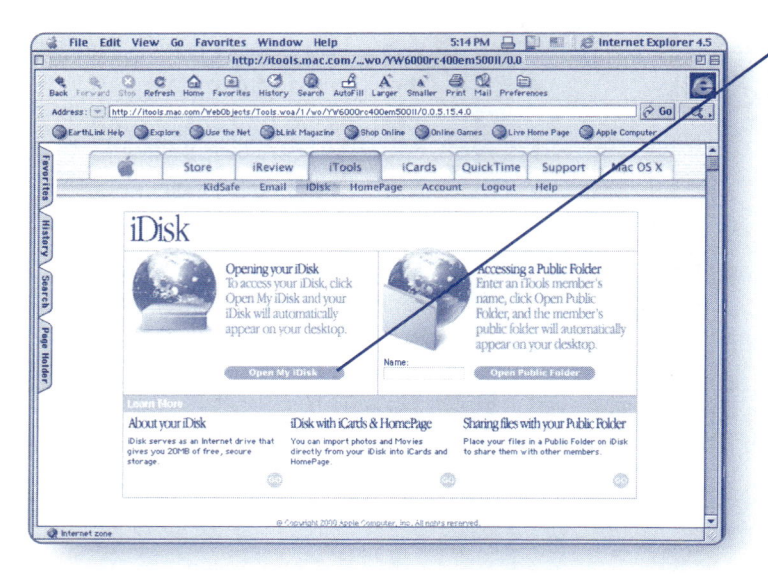

2. Click on the **Open My iDisk button**. After a minute or so, the iDisk icon will appear on your desktop.

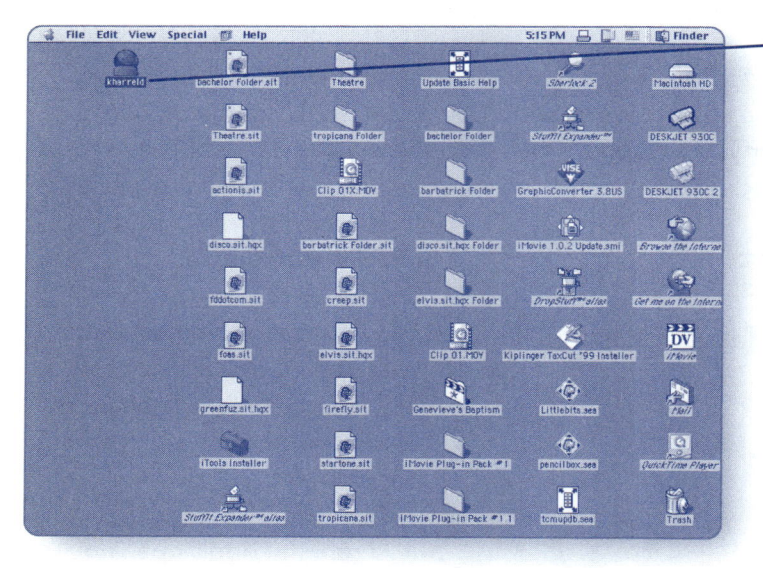

3. Double-click on the **iDisk icon**. Your iDisk dialog box will open. Your iDisk dialog box will have your user name in the title bar.

ACCESSING YOUR iDISK 275

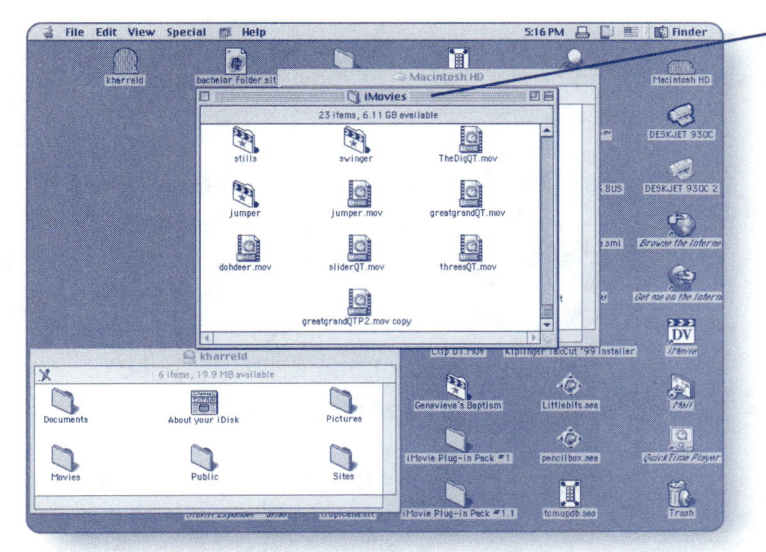

4. Open the **folder** on your hard drive that contains the QuickTime movie you want to post on your site.

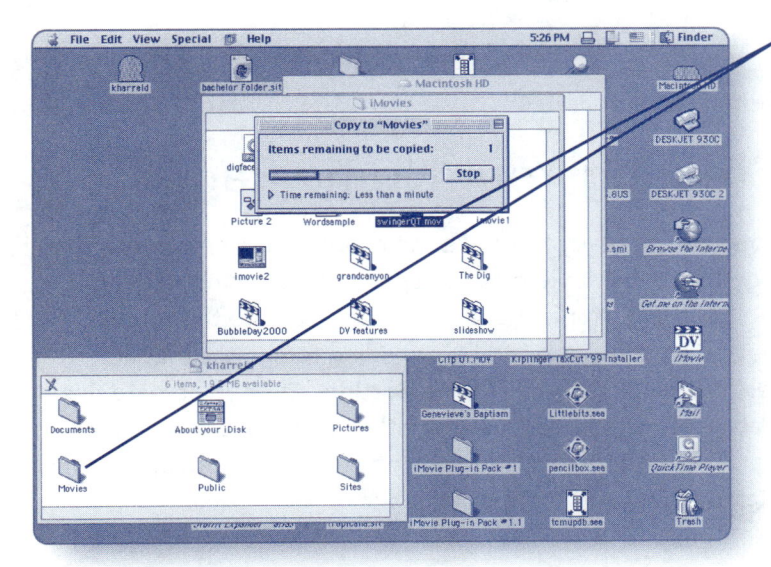

5. Press and hold the **mouse button** on the QuickTime movie and **drag** the **movie** to the Movies folder in the iDisk dialog box.

NOTE

Remember, to post your iMovies on the Web, you have to use the compressed QuickTime versions of the movies, which you learned about in Chapter 10, "Compressing and Exporting Your Movies." The raw iMovie files are too big to put on a Web site.

6. Release the **mouse button**. The movie will transfer to the iDisk. Depending on the size of the movie, this could take several minutes.

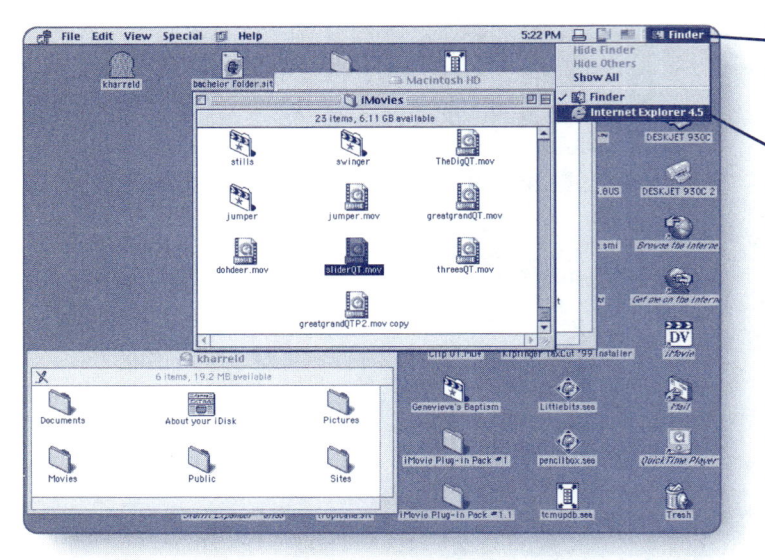

7. Click on the **Finder**. The Finder menu will appear.

8. Click on **Internet Explorer 4.5** (or whatever browser you use). You will be returned to the iTools page.

You now have access to iDisk, and you have a movie that is ready to be posted on your home page, which you will create next.

Creating Your Home Page

Now you are ready to create the online forum where you can showcase the iMovie that you spent hours filming, editing, and polishing. Apple makes it simple to create this iMovie theater on your Web site by providing templates that are designed especially for iMovie posting. After you create this Web page, feel free to use the other Web page templates that Apple offers (birth announcements and photo albums, for example) and add them to your site.

CREATING YOUR HOME PAGE 277

1. From the iTools opening page, **click** on the **Go button** at the bottom of the HomePage section. If you are still on the iDisk page, click on the Back button in your browser until you reach the iTools page again. The HomePage Welcome page will appear.

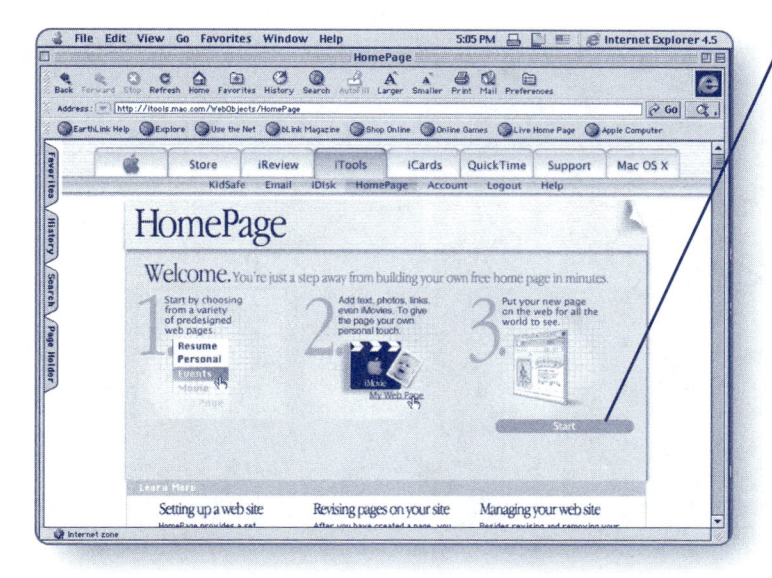

2. Click on the **Start button**. The Create a new page page will appear.

278 CHAPTER 13: GETTING YOUR iMOVIE ON THE WEB

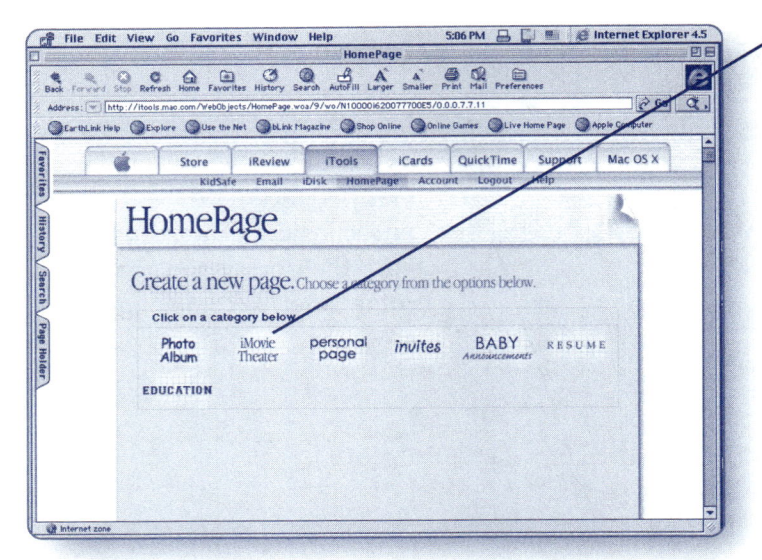

3. Click on the **iMovie Theater category**. Three themes will appear: iMovie Theater, iMovie Retro TV, and iMovie Drive-In.

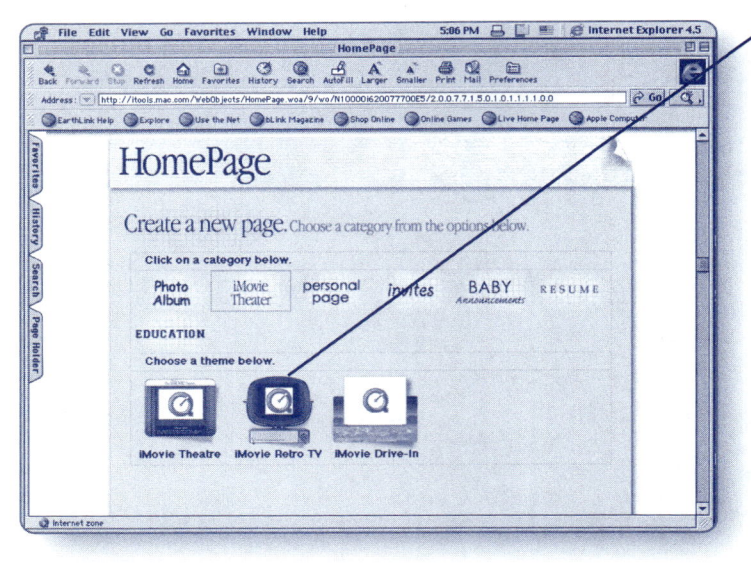

4. Click on a **theme**. The theme will be selected and your dummy page will appear.

CREATING YOUR HOME PAGE 279

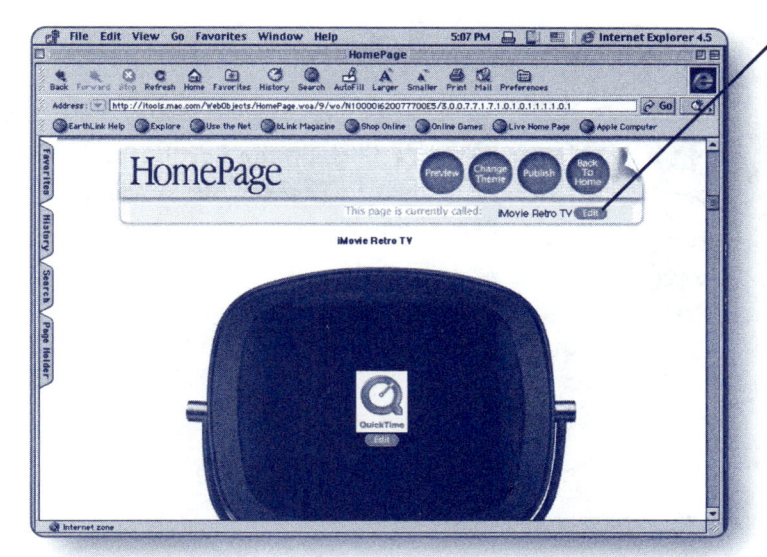

5. Click on the **Edit button** next to the This page is currently called field. A text box will appear.

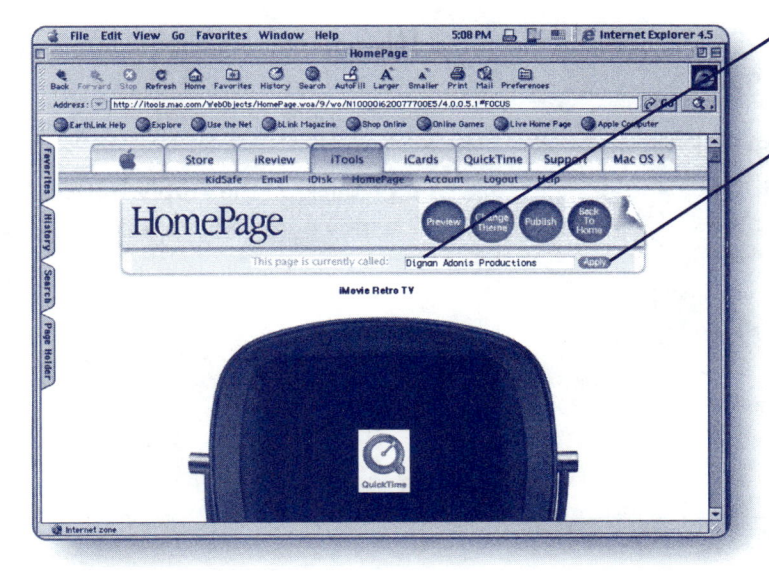

6. Select the **placeholder text** and **type** the **title** for your page.

7. Click on the **Apply button**. The title will appear at the top of the page.

280 CHAPTER 13: GETTING YOUR iMOVIE ON THE WEB

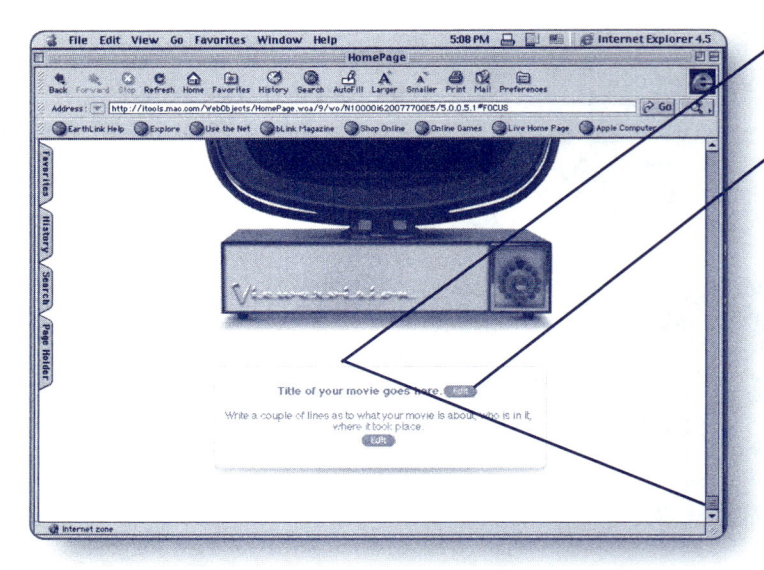

8. **Scroll** down to the **bottom** of the page.

9. **Click** on the **Edit button** next to Title of your movie goes here. A text box will appear.

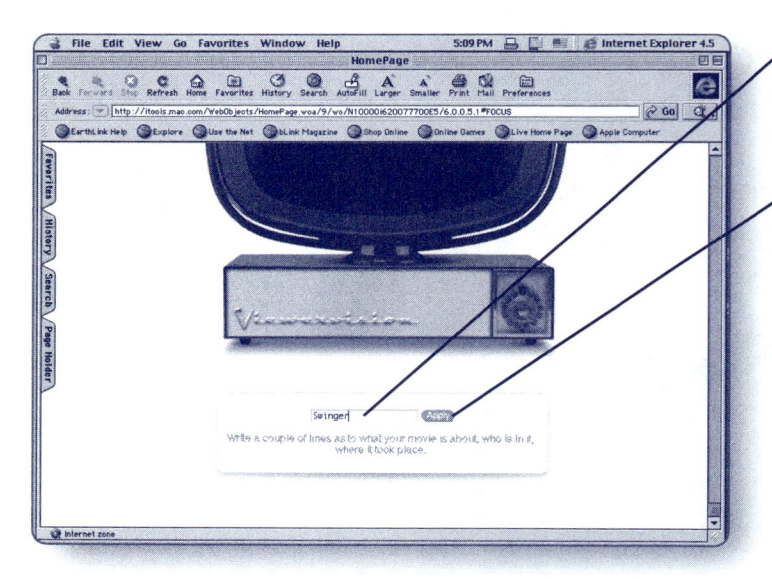

10. **Select** the **placeholder text** and **type** a **title** for the movie you plan to post.

11. **Click** on the **Apply button**. The movie title will appear.

CREATING YOUR HOME PAGE   281

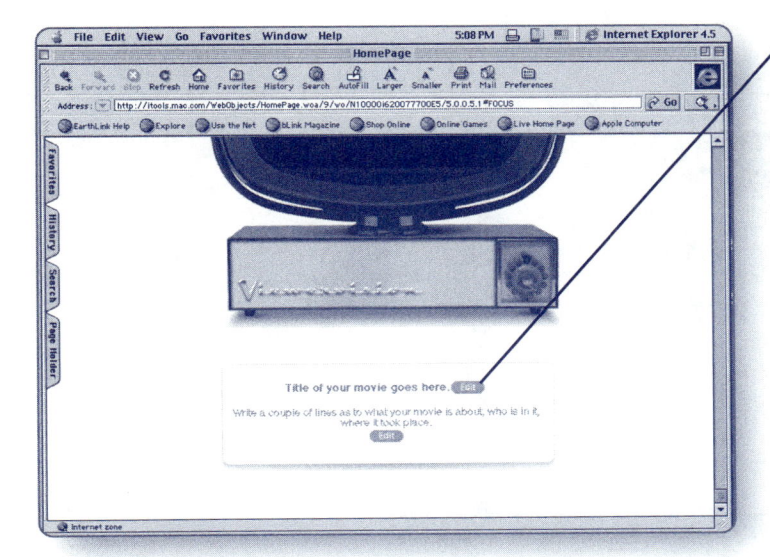

12. Click on the **Edit button** under Write a couple of lines as to what your movie is about, who is in it, where it took place. A text box will appear.

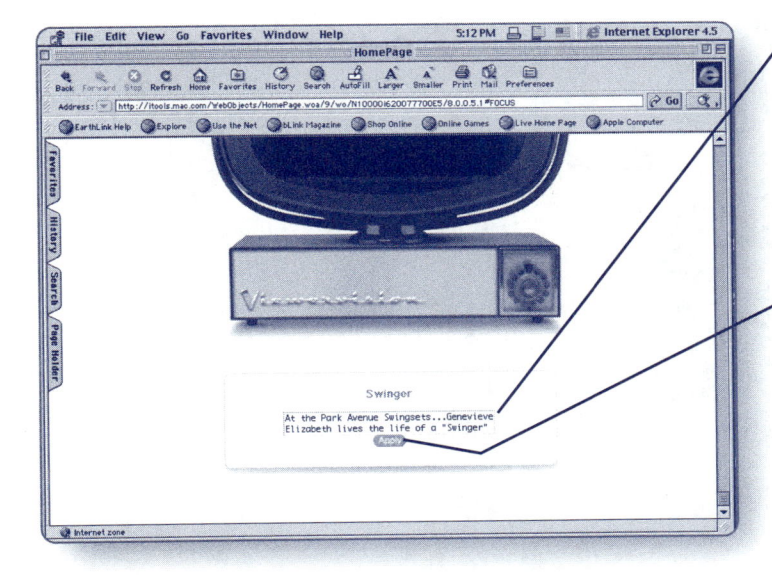

13. Select the **placeholder text** and **type** some **information** about your movie. Add the actors' names or a catchy tagline like in the movie posters you see at the theater.

14. Click on the **Apply button**. The text will appear.

282 CHAPTER 13: GETTING YOUR iMOVIE ON THE WEB

15. Scroll back up to the **middle** of the page.

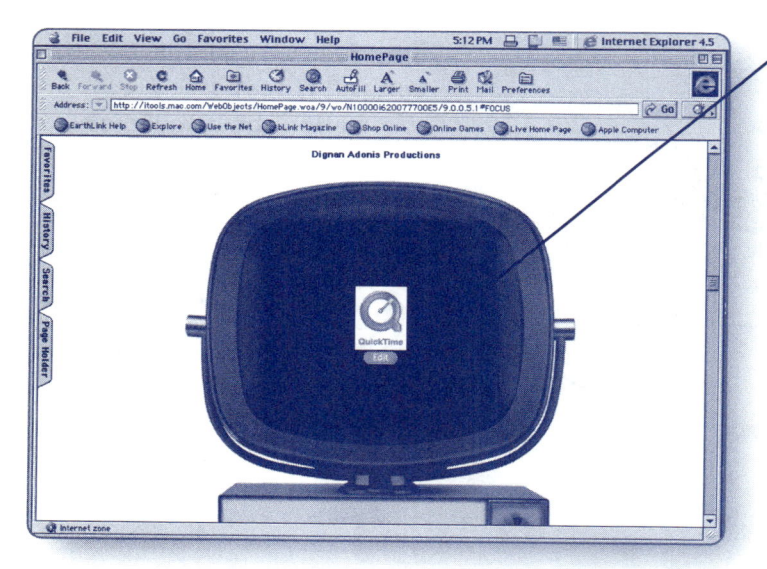

16. Click on the **Edit button** under the QuickTime icon. The Choose an iMovie from your iDisk page will appear.

CREATING YOUR HOME PAGE 283

17. Click on the **movie** that you added to your iDisk in the list box on the left side of the page. The movie will be selected.

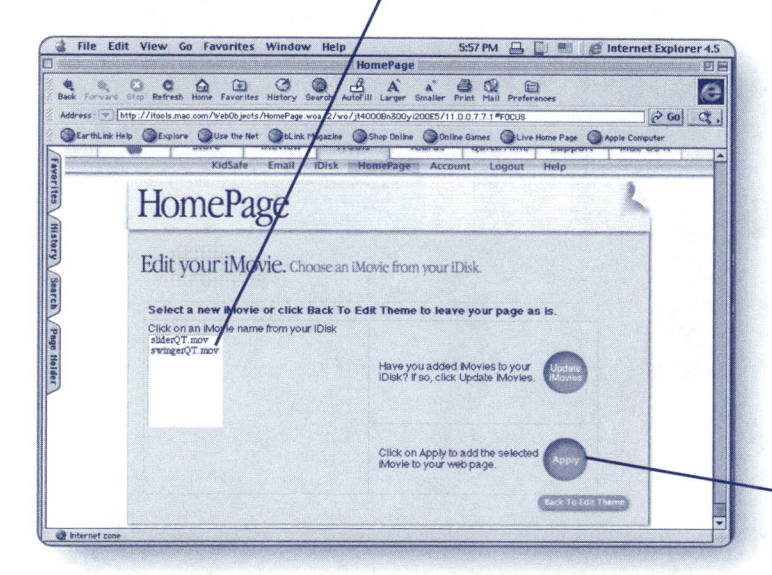

NOTE
This iTools page refers to your movies as iMovies, but it actually means your iMovies compressed into QuickTime movies. So again, make sure you are importing compressed QuickTime versions of your iMovies.

18. Click on the **Apply button**. The movie will be added to your Web site.

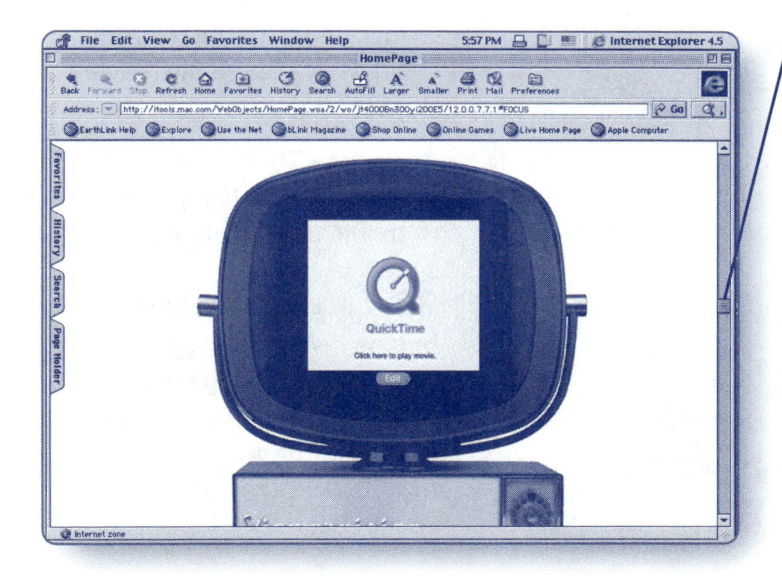

19. Scroll back to the **top** of the page.

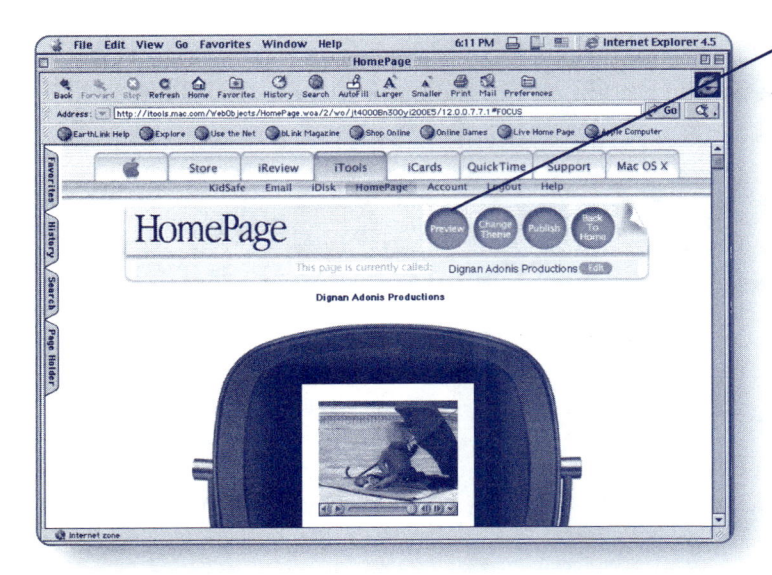

20. Click on the **Preview button**. The movie will play, and you will see your page as it will appear after it is published.

21. After viewing the page, **click** on one of the following **buttons** if you want to make any changes:

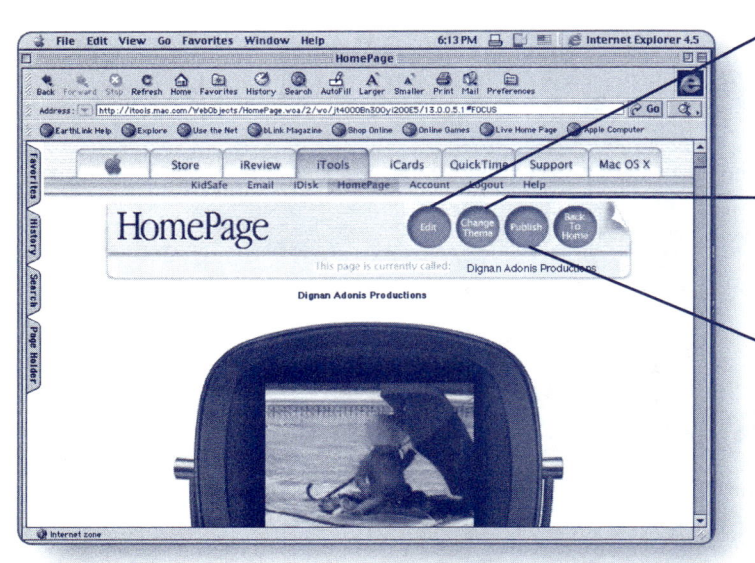

- **Edit**. This will allow you to make edits to the text or titles, or change the movie on your page.

- **Change Theme**. This will allow you to change the theme of your page.

22. Click on the **Publish button** if you are happy with your page. The page will be published to the Web, and you will see a Congratulations page that displays the address of your page.

CREATING YOUR HOME PAGE 285

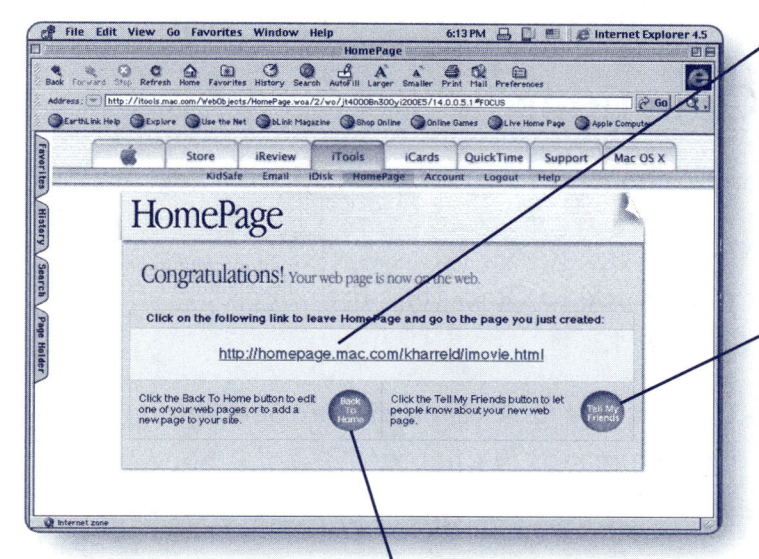

23. **Click** on the **link** to go to your Web page. You will be taken to your page.

24. **Click** on the **Back button** in your browser. You will return to the Congratulations page.

25. **Click** on the **Tell My Friends button** to send e-mails to friends announcing your new Web site.

26. **Click** on the **Back To Home button** to make changes to this page or add more pages to your Web site.

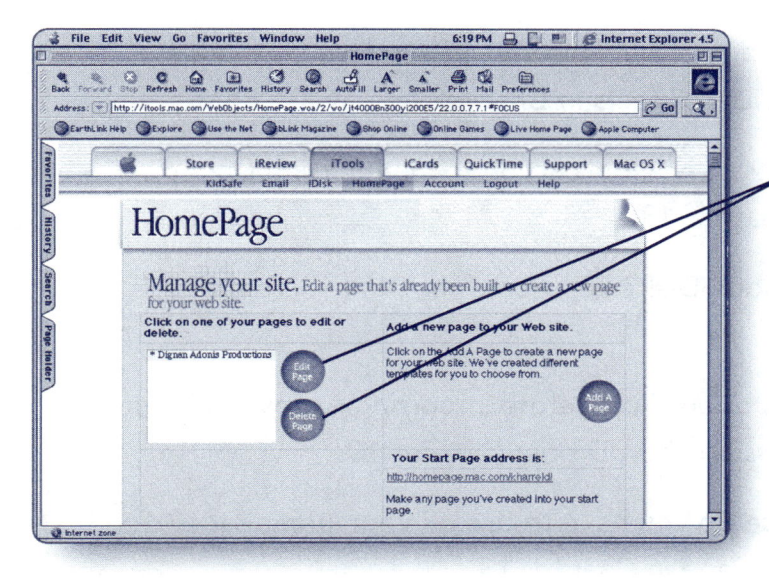

The page that you just created will appear in the list box on the left.

27. **Click** on the **page** and then **click** on the **Edit Page or Delete Page buttons** to edit or delete the page. You can also click on the Add A Page button to add a new page to your Web site. When you are finished working in iTools, you need to log out. Just click on logout on the iTools toolbar and you will return to the Apple home page.

Part IV Review Questions

1. How can you add more excitement to your text in iMovie? *See Chapter 11*

2. Why would you want to upgrade to QuickTime Pro? *See Upgrading to QuickTime Pro in Chapter 12*

3. How do you increase the size of a QuickTime movie? *See Sizing and Playback with Menu Commands in Chapter 12*

4. What editing features are available in QuickTime? *See Editing QuickTime Clips in Chapter 12*

5. How do you insert a QuickTime movie into iMovie? *See Importing QuickTime Clips into Your iMovies in Chapter 12*

6. What special effects are available in QuickTime Pro? *See Adding Special QuickTime Video Effects in Chapter 12*

7. What are the benefits of an iTools account? *See Setting Up an iTools Account in Chapter 13*

8. What's so special about iDisk? *See Accessing Your iDisk in Chapter 13*

9. Why do you need to open iDisk before importing a movie to your Web site? *See Accessing Your iDisk in Chapter 13*

10. How much free space do you have to use on your HomePage? *See Creating Your Home Page in Chapter 13*

PART V
Appendixes

Appendix A
　　Acquiring and Installing iMovie 289

Appendix B
　　iMovie Keyboard Shortcuts 299

A

Acquiring and Installing iMovie

Downloading and installing the free version of the iMovie program from Apple's Web site is a fairly simple task. This appendix will take you through this process step-by-step. You just need an Internet connection and a small amount of free time. In this Appendix, you'll learn how to:

- Download iMovie
- Install iMovie

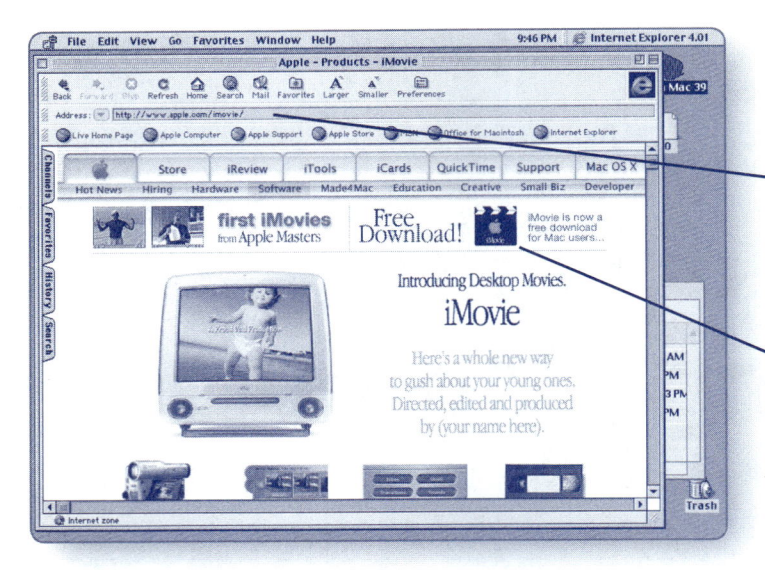

APPENDIX A: ACQUIRING AND INSTALLING iMOVIE

Downloading iMovie

1. Go to **Apple's Web site** and **navigate** to the **iMovie page**. You will see a page introducing iMovie.

2. Click on the **Free Download icon** at the top-right corner of the page. The Download iMovie page will appear.

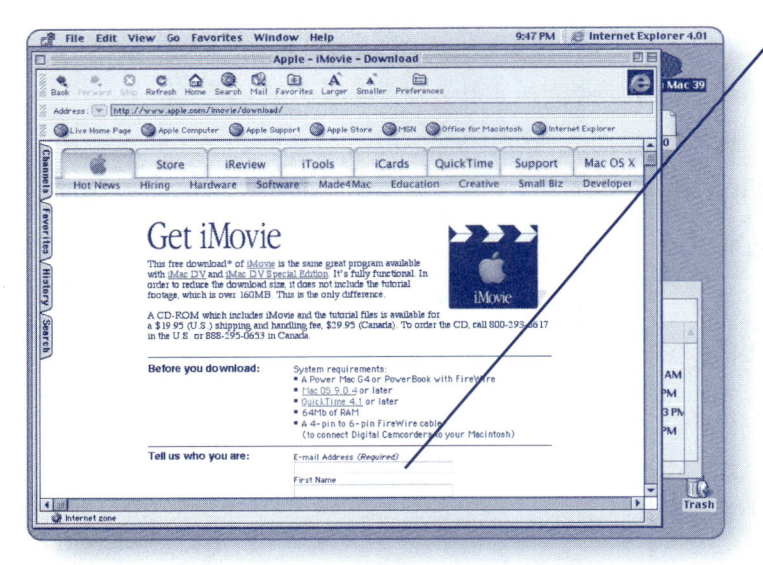

3. Type your **e-mail address, first name, and last name** in the corresponding text boxes.

DOWNLOADING iMOVIE

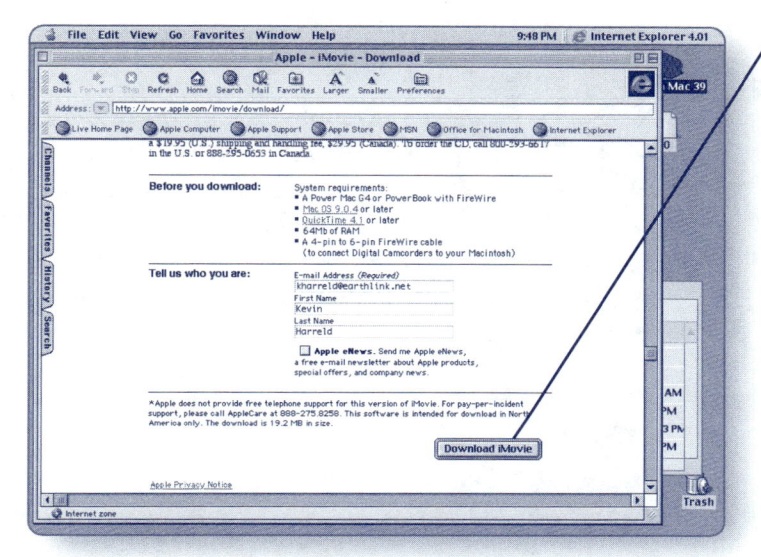

4. Click on the **Download iMovie button**. If Internet Explorer is your browser, the Download Manager will appear showing you the progress of the download. You can sit back and relax, because it will take a while.

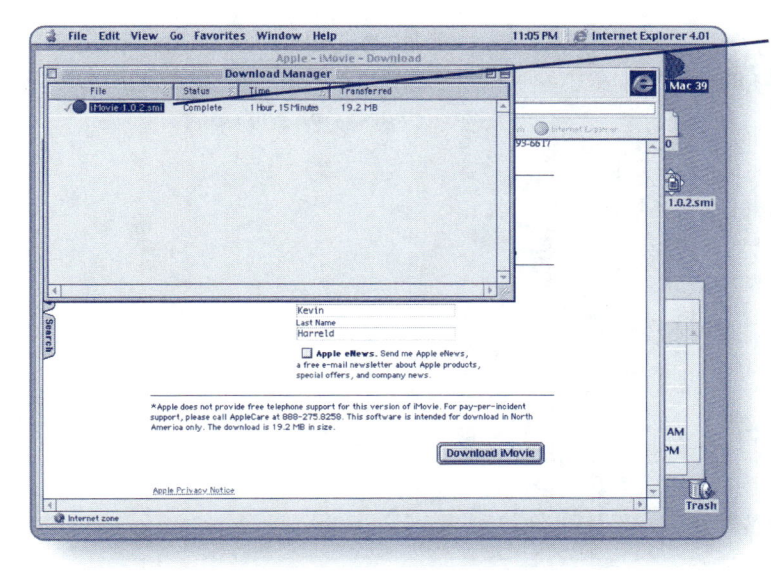

If you are using Internet Explorer, the Download Manager will indicate when the download is complete. An iMovie icon will appear on your desktop.

APPENDIX A: ACQUIRING AND INSTALLING iMOVIE

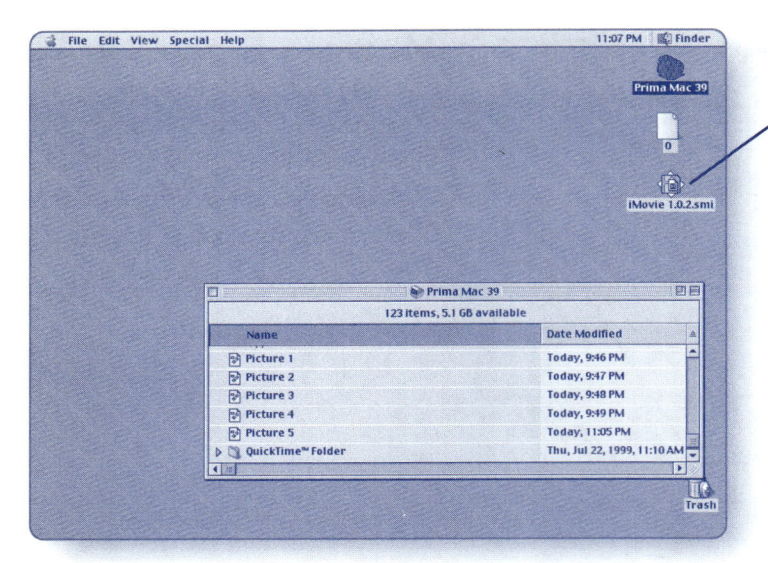

Installing iMovie

1. Double-click on the **iMovie icon**. An iMovie program icon will appear on your desktop and the iMovie dialog box containing the iMovie install icon and read me files will open.

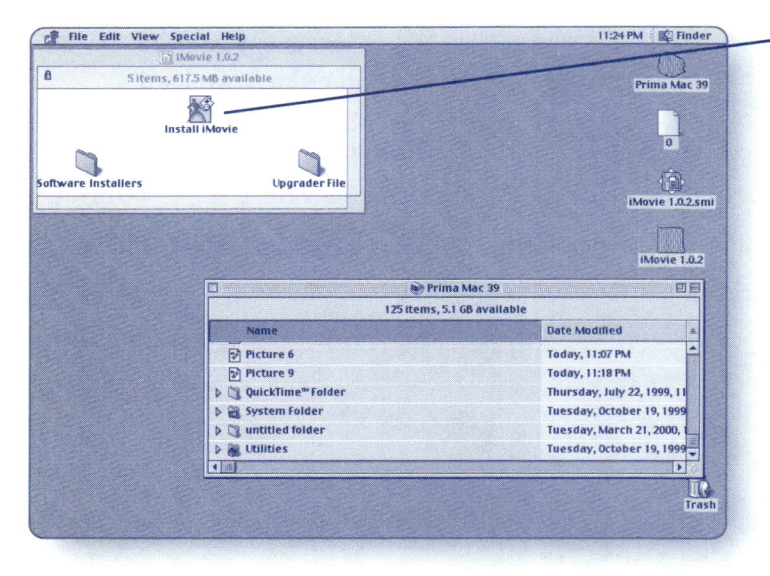

2. Double-click on the **Install iMovie icon**. The Install iMovie dialog box will open.

INSTALLING iMOVIE 293

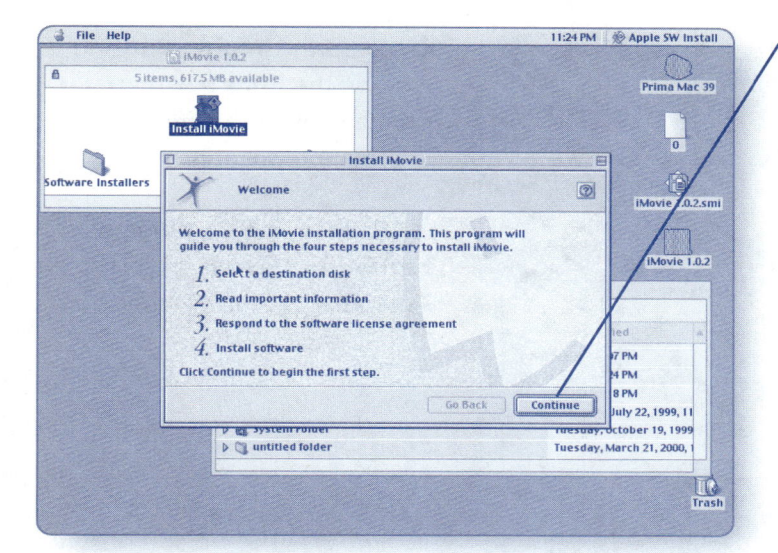

3. Click on the **Continue button**. The Select Destination page of the Install iMovie dialog box will open.

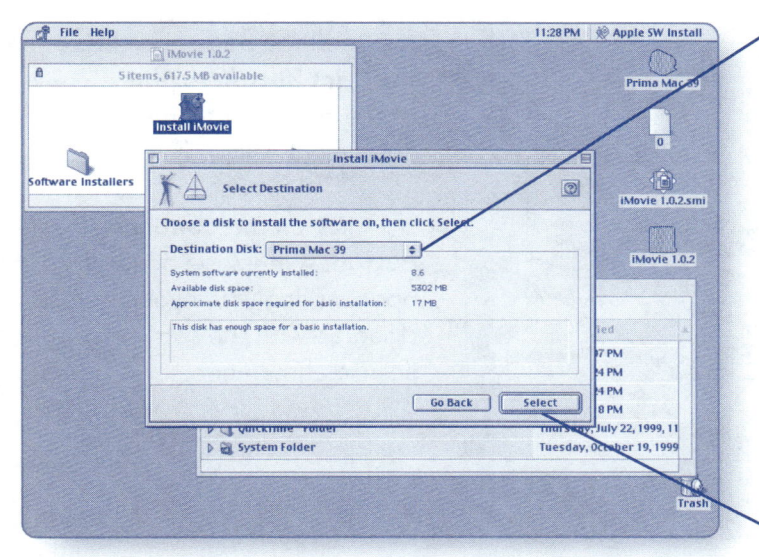

4. Click on the **up and down arrows** to the right of the Destination Disk list box and select the disk on which you want to install the iMovie software.

NOTE
The best place to install iMovie is on your Macintosh hard drive (HD).

5. Click on the **Select button**. The Important Information page of the Install iMovie dialog box will open.

294 APPENDIX A: ACQUIRING AND INSTALLING iMOVIE

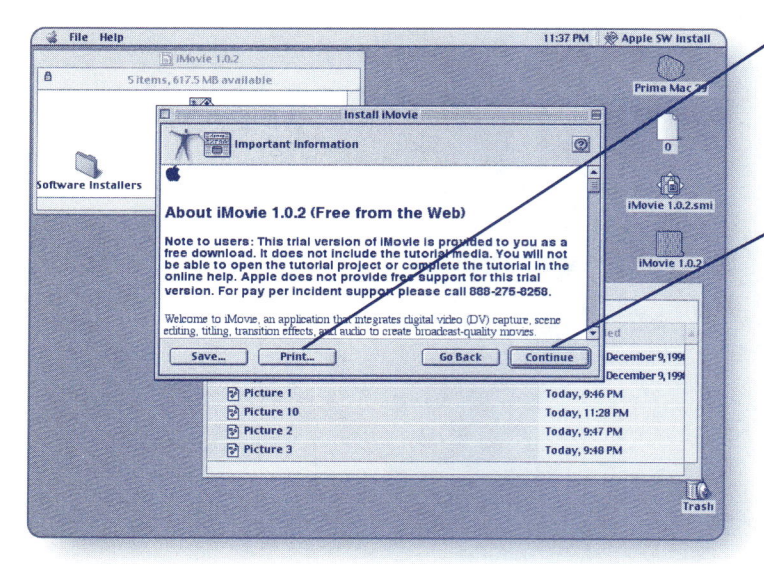

6. Read the **information** and **click** on the **Print button** to print a copy of the info. The information will print.

7. Click on the **Continue button**. The Software License Agreement page will open.

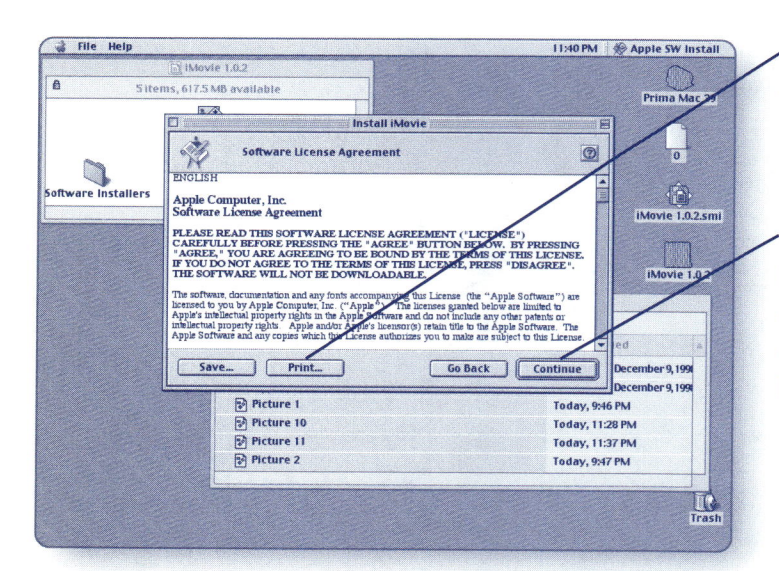

8. Read the **page** and **click** on the **Print button** to print a copy of the agreement. The agreement will print.

9. Click on the **Continue button**. A message box will open, asking you if you agree or disagree with the software license agreement.

INSTALLING iMOVIE 295

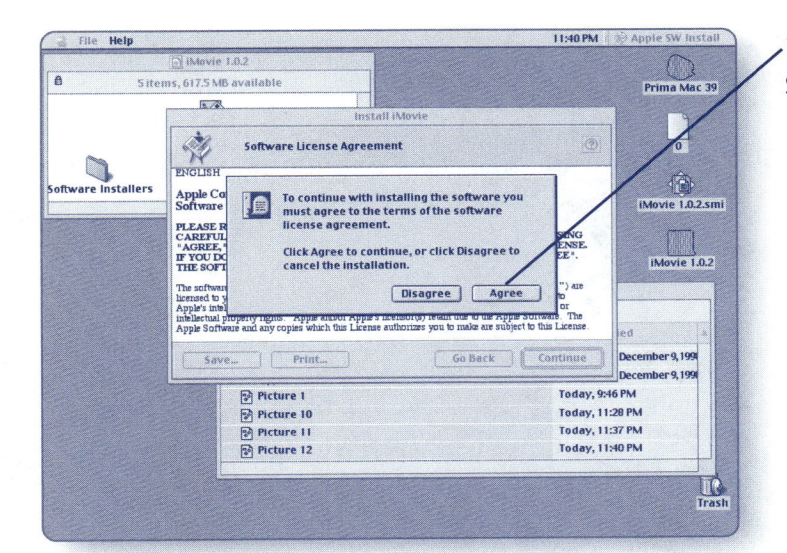

10. Click on **Agree**. The Install Software page will open.

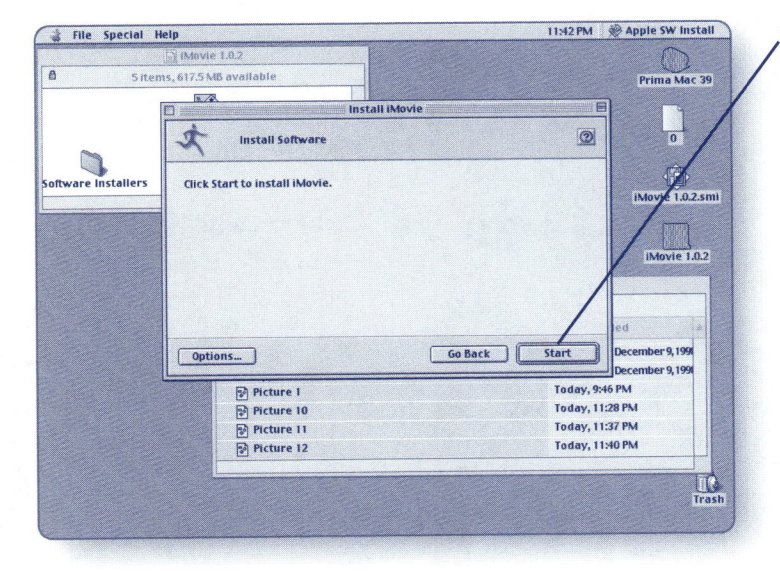

11. Click on the **Start button**.

APPENDIX A: ACQUIRING AND INSTALLING iMOVIE

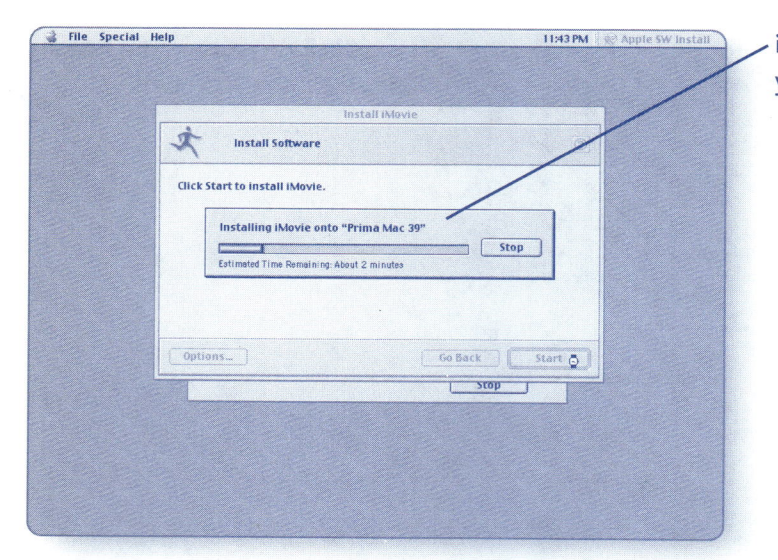

iMovie will start to install on your hard drive.

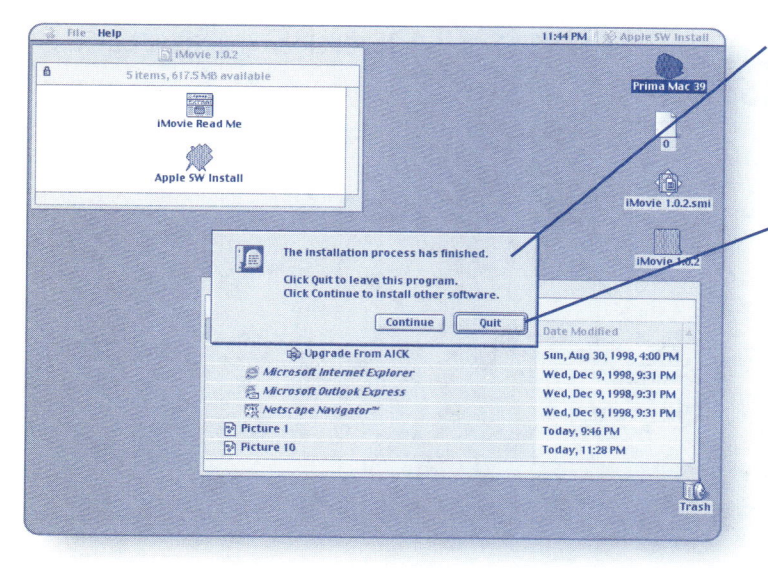

When the installation is complete, a message box will appear to let you know that the process has finished.

12. Click on **Quit**. The message box will disappear.

INSTALLING iMOVIE

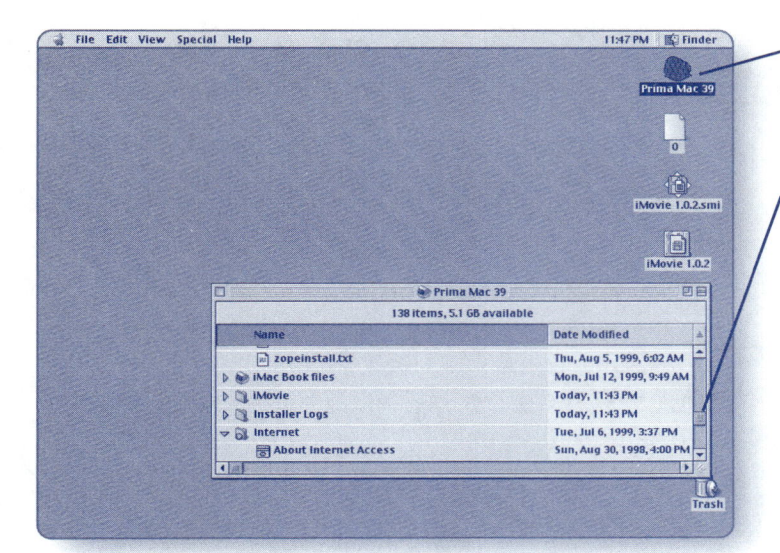

13. Double-click on your **hard drive icon**. The hard drive dialog box will open.

14. Scroll down to find the **iMovie folder**.

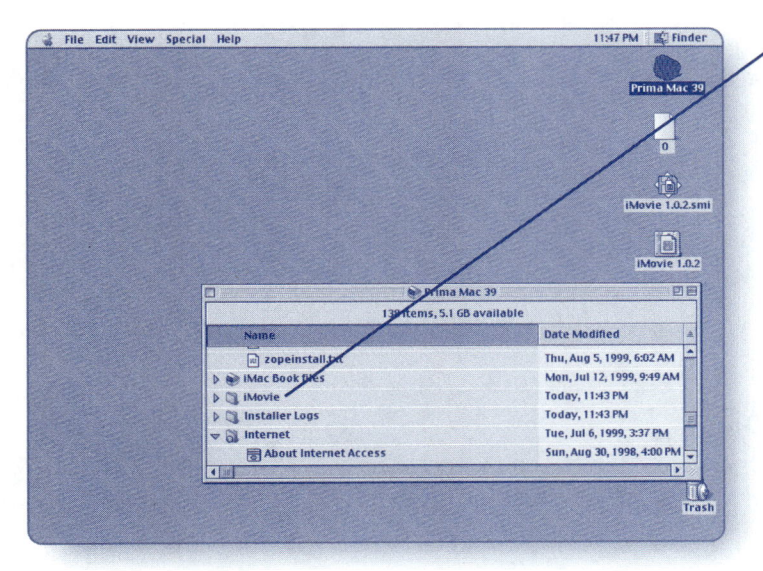

15. Click on the **iMovie folder**. The iMovie folder will open.

16. **Click** on the **iMovie icon**. The program will open, and you can begin using iMovie.

B

iMovie Keyboard Shortcuts

There are numerous keyboard shortcuts available in iMovie. Shortcuts for menu functions and navigation make using iMovie even easier!

File Menu Functions

Action	Shortcut
New project	Command + N
Open project	Command + O
Save project	Command + S
Export movie	Command + E
Save Frame As	Command + F
Import File	Command + I
Quit	Command + Q

Edit Menu Functions

Action	Shortcut
Undo	Command + Z
Redo	Shift + Command + Z
Cut	Command + X
Copy	Command + C
Paste	Command + V
Crop	Command + K
Split Clip at Playhead	Command + T
Select All	Command + A
Select None	Command + D

iMOVIE KEYBOARD SHORTCUTS

Navigation Shortcuts

Action	Shortcut
Play/Stop and Start/Stop capture	Space bar
Playhead to beginning of movie	Home
Playhead to end of movie	End
Forward one frame	Right arrow
Forward 10 frames	Shift + right arrow
Fast Forward	Command +]
Back one frame	Left arrow
Back 10 frames	Shift + Left arrow
Rewind	Command + [

Selection Shortcuts

Action	Shortcut
Multiple Selection	Shift + Click items
Range of Selection	Click first item then Shift + click last item in range

Moving and Cropping Shortcuts

Action	Shortcut
Move audio clip	Click clip + left or right arrow
Move audio clip 10 frames	Click clip, then Shift + left or right arrow
Move crop marker	Click marker, then Shift + left or right arrow

Glossary

AIFF audio file. Audio Interchange File Format. A digital audio file that can be used in iMovie.

Alignment. The position of the text in your iMovie project.

Analog video. Common video formats such as VHS, SVHS, 8mm, and Hi8.

Audio Viewer. Where you edit your audio. Displays audio clips in three tracks for music, narration, and DV sound. It is located at the bottom of the screen, along with the Clip Viewer, and has a musical note icon on the tab.

Browser. A program designed for viewing Web pages on the Internet.

Clip. Media file that contains audio, video, or still images.

Clipboard. Temporary storage containing the last item you copied in iMovie.

Clip Viewer. A timeline that displays your video clips, titles, and transitions. It is located at the bottom of the screen, along with the Audio Viewer, and has an eye icon on the tab.

Close-up shot. A zoomed in, tight frame of an object or subject.

Compression. Reduces the data size of a file.

Copy. Takes a video or audio clip and duplicates it on the Clipboard.

Crop. Cuts the unwanted video or audio off the beginning and/or end of a clip.

Download. To copy a file or application from the Internet.

Cut. Takes a video or audio clip and moves it to the Clipboard.

DV. Digital video format. DV stores video and audio information as data in a digital form.

Edit. To assemble your movie by cutting, rearranging, altering, and refining your video and audio clips.

Effects Palette. Palette that contains titles, transitions, music, and sound effects.

Export. A command used to convert your iMovie files into another format, such as QuickTime or digital/analog videotape.

File. Information stored on a single disk under one name.

File Format. A generic term for describing the way a file is saved. JPEG, PICT, and AIFF are different types of graphic and audio file formats.

Filter. Programs such as Photoshop and QuickTime Pro include image-editing filters to adjust contrast and brightness, and add other types of special effects to improve your video images.

FireWire. Apple Computer's multimedia peripheral that allows you to import and export video and audio from your camcorder at tremendous speeds. Also known as iLink or IEEE 1394.

Folder. An organizational tool used to store files.

Font. A character set of a specific typeface, type style, and type size. Some fonts are installed with the operating system on your computer.

Frame. A single image from a video clip.

Frame rate. The number of frames per second displayed onscreen.

Full-screen button. A button under the Monitor Window that allows you to view your movie on the entire computer screen.

Full shot. A video shot that gives the audience the setting of the scene and establishes how the subject of your movie fits in with the background or surroundings.

Hard Disk. A hardware component in which you can store files and folders of data.

Help. Feature that gives you additional information and instructions about iMovie.

Image. A bitmapped matrix of pixels that represent a picture.

Import. A command used to convert digital video, still images, and audio files into iMovie.

JPEG. Joint Photographic Experts Group. Compresses images into smaller file sizes. This format is mostly used in still image files sent as e-mail attachments, or for use on the Web.

Kilobyte. Commonly referred to as KB. Equivalent to 1,024 bytes.

Megabyte. Commonly referred to as MB. Equivalent to 1,048,576 bytes.

Media. All of your files, including images, sounds, music, and stills.

Medium shot. A video shot that shows one to three players within a small area, including their gestures and expressions.

Memory. Also known as RAM. Refers to the amount of physical memory in your computer. Virtual memory is the amount of memory or hard disk space allocated

GLOSSARY

for use by the operating system and applications on a computer. In regard to iMovie, memory represents the amount of space required for the program to run.

Menu. A user-interface element originating from the operating system, containing commands for an application.

Monitor Window. The large preview area located in the top-left corner of your iMovie screen. Includes playback controls, volume control, and a Scrubber bar.

Mode switch. Buttons under the Monitor Window that allow you to switch between camera and edit mode.

Narration. Using your voice as a storytelling effect in your movies.

Pan. Rotating the video camera slowly and steadily along a horizontal line from right to left, or vice versa.

Paste. The process of retrieving the information stored on the Clipboard and inserting it into your project.

PICT. Macintosh picture file format. Doesn't compress an image, therefore the image maintains the same quality as it is copied.

Playback controls. The Play, Pause, Fast Forward, Rewind, and Stop controls under the Monitor Window and in the Music Palette.

Playhead. The small monitor icon in the Scrubber bar. Indicates the starting point of a video or audio clip playback or recording.

Preview. A feature in iMovie which enables you to see what a title, transition, frame, or completed movie will look like before you render or save.

Processor. The central processing unit of a computer. A faster processor will run iMovie faster than a slower processor.

RAM. See Memory.

Rendering. Adding elements together (for example, adding text to a clip or transitions between clips) to change the visual information on a frame of video.

Resolution. The number of horizontal and vertical pixels that make up a screen of information.

Save. A command used to convert your iMovie projects stored in memory into files.

Scroll bar. A set of window controls consisting of up and down and left and right arrows, a scroll button, and a scroll bar that can be used to navigate a document window.

Scrubber bar. The bar used to position the playhead; it is located under the Monitor Window and in the Audio Viewer.

Shelf. The warehouse, in the upper-right portion of the iMovie screen, where your video clips are temporarily stored.

Size. The file size of a document. iMovie files are very large, and eat up several MBs of hard disk space on your computer.

Submenu. Also known as a cascading menu. A secondary menu containing a list of menu commands.

Transition. The effect of blending or smoothing out the cut between two separate video frames.

Trash Can. Where you drag your unwanted clips to delete them from your movie and free up hard disk space on your computer.

Undo. A menu command that enables you to reverse a previous action you made in the document window.

Viewer. The timeline at the bottom of your iMovie screen. Includes the Clip Viewer for editing and viewing DV clips, and the Audio Viewer for editing music, narration, and sound effects.

Web. The World Wide Web. A group of computers running Web server software connected to an extended network around the world.

Zoom. To slowly move toward or away from the subject in your video.

Index

4-pin connectors, 9
6-pin connectors, 9

A

accessing iDisk, 273–276
acquiring iMovie, 7
adding
    music from CDs, 129–132
    narration, 134–136
    sound to slideshows, 164–166
    sound effects, 132–134
        to folders, 145–149
        to silent movies, 222–228
    still images, 154–156
        to iMovie, 200–202
    titles, 199–120
        to slideshows, 162–164
    transitions, 90–91
        to Effects palette, 97–103
    video effects, QuickTime, 256–262
adjusting
    duration of title, 115–116

video playback quality, 52–53
volume
    of clips, 141
    within single clips, 142–143
aligning titles, 116–119
analog video, importing, 58–61
analog video converters, 9–10
Apple iMovie Web site, 4
Apple Web site, 98
Application dialog box, 147
audio clips
    cropping, 137–138
    moving, 138–139
    renaming, 139–140
audio levels, QuickTime Player, 235
audio tracks
    deleting, 140
    muting, 143–144
Audio Viewer
    clips, types of, 125
    tracks, types of, 124

B

Back To Home button, 285
backgrounds, 109–111
Better Image, 53
buttons
    See More, 265
    Back To Home, 285
    Download iMovie, 291
    Fast Forward, 33
    Full-Screen, 36
    Mode, 36
    Open My iDisk, 274
    Pause, 33
    Play, 33
    Publish, 284
    Rewind, 33
    Shirt, 235
    Stop, 33
    Submit, 272
    Tell My Friends, 285
    Titles, 106
    Transitions, 86
    Update, 94

C

Camera sound clip, Audio Viewer, 125
canvas preparation for opening film countdown, 186–187
CD-ROM Movie, Large, 176
CD-ROM Movie, Medium, 176
changing
    titles, 120–121
    transitions, 93–94
Choose Video Filter dialog box, 259

clips
    copying, 72–73, 242–247
    cropping, 67–69
    cutting, 242–247
    editing, 242–247
    importing, 44–46
    inserting
        connected by transitions, 96–97
        new among multiple, 77
    moving
        from Shelf to Viewer, 74–77
        via Edit menu, 77–78
    pasting, 242–247
    renaming, 65–66
    selecting, 64–65
    sorting, 70–72
    storing, 47–48
    trashing, 79–80
    volume, adjusting, 141-143
Close button, QuickTime Player, 234
close-up shots, 14, 21
Color Picker dialog box, 188, 208
connecting camcorder to computer, 26
converter box, 9–10
copying
    clips, 72–73
    movies, 168–171
        on VHS tape, 174
counter, QuickTime Player, 235
Create New dialog box, 31
Create New Project dialog box, 156
creating
    countdown numbers of silent movies, 196–200

INDEX 309

home page, 277–285
New Project, 30–32
opening film countdown
    canvas preparation, 186–187
    first number of, 188–195
    images, adding to iMovie, 200–202
    other numbers of, 196–200
    titles, creating, 207–213
    transitions, adding between images, 203–204
slideshows, 156–157

cropping
    audio clips, 137–138
    clips, 67–69
    shortcuts keys for, 301

Cross Dissolve transitions, 92
cut zoom in/out, 15

D

deleting
    audio tracks, 140
    sound tracks, 250–251
    titles, 121
    transitions, 95
    video tracks, 250–251

dialog boxes
    Application, 147
    Choose Video Filter, 259
    Color Picker, 188, 208
    Create New, 31
    Create New Project, 156
    Delete, 250
    Enable Tracks, 251
    Export Movie, 172

Export QuickTime Movie, 178
Extract, 247
iDisk, 274
iMovie Help, 37
Import File, 155, 157, 201
Layers, 196
Movie Settings, 258
New, 186
New Folder, 30
Open, 232
Open Existing Project, 56
Present Movie, 241
QuickTime Settings, 230
Search Results, 38
Type Tool, 193, 197

digital video cameras
    connecting to computer, 26
    types of, 4–5

Disk-Space gauge, iMovie screen, 36
Download iMovie button, 291
downloading
    iMovie, 7, 290–291
    Plug-in pack, 97–100

duration
    of still images, setting, 160
    of titles, adjusting, 115-116

E

edit menu functions, shortcut keys, 300
editing. See changing
Effects palette, iMovie screen, 35
Email Movie, Small, 176
End of clip, Audio Viewer, 125
establishing shots, 12

exiting iMovie, 54–55
expanding Shelf, 49–50
Export Movie dialog box, 172
Export QuickTime Movie dialog box, 178
exporting movies
    to camera, 172–173
    to QuickTime, 175–180
extracting
    sound tracks, 247–250
    still images, 152–154
    video tracks, 247–250

F

Fade transitions, 92
fading music, 144
Fast Forward button, 33
Favorites drawer, QuickTime Player, 235
file menu functions, shortcut keys, 300
Fill or Paint Bucket tool, 189, 208
film dialog placards, inserting in silent movies, 214–221
FireWire
    bandwidth, amount of, 8
    connectors, 9
    defined, 8
font colors, selecting, 112–115
Full-Screen buttons, 36

H

Help features
    iMovie Help, 37–38
    iMovie Tutorial, 40–42
    Show Balloons, 39–40
home page, creating, 277–285

I

iDisk, accessing, 273–276
iDisk dialog box, 274
images. *See* still images
iMovie
    acquiring, 7
    copying, 168–171
        on VHS tape, 174
    downloading, 7, 290–291
    exiting, 54–55
    exporting
        to camera, 172–173
        to QuickTime, 175–180
    screen features of, 34-36
    installing, 292–298
    saving, 168
    starting
        from desktop, 27–28
        from folder, 28–29
iMovie Help dialog box, 37
iMovie Plug-in Pack link, 98–99
iMovie Web site, 4
Import File dialog box, 155, 157, 201
importing
    analog video, 58–61
    clips, 44–46
    QuickTime clips, 252–255
Info button, QuickTime Player, 235
inserting
    clips connected by transitions, 96–97
    film dialog placards in silent movies, 214–221
    new clips among multiple, 77
installing iMovie, 292–298

INDEX

iTools account, setting up, 264–272

J
jump cut, 15

K
keyboard shortcuts, 300–301

L
Layers dialog box, 196
Length of clip, Audio Viewer, 125
lighting of shots, avoiding bad, 18

M
Macintosh, minimum system requirements, 8
Macintosh HD icon, 100
medium shots, 13
Mode buttons, 36
modes, switching, 44
Monitor window, iMovie screen, 34
Move tool, 194, 210
Movie Setting dialog box, 258
movies
    copying, 168–171
        on VHS tape, 174
    exporting
        to camera, 172–173
        to QuickTime, 175–180
    saving, 168
moving
    audio clips, 138–139
    clips from Shelf to Viewer, 74–77
    clips via Edit menu, 77–78
    shortcut keys for, 301

music
    adding
        to slideshows, 164–166
        to Sound Effects folder, 145–149
    adding from CDs, 129–132
    fading, 144
Music clip, Audio Viewer, 125
Music palette, features of, 126–127
Music track, Audio Viewer, 124
muting audio tracks, 143–144

N
Name of clip, Audio Viewer, 125
narration, adding, 134–136
Narration clip, Audio Viewer, 125
Narration track, Audio Viewer, 124
navigation shortcut keys, 301
New dialog box, 186
New Folder dialog box, 30
New Project, creating, 30–32

O
Open dialog box, 232
Open My iDisk button, 274
opening
    projects, 56–57
    QuickTime movies, 231–233
    Titles palette, 106
opening film countdown
    canvas preparation, 186–187
    creating
        first number, 188–195
        other numbers, 196–200
        titles for, 207–213

opening film countdown (continued)
    images, adding to iMovie, 200–202
    transitions, adding between images, 203–204
Oval marquee tool, 189

P

panning, 16
Pause/Stop button, QuickTime Player, 234
Play button, QuickTime Player, 234
playback, adjusting quality of, 52–53
Plug-in pack, downloading, 97–100
Polygon Lasso tool, 223
positioning titles, 116–119
Present Movie dialog box, 241
previewing video, 33–34
projects, opening, 56–57
Publish button, 284
Push Right transition, 92

Q

QuickTime
    clips
        copying, 242–247
        cutting, 242–247
        editing, 242–247
        importing, 252–255
        pasting, 242–247
    exporting movies to, 175–180
    opening movies, 231–233
    tracks
        deleting, 250–251
        enabling, 251–252
        extracting, 247–250
    video effects, adding, 256–262
    viewing movies, 241–242
QuickTime Player, features of, 234–237
QuickTime Pro
    playback menu commands, 240–241
    sizing menu commands, 237–239
    upgrading to, 230–231
QuickTime Setting dialog box, 230

R

Rectangular selection tool, 216
renaming
    audio clips, 139–140
    clips, 65–66
rendering, 90
Resize handle, QuickTime Player, 235
Rewind button, 33

S

saving movies, 168
Scene Detection feature, 51–52
Scroll bar, QuickTime Player, 234
Search Results dialog box, 38
See More button, 265
selecting
    clips, 64–65
    font colors, 112–115
    title background, 109–111
    title style, 106–107
    transitions, 86–88
Selection handles, QuickTime Player, 235
selection shortcut keys, 301
setting transition speed, 88–90
setting up iTools account, 264–272

INDEX

Shelf, expanding, 49–50
Shirt button, QuickTime Player, 235
shortcut keys
    cropping, 301
    edit menu functions, 300
    file menu functions, 300
    moving, 301
    navigation, 301
    selection, 301
shots
    angles of, 17–20
    close-ups, 14, 21
    establishing, 12
    lengths, 17
    lighting of, 18
    medium, 13
    panning, 16
    tracking, 19
    zooming, 15
Show Balloons Help feature, 39–40
silent movies
    canvas preparation, 186–187
    creating
        first number, 188–195
        other number, 196–200
    film dialog placards, inserting, 214–221
    images, adding to iMovie, 200–202
    sound effects, adding, 222–228
slideshows
    adding
        sound, 164–166
        titles to, 162–164
    creating, 156–157
    Push Right transition, 161
Smoother Motion, 53

Sony Web site, 9
sound
    adding
        to slideshows, 164–166
        to Sound Effects folder, 145–149
    audio clips
        cropping, 137–138
        moving, 138–139
        renaming, 139–140
Sound effect clip, Audio Viewer, 125
sound effects
    adding, 132–134
        to silent movies, 222–228
Sound palette, features of, 128
Sound track list box, Music palette, 126
sound tracks
    deleting, 250–251
    enabling, 251–252
    extracting, 247–250
speed of transitions, setting, 88–90
splitting clips, 70–72
Start of clip, Audio Viewer, 125
starting iMovie
    from desktop, 27–28
    from folder, 28–29
still images
    adding, 154–156
        to iMovie, 200–202
    extracting, 152–154
    setting duration of, 160
Stop button, 33
storing clips, 47–48
style of title, selecting, 106–107
Submit button, 272
switching modes, 44

T

Taskbar, iMovie screen, 36
Tell My Friends button, 285
titles
    adding, 199–120
        to slideshows, 162–164
    adjusting duration, 115–116
    backgrounds for, 109-111
    changing, 120–121
    deleting, 121
    font colors for, 112-115
    opening palette, 106
    positioning, 116–119
    style of, 106–107
    typing text of, 108
tools
    Fill or Paint Bucket, 189, 208
    Move, 194, 210
    Oval marquee, 189
    Polygon Lasso, 223
    Rectangular selection, 216
    Type, 209
transitions
    adding, 90–91
        new to Effects palette, 97–103
    changing, 93–94
    deleting, 95
    inserting clips, 96–97
    overusing, 93
    selecting, 86–88
    setting speed of, 88–90
    in slideshows, 161
    types of, 93–93
Trash, iMovie screen, 35
trashing clips, 79–80
tripods, 18
Type Tool dialog box, 193, 197

U

Undo Crop, 69
Update button, 94
upgrading to QuickTime Pro, 230–231

V

video, previewing, 33–34
Video camera soundtrack, Audio Viewer, 124
video cameras, digital, types of, 4–5
video effects, QuickTime, adding, 256–262
video tracks
    deleting, 250–251
    enabling, 251–252
    extracting, 247–250
Viewer, iMovie screen, 35
voice-over, adding, 134–136
volume, adjusting clips, 141-143
Volume wheel, QuickTime Player, 234

W

Wash transitions, 92
Web Movie, Small, 176
Web Movie, Small (QT3.0), 176
Web sites
    Apple, 98
    Apple iMovie, 4
    Sony, 9

Z

zooming, 15

Looking for something to do this weekend?

Want to create your own Web page? Organize your finances? Upgrade your PC? It's time to put your weekends to work for you with PRIMA TECH's In a Weekend® series. Each book in the series is a practical, hands-on guide focused on helping you master the skills you need to achieve your goals. While you have the time, let our In a Weekend series show you how to make the most of it.

**Write Your Will
In a Weekend**
0-7615-2378-2
$24.99 U.S.

**Tune Up Your PC
In a Weekend**
0-7615-2451-7
$19.99 U.S. • $29.95 Can.

**Create Your First Mac
Web Page In a Weekend**
0-7615-2135-6
$24.99 U.S. • $37.95 Can.

**Create Your First Web Page
In a Weekend, 3rd Ed.**
0-7615-2482-7
$24.99 U.S. • $37.95 Can.

OTHER HOT TOPICS

**Build Your Home Theater
In a Weekend**
0-7615-2744-3
$24.99 U.S. • $37.95 Can.

**Create FrontPage 2000
Web Pages In a Weekend**
0-7615-1929-7
$24.99 U.S. • $37.95 Can.

**Increase Your Web Traffic
In a Weekend, 3rd Ed.**
0-7615-2313-8
$24.99 U.S. • $37.95 Can.

**Learn Access 97
In a Weekend**
0-7615-1379-5
$19.99 U.S. • $29.95 Can.

**Learn HTML
In a Weekend, Rev. Ed.**
0-7615-1800-2
$24.99 U.S. • $37.95 Can.

**Create Flash Pages
In a Weekend**
0-7615-2866-0
$24.99 U.S. • $37.95 Can.

**Electrify Your Web Site
In a Weekend**
0-7615-2505-X
$24.99 U.S. • $37.95 Can.

**Jumpstart Your Online
Job Search In a Weekend**
0-7615-2452-5
$24.99 U.S. • $37.95 Can.

**Learn Digital Photography
In a Weekend**
0-7615-1532-1
$24.99 U.S. • $37.95 Can.

**Set Up Your Home Office
In a Weekend**
0-7615-3054-1
$24.99 U.S. • $37.95 Can.

DO IT In a Weekend

PRIMA TECH
A Division of Prima Publishing
www.prima-tech.com

**Call today to order!
1.800.632.8676, ext. 4444**

fast&easy web development

Getting Web developers up to speed

Less Time. Less Effort. More Development.

Don't spend your time leafing through lengthy manuals looking for the information you need. Spend it doing what you do best—Web development. Let PRIMA TECH's *fast & easy web development* series lead the way. Each book in this series contains step-by-step instructions and real screen shots to help you grasp concepts and master skills quickly and easily. Fast track your Web development skills with PRIMA TECH.

XHTML *Fast & Easy Web Development*
0-7615-2785-0 ▪ CD Included
$24.99 U.S. ▪ $37.95 Can.

Dreamweaver® *Fast & Easy Web Development*
0-7615-2905-5 ▪ CD Included
$24.99 U.S. ▪ $37.95 Can.

ASP 3 *Fast & Easy Web Development*
0-7615-2854-7 ▪ CD Included
$24.99 U.S. ▪ $37.95 Can.

CGI *Fast & Easy Web Development*
0-7615-2938-1 ▪ CD Included
$24.99 U.S. ▪ $37.95 Can.

ColdFusion® *Fast & Easy Web Development*
0-7615-3016-9 ▪ CD Included
$24.99 U.S. ▪ $37.95 Can.

Director® 8 and Lingo™ *Fast & Easy Web Development*
0-7615-3049-5 ▪ CD Included
$24.99 U.S. ▪ $37.95 Can.

Fireworks® *Fast & Easy Web Development*
0-7615-3082-7 ▪ CD Included
$24.99 U.S. ▪ $37.95 Can.

Flash™ X *Fast & Easy Web Development*
0-7615-2930-6 ▪ CD Included
$24.99 U.S. ▪ $37.95 Can.

Java™ 2 *Fast & Easy Web Development*
0-7615-3056-8 ▪ CD Included
$24.99 U.S. ▪ $37.95 Can.

PHP *Fast & Easy Web Development*
0-7615-3055-x ▪ CD Included
$24.99 U.S. ▪ $37.95 Can.

PRIMA TECH
A Division of Prima Publishing
www.prima-tech.com

Call now to order!
1.800.632.8676, ext. 4444

Learning Microsoft® Office 2000 is a breeze with PRIMA TECH's bestselling *fast & easy* guides

Offering extraordinary value at a bargain price, the *fast & easy* series is dedicated to one idea: To help readers accomplish tasks as quickly and easily as possible. There's no need to wade through endless pages of boring text. The unique and carefully developed visual teaching method combines concise tutorials and hundreds of WYSIWYG (what-you-see-is-what-you-get) screen shots to dramatically increase learning speed and retention of the material. With PRIMA TECH's *fast & easy* series, you simply look and learn.

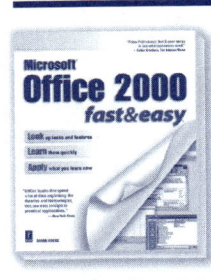

PRIMA TECH
A Division of Prima Publishing
www.prima-tech.com

Call now to order
(800) 632-8676
ext. 4444

Prima Publishing and Fast & Easy are trademarks of Prima Communications, Inc. All other product and company names are trademarks of their respective companies.

Microsoft® Office 2000
0-7615-1762-6
$16.99

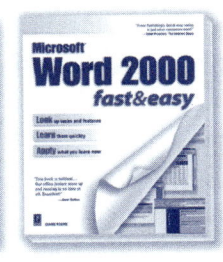

Microsoft® Word 2000
0-7615-1402-3
$16.99

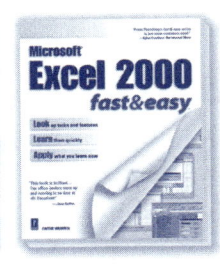

Microsoft® Excel 2000
0-7615-1761-8
$16.99

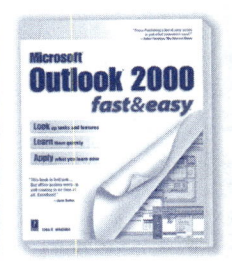

Microsoft® Outlook™ 2000
0-7615-1927-0
$16.99

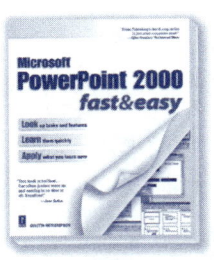

Microsoft® PowerPoint® 2000
0-7615-1763-4
$16.99

Microsoft® Publisher 2000
0-7615-2033-3
$16.99

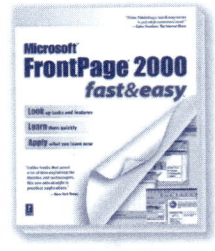

Microsoft® FrontPage® 2000
0-7615-1931-9
$16.99

Microsoft® Access 2000
0-7615-1404-X
$16.99

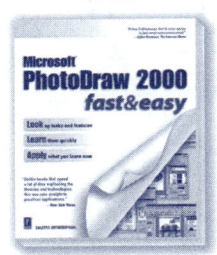

Microsoft® PhotoDraw 2000
0-7615-2034-1
$16.99

Microsoft® Internet Explorer 5
0-7615-1742-1
$16.99

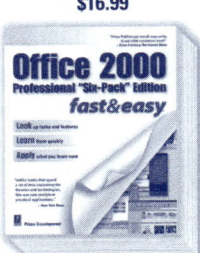

Microsoft® Office 2000 Professional "Six-Pack" Edition
0-7615-2032-5
$29.99